The Fetch

By

Janet Pugh

Copyright © 2023 by – Janet Pugh – All Rights Reserved.

It is not legal to reproduce, duplicate, or transmit any part of this document in either electronic means or printed format. Recording of this publication is strictly prohibited.

Dedication

I dedicate this book to my family and the organisations and individuals who support me.

Acknowledgment

I would like to thank my sisters for their endless support and my dear friends Andrew, Sonia, and Anne. They have encouraged me that, at times, the pen ran dry, and I needed some feedback. A big thank you to my dad, who encouraged me to get my book published. To Rosie, Fudge, and Milly, my pets, for putting up with me when I read chapters out aloud and stopped getting stroked when I had a brain wave. Finally, a big thank you to Mind and viewpoint and Hitchin CMHT, who picked me up when I was knocked over. Last not least, my greatest thanks to Lynn, Rachael and Jo.

About the Author

This is the first and probably the only book I have written. The idea of writing about a disabled-friendly world was attractive to me as a person living with a disability. I based the main character, Janet, on myself, sharing an age, name, and sex. All of the characters in the book are named after people I know, but that's as far as it goes. There is no resemblance in age and mannerisms.

I live in a rural location in southeast England with my two little dogs, Fudge and Rosie. I have struggled with disability for a large part of my life, so it was good to explore, in the book, life as a disabled person.

I am in my late fifties and live in a generation that is invisible. We go about our day-to-day life with no one really realising we are here. I thought I would see if my main character was far from invisible but a key member of her group of friends.

I hope you enjoy reading 'Fetchers' as much as I enjoyed writing it.

Table of Contents

Dedication ii
Acknowledgment iii
About the Author iv
Chapter 1 The Fetchers 3
Chapter 2 Induction 16
Chapter 3 Newbie 39
Chapter 4 Yellow to Green 53
Chapter 5 Mind over Matter 75
Chapter 6 Moving On 104
Chapter 7 Being a Brownie 135
Chapter 8 Sherlock Holmes 160
Chapter 9 Big Brother 191
Chapter 10 Wearing Grey 208
Chapter 11 Grey on Grey 232
Chapter 12 Changes 267
Chapter 13 Graduation 297
Chapter 14 Hurt 320
Chapter 15 Resistance 348
Chapter 16 Happy Birthday 369
Chapter 17 Graduation Day 389
Chapter 18 De Ja Vu 414
Chapter 19 Back Home 441
Chapter 20 Home 449
Chapter 21 Reunion 460
Chapter 22 Prologue 478

Chapter 1
The Fetchers

She lay on the gurney, covered only with a sheet. The room was quiet except for a gentle hissing sound which was unobtrusive. The room was lit by a couple of strip lights which burst through the otherwise gloom of the room. The room was bare, with no other furniture taking up space though there was a small sink in the corner of the room near the gurney. The temperature in the room was comfortable though there were no radiators on the walls and no obvious means of heating the room.

There was one door opposite the foot of the gurney, which had no doorknobs or any other means of opening it. There were no windows, no pictures, and no shelving. For all of the bareness of the room, it appeared to be sterile and medical. The woman on the gurney lay peaceful in her slumber. She lay on her back with a pillow under her head. The pillow was white, as was the sheet that gently moved with each breath. The woman looked like she was asleep; her face looked peaceful and relaxed.

After about an hour and a half, she lay there unmoving. Then her breath quickened a bit, and she started to stir. After a few moments, she tried to open her eyes but found the effort too hard, and she fell back into her slumber. A little later, her eyes opened again, and she moved to stretch her body. She winced with the pain of moving and then quickly scanned the room. She couldn't see anything hostile, so she drew her attention back to herself. She moved the sheet away from her body, then when she realised she was naked under the sheet, drew it back up again.

In doing this action, she managed to take a glance at her legs. They were caked in blood and looked irregular. She moved the sheet off them again to take a better look and drew in a deep breath when she saw the mangled remains of her legs. She felt fear, her breath came as gasps, and she felt her head spin. She moved the top part of her body in such a position that she could see her legs clearly. She saw a bone sticking out through the skin in two places and large gashes on both legs. She didn't dare touch the wounds, though nature was telling her to, but she was fearful of the pain. She covered up her legs with the sheet and lay back down on the gurney.

She wanted to cry out for help, but when she tried, her voice came out squeaky. She gave it a few goes; each attempt brought some strength to her voice, but no one seemed to hear her. She was at a loss as to what to do. She could hardly get out of bed to see if she could find a nurse, and calling one wasn't working. She looked around to see if there were any means of summoning help, like a call button. All hospitals had them, didn't they? She checked the best she could but could not see anything resembling one, so she lay back down on the gurney, trying hard not to give into the growing sense of fear engulfing her body. At that point, she heard a strange whooshing sound; she quickly looked over at where the sound was coming from and froze. The door opposite where she was lying had opened with a young man being framed in the door frame.

"Hello Janet, I'm Mark; I'm your Fetcher," the man said. "Please don't be afraid; I am friendly and here to help you." He walked over to the gurney and placed a calming hand on her arm. "Are you in pain?" he asked her.

Janet found it hard to find her voice, let alone say anything legible. She tried to speak but, in the end, just shrugged.

"That's OK; just nod to let me know if you are in pain," he said. Janet shook her head, indicating no, and then quickly reassessed what she had just done. She had two smashed-up legs; she should be in pain. Either that or they have bloody good pain medication.

Mark seemed to pick up on her thoughts and motioned to her to see if she was happy for him to look at her legs. Janet nodded and started to move the sheet away from her body until she remembered that she was naked under the sheet. She held the sheet over her upper body to cover her breasts while Mark gently pulled off the sheet from her legs. He hummed and harred a bit as medics do, then pulled the sheet back over her legs. "Do you want a drink?" he asked her.

"Yes, yes, please. That would be nice," Janet said, finally finding her voice.

"Tea?" asked Mark.

"Yes, please, no sugar," she said.

Mark moved to bring up the head of the bed so she would be in a seated position, then left the room through the whoosh door to make her a tea. Janet felt reassured by his matter-of-fact attitude though she had so many questions she wanted to ask him. Hopefully, she thought, she would have that opportunity later. Mark returned to the room a few minutes later, holding a mug of tea for Janet. He offered her the mug and a couple of biscuits in a paper napkin. She smiled at Mark in thanks, and then took hold of the napkin.

"Now, we have a few things we need to do before the induction meeting. Firstly, I have to do this, but well. Here goes. Did you know you are dead on the earth? You died." He stopped speaking to gauge her reaction. Janet just looked at him, wondering what the hell he was going on about.

"You died from your injuries when you committed suicide. The medical team could not mend you, so you have come to us to stay here on Second Chance." He again paused to see if she had taken in what he had said.

"So, this is heaven?" she asked.

'No," he replied.

"Hell?" she said.

"No, its neither; Second Chance is a place where people who die too soon get to live out their lives until they retire and Graduate," Mark explained, looking at her.

"So, what you're saying is that I am neither dead nor alive? I am a zombie?"

"No, you are not a zombie. You are not on earth, anyway; you will find out more about that later on today. For now, I need to find my pal Bonnie to give me a hand to set your legs and clean you up. Then you should be ready for Induction. Are you still hungry?" he asked her.

Janet shook her head no, then watched as he walked out through the door into the corridor beyond. She had no thoughts in her head but felt a sense of dread. *What if she hadn't died when she jumped from the height? Maybe this is the kind of place they send people to who have been near death.*

So many what-ifs made her head spin. After about ten minutes, the door opened, and Mark walked in with Bonnie. Bonnie was a pretty petite woman dressed like Mark in a light blue uniform. Mark and Bonnie had come in with a trolley covered in bandages and other odds and sods, as well as a bowl of water.

Bonnie said hello to Janet and then asked her permission to see her legs. Janet agreed for them to do this, thinking it was nice to be asked, then layback to let them do their work. Bonnie carefully cleaned her legs taking special care to clean the gouges in her legs where the bone was coming through. Once they were clean, Mark stood at the bottom of the bed and took hold of her left ankle.

"This shouldn't hurt, you will probably hear some odd noises, but we have to reduce your fractures. Are you ready for this?" Mark asked. Janet nodded her assent then Mark pulled her left leg while

Bonnie manipulated the bone into alignment; after a few failed attempts, they were happy that her limb was straight; then Bonnie dressed the wounds then wrapped a crepe bandage around her leg. Finally, she fitted on a Velcro splint that held the leg straight to allow it to heal.

Once the left leg had been done, they did the same with the right leg. They checked the circulation in her toes to make sure the supports were not too tight. Then satisfied, they tidied up the used dressings and took them away on the trolley. A few minutes later, Mark and Bonnie came back in carrying something. Janet looked over at them and smiled a small smile. She felt sure these were nice people. Even though she had no idea of what they were going on about.

"Just to check, I am dead but alive?" she asked, staring intently at Bonnie.

"I know it sounds confusing, but basically, yes. On earth, you would be seen as dead, but you are alive here on Second Chance," Bonnie exclaimed patiently.

"What is this Second Chance? Where is it?" Janet asked.

"This is the place where you will live now; it's a place giving what it says on the tin *a second chance at life*," Mark said, flicking his blond fringe off his face. "Anyway, the next thing to do is to remove that canula from your neck. Are you OK with me doing that?"

"Yes, of course, thanks for asking," Janet replied, tilting her head to one side to allow him easy access. He deftly removed the needle and then placed a small plaster over the wound. Bonnie came over to Janet; she was carrying something in her hands that looked like clothes.

"The next thing on the list, Janet, is for you to get dressed. I can help you with that if you like, and we can ask Mark to leave us with it. What do you think?" she said.

Janet looked at the clothes she was carrying. It looked like a yellow outfit and some underwear. Janet asked Bonnie to help her, and they waited until Mark had left the room before Bonnie showed her the clothes. "All our new people or newbies wear yellow. Everything here is colour coded for ease. Mark, as Fetchers and I wear light blue, it is so you can tell us apart. We have been in the position you are in now, so I can really empathize with you. Anyway, let's get you dressed."

Bonnie handed her the garments and helped her when needed. The yellow tunic and trousers looked well-made and were surprisingly nicely tailored. The underwear was not new, they looked a bit greyish, but they fitted fine. Someone had a good eye for size as everything fitted well. "Do you want anything to eat, Janet?" asked Bonnie standing by the door. "I could go get you something light, like a sandwich?"

"Yes, that would be nice, thank you," Janet, replied.

"Great, everything here is veggie. How about cheese and tomato?" Bonnie said, looking at Janet.

"That would be great," said Janet, really wanting more than anything else to be left alone for a little while. She needed to get out of there and needed to suss out how to do that. She was not sure if she could walk with her legs broken like that, but she had to give it a go.

Once Bonnie had gone, Janet carefully swung her legs over the side of the gurney and gingerly lowered them to the ground. She put a bit of weight on them, and it seemed to feel OK, so she tried a bit more. The bit more was a bit too much, her legs crumbled, and she found herself on the floor. Still determined to escape, she crawled along the floor towards the door. She didn't want to be caught in case she would get into trouble.

She made it commando style to the door expecting it to open as it had for Bonnie and Mark. She tried everything she could to get the door to open, from waving her arms at the door to seeing if there was any kind of a sensor. She wondered if she made her way back to the gurney, it would be embarrassing if they caught her like that. She turned around and dragged her legs back to the gurney using her upper body. She was not entirely sure how she would get back onto the gurney but guessed she could always tell them that she had fallen. She lay there for a few minutes before the door opened, and Mark walked in.

"Oh my god, are you OK? Did you fall?" Mark said, coming right over to where she lay on the floor. "Let me check your legs; stay still now." With that, he gently ran his hands over both of her legs, feeling for any irregularities. He undid the fastenings of the trousers to check the splints, then finally, satisfied no damage had been done, told her he would just get Janet a wheelchair.

As he left the room, Janet watched intently to see if she could determine how the door opened. She couldn't see anything obvious on or around the door but had noticed that Mark had a fob key attached to his tunic that looked a bit like a watch. Mark was back within minutes with a manual wheelchair. He moved it near to where Janet lay on the floor and put on the brakes. He then instructed Janet to put her arms around his neck and allow him to take her weight.

He expertly lifted her up and swivelled around so she could sit on the chair. He then placed her feet on the footrests and moved the chair around to face the door. The door opened, and Bonnie walked in carrying a plate with a sandwich on it.

"Is everything OK?" she asked, handing the plate of food to Janet.

"Yes, it's all OK now. How long have we got until Induction?" he asked.

"About an hour, enough time to show Janet around," she replied, smiling kindly at Janet. With that, she waved them both goodbye and left the room.

"Now, do you mind telling me what really happened?" he asked her trying to look firm.

"I fell," Janet said, not meeting his gaze.

"Yes, and I'm an old queen. Now, what happened?"

"I tried to get up; I needed to get out of here. I don't want to live or live, die or die die, or whatever the fuck is going on around here. I just want to go; you can't stop me." Janet said with emotion in her voice.

"No, I can't stop you, but there is nowhere to run. I know this is all of a bit much for you at the moment; you did take your life; it must be a real bummer to find out you are not dead dead."

"I don't understand. Why was it not my time to die? When is it my time to die?" Janet said through a tirade of tears.

She stopped speaking for a moment to try to get her emotions in check; still, the tears fell. Mark tried to comfort her by placing a hand on her shoulder. He would have liked to have held her but was as yet uncertain how she would respond.

"I know, I do know. When they told me that I was not dead, it made me laugh. Everyone responds differently. Now, eat your sandwich, and could you do with another tea?"

"Yes, please," she said, looking up at him gratefully. He turned around and left the room while Janet composed herself. He might be a lot younger than her, but he had been through it himself, so he could say with certainty that he understood. He went into the kitchen down the corridor to make her a brew and almost collided with Bonnie.

"Is she OK?" Bonnie asked Mark.

"Think I am going to have to keep quite an eye on her; she is so vulnerable," he said, watching the kettle boil.

"Yes, do you feel that she can relate to you?" she asked.

"No, I don't think so; it is going to be hard to gain her trust," Mark said, pouring the hot water from the kettle into a mug that had a tea bag in it.

"I've got one coming in, should be here around twelve tonight; if you need my help, just let me know," Bonnie said as she left the small room. Mark dunked the tea bag until it got to good colour, then removed it, discarding it into a trash bin. He got out some milk from the fridge and poured a small amount into the mug, and replaced the milk in its place. He carried the mug to the door, took a deep breath in then zapped the whoosh door open. Janet was in control of her emotions by the time he returned and apologized as he handed her the mug.

"Please don't worry; you don't have to apologize. It's hard. I know. I know." Mark said tenderly. He sat down on the gurney and then checked his fob watch.

"Are you comfortable? Would you like to move to lie on the bed?" he asked her.

"No, this is fine; you have to watch your back," she said.

"Tell me about yourself, Janet. Do you have kids?"

"No, I didn't meet anyone whom I felt would make good husband material. I married the job instead."

"What did you do?" he asked.

"Me, I was a nurse. I loved my job, but back in the eighties, they didn't like to have people with mental illness on the books. I was persuaded to leave by the head of nursing. I have spent years in the mental health system with bipolar disorder. I still get bouts of depression; that is what happened this time. Only, I didn't account for this, this keeping me here" she felt the tears coming again, so she twisted her body around so Mark couldn't see her crying.

"It will be OK. You will settle in brilliantly; you will see," Mark said reassuringly. 'Now, you are due for your induction any time soon, so we had better get you to the hall where it all happens. Do you feel ready to go?"

"What goes on in this induction? What should I expect? Will there be other people there?" Janet asked with rising anxiety.

"They will give you the lowdown on Second Chance, what to expect, some of the rules, and yes, there will be other people there. Many of them came here the same day as you. Just be prepared; many of them have pretty serious injuries. I'm sure you can deal with that," Mark said, then slapped his thighs and got up off the gurney. Now, how do you look? Think we need to find a comb or a brush for your hair. Leave it to me, I'll be back in a sec" with that Mark went out of the door giving Janet a tantalizing glance of the corridor beyond. He came back with a hand mirror and a hairbrush and then ran the bristles through her hair gently. He managed to get rid of the tangles and make her look half decent, then showed her the results in the mirror.

"Look at my face; it's all blotchy; what will people think of me if I go out looking like this" Janet said, looking at her face.

"Don't worry about that. The light in the room they use is not that brilliant; you will look fine. Now we must get going. Are you ready?" Mark asked her, taking the mirror out of her hand and putting it next to the mirror on the gurney.

"OK, let's do it," Janet said, pointing forward with her right hand. Mark moved the chair so he could get to the handles, then started to push her towards the door.

"How do you open the door?" asked Janet.

"I have a fob key in my watch; you will get one soon, so you can come and go." He said as he pushed her through the open doorway. Janet looked down the corridor; it had strong strip lights like the one in the room and looked sterile. It was spotless but didn't have that weird smell you get in hospitals. There were about ten doors coming off the corridor; some had a light above the doorway, others were numbered, but they were all closed. The only door open was the one to the small kitchen where Mark had got her tea. Janet made a mental note of things like that, but there was one room she felt she really needed to visit sooner rather than later.

"Mark, I really need to wee; where is the toilet?" she said, turning her head to speak.

"OK, are you happy if I help you, or I could go and find Bonnie, or can you wait until after the induction? They are your options. What do you think?" Mark said, stopping the chair.

"How long does the induction take?" she asked.

"Good question. Probably about half an hour. Can you wait that long?"

"No, I need to go now," she replied. "I'm OK with you helping me." Mark approached one of the doors with a light above it and then keyed some numbers in a keypad on the frame of the door. The door clicked open then Mark skilfully wheeled the chair into the space beyond the door. It was pretty big; with the throne taking centre stage, it had a hoist over the seat and grabbs handles on either side.

Mark positioned the chair next to the toilet and then lifted her up and over using the same technique as before. He left her to lower her garments and then set her down on the pan. He then withdrew from the room, asking her to call him when she was done. After she had pissed, she called Mark, who came in promptly. He moved her into the wheelchair and then moved her over to the sink so she could wash her hands. Once done, Mark moved her out of the toilet cubicle and back onto the corridor. Mark pushed her carefully, but the passageway was smooth and still oh so clean.

Janet was impressed by that; despite having worked for the NHS and knowing how clean they kept things, the room and corridors never looked clean. Everything looked old and drab. Here, you could see your reflection on the floor; it was so clean. At the end of the corridor was a set of double doors that whooshed open as Janet and Mark approached. He turned left down another corridor, then a right, then a second right.

Janet was struggling to remember the route and had seen no signs of the outside. It felt like they were in the middle of a complicated building. Mark turned left through another set of doors where they saw a man being pushed by two Fetchers in a gurney. They were making slow progress along the corridor, and the man kept calling out for them to be careful as they went along. Mark called out to the Fetchers by name, who turned around to say hello. They stopped to talk for a moment, and Mark introduced Janet to them, Richard and Philip. Janet looked at the man on the gurney. It was hard not to stare. He appeared to be just a torso with one arm. The man seemed jolly despite his horrendous injury, which put her broken legs into some kind of a perspective. Mark followed Richard and Philip down the corridor to another double door. This one whooshed open into a large room. Janet fell quiet; all she really wanted to do was to sleep; she felt so tired and tried to convey this to Mark. Mark reassured her that it would not be long then she could sleep and that they insisted all newbies attend.

"Newbie, what is that then? Is that what they call us here?" she asked.

"Yes, that is what we call our new intake.

Chapter 2
Induction

They approached the door then Mark stopped pushing her as they waited for the door to open. This door opened like the other one with a whoosh.

It opened into a large hall with several doors coming off it and a small stage at the end. The room was brightly lit with strip lights on the ceiling, and the room felt warm. A bit too warm for Janet, who wished she had a layer she could remove. Janet saw the same hazy light coming from the walls as she had seen in her room. Despite the warmth, she was also aware of the noise in the room. It hit her like a wall of sound and came from the chatter of many people. The room had a good twenty to twenty-five people in it, some wearing yellow and others dressed in blue like Mark.

Janet looked around her at the people in the room. She saw some in wheelchairs, a couple in beds, some walking with aids, and many just standing. All appeared to be talking in anticipation of something or someone. Many of them had obvious disabilities or injuries; the man next to her was missing an arm, the stump dressed with a pad and bandage. No bleeding, just gone. It looked like it had been torn off. "Got hit by a train, dragged down the track, I apparently died, bit weird, isn't it?" The man spoke in an upbeat manner for something so dramatic, but Janet didn't say anything, just smiled at him.

She didn't want to appear to be staring at anyone as it would be awkward, but she couldn't help herself. She could see a young woman with what looked like an eye on her cheek; shame that Janet thought she was stunning. Janet looked away so she couldn't be accused of staring and rested her gaze on a young man in a wheelchair who had lost three limbs. His short haircut and demeanour left Janet to think he was from the military. She wondered what had happened to him to get so seriously disabled. Janet turned around in her chair to look at Mark, who was waving to someone in blue near the front of the room.

"Are these all Fetchers?" Janet asked Mark gesturing towards the light blue coloured uniformed persons, "Yes," he replied, "The rest are Newbies like you. They all died today."

"They can't be dead; they are walking and talking. Are they ghosts? Am I a ghost?"

"No, you're not a ghost, just having a second chance. You were not ready for death." Mark placed a reassuring hand on her shoulder, "It will be made clearer."

The noise in the room subsided as movement at the far end of the hall indicated a couple of people climbing three steps up onto the stage. Both men wore brown informal suits, no ties, and open-necked shirts. One of them put out his hands and moved them up and down to settle the crowd. "Quite now, quiet, thank you."

The noise in the room abated, and all eyes were on the couple on the stage. One of the men had a missing arm; the other looked as if he might have a wooden leg from the way he walked. Janet looked at them with interest in what they had to say. She noticed Mark had left her and was now standing at the back of the room. She suddenly felt very vulnerable without him there but was in no position to do anything about it. With the people in the room now focused on the two men in brown, Janet waited with bated breath to see what they had to say.

"What is going on? Where the fuck are we?" shouted out a Newbie in the middle of the crowd; others in the crowd jeered at this. "Just tell me how to get home; there has been some kind of a mistake," spoke out a young woman with beautiful red hair.

"Yes, me too," said two other people. Janet was concerned that the two men were losing the attention of the people in the room. They needed to take back control before things boiled over.

"Please be patient; all will be made clear," said the other suited man.

"Will all The Fetchers leave the room, take a break, have a coffee, thank you," said the first suited man. Janet looked back at Mark, who gave her a quick smile, then he turned around and walked out of the hall with the other Fetchers. Janet felt afraid without him there; *what if things kicked off? She could get trampled.* She decided she would feel safer with a wall behind her, so she wheeled the chair to the back of the room. She had a good view from there and would be able to see if there was any trouble.

"Just get on with it, won't you?" shouted out a man standing right near the stage. The two brown-dressed men talked between themselves for a moment or two; it was difficult to understand what the delay was.

"What happened to you?" Asked a Newbie woman standing on Janet's left. Janet leapt in her seat when she heard that, then turned to face her. She felt herself immediately recoil in shock. The woman's face, or what was left of her face, smiled kindly through lips blooded and torn and a smile that ended in a deep, visceral gorge. One eye looked kindly at Janet; the other hung down her cheek, held in place by the optic nerve. "Gunshot, just one bullet, that's all it took; what about you, dear?" She spoke. Before Janet could string some words into a sentence, one of the suited men again appealed for quiet, which let Janet off the hook.

"First of all, welcome, all of you. My name is Tony; this is Stephen," said the first suited man, Tony.

"We manage the inductions of Newbies like yourselves. We were where you are, so I have an idea of what you may be thinking.

Now, hopefully, The Fetchers have let you know you are all dead. Most of you died today, and a few of you yesterday. We don't do the induction seminar on Sundays; even the living dead need a day off." He seemed to find this amusing, seemed to expect laughter from the crowd; it was a tough audience.

"Feel free to ask questions as we go; please sit, lie, or whatever you feel comfortable doing," said Tony. "Now, to get us all warmed up, let's do an exercise to get to know each other. Get into groups of four. Can everyone do that?"

"I don't know what you are on; just tell us where we are and what is going on," shouted out a man near the front of the hall.

"Yes, well, we will be getting to that in a short while," Tony responded.

Janet took in what was being said with a sense of disbelief. It felt surreal, otherworldly. She felt something huge was being trivialized by the two suited men. Why play a get-to-know-you game at a time like this? It, along with everything else, felt wrong, so very wrong.

Things have been going wrong for Janet for the last few weeks. She had felt the familiar creeping of depression engulf her body and mind. She felt tired, things became more of an effort, and she could not stop intrusive memories replaying over and over, being dissected, and analysed with no clear outcome. These thoughts became dominant, driving her mood down and interrupting her sleep.

Janet felt irritable, snapping at people, hating herself for reacting like this but feeling unable to stop things, only to isolate herself. All of this had happened to Janet many times. She had been diagnosed as having Bipolar Affective Disorder in her early thirties. Despite the familiarity of her depression, she still felt unable to deal with it due to the smothering effect of her mood and experiences.

On some occasions, it was just a case of riding it through; other times, Janet was able to alert her local Mental Health Team. A few times, Janet just wanted to switch her brain off through suicide attempts. On this present occasion, she had planned her death, taking strength from knowing it would all be over soon. She went to great lengths to organize the event like a pet project. She used her computer to draw up a database listing how much notice she needed to give commodities like gas and electricity so she could cancel them at the right time.

She wrote a letter to the housing association she rented her home from giving the notice to quit. Janet spent quite a bit of time getting rid of her stuff. She packed things in boxes to drop off at local charities and then made arrangements for a house clearance firm to take the rest of her belongings.

On top of all that, she managed to find new homes for her pets; that was a tough one, it took a while, but she found good places for them to go. It was hard saying goodbye to them, but at least they were going somewhere where they would be loved. With all her affairs taken care of, the last thing she needed to do was to finalize things with her family. On Sunday, she spent time writing letters to her loved ones. It was not easy to do. Her first draft sounded clichéd; the second one read like a heavy-duty novel. Finally, she produced something that read OK.

"Dear Mum and Dad, I am writing this for you to find out after my death. Neither of you is to blame for my death. It is my own selfish action. Depression keeps coming back, and each time it takes part of my soul. Please tell my sisters that I love them. My will is in the small drawer in my living room.

Yours truly,

Janet

Concise, direct, emotionless.

On a damp cold November day, she made sure everything she did, she did it mindfully as if it would be the last thing she did. She made herself a cooked breakfast to start the day. A bit later on, while listening to her radio on her iPhone, she sang along to the music. The disc jockey seemed to be playing her song list, a history in music, Janet thought.

In the afternoon, she went out to post the letters she had written to her family. Then in the evening, she ordered a takeaway, her favourite food as her last supper. Sunday evening, Janet changed into some clean clothes, putting the old ones in the bin, which she emptied ready for the bin man the next day. She dragged the waste bin up the path to the place it goes for emptying by the bin men.

She made herself a cup of tea, washed up the mug then got herself ready to go out. Janet pulled on her shoes and then wrapped herself up in her winter coat. She checked the time on her phone; it was eleven at night, perfect.

She turned off all the lights and locked the door posting the keys through the letter box. She walked down the path for the last time. The cold breeze brushed the hair off her brow and pushed the Pom Pom on her hat to the side. Janet reached inside the pockets of the coat for some gloves, which she put on.

She noticed every step, every breath, and every movement as it felt important to register them. How acutely aware she felt. It made her last walk monumental. It must be what prisoners felt on their walk to the gallows. Her footsteps on the pavement sounded noisy to her; she really didn't want to draw attention to herself, so she tried to walk quietly, which really didn't work.

But, no one was around; everyone was either in bed or watching the telly. People walk around at that time of the day, so why should tonight be any different?

It started to spit with rain; Janet felt the drops on her face as the haze of fog settled down. She could see OK and tried to avoid the puddles from the rain earlier in the day. A car passed her; she had not noticed the headlights coming up from behind her. She looked at it speeding along, feeling suddenly so alone. All the houses looked the same except for the displays of the lights. Some of the houses had lights on downstairs and some upstairs; she tried to imagine what they were doing on a cold, damp November night.

She delved in the pocket of her jeans for a paper handkerchief, and finding one; she dabbed her nose, which was dripping. She blew her nose and then put the soiled handkerchief into the pocket of her coat. She crossed the road at a junction and then turned right onto a lane. There were no houses down here; the road passed a popular dog walking place, the woods. She used to take her dogs there, and as she thought of it, it made her feel suddenly sad.

She refocused her mind on the task ahead and stopped for a second to look around her. The lane was deserted, which was why she had chosen this particular location as opposed to others she had considered. *Nearly there now*, she thought. All was still quiet. *Good.*

She spotted the old bridge over the old railway track, her destination. She crossed the road choosing to go to the centre part of the bridge, the highest point. She stopped, looked around, and then climbed up onto the bridge, so she was sitting with her legs dangling, and then she pushed down with her hands, sending her body crashing down to the bottom. *Janet died in the ambulance from internal bleeding*, they said. She had crashed, and CPR failed to put life in her body. She jumped and then crashed. That was it, the end of her life on Earth.

"Can I join your team?" said the half-faced lady. "My name is Melanie, Mel; my friends call me Mel," Janet introduced herself to Mel.

"What happened to you? Janet asked.

"Wrong place, wrong time. Looks all right here, doesn't it?" said Mel changing the conversation quickly. Janet smiled briefly at Mel while taking her in. She was probably in her mid-twenties, dyed blond hair with the roots showing her true colour and half a face. Janet could not help staring at her face. Intrigued to see muscles and blood vessels and flaps of cheek skin, a real-life biology class.

"That must really hurt," Janet asked Mel.

"You would think so, wouldn't you? What about you with your legs?"

"No, no pain, weird."

They were joined by two women who introduced themselves as Kim and Lisa. Lisa was in her early thirties; Janet could see no obvious injury; she assumed she had a hidden disability; sensing that, Lisa decided to help Janet out by pulling up her yellow tunic, revealing an open wound from below her ribs to her belly button. The hollow looked as if you could easily put your hands in; a bit of blood traced its way down her abdomen.

"Caesarean gone wrong," explained Lisa to the others, "I don't know what happened to my baby, Linda. She was taken away. They said she had the cord tight around her neck." All the woman exclaimed their sorrow for her loss and injury. She seemed to be very together for what she had been through. *Maybe that's the way she copes,* thought Janet.

"And you?" Asked Mel to Kim.

"RTA got hit by a car. Speeding it was, I had to be cut out of the wreckage. My spleen ruptured, and my broken ribs pierced my heart, got some lovely bruises coming out," replied Kim.

Janet felt as if she was on some warped coffee morning comparing outfits or nail polish; what on earth was going on? However, in light of the conversation, it could not hide the real fact that they had all recently died and died in horrific ways.

"Are we already in our groups?" called out Tony, snapping Janet away from her thoughts. "Excellent, now I want you to find four things you all have in common, for example, birthdays, favourite colours, you know, the kind of things. Keep it clean and light."

"Where are we?" Janet asked the group. "I have no idea what is going on."

"My Fetcher said that it is a place to give dead people a second chance; that's all I know," said Mel.

"But how? Nothing makes sense. I don't want to be alive," Janet cried out. "If I'm dead, that's it, the end, over!" Janet felt tears prick, trying hard to keep control. "Is this heaven?" she said through her tears. Kim came over to put a reassuring hand on her shoulder. Janet felt comforted by her effort and regained control of her waterworks quickly.

"Did you, did you kill yourself?" asked Lisa. Janet nodded yes, then felt an immediate regret as it seemed the ladies had recoiled. "You must have been desperate; my dad had depression. Is that what you get, Janet?"

"Yes, Lisa, I suffer from depression. I am not too sure how I should feel now. Did I succeed or not?" Janet said to the group. "Anyway, how about we get on with the task, things we have in common?"

They didn't find it too difficult to come up with four things. They decided that they were all female, they were all dead, they all dyed their hair, and they loved dogs. As Tony brought the room back to the stage, the girls stopped talking and turned around to listen. Tony asked for one spokesperson to call out the similarities. Janet agreed to do it for their group but kind of regretted calling out the fact that they were all dead as Tony tutted and asked for one, which was less hard-core. After a quick powwow, they all agreed they liked coffee which seemed to go down better for Tony. Once the silly icebreaker was over, the suited Stephen indicated for those who could sit and then outlined the contents of the induction.

"To start off, Tony will explain the role of The Fetchers, important people for you Newbies, then I will go through some house rules and the streams leading up to Graduation." He leaned forward, smiling as he looked at the sea of yellow, "Any questions, or shall we just get on with it? I appreciate some of you have injuries that make you tire quickly." *What an odd thing to hear,* Janet thought. But the whole scenario felt odd, not how she expected heaven to be, but as a non-believer, the concept of heaven is in the field of fantasy.

"Over to you then, Tony."

"Thank you, Stephen, so The Fetchers, hmmm. All of you have been paired up with a Fetcher. They are primarily there to take care of you while you heal. Some of you have such awful injuries that you will not regain full health, in which case your Fetcher will stay with you up to Graduation. Fetchers wear a light blue uniform; they have been trained to care for and rehabilitate. Please give them respect and treat them well. Your Fetcher will answer your questions and help you to understand how to get on around here. Any questions?" After a short time, someone called out.

"What happens if you don't get on with your Fetcher?" he asked. "Can I get a female one?" this caused a bit of laughter to eke out; Tony looked at Stephen before he answered.

"Thank you; your Fetcher is matched on not only their skill set but also with personalities. We do have a policy in place to deal with wrong matching, but we do encourage Newbies to take a bit of time with their Fetcher first; I hope that answers your question. Anything else?" Janet had a question but did not feel OK about asking it, so Mel did it on her behalf.

"Janet feels a mistake has been made, that she is in the wrong place. Can her Fetcher help her get back to where she should be?" The room fell quiet at that, and Janet held her breath as she waited for the reply.

"It takes some people longer to adjust; it will take time. Some people are in denial, especially about being dead. Second Chance is like a halfway house; it gives you a lovely place to live and work in a beautiful environment. In time, when you are ready, you will leave The Physical Complex to go first to the Mind Complex, then onto the main area of Second Chance," said Stephen. "Second Chance gives you the space to bring out your potential. It is a positive place where physical and mental disabilities and injury come centre stage; there is very little hierarchy here. Well, over now to Tony to take you through the main rules and expectations here on the Physical Complex."

"Thank you, Tony; now, the rules. There is quite a lot necessary to keep the ship rolling. First, and possibly the most important one, we need you to be inside between the hours of 5 pm to 9 am while you are a Newbie. This is for your benefit; pain relief is distributed along with antibiotics during that time. The amount is controlled by your Fetcher. If you are not undercover, we cannot be held responsible for your health.

Secondly, please be respectful of your Fetcher and other Newbies; please refrain from using bad language, and any kind of violence will not be tolerated. We have procedures in place to manage conflict. The fourth thing you need to know about is that we run a three-strike policy here; we hate having to discharge an offender; thankfully, it doesn't happen often. Well, these are what you need now. Your Fetcher will go through the day-to-day stuff; they will do their best to satisfy enquiring minds.

As mentioned, Newbies' primary role is to heal. Once your physical wounds have healed, you part company with your Fetcher, get a different colour outfit, a rather nice green." He smiled at the audience, "You go to the Mind Complex for the mending of the mind. Facing your daemons, acceptance, peace, reconciliation. Quite a tough call, much harder than being a Newbie."

He looked over at Tony, who nodded in agreement. "Most people stay there for about six weeks. It is an important step along your way and will help you, even to try to mentally adjust to a disability. The next level is work and self-development, learning new skills, maybe training and working as a Fetcher, going to the Control Centre, the corporate side. Maybe you like to clean, tend plants, cook, whatever is your cup of tea. Whatever you can bring to the table to keep this place ticking over. This you do until retirement and Graduation. Now, we have time to take a few questions." he again scanned the audience, responding with a nod when a hand shot up in the air. "Yes, go ahead."

"What is this place? Why are we here?"

"Excellent question. You are now residing in a state called Second Chance. It was established to give life and opportunity to people who die from trauma, the undeserving dead; you reside here until you die of old age, does that help?"

The noise in the room escalated. Janet joined in with her own questions and concerns. She felt confused and fearful. Thoughts whizzed around her head; she was in a place for the rest of her life, and she was not going back home. Her suicide attempt had worked; she was dead. This is not what she imagined death to be. Feeling overwhelmed, she started to panic; just then, she felt the wheelchair move gently backwards; looking up, she looked warily at Mark, who had entered the room with the uproar.

"Let's get you out of here," he said, wheeling the chair backwards and then steering it out of the room.

"Thanks," said Janet.

"You must be tired; let me take you to your room," he said kindly. Janet felt very overwhelmed. The noise in the room added to her vulnerability; she had never been good in crowds.

Mark pushed her without saying a word. Janet felt that she needed to break the silence but was not sure what to say, so she stayed quiet. The corridors seemed a bit different from the ones she came down; she swore the paint was a different colour; these ones were pale pink while the other one was magnolia, "Where are we going? This isn't the way. Where are you taking me?" Janet said with growing alarm.

"Not too far now," Mark replied, keeping up the speed, "Look, there's the kitchen," he said; Janet looked but was too late to see. Next to the kitchen was a door where he stopped. He activated his fob key, then when hearing a click, the door opened to show a nicely decorated room. The walls were pale pink, like the corridor; it had flowery curtains with matching duvet covers and pillow slips. The furniture was white and in this room there was a proper bed. Janet looked around, taking it in, and she nodded her approval. Mark applied the wheelchair brakes and then assisted Janet onto the bed.

"Do you want tea?" Mark asked her as he folded the wheelchair putting it near to where Janet could reach.

"Yes, that would be nice, no sugar," she said. Mark turned round to open the whoosh door, then turned right into the kitchen. At that point, the door closed, leaving Janet staring at a white door. She looked around the room again and then tried to see if she could look out of the window. She could not make out much, she was in the wrong position, and the angles were all wrong. There were a couple of pictures of dogs on the wall; the two dogs looked a bit like her two, the ones she had to rehome.

She looked at them again, really scrutinizing them and then giving up on the idea they were her dogs as it was too far-fetched. She turned her attention to the wall with the window. There was a small sink near the corner with a white towel hanging on a ring next to the facet.

Janet wondered if there was a toilet there but could not see anything to confirm if this was the case. Her bladder was telling her it was full, but she felt embarrassed at telling Mark; he was young enough to be her son. Still, she needed to do something about it; maybe, she thought, if she got to her chair, she could wheel herself to the toilet if it was not too far. But, despite stretching out, she could not reach the wheelchair. At that moment, Mark knocked on the door before coming in with two mugs of tea. He put them down on a dressing table opposite the bed.

"I bet you must be getting to the point of needing to wee; the toilet is opposite the kitchen if you want to go. I can help you, or I could ask for a female Fetcher to give you a hand. I have seen everything, you can imagine, so many very broken bodies." *How did he know,* she thought; *how did they know she was coming to get pictures of her dogs? How did he know she needed a wee.* She felt afraid of what else they know about her.

"Yes, I do need to go to the loo; I'm fine with you helping me; I lost my modesty years ago," she replied, feeling foolish at her past thought. It was all just coincident, that's all.

Mark walked over to the wheelchair and opened it out. He wheeled it over to Janet, who was still on the bed. He encouraged her to put her arms around his neck so he could lift her and swing her into the chair. Once in the chair, he wheeled her out of the room and into a large wet room. The toilet was nicely placed for her to transfer onto the seat, and Mark helped her to lower her clothes and knickers so she could have a wee. He left her to perform, then came back in when she called out that she was ready. They reversed the procedure then, once she was back on her bed, they settled down to drink their tea. They spoke little, with Janet giving short answers to his questions. She felt too tired to engage in small talk.

"I expect you are tired," said Mark. "How about I leave you to have a rest? Then I will get you your evening meal. How does that sound?" Mark asked as he took the mug from her.

"How did you know, you know, about the wee, the dogs, and now this? Are you psychic?" Janet asked in a rush.

"I'm just good at what I do, that's all," Mark replied, heading for the door, "Now, get some rest." She did feel tired, bone tired. Sleep would be very welcome, and when she woke, things would be back to normal, or so she hoped.

She woke up about an hour and a half later. It took her a moment to remember where she was and what had happened to bring her here. She could not believe the words that Stephen and Tony had said earlier that day. It's all a dream, she theorized; she would wake up properly any time soon. Mark knocked on the door heralding his entry and looked at Janet as she sat up in bed.

"Are you ready to order your food? I've got a menu here; then, I will pop down to the kitchen to bring it to you. The food here is vegetarian; they grow all the ingredients here on Second Chance. I would recommend the butternut squash and spinach lasagna."

"That sounds good," replied Janet without enthusiasm.

"What about pudding? There is sticky toffee pudding with custard, fruit trifle, or ice cream. What do you fancy?"

That's more like it thought Janet then ordered the pudding to go with her healthy lasagna. Lunch and breakfast hadn't happened as she was in the hospital dead, so she was hungry. Mark turned round in a mini spin and then left the room to get the food. She looked out of the window as far as she could, seeing that it was now dark. The clock said it was ten o'clock; she had slept longer than she thought, she said to herself. The cold, drizzly weather had passed, and it felt oddly warm for the time of year. Janet considered that global warming was to blame for that.

It felt more like a spring day. She made a mental note to ask Mark about that when he came back. He came back about ten minutes later with a covered plate and bowl. The smell coming from them started her mouth to salivate; she was looking forward to consuming them. Mark lifted off the lid of the plate and handed the tray they were on to her to put on her lap. The lasagna looked delicious, and when she tasted it, she forgot it was not meat; she enjoyed every mouth full. After consuming her dinner, she was set loose on the sticky toffee pudding. She ate it quickly, not wanting it to cool, enjoying the indulgence. Once finished, she put down the spoon and handed the tray back to Mark.

"Did you enjoy that?" he asked her.

"Yes, that was so good," Janet said, "I dread to think of the calories in that?"

"Yes, I don't think I would want to know," he said with a smile. "What do you want to know? I could show you the day areas." Janet nodded her agreement and then got into the wheelchair. Mark operated the fob key and then pushed her through the space left by the door. Just then, he stopped pushing her and reached into one of the pockets in his trousers. He pulled out a fob key which he handed to Janet.

"This is for you; it allows you entrance into all the places you need. Like the kitchen and toilet and of course this room." Janet took the fob key, which was on a ribbon, and hung it around her neck; then Mark started to push her, heading towards where the induction had been held. Further along, passed the hall, they came to a lounge area. There were a few comfy chairs and some tables. Someone had been working on a jigsaw and was nearly at the end. Naughtily she thought about hiding the last piece but didn't as she didn't want to get told off by Mark. There was a small bookshelf holding some novels and old magazines.

"What do people do in here?" Janet asked Mark.

"Socialize, they run a writing group here most evenings, you know, people write poems and short stories. A couple of people who are here presently run a music group; they tuned the guitar over there," he said, pointing to a space next to the bookshelves.

"Obviously, it's a bit late now for anything to be going on; if you can think of anything creative to do, you can always take a group. People are pretty willing." Mark wheeled her out of the room and went into a room next door.

Janet knew immediately what the room was for. It was a dining room with a serving hatch and several tables with chairs. Mark told her the opening times and that from now on, she would be having her meals there. Janet asked him how it worked, did they give their orders, then sat down or waited to be served.

Mark confirmed that they bring the meals to the table; you can see the tables have numbers on there. Generally, people use the same table each meal time. They left the dining room and took a left down a corridor. Down on the right of the corridor, Janet noticed a couple of rooms with nameplates on. Janet got close to reading them; they were in therapy rooms one and two.

"You will come here for your physio when your legs are ready," he explained. "There is also a small gym area that they use as well. It has things like a walking rail and weights and steps and things like that. I should imagine you will be coming here once your legs have healed. You know, to get you moving again. Newbies have physio once a day; it's an important part of your care." He turned the chair away and headed back to her room. She used her fob key to let them in then Mark asked her if she felt ready for bed.

"Yes, I am tired. Thank you for showing me what's what," Janet said to dismiss him. He said, "I will see you in the morning. Breakfast is served from half seven til half past eight." With that, he turned around, leaving her to take off her day clothes and change into her night clothes.

She moved the chair to go to the sink, where she washed her hands and face and cleaned her teeth. Once she had finished her toilette, she moved the wheelchair. Mark had shown her how to transfer from chair to bed and vice versa, which she did with ease. She took off her top, noticing a very large black bruise on her chest. It looked like someone had been jumping up and down on her chest; in fact, she thought that was probably what would happen if they tried to resuscitate her. She continued to change, then, when ready, got under the covers and laid on her back to sleep. She thought that she had done OK for a dead person. No major gaffs, nothing done to feel embarrassed about.

She planned the day ahead, thinking that she would love to go outside if it was allowed. Mark hadn't really said anything about the garden she could see from her window. She liked to be outside; one of her greatest pleasures was walking her little dogs in all weathers. They were always up for going out, which meant that she had to move despite the fact that sometimes she really didn't feel up to it.

Janet wondered how her dogs were getting on in their new home. She felt very guilty giving them up like that; she remembered the look on their faces when she dropped them off at their new home. But it had to be done. Janet tried to get her mind on something to induce sleep, and finally, she did some deep breathing exercises, focusing entirely on the movement in her chest, or that was the plan. In reality, her mind wandered off again and again until she gave up the effort.

Finally, she just allowed her mind free range to go where it wanted to go but to just acknowledge it, nothing more. Gradually sleep crept up on her; she had periods of blankness in the narrative, which allowed sleep in. She slept restlessly and fitfully until the morning when the sunlight in her room wakened her. She checked the time on the clock on the wall. It was seven-thirty; she rubbed her eyes, then looked again. She was not sure if she had to stay in her bed until Mark came or risk him coming in mid-wash or clothes change. She knew he was a nurse and all that, well used to the female form, but not hers. She was fifty-nine years of age; he was what, twenty-something?

She made up her mind to get up and see if she could get herself to the loo in the chair. She transferred over then, grabbed hold of the fob key then wheeled herself to the door. The door opened, allowing her passage to the toilet. She checked to see if the door of the toilet had a lock on it. She was tempted to lock it but was worried that if she had some difficulty, Mark would not be able to get in to help her. She decided to lock it; her dignity was worth more than 'what if's.'

When she had finished and went back to her room, she washed and dressed herself. She had every intention of trying out the shower in the wet room that evening but thought she would definitely need Mark as she may have to keep the splints dry. Mark didn't turn up mid-wash or dress; in fact, Janet began to wonder where he was. With breakfast time halfway through, she wanted to go to the canteen, so she set off, wheeling herself slowly along the corridors.

She remembered the route well, passing the day room, which had a couple of people sitting there. At the canteen, she went up to the serving hatch and asked the man manning it for the menu.

The cooked breakfast sounded lovely to Janet, but she stopped herself from ordering it because she really didn't want to get fat. She had a very sweet tooth which was her downfall, and she found that avoidance was the best policy for her. She didn't buy biscuits or sweets or sugary things because she knew she would eat them in one sitting. Janet asked for toast and butter and a mug of tea but was lost to what table she should sit at. Then she spotted someone waving to her. It was Mel; Janet waved back and then told the man who was manning the serving hatch that she was sitting with her; she pointed to the table.

"Table six," he said in a gruff voice.

"Thank you," Janet said, then turned the chair around to move slowly to where Mel was sitting. Mel greeted her warmly then asked her how she had slept; Janet answered her and then asked her the same question. Mel appeared to have slept better than her. Mel had a dressing over her eye. She was having problems with eating as the food came out of the hole in her face.

To counteract it, she used a pad of lint to block the hole as she ate. It seemed to work, but drinking fluids was still a problem. She had to really tip her head back to allow gravity to manage the flow of the liquid. Janet was amazed at just how well Mel seemed to take it. Maybe, Janet thought, she was not aware of just how bad it was.

Mel asked her if she had seen Lisa or Kim, and she said that she had seen them yesterday in the day room. They had held a quiz and were on the same team. She said that they cheated a lot, much to the annoyance of some of the other people. Mel seemed like a lovely person. Janet knew that they were going to become good friends. Janet asked her what she was doing that day. Mel was having her wound cleaned and her damaged eye surgically removed in one of the clinics. Also, they were making arrangements to get a plastic plug to go in the wound to block it to make it easier for her to eat and drink. Janet thought that all sounded amazing. Mel put down her mug and then leaned forward towards Janet.

"How does it look? Is it really terrible?" she asked. Janet was not sure how to answer. She should probably be honest, but she didn't know her well enough to know how she would react. If she lied to her, saying that it wasn't too bad, well, then Mel may hold it against her. Janet decided to be truthful.

"It looks bad, Mel, but I think with the steps they are taking, it will heal well, just leaving a bit of a scar."

"Thank you; I can't look in a mirror; I'm too scared to see what I look like," Mel said. Janet touched her gently on the hand to reassure her.

"I think I would be the same," Janet said earnestly.

"Look, isn't that your Fetcher," Mel said, pointing to the entrance of the dining room.

"Who, Mark?" Janet said as she turned her head to see. Mark spotted Janet and came over.

"Well done, you did it; I knew you could," Mark said to Janet.

"I may need a hand when I have a shower later on," Janet replied. Mark nodded his head at this, then told her that she had an appointment to see the physio later that morning and that they had to go together. She thanked him for passing on the information them let him know she was hoping to go outside for a while.

"It looks like it's a lovely day. I would love to explore the garden." She said. Mark suggested he take her as it was hard work wheeling the chair with her hands. He didn't want her to get blisters.

They agreed on a time to meet in the afternoon then he left her to go about whatever it was he did. Janet felt good having things to do that day; she was especially keen on going outside. The world felt like a better place out there as she could think clearer.

The shower went OK, and the physio focused on her being able to transfer to different chairs safely. The woman she saw said she would make arrangements about getting her an electric wheelchair instead of the manual to get around. Mark offered to go and pick it up from the medical centre that day if it could be arranged. Janet was pleased about that; it would give her independence and save her hands from getting sore. After the appointment, Mark pushed her down one of the corridors near the dining room. There was a door at the end which opened with a press of the fob key.

On the other side was another corridor, very short which led to a door to the outside. This one you had to push; Mark expertly navigated it by turning her around so he could use his body to move the door. He spun her around once they were through. To Janet's delight, she saw that it was more than a garden; it was a park. It had grass and flower beds and trees in a lovely landscaped place. There was a path leading from the door they came out of, which cut the park in two with, as far as Janet could see, small paths coming off it. The park was probably about three acres in size, It was clear it was well looked after, but one thing that surprised Janet was the weather. It was meant to be November. It felt like a lovely late spring day there. She asked Mark how come the weather was so good.

"It's always good here", that was it, her explanation. Janet vowed to find out how come the flowers looked like new this autumn. The trees still had their leaves on, and the grass looked as if it was still growing; and what's more, it looked as if it had been mowed recently. At the far end of the park, she could see little figures of people; they were not moving around, just up and down now and then. Mark told her that they were Brownies tending the garden. Janet found this interesting; she wondered if she could help. She used to love her garden at home. She tried her best to make it bee friendly and colourful. Her dogs always tried to sabotage her work by sitting right where she was working or climbing onto her lap if she was sitting down doing some weeding. She really missed them and hoped they had forgotten about her though she also hoped that they hadn't. Mark wheeled her back after a while, discussing what she had thought about her day. Janet was pleased it had been so productive and planned to make sure she had a full diary of activities each day. After dinner, Janet returned to her room with Mark. He opened the door and proudly showed her a power wheelchair in her room.

"It's all charged up and ready to go. Do you want to give it a go?" Asked Mark. Janet nodded her agreement and transferred from one wheelchair to the other. He quickly went through the controls with her, then left her to play. Janet was worried she would end up destroying the place but managed to turn it around to face the corridor.

"Of you go," said Mark as she disappeared off down the path. She mastered the controls quickly, then when she felt ready, head back to her room. She was getting tired; it had been a busy day, but a good one.

One thing that did hit Janet was the smell. It was a smell she could only relate to one thing; it was the smell of the death.

Chapter 3
Newbie

Janet was not sure how long she had slept; upon waking, she saw that Mark was in her room, pulling open the curtains. Sunlight tickled objects in the room and on her face. It felt nice. She had slept well, not like the nights of interrupted slumber she had been dealing with for the last month or so. Janet stretched out her arms, shoving away the last lingers of sleep. She felt surprisingly good as a dead person; she felt alive and looking forward, which is something she had been unable to do in recent weeks. Mark turned to look at her "you must be hungry; it's a bit late to go to the dining room. I could make you toast, he said."

"Oh yes, please, is it really that late? You should have woken me." Janet replied. Then she said sincerely, looking intently at Mark, "It can't be right; zombies don't eat breakfast."

"Well, you are not a zombie, so tea or coffee with your toast. I'm pretty sure we've got orange juice; do you want that?"

"Oh, a cup of tea would go down a treat, toast and orange juice if possible."

"Do you want marmalade or jam with your toast, and I have you down as a no sugar person, am I right?" he asked, standing up.

"Marmalade would be fine, thanks, and no sugar."

"OK, I won't be long; you do not have much to do today, just physio. You should meet some of the others in the lounge; I think they are having a debating session. That's usually good for a laugh, they choose ridiculous subjects to argue about, and it gets quite heated. Be back in a sec," Mark said as he turned around and left the room through the whoosh door.

Janet pulled herself up into a seated position. She tried to see if she could look outside through the window. She tentatively moved her legs over the side of the bed in order to improve the view. Then she stupidly tried to stand up instead of this, but her legs gave way, and she slumped onto the floor. She hit her head on the way down by crashing into the wheelchair. She rubbed her head, feeling annoyed at what she had done, but, realizing that she was stuck, called out for Mark. She cursed at herself as she remembered, too late, that the door made the room soundproof. She would naturally expect her legs to hurt after a fall like that; instead, there was numbness. Almost as if the pain was blurred. She tried to inflict pain on herself by pinching the skin and hitting her legs. But there was nothing except for the pressure of the blows. She knew that they administered pain relief, but she was just frustrated at being infirm and reliant on Mark. How can you break your legs and not be in pain? Janet thought over and over again. She had a feeling that today was not going to be good. She felt a bump on her head where she had knocked herself on the way down, but there was no bleeding. Janet felt some tears dropping down her face, and she brushed them away angrily; this really was not the time to cry, she thought. She tried to get herself up by holding onto the chair to heave herself up but lacked the upper body strength. Slumping back down, she tried to work out what would help the situation. What helped the situation came in the door; Mark entered the room carrying a tray about ten minutes later. Seeing her on the floor, he immediately set down the tray to go to her aid. She offered an explanation while he examined her legs. "I can't see any more damage, so when you are ready, we will get you up," He instructed her to put her arms around his neck while he lifted her up and onto the bed.

"Thank you," said Janet, "I'm sorry."

"Don't apologies; no harm done." Said Mark as he moved the tray nearer to her where she could reach. "If you like, we can go out into the garden later on; it's a beautiful day,"

"Is this heaven, Mark?" asked Janet.

"No, it's not heaven. This is a place where people who die too soon from trauma come to live out their lives to old age and Graduation. Now, eat your breakfast," Janet pulled the tray towards her, lifted a half slice of buttered toast, sniffed it, tentatively nibbled a corner, then, satisfied it was kosher, took a larger bite followed by a mouthful of juice.

"Enjoy," said Mark. "I will be back soon," he left the room content his charge was ok. Janet ate her breakfast quickly; she was surprised at just how hungry she was. The tea particularly went down well. When she had finished her food, she wiped her mouth to dislodge the crumbs with the back of her hand and then had a bit of a stretch. She began to get her head around getting washed and dressed but knew she needed Mark to help her with that. She checked the lump on her head gingerly and then looked at the fingers to see if there was any blood. She was satisfied that it was not a major injury; she had no signs of head trauma, so she would live another day, even though she wouldn't'. Janet found it hard to get her head around that concept, and it just seemed to get her into confused mind talk. She realised that she was doing a lot of mind talk and tried to drag herself to the here and now. Mark came in at that point and removed her crockery and cutlery and put them on the dressing table. He said he would get her a bowl of hot water and some towels so she could give herself a strip wash. He gathered her up some clothes to wear and then left to get the water. He was back in next to no time, placing the large wash bowl on the seat of the wheelchair.

"Do you need me to help you?" he asked.

"No, I should be fine," she replied, then waited until he had left the room to remove her night dress. She looked down at her chest, seeing the bruising from the accident. It looked less dark than yesterday. It looked purple around the edges. Signs that it was dispersing, she thought. She, for some reason, decided to touch the bruised area expecting to feel something. She felt her fingers on the skin but no pain. That is seriously good stuff they use, she thought. Grabbing the wash towel, she dipped it in the water and then scrubbed the towel onto the soap. She gently washed her body bit by bit until she had cleaned all she could reach. Satisfied that she would pass as clean, she dressed quickly as she did not want Mark to come in a mid-dress. She knew he was a nurse and had seen it all before, but to her, he was a young man. She debated with herself if she would feel different about it if she was young and gorgeous instead of old and ugly, but no, that wouldn't work either. She would still feel awkward. Mark came in through the woosh door and looked over at Janet.

"All done?" he asked.

"Yes, I feel so much better after that," Janet said, gathering up the washing implements and handing them to Mark. She did feel better after having a wash, but she also felt drained. Janet's day as a Newbie wasn't as productive as the last. She spent a lot of her time in her room, drifting in and out of sleep. She did not get out into the garden but spent periods of time looking out of the window at the garden from her room. While sitting in the powerchair, she was able to observe people wearing various coloured tunics. Some, those with brown tunics and trousers, tended to the plants; others in yellow tunics were just enjoying the space; Janet was happy to just watch. She went inside herself, distancing herself beyond the window into the garden. In her inner world, she saw life as a spectator like a ghost, invisible to many, visible to the few. As evening approached, yellow-clad Newbies headed inside to comply with the curfew. Mark popped in every now and then throughout the day to check on her. He was concerned about her mood; she seemed low to him. He planned to sleep in the spare room a couple of doors down that night so he could see her throughout the night. On one of his visits, he came in carrying a tray with a sandwich and a mug of tea on it. She had barely eaten that day; he hoped she would have the food. Janet was sitting in the wheelchair, just staring out of the window; she asked him about the curfew; it seemed odd to her that it would be frowned upon to be outside at five o'clock in the afternoon. There was so much of the day left, so much time to have the benefits of fresh air and sunlight.

"I know it must sound odd, but various drugs are pumped through the walls."

"What drugs, what do you mean?" asked Janet.

"Pain relief and antibiotics. The walls are porous; they infuse through the walls they keep the pain at bay to support healing. I can adjust how much you need using this dial here," he said, indicating a small round dial on the wall by the door. "As you heal, I adjust how much you have.

"So, the glow I see coming out of the walls, is that? Asked Janet.

"Yes, that's right. It really is not anything to be fearful about," He pointed to the tray of food, 'Don't forget your tea," Janet picked up the mug of steaming tea, sipping it carefully. Mark explained that the Fetchers worked on a one-to-one basis with Newbies because they are at risk, as I was earlier that day, of injury or causing further damage to themselves because the pain had been eradicated. The Inner Circle had regular reviews of this treatment to see if the positive benefits outweigh the risks.

"The Inner Circle, what's that when it's a home," she asked.

"They are the top guns who live and work in the Nerve Centre. The place where all the big decisions are made." He said, pointing at the sandwich.

"What about you, Mark? What's your story." She asked Mark as he helped her get back in her bed,

"It will only bore you; we need to focus on you," he responded, plumping up her pillow

"No, tell me, come sit down," she patted the bed; he relented, sat down, took a deep breath, exhaled, and then began his story.

" I was killed when I came off my motorbike. My helmet was not fastened properly; it flew off, my head took the impact, my neck broke, and death was quick."

"How come you are able to walk?" Janet enquired, "surely a broken neck would paralyze you; why can you walk? I don't understand."

Mark took another deep breath before continuing his narrative.

"My injuries were incompatible with life on earth, but here," he gestured, taking in the room, " the rules are different, it took time to heal and recover, but I walk well, have most of my sensations back, as they said in your induction some bodies are too damaged leaving degrees of disability. I did OK; I got away with it. Now, do you want something to drink before bedtime" he enquired?

" Yes, please!"

"Let me guess, tea?"

"Yes, please," replied Janet, already feeling drowsy; it was hard work recovering. She settled down early to sleep that night. Mark popped his head around the door throughout the night to make sure she was OK. She had been through so much these last few days; it was not surprising she wasn't coping too well. She slept deeply as if her body knew there was much healing to be done, mentally as well as physically. Her dreams were her memories, delving into her life on earth, where everything was roses. Only it wasn't all roses, yes, some of it was, but the rest was bloody hard work. She always felt like she had to be a people pleaser. She bent over backwards to be helpful, even if it was to the detriment to herself. Anything to get love and attention. She was always a needy person, but that desire was met in the gratitude of others in her acts of kindness. Janet would have been classed as complex if anyone was classifying her, but despite feeling as if she always put others first, she did OK. Her life on earth was OK. But here, on Second Chance, the rules were different. She didn't know the rules here. It would take her time to get used to how things work here. So though her sleep was deep as her body healed, her dreams were healing her mind. In the morning, she woke up with a promise to herself to achieve more this day. She did her toilette in good time to be decent when Mark came in. He got his timing right by knocking on the door to herald his arrival just as she was folding her night clothes and putting them on her pillow.

"Are you OK, Janet? Do you feel up to going to the dining room for your breakfast?" Mark asked her.

"Yes, I can go to the dining room; now I've got the wheelchair; I need to make the most of it. Am I allowed to go into the park on my own?" she asked.

"Yes, of course. I have got you a new fob key. This one not only unlocks the doors but summons me if you need help. You press this button here, can you see?" He bent down, showing her the button on the side of the key. She took it and hung it around her neck, then neatly transferred from her bed into the power wheelchair. She got hold of the tiller, moving it forwards to move the chair. Mark came with her to the dining room to make sure there were no obstacles and also to give her a hand with her tray. Janet spotted Lisa and Kim already seated. They looked up as she came in, and they beckoned her over. With a bit of scraping of chairs, they made room at the table for her and the chair. Mark went up to the counter to order her breakfast and then brought it over to her when it was ready.

"I'm going to leave you three to chat; if you need anything, Janet, just press the button," with that, Mark turned around and exited the room. Kim and Lisa filled her in on the gossip, not that

Janet knew who the person was who apparently kicked off in the dining room yesterday. Apparently, he hurt one of the Fetchers who needed medical treatment. They sedated the man and then put him on suicide watch. Janet was amazed at the level of detail they seemed to know. They must have been present, thought Janet. Janet didn't engage much in conversation. She was happy just listening to their chatter. Lisa was quite animated at times; however normal all this seemed, it felt false to Janet; all of it, it was all wrong. She didn't share any of that with the two girls but just smiled and nodded at the right moments. After breakfast, she had time to kill before her appointment with the physio, so she used the time to go outside into the park. She had no problems negotiating the doors and the corridors. Even the push door to the outside was not too heavy for her to manage. She found steering the chair pretty easy. It was very responsive with a small turning circle. She was determined to go over to where she saw the people in brown working the day before. When she looked, she could not see anyone there but made her way over non the less. The day was the same as when she was last out there, a warm spring day. She had lost track of the day of the week; she would have to ask Mark when she saw him next. He was bound to know. She stopped the chair under the leaves of a large oak tree. No one was around; she felt very alone, and she was not in a good place. However, she recognized that she was at a loss as to what to do.

The next couple of days passed quickly; Janet had gotten into a routine that seemed to serve her well. Mark continued to keep an eye on her, not convinced she was telling the truth when he asked her how she was. He had enough nursing experience to know when something was wrong. She was quite evasive when he questioned her; she avoided his eyes and mumbled her answers. Nevertheless, Janet continued to go outside into the park at least once a day; she loved the feeling of the fresh air on her face. Mark, as always, was very attentive; in her room, he seemed to know when to go to her aid and when to let her try to manage things. He was a sweet person, very kind and gentle, and he was very skilled when he nursed her having to be so aware of her vulnerability. On the fourth day, Janet woke up, opened her eyes, then closed them, and slumped back on the bed, groaning. She didn't want to get up and face the day; she sighed, sat up again and called for Mark using her pendant. Mark entered the room a few minutes later. Seeing her, he immediately went to bed and gently placed a reassuring hand on her shoulder. "I guess the honeymoon period is over," he said "people generally crash on the fourth or fifth day. When he said that, Janet dissolved into tears. She cried from the bottom of her stomach. Deep, heaving sounds left her body as she uncontrollably let everything out. Mark held her to him, letting her cry it out. He was pleased she had been able to do this; it may help her, he thought. When she finally stopped crying, Mark handed her a tissue from his pocket so she could blow her nose and wipe away the tears. Janet was exhausted but looked haunted, distraught. Mark let her go, then stood up,

"Let me get you some tea." He said, then left the room. Janet moved her encased legs over the side of the bed and then expertly moved her body into the wheelchair. She drove it to the space by the window in the hope the daylight would lift her spirit. She watched the nameless people moving around outside in the garden, feeling so distant, so alone. The shape of their bodies now getting familiar from regular viewing, she contemplated, not for the first time, that this place was wrong; none of it made sense; why was she here? Thinking this way made her feel tired and sad. She wished her suicide attempt had worked, but it had; no, it hadn't. No. She was losing herself in this pointless argument. Fortunately, Mark came in with her tea and breakfast, which, at least for a short while, broke the circle of thought. Janet accepted the tray. She picked up the cup, circling her hands around it. She felt the onset of tears again; she cried the silent cries of those who had reached the end. She looked at Mark, crying, "I don't understand why this is happening. I am dead. I killed myself. I don't want to be alive."

Mark motioned for her to drink her tea. "I have put something in your tea to help you," he said. Janet just nodded, feeling a bit of her autonomy drift away; no change there, she thought, that happens on earth. She felt too tired to kick up a fuss. Instead, she sunk in her chair, giving consent to Mark to steer her to her bed. He helped her to transfer over and then tucked her in. he kissed her on her forehead as the drug took hold. Her body quickly relaxed into the bed and her eyes closed as they entered an induced slumber. She needed to rest, thought Mark. She has a lot on her plate. Once he was satisfied she was sleeping, he popped out for a moment to go to his temporary room, where he grabbed a magazine. He returned to her bedside and sat down in a chair next to the dressing table near the window. He flicked through the pages, now and then looking up to check on Janet. He would let the physio know soon that she was not up to coming that day and make arrangements for fellow Fetcher Bonnie to come and sit with her while he grabbed something to eat. It always seemed odd to him that they call this suicide watch, as the dead are already dead and can't re-die through suicide. However, her level of distress was such that he wanted her to feel reassured that she was not on her own.

Janet slept all morning and the first part of the afternoon deeply. She finally woke up when the drug had left her system. She opened her eyes briefly, feeling as if they were full of grit. She rubbed her eyes and then looked around her. She saw Mark sitting by the window, looking over at her.

"Are you OK, sweetheart?" he said, standing up and coming over to the bed. She felt drained, but at least her thoughts were behaving themselves.

"What time is it?" she asked him.

"It's four-thirty. Do you want something to drink?" he said.

"Yes, just some water, please."

"OK."

She considered her next step; she felt that she had to mark the day somehow to achieve something. "It will get better, you know," Mark said as he came over with some water in a glass. He moved a lock of her hair off her face. It felt too intimate for Janet, who gently pushed his hand away.

"Do you want anything to eat?" Mark asked her.

"Yes, something light, a sandwich," she replied. Mark stood up and walked out of the room, leaving Janet to her thoughts. She felt annoyed that Mark had drugged her; she would have liked to be asked. It took her back to being a patient in a psychiatric hospital when giving out drugs like smarties were commonplace, with or without patient consent. She hated it then, despite knowing that it was done with her welfare in mind. The action was dehumanizing and paternalistic, like her own mind and decision-making abilities were questionable. Janet considered the mode of delivering pain relief and antibiotics through the walls in the rooms and corridors. There was no easy escape from it; all this made her feel deeply uneasy. She was missing her freedom. She came to this place with no consultation, no choice and expected to stick to the rules and play the game. Janet had always been a rebellious type; she kicked up about injustice and powerlessness, whether for herself or affecting others. She thought about Mark, who seemed nice enough; he made a good carer. She was concerned about becoming dependent on him; she realised the need to talk to him about this and the other things occupying her mind. When he came in with her sandwich and mug of tea, she smiled thanks to him, then thoughtfully ate her food, silently running through the conversation to lay her concerns on the table. For some reason, she felt uneasy about doing that because it clashed in her brain with the sense of things being unreal, not knowing the rules, what's OK, and what's not. Maybe she should shelve the conversation for now.

Janet felt stronger each day. She was able to manoeuvre well in the wheelchair and cope with being non-weight bearing with transfers. Her upper body strength was improved by doing twice-daily exercises with weights set by the physio, which Mark talked her through. Sometimes he joined in; it was a fun time, especially when he brought music in via a cd player. They did bicep curls to nineties dance tracks. It lifted Janet's spirits for a while. She had met up with Mel and the others in the day room a few times. They seemed to be doing OK. One day Mark suggested they go to a social event in the induction room hall. They were holding a karaoke evening, and every newbie was invited. Janet was in two minds about going. She always felt awkward at these kinds of events because she had a crap singing voice and dreaded someone suggesting she sing a song, but on the other hand, it would be good to be around others for a while. In the end, she agreed to go thinking it would be nice to see Kim, Lisa and Mel again. Mark brushed her hair for her, carefully manipulating it into a French plait. She was pleased with the result and thanked him for doing it. After curfew, they left her room and journeyed down the numerous corridors to the hall. She heard the sound of a party before they got in the room. Janet felt a bit excited, which she declared to Mark. The door to the hall opened, which amplified the sound of music and chatter. There was a good number of people there, a few she recognized from her induction, others that she knew from going in the garden. She scoured the faces looking for the girls hoping that they would attend. Just then, she heard someone shout out…

"Janet, Janet, how are you? It's so good to see you." Janet looked around for the person who had spoken. Then she spotted Lisa waving at her. Janet moved the chair over to where Lisa stood, who in turn called out to get Mel's attention. Mel was dancing with a bloke who looked as if he had been run over. Literally, his torso looked squashed in. Mel, hearing her name being called, turned around to face Janet and Mark; she immediately moved over to them, and she came over to Janet and gave her a hug. Mel's face looked less gory as it healed; there were signs of scar tissue growing around the hole. Janet and Mel fell into friendly chatter; at that point, Mark took his leave, satisfied that Janet was in good hands. Janet asked Mel if Kim was there; Mel replied the negative but explained that she was having a tough time. The chatter was mixed in with sing-song and dance. It was noisy and busy but a whole lot of fun. After a while, Mel went off to get Janet a drink, they could not serve alcohol there, but the fresh lemonade was proving to be very popular. Janet took the opportunity to ask both Mel and Lisa how they were settling in and to share some of her concerns. They were both very impressed with their care and treatment and were sympathetic to Janet's mild paranoia if, indeed, that is what it was. Nothing was at it first seemed in this strange new world. Maybe, thought Janet, she is reading too much into everything. Satisfied, Janet joined in the girly banter. Then Mel left them to get on the small rectangular stage to sing. She had a beautiful singing voice doing 'I will survive' justice, with near enough everyone in the room joining in, including Janet. Lisa and Mel did a duo which was fun; Janet declined to join them, which was not a big deal. The evening was going well, Janet was pleased she had gone, but halfway through the evening felt her energy plummet. She felt very tired, so tired she was experiencing mind fog, giving odd answers to questions posed to her. She realized she needed to rest. She pressed the button to summon Mark, who appeared about ten minutes later. On seeing him, she apologized to him for disturbing him, which he shook off. He asked her how she was, but she really didn't need to answer; he could guess just by looking at her. Her face was pale, and she was shaking. Mark walked with her as she said her goodbyes and headed back home. He helped her to undress and then settled her in her bed. After saying night, he left the room after turning off the light. She fell asleep almost immediately. Her dreams were vivid and wild; she woke up at one point sweating but soon drifted off back to sleep.

Mark stayed in the spare room that night but popped into her room every now and then, checking her out. He watched her sleeping, wondering what was going through her mind. Bonnie, another Fetcher, was due to come and sit with Janet for a while so he could get something to eat and have a sleep. When she came, he gave her a quick handover and then left Janet with Bonnie while he went to the canteen to see if there was a sandwich with his name on it. Bonnie sat near the window by the dressing table where she could check Janet without being on top of her. She had been warned by Mark that she was a high suicide risk, so he was taking no chances by staying with her. Janet tossed the sheets in her sleep. She was moving about so much that she risked trapping her body in the bedcovers. She woke up with a start on a couple of occasions; Bonnie got up from her chair and went over to the bed to soothe Janet and reassure her that she was not alone. She hated to see someone so troubled. There was so much anguish there, so much confusion, so many questions.

Chapter 4
Yellow to Green

Janet improved day by day, both mentally and physically. She mastered everything coming her way well; she had absolutely every right to be pleased with herself. She tended to the daily physio appointment and was delighted when she was told her left leg had healed enough to remove the strapping. Janet was delighted by that but asked her about her right leg. The physio explained that the leg had taken the brunt of the fall and had more complicated fractures, so it would take a bit longer to heal. The day she had her brace removed was the day she had been waiting for for ages. It meant that she could start to weigh bare and hopefully ditch the wheelchair.

So, Janet whooped with delight when Mark entered her room with a pair of crutches. For Janet, it was huge progress. She would need to use the wheelchair occasionally as, Mark had said, using crutches was hard work. She reached for the support, eager to give them a try. She used them to stand up, then took a tentative hop forward onto her left leg. It marked her next step to independence. However much she had come to love Mark, she knew she had to find ways to manage without him. Janet took a few more steps, gaining confidence. Mark looked on like a proud parent, just staying close enough to catch her in case she fell. Janet pointed to the door with the crutch in her right hand, "can you open the door please, Mark,"

"Of course, just don't overdo it," He used his fob key to open the door, which opened with a satisfying familiar whoosh. Janet hopped out into the corridor, gaining speed.

"Slow down, take care," shouted Mark, who followed her out, steering the wheelchair. He started to get worried when she went zooming up the corridor; she could so easily slip on this surface. Just then, his fears were realised when Janet's foot slipped on the glossy floor. She stumbled and then fell to the floor in a heap. Mark rushed over to her, expecting the worse. He was worried she had re-fractured her leg; Janet, winded, turned her head and looked up at Mark with a huge smile on her face. She accepted his help to assist her in climbing into the chair, holding the pair of crutches in her left hand. Mark accompanied her back to her bedroom, not saying a word. He knew if he told her off, it would fall on deaf ears, so he didn't bother.

He knelt in front of her to examine her, taking care to see if she had sustained an injury from the fall. The infused painkillers wiped out the main symptoms of trauma, which made it harder to detect. Mark gently felt down her legs for irregularities, finding nothing out of the ordinary. He breathed out harshly with relief. He had got to know Janet in the time they had worked together to know that telling her off would not work. Instead of chastising her and suggesting she take it easy, he just asked her if she was OK.

"I'm fine, sorry about that, and I went too fast. I will try again later," said Janet. Satisfied with her answer, he helped her get on the bed and moved the crutches to the side next to the top of the bed so she could reach them when she was ready. He asked her if she needed anything before leaving her to rest. Janet smiled to herself as she snuggled down on the bed, appreciating the comfort and warmth. She was so pleased to be making progress and be less reliant on Mark.

She had been living in Second Chance for nearly six weeks now. Her body was mending well though her legs would not win her any prizes in a beauty pageant. The internal injuries were not causing her too many problems; her stomach objected to some types of food, causing constipation and excess wind. Mark and Janet had devised a wind language to lighten the mood and remove any embarrassment she experienced. But it still concerned her a lot and often impacted on when she mixed with others. Still, sticking to foods that caused her less of a problem was the right thing to do, and thankfully, there was a good choice of food in the dining room. Her depression still lurked under the surface; she was still frequently plagued with intrusive thoughts, which she kept to herself, still uncertain about disclosing them to Mark. Mark delighted in his charges practice using the crutches; he hoped it would keep her mood good. He had been aware of the times she looked pained. He was hoping and waiting for her to find the strength to talk to him about it. He had reduced her intake of pain relief bit by bit over the past few weeks. She was not showing any signs of withdrawal and did not complain of pain, so it was working for her. They would spend a lot of time chatting, and he felt he had a handle on her moods. She was sceptical about Second Chance as she still felt cheated of death. It must be hard, he thought, being kept in a place where you don't want to be. Still, he was proud of her progress and was always willing to listen to her moans.

Mark had always been a good listener. He was the quiet, thoughtful member of the family, or 'sensitive' as they liked to say. He was the youngest of three siblings, the much-wanted boy, but it soon became obvious that he was more effeminate than his two sisters. Coming out as gay took time; he was worried about the reaction from his conservative parents. But, when he finally found the courage to tell them, he was pleasantly surprised at how accepting they were. His father appeared to be proud of his courage to say he was gay. Mark's mum told him that she knew he was gay from when he was a young boy. So, it did not come as a surprise to her. It was a pleasant surprise when he was asked what he wanted for his 18th birthday. His parents thought his request for a motorbike made him manly. Lo and behold, he was duly given a red 125cc Suzuki bike that became his constant companion. He named her Dorothy after the character in East Enders and took his CBT training before being let loose on the roads. Unknown to his parents requesting such a machine for his birthday served two purposes, his escape and a sweetener for his family for when he dropped the bombshell, his intention to study and train as a nurse. He thought there would be fewer homophobic comments, and it worked.

He knew he had found his true vocation as a nurse; he felt fulfilled. His workmates accepted him, his patients thought him caring and kind, and he was doing OK. Just one thing missing in his life, the 'one', a partner to settle down with. He had the odd date, meeting some really nice people but no one whom he could imagine spending the rest of his life with. Nothing serious until he met Ron in a pub. Mark went to the Frog and Carrot on a regular basis to meet up with his friends. On this occasion, he was out with Rebecca and Ruth, his sisters, for the evening. While he was drinking his beer at the table near the gents, Ruth told him that there was a bloke at the bar giving him the eyes. They urged him to look and see if he was the kind of person he went for, but he got embarrassed, so he focused on his drink instead. Rebecca called the man over, much to Mark's annoyance and nearly died when this rather handsome man came over.

"Hello girls, who is this you are with?" he asked. Rebecca introduced Mark to him and then asked him his name and if he was available. Mark kicked her under the table in the hope she would shut up, but she carried on talking to the man. Eventually, Mark felt confident enough to turn around in his chair to look at him. He was a rather good-looking blond, nice tan, lovely bum, he thought.

"Hi Mark, I'm Ron. Can I join you?" asked Ron.

"Yes, of course. Do you want a drink?" Mark asked as he finished his beer and stood up to go back to the bar.

"No thanks, I'm driving; I've had enough," Ron said, putting his coke on the table. At that point, they shared some get-to-know-you questions then chatter peeled off very naturally. Rebecca and Ruth left them chatting to go to the bar and get drinks. They left the men until it was time to go home. Ruth made sure Mark gave Ron his contact details before they left. Ron offered to give Mark a lift home which he declined. He felt it was too soon to be doing that kind of thing; he was a very old-fashioned kind of a man.

Mark hoped Ron would contact him; he didn't expect him to, so when he rang the next day, he was delighted. The rest, as they say, is history. Ron proposed to Mark on his twenty-first birthday; Mark burst into tears at the proposal; he had never imagined that this could happen to him. Mark said Yes, quite a few times in succession, then threw his arms around him with delight.

Mark's parents were, thankfully, impressed by Ron. They could see them both together as a couple. Mark was at first concerned about their reaction; often, the good-natured teasing from his father about him being gay wore a bit thin and cut to the bone. His sisters were vocal with their thoughts that Ron was too handsome not to be straight and teased them both relentlessly by flirting with him in Mark's presence. Mark knew it was play and joined in the game by pretending to dump Ron to free him up for his sisters. All was good with talk about civil partnership and babies; Ron and Mark were good together.

Two years into their relationship, they were busy getting the final tasks ready for their marriage the next day. The identical smart suits hung up on the wardrobe with highly polished shoes all ready for smart socked feet. They had thought of everything to make sure the day went as planned. Mark's two sisters were bridesmaids wearing rainbow-coloured dresses. The hair designer was coming in the morning to do all their hair, including his mum, who was going to walk him down the aisle. Ron's mum was walking Ron down the aisle, so she was having her hair done at the same time. Both mums were going to wear matching outfits in style but in different colours.

They had planned out everything and planned contingency plans in case the first plan got scuppered.

The day was going to be perfect. They had chosen the music carefully, picking out songs that meant something special to them. So, they had near enough done all they could for the day, and they were hoping to get to bed to have a good night's sleep. They were sleeping in separate rooms that night in time honoured tradition. Both of the boys felt nervous mixed with heightened excitement mixed with alcohol-fuelled work, until work had to stop because something had been forgotten.

The Party Favours were in the wrong place at Ron's mum instead of the lover's flat. Mark pulled on his helmet and then left the flat to make the short journey on Dorothy to pick up the gifts. That was the last time Mark saw Ron. On the way back from picking up the gifts, Mark hurried home. The weather was unpleasant, and he had full element overload on the bike. His visor was steaming up from the cold drizzle despite Mark trying to de-fog it. Then the bike slid on black ice, catapulting Mark in the path of a car driver. His helmet fell off from where he had been trying to de-fog; it landed on the ground, rocking a bit before it lay still on the road. The distraught driver got out of his car and hurried over to where Mark lay and tried to see if he could help. There was a pool of blood underneath Mark's head where it had taken the impact, and his neck looked like it was at an odd angle. The man felt for a pulse on the writs; not feeling one, he tried the carotid artery. He thought he could detect something and relayed that to his passenger, who had also gotten out of the car.

The passenger used his mobile phone to call for an ambulance which only took a few minutes to arrive. Unfortunately for Mark, within one minute of that time, his pulse registered nil beats per minute, and he had died. Mark's last journey opened the door to Second Chance. In time his body had mended, and his life had meaning, but the loss of love stayed deep in his heart. He was a natural being a Fetcher. He had always been good around people and enjoyed the challenge.

Janet certainly was a challenge; she was very angry at the world; he just wished she would open up to him. He might not always have the right things to say or a way to put things right, but he was a good listener. Janet could not see that she was angry; anger is something Janet doesn't do. Experience as someone who used mental health services had left her in denial about strong emotions like anger and hate. They were way too strong and had negative connotations and were things she had learnt to suppress. As well as her ongoing struggle in the internal world, she was increasingly disturbed by this place called Second Chance. She absolutely disliked the lack of choice about medication with the infusion of painkillers and antibiotics through vents in the walls.

This, she felt, disempowered her and made her concerned about what else the establishment did to keep the natives compliant. Maybe they infused sedatives, antidepressants or narcotics. The list of possibilities frightened her and made her deeply concerned. She had had the experience of being detained by the mental health act before, which gave the medical profession the right to administer medication to her if she refused. This had seriously worried her and undoubtedly caused long hard scars in her mind. Janet also often felt annoyed by Mark's attentiveness but didn't feel able to talk to him about it. It felt like Big Brother; she particularly was concerned about whom he reported to and what he reported. She didn't know the hierarchy and where she fits in in the strange place of Second Chance.

Janet felt uneasy around other Newbies as they all seemed false. They seemed to be settling in better than her. Both Lisa and Mel were enamoured with Second Chance; they were having fun. Janet questioned what there was to have fun about but kept her thoughts to herself. Most of the Newbies, accompanied by their Fetchers, went to the various social events held in the induction hall. Occasionally the two suited men, Stephen and Tony, joined them, circulating to chat with people. They played indoor bowls or indoor Curling, cards, dances, and storytelling.

Some people took part in self-improvement sessions, including Mindfulness and Yoga. Mark gently urged Janet to participate in these, but Janet refused, saying it was not her cup of tea. Janet looked on at the others, shaking her head, thinking what was wrong with them. Once she took Mel to one side, asking her if she had given up on her past life, Mel shook her head no, explaining that she has had to accept there is no going back. This, Janet tried hard to understand; no doubt the fact that she took her own life would make this concept difficult. She tried to leave the earth and her existence, so going back to it would go against everything she had meticulously planned for. The thought of going back could not be on the agenda, and by the look of it, not happening. She had been told that in Second Chance, people only die from old age; she had no choice but to buckle down to living a life here. For someone who liked to be in control, all this was proving very challenging and gave Janet every right to be angry.

Over time Janet noticed that the social events were attended by new Newbies, and the ones that she knew stopped attending. It was the same in the dining room and the lounge. She had not seen Lisa and Kim for a while, which was odd as they were always around. Two days later, she met Mel in the corridor; she was making her way to the induction hall to join in with a quiz, and Janet was on her way out into the garden. Janet stopped to chat with her listening intently as she filled her in with all her news. Janet took the opportunity to ask Mel if she had seen the girls.

"Oh, hadn't you heard," she said, "they've been moved on; they were ready to go to the next place,"

"Really, when did that happen," asked Janet.

"Kim went Monday, Lisa yesterday. I'm off next week. Do you know when you're moving yet?"

"No, not yet. Mark said I had to be able to weight bare on both legs and not need the crutches,"

"That should not be too long; you are doing so well," said Mel. They caught up on some gossip and then went on their way with a smile and a wave. Janet hopped down the corridor taking the first door down a different corridor that led to the entry to the garden. It was a place she liked to be. It gave her the chance to think and calm down. The weather was always good, the temperature was always nice, and the sun always shone; it was reliable and constant. She always hoped some of that would rub off on her. She lowered herself down onto the lawn, amazed at just how well she now managed on the crutches. Mark rarely accompanied her anywhere nowadays, probably, thought Janet, part of the separation process. The last thing she needed was to lean too much on him. Lying down, she looked up at the sky. As her body relaxed and her mind was soothed, she drifted off to a half sleep. Part of her was still aware of her surroundings. The other part succumbed to the relaxation. She remained like this for a good couple of hours. Once fully awake and ready, she weaved her way down the corridors to her room in good time for the curfew of five o'clock. She made an effort to go to the gardens every day; it helped her to stay sane and well-balanced. She felt at peace watching the plants nod their heads with each gust of wind. The grass was beautifully manicured, and the beds were immaculate. Brown-clothed Second Chancers worked quietly, keeping the gardens beautiful. The air filled her senses with a light breeze tickling her skin which was refreshing, and a light perfume rose from the flowers.

One day, Janet was sitting on a bench in the garden, feeling the sun on her face. She bent down to pick a flower and raised it to her nose when she suddenly thought of something. *Where were the insects? Where were the bees? No butterflies, no ants.* The flower beds were just too perfect, the lawn too regular. Janet felt her good mood evaporate when she looked around her in dismay. She felt sick, nausea unsettled her stomach, and she dry heaved, nothing able to come up. She got onto her crutches and hurried indoors, feeling that the outside was as false and controlled as everywhere else in this godforsaken place. She felt tears make their way down her cheeks, which she tried to wipe away with her sleeve. She could not stem the flow, so she stopped trying; she used her energy to make her way back to her room without anyone stopping her to ask her if there was anything wrong. It was all wrong. Mark saw her enter her room; he immediately went to her side to find out what had happened. Tears still rolling down her face, she lowered herself onto the chair in her room. She carefully placed the crutches down on the ground next to the chair, then looked up at Mark, too distressed to speak and not sure how safe it was to tell him what she felt.

"Let me get you some tea, then let's chat, OK?" said Mark leaving the room to go to the kitchen a few doors down. Janet appreciated him leaving so she could compose herself and try to work out what she needed to say. Drying her eyes and blowing her nose, she moved the fallen crutches from the floor to the place they belonged next to the bed. She used the arms of the chair to lift herself up, taking care to lift her still-mending leg. She moved to sit on the bed. Mark came in at that point, carrying a mug of steaming tea. He handed it to her, which she took with gratitude and a small smile. He moved to the bedside cabinet on the far side of the bed to get Janet some clean paper handkerchief, which she took before taking a mouthful of the liquid.

"This is just tea, isn't it?" She asked.

"Just drink it; you will feel better," he replied, lifting her hand and holding the mug to her lips.

"No, Mark, no, you can't do that to me, please." Janet felt the tears start up again as she felt the familiar wave of sedation run like fluids over her body. She stared at Mark shaking her head "no, no, no." Confident the drug had taken hold; he gently pulled the covers over her before kissing her gently on her forehead.

"I'm sorry; sleep well," he said, looking at her before leaving the room.

The next day Janet was subdued, partly due to the medication she had taken and partly because she was upset with Mark. She barely made eye contact with him when he was helping her with her shoes. She knew where the power lay in this relationship, and for now, she would go along with it. At the earliest possible time, she took herself off to the garden where she could get peace and in order to reflect, evaluate and plan. She chose her favourite spot under the cherry tree, sat down and started to make a daisy chain. As she pierced the stem and threaded the next one through the gap, she quickly entered a focused point of mind.

Her thoughts, once focused, rocked between this life, death, life scenario. She had no idea what to believe except that she really did not want to be here in Second Chance. She felt oppressed, confused and powerless. She knew in her heart that Mark was putting her wellbeing at the centre of his care; she was pretty sure he worked under the instruction of others higher up the chain. It all felt familiar; she recalled the times she was a patient in psychiatric facilities with the sense of having to comply and be good in order to gain privileges and liberty. All Janet wanted was to rebel against the control, the liquid cosh, the isolation cell. The whole system suppressed people to not rock the boat and to be model patients. Anger so much anger that they, the powers that be, called mental illness. That's why Janet does not do angry. It segregates you away from society breaking you down and then building you up into a life of dependency. But today, she worked out what she needed to do, a plan to regain control.

Later that day, back in her room, she told Mark that she was tired and was going to rest for an hour or two. He left her to rest, taking the opportunity to get himself some lunch. He looked at her at the door of the room, flashing her a killer smile. He had a feeling she had the stuff to work through; maybe she would share it with him, maybe not; it was hard to tell with Janet. Once Mark had left, Janet reached over to open the small drawer on her bedside table. She felt around inside it, trying to locate something that was eluding her.

She moved closer to the drawer to see if she could reach better, then finally found what she had been looking for. She picked up a pair of nail scissors, then quickly shut the drawer and re-centred herself on the bed. Casting a quick glance at the door opposite her, she held the scissors in her right hand and deftly and deliberately stuck them into her left wrist, slashing multiple times at the skin. The blades cut through muscles, tendons, nerve fibres and blood vessels. She had a look into the wound, which was gaping open, quickly identified the ulnar artery and used the scissors to cut the major vessel. But despite the severing of the artery, no blood came out, yes, a liquid did spurt out, but it was not quite the right colour of red to be blood. She dropped the scissors, not really understanding what had happened. The flow of the liquid subsided quite quickly despite her attempts to keep it going. She put two fingers from her right hand into the wound, keeping it open to maintain the flow, but still, it remained a mere trickle. Janet expected to feel pain, but thanks to the infusion of pain relief, this also was denied to her. Thanks to the regular infusion of pain relief, she felt no pain, just slight discomfort. At a loss as to what to do, she decided to wrap up her arm in a towel for now. Mark may well come in and see the staining on the sheets from the wound. She had no idea what was in her veins, but it certainly wasn't blood. She took the towel away to inspect the damage she had inflicted on herself. It looked like a biology lesson with all the structures in her wrist exposed. She watched in interest as she saw the mechanics when she moved her hand. Just then, she heard Mark knock on the door; she quickly moved to cover up the wound with no idea of what she was going to say to him. She sat on the stain on the sheet, but for all that she had done to disguise her action, he came in and looked at her.

"What have you done, Janet? Let me see," he said, coming over to her. He picked up the scissors and put them on the cabinet next to her bed. "let me see," he said again as he reached over to see what she was trying to conceal. Janet reluctantly showed him her wrapped arm. She allowed him to take the towel off to inspect the wound. He looked at it; then he looked at her. "Are you injured anywhere else?"

"No," Janet replied, feeling very sheepish.

"OK, I will go and get what I need to close the cut. Are you OK to be left?" he asked with no sign of annoyance. "I will take the scissors with me; I won't be long," he said, then picked up the small scissors before leaving the room. Janet examined the area again, trying hard to make sense of what had just happened. She needed to ask Mark what was in her blood, what they had done to her. She felt deflated as she moved to free up the sheet that she was sitting on. She would need a clean one, she thought as she removed it from the bed. At that point, Mark came in with Bernadette, another Fetcher. He had a look at the sheet and then told Janet he would get a clean one once he was done. He needed the other person to hold the arm steady while he sutured the wound. Before suturing, he thoroughly cleaned the area and then selected a thin thread to mend the artery before stitching the skin. He did it quickly and expertly, saying very little to Janet except for asking her if she was OK. When the last stitch had been cut, he put down the forceps and needle on a sterile tray and then wrapped a gauze bandage around her lower arm. Once done, he said thank you to Bernadette, who left the room with the dirty sheet. Mark sat on the bed next to Janet; he seemed to be finding it hard to know what to say.

"Are you angry with me?" Janet asked.

"No, I am just sad that you felt you needed to do that," said Mark looking into her eyes. With that, she broke down sobbing; she cried until there were no more tears. Mark stayed sitting by her the whole time. He did not put a reassuring hand on her shoulder like he normally does. Janet took it that he didn't like her anymore; her thinking was far from logical. When Janet felt composed, she lent back against the bed backboard.

"I did not bleed blood. What is there in my system?" she asked him, looking at him in the eye almost like a dare.

"No, you don't have blood in your veins. None of us does. We are embalmed before we get to Second Chance. What came out was embalming fluid." Said, Mark.

Janet was not expecting that; she recoiled in shock, really lost for words.

"OK," she managed to find in her hazy brain. She felt like she should have more questions to ask him, but that was enough for now. She would have to work through that bombshell.

"Do you want tea?" Mark asked her, then got to his feet. He picked up the tray of surgical implements and headed to the door.

"Yes, please," replied Janet; it almost felt like nothing had happened.

"OK, I won't be long. Are you OK with me to leave you?" he asked.

"No, I'm fine," she said, then watched him as he left the room with the tray and soiled sheet. She allowed his explanation of the fluid in her body to rattle around her thoughts. She imagined that they arrived at Second Chance when they were in the hospital, not the funeral home. She understood better how the dead couldn't die, having been unable to kill herself. She felt ashamed to have tried that now; she hated the fact that she had caused Mark to put himself out for her. When he returned, she apologised to him; he said she had nothing to apologise about, which made her feel worse. Mark decided he had to move back to the spare room near Janet's room again, just so he could keep a good eye on her for a while. Bernadette would help when he took breaks, and he was going to ask one of the doctors to come and see Janet to see if there was anything else they could be doing to help her. He finally left her to sleep and then made the necessary arrangements to manage this situation. In the morning, Janet woke up with a very bad headache. She felt nauseous and achy as if she had been through rounds in the boxing ring. Mark came in pushing the power chair, which had gone back to the store's area. Walking with crutches would not be possible with the wound on her arm; there was a high risk of it bursting from the strain. Janet got out of bed to wash and then, accompanied by Mark, went to the dining room for breakfast. She still felt very fragile but was hoping that food would ease her bad head. She selected tea and toast for her meal and then went to find a free table. Mel was in the room; she called Janet over. When she saw the bandage on her wrist, she took hold of Janet's hand to offer her some reassurance. It was obvious what she had tried to do.

"Oh Janet, things are really that bad for you," she said. Janet felt like she was going to cry again but tried hard not to; she didn't want to draw attention to herself. She didn't respond but offered a small smile which said thank you to Mel. Mel talked to Mark about something or anything while Janet ate her toast. She felt able to join in the banter a little; the atmosphere felt good. Once she had finished her food, she asked Mel what she had on that day,

"Well, today I'm going to the Mind Complex. They brought the date forward as I'm doing so well. I think I may ask if they can cancel it so I can be around for you," she said. Janet felt blown away that Mel would even think about doing that for her. She was not used to that. She usually felt like she was in the way.

"Mel, you should go. Janet will be fine with me, won't you, Janet?" Mark said, looking first at Mel, then at Janet, then back again.

"Of course, you should go. I will be coming soon. Mark will look after me," Janet replied. Mel looked at her and then said, "Are you sure? I don't mind."

"No, Mel, you should go," said Janet decisively. Decision made; Mel leant across the table to hug Janet. She then said goodbye to Mark as she got up to leave the dining room.

"Right, you know I need to stay with you for at least today. How about we go to the day room, so you are around other people? We could go outside a bit later on. How does that sound?"

"It sounds good. Maybe we can find some people to play cards with," Janet said. Once she had finished, they left the dining room and entered the day room. There were a couple of people already there, Janet did not recognise them, but from the sound of their chat, it sounded like they were new. Mark said hello to them both and introduced himself and Janet to them. They gave their names and then asked Janet how long she had been there. The chit-chat continued until Mark noticed the time. He reminded Janet that she had an appointment with the doctor to go to. He accompanied her to the interview room, where a very kind-looking doctor looked at her sutured wrist and checked that everything was working ok. There was no sign of ligament or tendon damage and nothing obvious to say that she had nerve damage. The doctor asked Mark to stay on a one-to-one for forty-eight hours and then to come back to see him again. Mark asked her if she was OK with that; Janet shrugged her shoulders and then said that it sounded alright. At the end of the appointment, Janet and Mark went out into the park for a walk. Janet kept quiet during their exercise, lost in her own thoughts.

"Penny for them," Mark said. Janet looked up at him, then looked forward,

"Do you have a problem with me?" he asked her. Janet was quiet for a few more moments, then said, "I expected you to be rude when I cut myself. I am used to people being angry with me when I have self-harmed in the past."

"I am not people; I am me," he replied.

"Don't you feel as if I have let you down?" she said with true feeling.

"No, I feel that you are struggling," he said, looking straight ahead.

"I would be angry with me," she said, then realised just how stupid that sounded.

"I can understand that. It hurts me that you are hurting," he replied.

"I'm sorry for that; I didn't want to hurt you," she said.

"I know you didn't; that's not what I meant," Mark said. Janet stayed quiet as she tried to make sense of the conversation. She could see how she was twisting his words, almost like she wanted him to say that she made him angry. She apologised and then suggested they go in and get a coffee.

"Good idea Janet; I could kill a cappuccino; what about you?"

"Skinny late," she said as she turned the wheelchair around with the tiller.

Over the next few weeks, the wound on her wrist healed quickly, leaving a scar to remind her of her fight. The bones in her legs had knitted strongly and were now able to take her weight. She was pleased to give up the crutches, and although her legs were mended, Janet half expected her legs to give way. It would take a little while to get her confidence up. Her relationship with Mark had improved since she failed her suicide attempt. She felt better about sharing stuff with him; he was a good listener and respectful of her feelings. Janet was aware that her time with Mark was limited as she was ready to take the next step. Mark had been dialling down the level of pain relief coming through the walls in her room. She did not notice the difference, but for Mark, it was a sign that she was on the point of being ready to leave. He talked this through with her when his seniors agreed with him that she was ready. He was a bit concerned about how she would cope with the change now that she was on an even path. He was worried that moving her would cause a relapse in her mental health. But she was going to be moving to a place that dealt with all of that. He prepared her the best he could by not being around so much. He kept a paternal eye on her, nevertheless. The day before becoming a Greenie, Janet and Mark walked together in the gardens for a while. She hoped that there was an open space in the new place she was going to. Mark was able to assure her that they had a park there, which was just as lovely as the one she was used to. After dinner that night, they went into the induction hall for a social gathering. Tonight, it was a sing-song singing popular songs from the '80s and '90s. Song sheets were handed out to the attendees, and people were encouraged to sing solo or in small groups if they wanted to. Janet looked at the song titles. They were all songs that had memories for her of better times before everything started to go wrong. The evening was uplifting and fun, and Janet felt glad to be part of it. She didn't volunteer to sing solo. She was happy being part of the crowd. She did not expect to enjoy the evening, but Mark made it a great experience; his singing was as bad as hers, so they had a competition between them who could sing the worse. Other people looked at them when they sang the lyrics out of tune, but Janet didn't care. This was her last night with Mark;

he would be assigned to a new Newbie to fetch, carry and care for once she had moved on. Janet felt a stab of jealousy when she thought of Mark's time spent with another. She felt quite sad about saying goodbye to him; despite his attempts to initiate a discussion about ending their relationship, she was unwilling to share her thoughts, so he let it ride. After the social, they walked back together to her room. Janet thanked him for going with her, then let herself in her room to get ready for bed. She noticed something on her bed that was not there before. It was some green clothes, a tunic and some trousers on lovely green grass. She picked them up and held the tunic to her to see if it fitted her. She looked at it in the mirror and then put both garments onto the chair to change into in the morning.

She went to bed, a Newbie wearing a yellow tunic and trousers and woke up with a new green tunic and trousers to change into. This marked her transition from a Newbie to a Greenie. Janet checked her appearance in the mirror on the wall of her room. She looked OK; green was never her colour, but she would have to get used to it. She looked poignantly around the room, wondering what her next accommodation would look like and who would be moving in here. She picked up a used mug and left her room to clean the mug in the kitchen. She took her time cleaning it, trying to eke as much of the day as she could. She wanted to remember everything there was to remember. Once the mug had been thoroughly washed, she put the kettle on to dirty it with a brew. She took the filled receptacle back into her room and sat down at the vanity desk, looking out of the window. It reminded her of her first day here when she watched people come and go out of her field of vision. She heard Mark knock on the door before he opened it,

"Hi Janet, are you ready for your big day?" he asked her.

"Yes, just need to get breakfast," she replied, barely able to look him in the eye in case she cried.

"Want me to come with you?" Mark said.

"Would you? That would be nice, thanks!" Janet said, then headed for the door. They walked together down the now familiar corridors to the dining room. At the counter, she ordered scrambled egg on toast, tea and orange juice, then went to find a seat. She missed not seeing her friends there at their table; now, it was occupied by goodness knows who. The canteen worker brought over her meal and put it on the table near to her. She thanked him and then took a sip of the orange juice. She thought she should be saying something profound to Mark, but instead of that, she just asked him how his porridge was. He was one of those odd people who put salt in his porridge. Janet had previously asked him if he was of Scottish decent, which he denied. She did try it once, but the step from savoury to sweet was a step too far for her. Mark tried to start small talk, but Janet just replied with 'yes' or 'no' when required; she was not in the mood for talking. The truth was, she was really worried about leaving Mark and stepping from this complex into the next. She didn't want him to know that but felt that he deserved something, anything, from her.

"How's your food?" she asked, then chastised herself for saying something stupid like that.

"Good, how's yours?" he replied, putting the ball right back into her court.

"Yes, thanks, it's good," she said, then regretted it was hardly enlightenment. "Mark, do I have to go today? Can't we wait a bit," there it's been said, she thought to herself.

"Yes, you do, hunny bunny; you're ready now," he said.

"I may be ready physically, but I'm not ready mentally," she said, looking down at a particular piece of toast.

"That's why you're going. The Mind Complex is designed to give you skills to overcome fears and anxieties. It's not just for those who have a mental illness like you; it's for everyone who comes to Second Chance. Just think, Mel, Kim, and Lisa will be there; they will help you settle in," Mark said in a reassuring tone.

"But you won't be there" finally, she was able to say it.

"I know, but when you leave the MC, we may see each other when you are a Brownie. So, it's not really goodbye at all. I often bump into people I fetched for on my days off," He made an awful lot of sense, thought Janet. She nodded at him, then signalling that she had finished with her breakfast, they both stood up to go out of the room. "We need to get your things," he said as they walked back to her room. Not that she had a lot to take. Just a few clothes and some things Mel had made her. Once back in her room, she gathered her belongings while Mark found a bag to put them in. He found a cotton bag with a picture of a cat on it. It reminded Janet of her Milly Moo, the cat she had given to someone to look after. Janet fingered the image for a moment or two as she reminisced, then put her belongings in the bag. Mark took hold of it and then asked Janet to give him her fob key. He took it and put it in his pocket. Now she was ready to go. They went via the garden so she could say goodbye to it. This Mark indulged, now fully aware of her need for space. She was never very good in crowded places. She would only go if there was a clear way out of the room. She would stand at the back near the exit so that if things got too bad, she could get out fast. After seeing the garden, they walked through several whoosh doors and past the therapy rooms. Janet walked quietly by side Mark, marvelling at how he knew the way down all these identical walkways. She had not been down as far as this when she was exploring, but now, she just wished she was back at home, not home. Just home. On some of the walls at junctions, there were signs indicating which way to go. She spotted one saying 'Mind Complex' with an arrow pointing first straight, then around to the left. Janet thought that they must be nearly there, but they kept walking and walking. Eventually, Janet saw a door straight ahead of them. It had a sign on it saying 'Entrance'.

"This is it, Janet. Are you ready?" Mark said, then he tapped a numerical code on a pad on the door. He pressed 'Enter' then they heard a click as the door unlocked then opened, no whoosh, which surprised Janet. Mark went ahead of Janet down a short and narrow walkway that opened up into a reception area. Janet felt a stab of nervousness when they walked in; she had no idea what to expect. But, once in, Mark gestured for her to go through the door on the right marked 'Office'. There, Janet saw a young woman sitting at a desk which was piled high with papers and files. They seemed to be in some order, but the pure volume looked like it would buckle the desk. Mark smiled at the lady; she had a name badge attached to her tunic; it read Rose; she smiled back at Mark, asking him how he was.

"I'm doing OK, thank you, Rose. This is Janet," he said, indicating towards her with his hand. "Janet, this is Rose; she is your Minder," he said; with the formalities out of the way, Mark gave Rose a pocket history of his time as Janet's Fetcher. After that, Mark turned to Janet to say his goodbyes. Janet thanked Mark for everything then they fell into a long hug. Finally, Mark pulled away, "Be good," he said, holding her hands.

"You too," said Janet. With that, he walked back out of the whoosh door, leaving her in the hands of Rose.

Chapter 5
Mind over Matter

Janet felt an attack of shyness when she was introduced to Rose; she was an attractive young woman who had, by the look of it, a false leg. The prothesis inhibited her walking, so she used a walking stick to get her balanced. Janet watched Mark go until he was out of her sight. She clutched the bag of her belongings close to her body despite Rose asking her if she wanted to set it down while she took on her a quick tour of the wing.

Rose explained that in this particular wing, there were eight dormitories with four beds in each room with a small kitchen area and bathroom. Janet was dismayed by the thought of having to share personal space and asked Rose if there were any single rooms.

Rose said that each wing had a couple of single-use rooms, which they save for people who need intensive care. She went onto explain that the Mind Complex had four wings, all were near enough the same as the one Janet had been assigned to. Away from the wings were the studios, meeting rooms, activity rooms and a gym.

The new complex was much bigger than the one for the Newbies. Janet tried hard to remember where everything was and failed miserably. Fortunately, the signage was good and clear, which helped her massively during her first few days. The space was bright and, despite its size, felt welcoming.

There was no light coming from the walls; instead, works of art hung there with the name of the artist underneath. Despite the decor, it still felt like a clinical institution. Rose showed her the four bedded dormitory she would stay in during her time in the Mind Complex.

To her relief, she found out from Rose that she would be sharing with the three women she knew as a Newbie, Kim, Mel and Lisa.

Rose pointed out her bed in the four bedded dorm and showed her where she could store her meagre belongings. She left Janet to settle in and explore the ward.

Janet was quite impressed when she saw the amenities. The social areas were beautifully decorated and had proper furniture in them than the standard seating usually found in an institution. The sofas and armchairs were comfortable and nicely arranged; there were several coffee tables and two desks.

One of the desks had a partially completed jigsaw puzzle on it, and the other was bare. Janet noted that there was no television or radio in the lounge, but there were a couple of bookshelves full of reading material; interested, Janet explored the shelves to see if there was anything there that she wanted to read.

She found a novel but was then unsure if you could just take it or if they had a loan system. She replaced the book on the shelf at the end so she could find it easily once she knew how it worked. She really didn't want to tread on anybody's toes. She moved out of the lounge and head back to her dorm. She used the toilet in the bathroom and contemplated having a shower so she could get it done before the others returned. She was not the type of person that felt comfortable being nude around others. Just then, Rose knocked on the door of the dorm and came in when invited by Janet.

"Are you hungry? The canteen is open now. Would you like me to take you there" she asked.

"No, it's OK, I will try to find it by myself, thanks for asking," said Janet smiling at her.

Rose turned to go, then turned her head back, saying, "Remember, anything I can do to help, just ask."

Janet did not feel particularly hungry but went anyway. Fortunately, there was good signage she made it to the canteen after two failed attempts. All the corridors looked the same bar the works of art. Once there, she took in a deep breath and made her way to the serving hatch and selected a sandwich for her lunch.

Turning away from the hatch, she spotted Mel waving at her; she made her way there, swerving around occupied chairs and tables. The canteen was busy with lots of people milling around. It looked clean, which is something that pleased Janet. The canteen had plenty of space for wheelchair users, and the tables were well spread apart, giving room to manoeuver. She arrived at the table occupied by her friends and then sat down, placing her sandwich in front of her on the table.

"Janet, how are you? It's good to see you," said Mel. "We heard about your attempt through the grapevine. Are you OK"

"Yes, I'm OK," she replied. "I'm in your dorm." She said, rapidly changing the subject. She dared not share with her friends that they all had embalming fluid going through their veins; they would think she was crazy.

"Great, we have dorm parties all the time," said Mel before she took a mouthful of veggie burger. Janet wished that she had taken something hot for her lunch, her sandwich was OK, but she could not help but look at the burger. Mel seemed to pick up on that; she offered to go to the serving hatch to get her burger and chips. Janet said thanks, but she would make do with her sandwich.

"So, what is it like here? What's Rose like? She looks fierce," said Janet, unwrapping her food.

"She is OK; we have lots to do, you know, learning how to move forward, acceptance, all that kind of stuff. It can get quite heavy; that's why they run fun things to balance it all out. Anyway, I see your walking, are your legs healed, OK?" Asked Mel.

"Yes, they are good and solid. Though there are quite a few scars, and my legs are lumpy in places. I daren't wear shorts or a skirt." Janet said, then bit into her sandwich. The food tasted lovely; she was less bothered now about having made the wrong choice. She ate her sandwich quickly and had some sips of her juice before tucking it into her pudding. She had chosen an apple pie with custard. She always opted for the sweet stuff; it was probably her only vice.

"Lisa, tell her your news," said Mel to Lisa, who was struggling to open a carton of juice.

"What's that, Lisa?" asked Janet.

"Yes, I heard the news about my baby; she's here and doing OK," Lisa said, putting down the carton in defeat.

"Give it here," said Janet, who picked up the offered carton and deftly opened it before returning it to Lisa. "Where is she? Have you seen her?" asked Janet.

"I've been expressing milk for the babies; someone noticed we had the same sir name and we look alike, which was lovely to hear" Lisa took a sip of her juice.

"What's that lovely smell?" asked Janet, looking at the various dishes on the table.

"Sticky toffee pudding," said Kim.

"Mm, I love sticky toffee pudding," she replied.

"Let me get you some," said Kim getting to her feet. "It's to die for; sorry about the pun," she looked at them sheepishly then they all burst into laughter.

Kim went up to the serving hatch and then returned with the pudding in a bowl for Janet. Janet felt like a real pig having not only sticky toffee pudding but apple pie. The sticky toffee pudding was a good as it looked. She ate it quickly and then scraped the bowl with the spoon to get out as much as she could. Janet could not help but stare at Mel eating her food. The muscles used in mastication were visible in her mouth from the damage caused by the bullet. Healing had tidied up the edges of the wound, and her eye had been replaced in the socket by a false one. It was amazing she seemed so upbeat with tremendous injuries like that, especially her face.

Melanie Shift, or Mel, as she was known to family and friends, was an outgoing person who lived life to the full. She left school at sixteen, finding work as a receptionist at a car dealership. She enjoyed the work and openly flirted with her male colleagues and the punters. She had no ambitions in life, just randomly selected opportunities in life without regret.

Mel was a real beauty; she had a fabulous curvy figure and luscious long black hair. Her ebony face was exquisitely shaped. She was very much the party animal and had loads of friends and admirers. She fell in love with the love of her life when she was twenty-one. His name was Richard or Rick, and he treated her like a princess. She was not too sure about his line of work and was suspicious of the legality of it. She wisely kept her mouth shut.

He often came home with cuts and bruises, which she lovingly cleaned and dressed. She asked no questions as she went about tending to him but was worried for him. One day he might not make it home; he could be injured somewhere by someone. He seemed to always have lots of money on him which he often gave to her to go out and buy herself something pretty.

She had a good life, helped by the fact that she did not pry into his business. She heard his side of telephone conversations which were punctuated with threats or promises to whoever was on the other end. She took it all in her stride but often cried at night when he didn't come home. She was beginning to think he had someone on the side but dare not confront him about it. Sometimes she went through his pockets to see if there was anything to give her an idea of what he did.

She feared being caught; he was well known for having a short fuse she did not want to anger him. So, she kept quiet and made sure she always looked good for him and cooked him great meals in the hope that he would stay with her. Despite all this, she loved him and hoped to bear his children sometime soon.

One day, he came home early in the afternoon, yelling at Mel to quickly pack a bag. He told her that someone was after him, that they had to leave now. She grabbed a few belongings quickly, stuffing them in a bag. She packed the essentials remembering passports and an envelope of currency notes that was tucked away in one of the drawers in the bedroom, set aside for this kind of emergency.

Mel was petrified but had mentally practiced this for ages. Rick shouted to her to get moving, and they headed out of their house via the back door with the aim of getting in the car. Rick opened the lock on the door with his fob key; Mel ran to the passenger side, looking back over her shoulder as she moved to see if anyone was following them.

She saw movement in the driveway but could not clearly see who it was. At that point, a shot was fired. She heard Rick cry out and then fall on the floor. She froze for a second, then tried to get to the driver's side of the car to see if she could help him; he wasn't moving or breathing.

Mel panicked, and she moved to get in the car to see if she could drive away; it was at that point Mel got hit by a bullet from a gun. She heard the sound as the bullet left the chamber of the firearm and heard the crack as it hit and broke her jaw, exiting her head near her ear. She died almost immediately; she was aware of pain then as she neared death, the pain melted away.

She was aware of someone standing over her. She tried to ask for help, but the words were not coming out. She died a short time later. Mel seldom spoke about her husband and was always vague about what had happened. She was surprised that she didn't really miss him but always questioned why she ended up at Second Chance but not Rick.

She knew that people ended up there who were not ready to die, but Rick lived on the edge; he lived life to the full, and surely someone like him wasn't ready to die. Mel took the opportunities in Second Chance with the same vigor she faced life on earth. She didn't speak about how her life ended, and she was not alone in that.

Few people willingly shared their loss with others. There was no real reason for that; it just felt like a no-go area. The Mind Complex was there to provide a safe environment for people to look at what they have lost or whom they have lost. Mel, though, kept it to herself but engaged with enthusiasm with all that Second Chance had to offer. She was a delightful, bouncy, upbeat person in life and in death.

Mel took Janet under her wing for the first few days. The girls held a dorm party the first night Janet was there. They had an old CD player to play music on, and the range of CDs was limited, but they had found one with music from the 80s which they could sing along to or mime.

Everyone joined in, and several other people from other dorms came to join the party. Rose found some crisps and coke, which she donated to them, nothing stronger as there was a strict no alcohol rule in the Mind Complex. The participants got high on the atmosphere and laughed until it was painful. Janet felt herself swell with joy at having found such lovely people. It was good to let go and be in good company. She was pleased she had friends.

The party had to end at ten o'clock, bedtime. The music had to stop, but the chatter went on until the early hours, with Janet and the others joking and giggling in their beds. They heard someone from a different dorm call out for them to stop the fucking noise, so the girls turned their volume down a bit.

Eventually, they settled down to sleep; Janet felt happy, something she had not felt for a long time. The next morning, Janet woke early; she looked around at her sleeping friends and then got out of bed, trying to be quiet so as not to disturb them. The clock said six thirty in the morning; normally, if she woke that early she would try to get another couple of hours of sleep, but today, she considered that she didn't have any more sleep left, so she decided to get up. Why does it happen, she thought, that when you try to be quiet, you seem to make more noise?

She first dropped her toiletry bag on her foot, which nearly made her yell out. Then she banged her shoulder on the door frame of the shower room, which nearly made her curse. She washed in the shower room, enjoying the sensation of the water on her naked body.

After washing and rinsing her hair, she dried it as best she could with the towel and then rubbed it over her body. Once she was dry, she dressed in the bathroom, still taking care not to disturb the others.

Quietly she left the dorm, ready to start her day and made her way to the canteen. Rose had shown her the way to the canteen, but for the life of her, she could not remember the way. She tried out a couple of routes that took her to what looked like stock rooms. She made her way back to the dorm and then tried a different route. This one took her past the staff office space; again, it led to nowhere she wanted to be.

Finally, after another wrong turn, she found the canteen. She walked in and had a brief look around her. There were a couple of people in there in various stages of eating and drinking. She returned the greetings she received from them, absolutely surprised at people's friendliness. That was something she had noticed about being here on Second Chance. It made her feel welcome having perfect strangers saying good morning. Janet went over to the counter and selected scrambled eggs on toast, and a mug of tea for her breakfast, then sat down at the same place she sat last time she was there. She thought that if she sat in the same place, she was reserving it for the girls when they arrived. She looked at the clock on the wall; it was seven-fifteen. She couldn't imagine that the girls were early birds, but she had made an effort to save the seats if they came. The kitchen worker brought over her hot food and placed it down on the table with a smile.

"Thank you," said Janet looking up at her and smiled. The worker turned back around to go back to the kitchen. Janet ate her food savoring the taste of the eggs. She wondered what they put in it to make it so creamy; maybe, she thought she could ask the kitchen staff when she returned the plate. After finishing her hot meal, she turned her attention to the mug of tea. She stuck her finger in it to gauge the temperature, then lifted it up to her mouth to drink.

She took her time over it as she had a couple of hours until she had to attend to anything. She planned out what she could do to pass the time, with the top priority being to find the exit to the garden. Mark had told her that the outside area was bigger than the one in the Physical Complex, but she had no idea how to get there. Once she had finished her meal, she carried the plate, mug and cutlery back to the counter. She deposited it in the dedicated area on the serving counter then she made eye contact with one of the staff members.

"Hi," she asked the server, "Can you tell me how I get to the garden? I'm new here."

"Yes, of course, it's really easy. Just go out of the canteen, go left then first right, you will see the door to the garden ahead of you," said the server.

"Thank you" Janet smiled at him, then left the dining room to follow the instructions. He was right. It was easy to find the entrance to the garden. But to her surprise, when she looked through the entranceway, it looked more the size of a park than a garden. There was a large expanse of grass undulating with small hills and dips, giving it a truly natural feel. There were flower beds here and there with stunning colours and scents. She stopped for a moment to sniff the flowers and cup the heads in her hand.

Looking up from one of the beds, she noticed a lake in one of the dips of the landscape. It was a good size, and she thought about walking around it. She could see a couple of benches overlooking the lake, and Janet decided to make her way to the nearest one to sit and enjoy the view.

She noticed a few people doing exercise on the opposite bank of the lake. One person was moving in a way that Janet thought was Tai Chi. Janet watched the fluidity of the movements. The person was truly engrossed in the ritual, and Janet felt lost watching the movement. Then her attention was diverted onto two other people who were walking around the lake using a path. They were doing a fast-paced walk, nearly but not quite a run, Janet thought as she watched them exercise.

Janet sat for a good hour just watching the water in the lake. Little ripples disrupted the surface making the water alive with movement. There was a small island in the lake with a weeping willow tree in the centre. The shadows of the tree on the water were beautiful to observe, especially with the light breeze. The sky was sky blue and the grass green, everything she would expect it to be; it was hard to believe she was not on Earth. If she had invented

Second Chance, she would have made things different, the other way around, so the sky would be green and the lawns blue.

Everyone would just eat puddings and would at least try three in a bed. She smiled at herself to see how her mind worked, then pulled herself back to the here and now. The person who had been meditating stopped moving and sat down on the grass, which sloped down to the lake. She looked so serene, Janet thought. She had taken lessons in Tai Chi a good number of years ago. She thought then as she did now that it was just like learning a technical dance. She had not gotten to the point where she knew all of the moves when she stopped as she was falling behind the others.

Anyway, she thought, she had really sat and looked over at the lake; that was her kind of meditation. Janet sat on the bench a little bit longer, then set off along the path that circled the lake. She took her time to look at the scene, which relaxed her and focused her. She sat back down on the bench and thought about her day ahead. Today she would be attending her first therapy group session. Janet thought that by centralizing herself, she would fare better in the group. She recalled in her past life how deep some of these sessions were. How intense they can get, she wanted to be prepared. She would join in when suitable but often was told that she was dominating things. This time around, she thought, she would just listen.

Having now a strategy, she finally got up from the bench and retraced her steps back to the door near the canteen. She heard the babble of voices in the corridors. She thought they were engaging in morning banter, you know, the did you sleep well question where no one actually cared about an answer. She looked in the canteen on her way past to see if Mel and co were there. Janet saw them sitting at their table eating breakfast. Lisa spotted Janet at the door and beckoned her to join them. Janet went over to the table, explaining that she had already eaten but could get another mug of tea. She then made her way to the serving hatch to request the beverage. Mug in hand, she returned to the table and joined in the chatter. Mel offered to show her where to go for her group session, which Janet gratefully agreed to. Tea drunk, Mel ready, they left the canteen, taking the corridor passed the entrance to the garden. The room was not too difficult to find; there were several small rooms in the area, all looking out onto the park. Mel was attending a session in one of the other rooms but pointed to the one Janet was in on the way.

"Good luck," Mel said as they parted company. Janet, at that, felt nervous about what was coming up next. She walked quietly into the room, hoping that no one would see her. Six people looked over to her and smiled a welcome. Maybe it won't be so bad, she thought as she selected a seat furthest away from the seat saved for the therapist. They sat in a circle in silence, waiting for the therapist to arrive. About five minutes later, the door opened. Janet saw a young woman enter who came in and sat down on the empty chair. She apologized for being late and then introduced herself to the new Greenies.

Each person in the room were new to the Mind Complex. The sessions they had with Natalie were an assessment to place them into a group specific to their needs. Natalie invited each group member to say their name and a little thing about themselves. Each person spoke in turn, but Janet didn't listen to what they were saying.

She was busy trying to work out what she was going to say. When the eyes of the room fell on her, she stuttered, "My name is Janet; I am not meant to be here; it is a big mistake." With that, she fell silent, which matched the quietness in the room. Janet wondered what Natalie would make out of what she had just said. What had come out of her mouth was not what she wanted to say. Her words silenced everyone. Natalie invited the last person left to speak to share with the group, but Janet felt mortified. She was more nervous than she thought. Once everyone had spoken, Natalie smiled at members of the group,

"Let's do a spot of relaxation to prepare ourselves for the disclosure." With that, she clicked a button on the CD player she had by her feet, which admitted a soothing, pretty, monotone sound. She guided everyone through an exercise that Janet found quite easy to do. She was still in a relaxed mind following her stint in the park. But she followed Natalie's instructions in controlling her breathing and relaxing muscle groups. At the end of this part of the session, the room felt calm and ready for what was happening next. Natalie prepared the room, saying, "This group is for new people in the Mind Complex; let me tell you what we are going to do now. Disclosure is about telling the room something about yourself that you feel holds you back. The theory is that unburdening yourself moves you forward as a person. Now, I know this sounds daunting, but it is not compulsory for you to speak; it is often something you have to build up to do and feel this is a safe space." Janet had already decided for herself that she was not going to join in. At least she would not be forced or confronted to speak. This immediately felt like a safe place for Janet.

Most of the participants took time to tell their stories with a heavy theme running through loss. This is something Janet could identify with. Everyone in the room and, in fact, Second Chance could relate to that; still, listening to the others as they told bits of their stories, Janet felt less alone. Mel was right; it was heavy duty. Towards the end of the session, Natalie thanked everyone for attending and then asked each person in turn how they were feeling about checking out. Janet tried to think of something that had not already been said. Being as she was, she sat next to Natalie; she was last to speak. Not wanting to repeat anything, she mumbled something in the hope it would do.

"Sorry Janet, can you repeat what you said," asked Natalie.

"I found it interesting; I feel OK," she said, hoping Natalie would not ask her to elaborate. Fortunately for her, Natalie dismissed the attendees who filed out of the room. Mel was waiting for her outside. She smiled at Janet, who grimaced back.

"Was it really that bad? Did you speak?" Mel asked as she linked arms with Janet walking her down the corridor back to the canteen. They grabbed a coffee and biscuits and then sat down at their table. They chatted back and forth, putting the world to rights. Once the coffee had been drunk, Mel suggested Janet and her go to the gym.

"It's a good place for getting rid of pent-up feelings," she said, selling the idea to Janet.

"What do they have down there?" asked Janet.

"Usual stuff, an area to do resistance work, boxing space, gym floor for team sports. I usually go on the treadmill; a good run makes me feel better." Mel led Janet through numerous identical-looking corridors and through numerous whoosh doors. Janet could not imagine a time when she would learn where all these corridors led to. Eventually, a double door on the right had a sign saying Gym on it, which they entered. It was a large space with separate areas for boxing and resistance machines. There were several people playing basketball; it looked odd to see people with clear deformities from injuries finding their way around the hall. Janet still found it odd to be around people with disabilities; she wondered about their stories, who and what they were before ending up at Second Chance. She stopped herself from staring; she did not want to draw attention to herself, so she followed Mel to the torture machines.

"Do you know how to use this," said Mel pointing to a couple of treadmills.

"Yes, I have a gym membership; sorry, I had a gym membership," replied Janet climbing up on the belt and pressing the start button on the touch screen. The machine started up immediately, and Janet set the speed to start exercising. Mel used the treadmill next to Janets, quickly accelerating the speed, so she was running at a fair pace.

"Are you going to run?" asked Mel.

"Not sure if I can with my legs; I'm a bit worried they won't be up to it," replied Janet. She put the speed higher, finding it hard to move from a fast walk to running. She just didn't feel confident about running, so she settled for walking. She was soon panting and puffing, but her sense of competition prevented her from ending her workout ahead of Mel. In time, Mel brought her treadmill to a halt, looking like she had when she started, unlike Janet, who felt sticky with sweat and had a red face. She had not realized how out of condition she was, but it had been quite a time since she last exercised. After a few minutes, Janet slowed the pace to an amble and then stopped the machine. She looked around at the other pieces of equipment, opting to use one exercise muscle in the arms. She selected the desired weight and settled into the activity. Mel stopped her run, wiping her face with her sleeve; she had worked up quite a sweat. She went over to the free weights selecting three-kilogram dumbbells. Both were too engrossed to chat, but it felt OK.

After using a couple of other resistance machines, both girls stretched out and then set off to return to the dorm. Mel wanted a shower before the last session of the day. Janet showered after Mel wondering if there was anywhere where she could get gym clothes and shoes. She made a mental note to ask Rose the next time she saw her. Kim was in the dorm sorting out her dirty clothes to be washed. Greenies had to put the washing in a bag and leave it outside of the dorm by the door for it to be taken away and washed. Janet asked Kim how long it took to get them back, and Kim replied that it was usually a day.

Kim asked Janet if she felt like doing some craft work. They had a fully stocked room where you could use whatever you wanted to be creative. There was also a room for pottery, one for woodwork and another for dressmaking. Janet was impressed with the facilities and liked the sound of a craft group. She went with Kim along a corridor that was labelled with the various activity rooms. When they reached the right door, they went in to see what they wanted to do.

A birdy had told Janet that Mel's birthday was a few days away, so she thought she would make her a card. Kim pointed out where the various materials and paints were that may be helpful in creating the card. Janet found cardboard which would be suitable to use as the card, then found some ribbon and some old magazines. She figured she might find some pictures she could use in them, or maybe she could cut out letters to make a message. With a plan sorted out, she set about putting her creative skills into making the birthday card. She looked over to Kim, who was sitting back in a chair knitting.

"What's that you're making, Kim?" she asked.

"I'm making baby clothes for Lisa, little one," she answered as she tackled some complicated ribbing.

"What is it, a cardigan?" Janet said.

"No, it's a christening blanket; Lisa is hoping to get her properly named in the chapel. It's happening the week after next which gives me plenty of time to finish it. She doesn't know I'm making it, so please don't mention it," said Kim.

"Mums, the word," Janet replied as she cut out an 'L' and an 'H'. At this rate, it would take her ages to make the card, but she wanted it to look good. Janet was very competitive; she would set herself targets and then bend over backwards to exceed them. She wanted to do all the lettering today then she would work on finding some suitable images to add to it. She lost the sense of time then Kim stopped what she was doing, saying that it was lunchtime. Janet asked her if it was OK to leave things out or if she should tidy them away somewhere.

"No, you can leave it out; no one will take it, anyway; I'm coming back later on in the day; I can keep an eye on it. They walked together to the canteen and then selected their dinners. Janet opted for a vegetable curry with rice and baked rice pudding. She realized too late that she was going to have two rice dishes but chose not to change them; she justified it by having had a workout at the gym. They sat down at their table and started to eat. Just then, Lisa and Mel turned up, grabbed their food then joined them at the table.

"How did the group go, Janet?" asked Lisa.

"Yes, it was OK; I didn't say much, though," Janet replied.

"It took me a couple of weeks before I said anything," Lisa said as she pushed the food around her plate with her fork. Finally, she pierced a bit of potato and then put it in her mouth.

"Did you find it got easier the more you did it?" Janet asked Lisa.

"No, not really. I still struggle with it, but generally, I find it helps, you know, disclosing." The others agreed with her then the subject turned to talk about the handsome new Greenie who came the same day at Janet. At that moment, the subject of the discussion entered the dining hall, which made the girls giggle like they would have done at school. Mel dared Kim to go over and introduce herself to him and invite him to come to our table.

"I can't do that!" she replied, going red in the face; you do it," she pointed at Mel at that point. Straight away, Mel got to her feet and quickly went over to the man. She asked him if he wanted to sit with them, gesturing towards the table where the girls were sitting. Janet saw him shake his head 'no' and then watched as he turned around to sit at a table at the front of the dining room. Mel turned around to come back to the group. She told them that his name was

Andrew, then sat down to indicate that that subject was closed. They started to talk together about the steps after they were Greenies. They wondered what the main Second Chance complex had to offer. They had had little contact with the Brownies who lived and worked there. Janet found this interesting. She had seen Brownies working in the gardens and could imagine herself doing that. She asked the others what they would like to do when they left the Mind Complex.

"I'd like to be Linda's mum full-time. I only get to see her once a day. I feel as if I hardly know her," said Lisa.

Mel replied to the question by saying that she would like to work in a gym as an instructor and that she would make it hell on earth for some of the attendees. The others laughed at that.

'What about you, Kim?" Asked Janet.

Kim put down her fork and then wiped her mouth with the back of her hand. "Me, I would be happy working in an office; it's what I used to do at work when I was on Earth." After lunch, they had a break before the last session of the day. Kim and Janet filled in the time in the craft room, working on their secret projects. Janet was engrossed in her work, forgetting about the time. They had been in there for over an hour before one of them checked the time on the clock on the wall above the door. It was, according to the clock, half past two, and they were going to be late for the session.

They both quickly packed up their things and then hot-footed them back to the therapy rooms. They got there by the skin of their teeth and then separated to go to different rooms. Janet was with the same people she had met earlier in the day, but there was a new person sitting in the therapist's seat.

He introduced himself as Anayat and asked each person to say their name. Janet introduced herself when his gaze landed on her then the session began properly. This session started with a guided meditation by Anayat. He had a delightful accent and led the exercise with a melodic lilt. Janet could feel herself letting go; it seemed like the right end to quite a busy day.

After the relaxation exercise, they had a discussion about what people did to relax; Janet joined in with the talk offering her own experiences. After the session, she went out into the park to sit and ponder the day. She walked around the lake and then went in for dinner, which was being served in the Dining room. Janet selected a mushroom omelette with salad. There was a proper chocolate sponge for dessert, which reminded Janet of her grandmother, who used to always bake it when she visited. After food, Janet decided she needed a bit of me time, so she opted to go back outside in the park until it was time to go to bed at ten. She sat back down on the bench, looking over the lake. She really missed the sound of the birds and insects. She would never have imagined a world with no wildlife. She reflected on the highs and lows of the day and then got lost in her thoughts. Suddenly she was jolted back to the here and now by someone calling her name. She looked over her shoulder seeing Lisa standing there.

"Can I join you?" she asked.

"Of course," replied Janet patting the bench next to her. Lisa sat down, smiling at Janet.

"How was your first day?" she asked.

"Not too bad; it was pretty much what I expected," replied Janet. "When can you see your baby?"

"I saw her today. It was pretty tough; I thought I would feel something, anything, but nothing."

"It may come in time; you have been apart for quite a while. Was there a bond?" Janet asked.

"No, I thought there would be. I found it hard to recognize her. Also, she is badly disabled, being premature and dead." Kim's voice broke at this point, dissolving into tears. Janet reached out to hug her. *It must be very difficult for her. She has been through so much,* thought Janet.

Lisa was a quiet and shy young woman who lived on her own in a ground-floor flat not too far from where her parents lived. She held down a good steady job that satisfied her and gave her a good income. Life was going OK, so it came as a surprise to her and her family when she learnt she was pregnant. She had been dating a young man called Adam. When she told him about the pregnancy, he legged it. He up and left the area, never to be seen again. Lisa tried phoning him, but he had changed his number. In the end, Lisa accepted the fact that she was going to be a single parent. Her immediate family rallied around to get things ready for the birth. Her parents were sure Lisa would make a great mother but had hoped she would do the dating, have a long engagement and marry a bit before having a baby. Lisa was fearful of having to look after a baby; it was a huge responsibility.

She worried endlessly about her abilities but also felt a sense of excitement as her due date crept near. She would have liked to have someone to share this with, but she knew in her heart that the chances of that happening were small. She spent time on the baby's pre-arrival kit, burp cloths, clothes, nappies etc. She kept smoothing down the tiny clothes, folding them carefully and packing them into her hospital bag. Her mum said Lisa was nesting, a clear indication that the baby was due very soon. Then, the baby didn't move.

No more kicking her bladder, sending her rushing to the toilet. Lisa rang her mum for advice, who came over to drive her to the maternity unit at the local hospital. Lisa felt panicky; her mum tried to reassure her even though she was apprehensive, which she tried not to show. Arriving at the hospital, they had a short wait before a midwife called her into the examination room. Lisa lay down on the couch and tried to control her breathing.

"Baby is in distress; I will ask the doctor to come and examine you; it won't be long," said the blue-clad midwife. It felt like hours before the obstetrician entered the room. He felt her abdomen and requested an immediate scan which indicated the baby had the cord around its neck.

"Well, my dear," said the doctor, "we need to get this baby out now. We need to do an emergency Caesarean." With that, he turned around, walking out of the bay. Lisa had some questions she wanted to ask but could sense the urgency in the gestures of the doctor and the midwife.

"Don't worry; you will be out when the baby comes. When you wake up, you will have your beautiful little girl to hold," said the nurse.

"But it's too soon; I've still got eight weeks to go," Lisa cried out. The nurse smiled gently at her and then got busy checking her blood pressure and oxygen saturation level. Lisa succumbed to tears; she felt so scared. This was not what she expected. A few minutes later, Lisa was taken into the operating theatre, and people surrounded her doing this and that. She let them do what they needed to do and then just lay back. She had a bad feeling about this. She drifted off to sleep, leaving her body in the hands of strangers. They did their best to save the baby, but unfortunately, she was strangled by the umbilical cord. It was too late to save her. She had been deprived of oxygen for too long. Just after they had removed the body of her baby, Lisa started to haemorrhage.

The medics gave her an emergency transfusion and administered Ergometrine, but it was too late. Despite all of these interventions, she crashed and died with her belly still open from under her ribs to her belly button. It was a sad day for all. Her parents were distraught. Lisa's mother could only sit on a chair rocking backwards and forwards, fingering a baby grow. Her father set about being busy so he wouldn't have to confront the truth. He set about tidying his garden shed and sharpened all the tools. Her parents never talked about the day they lost Lisa and baby Linda, but on each anniversary, they brought a huge bunch of flowers to put in Lisa's favourite vase in the lounge.

Lisa knew her baby was dead; she felt incomplete without her, despite never holding her or smelling the smell of newborns. On Second Chance, she was told that there was a place for dead babies, some still so young they needed mummy milk. She willingly agreed to express her breast milk for these babies, taking comfort that she was able to help them. This knowledge enabled her to accept where she was. When Rose told her that her baby was one of those she had fed, she felt that sense of completeness and calm. She would be reunited with her when she left this complex, but she could go and see her anytime. Unfortunately, the lack of oxygen had caused the baby to have serious problems; she was mentally and physically disabled. She would be dependent on others all her life. When Lisa saw her baby for the first time, she felt a wash of love gush out of her and into Linda. She looked just perfect to Lisa. She wanted to take care of her now and forever and could not see anything wrong with her. Truth be told, Linda was seriously disabled. She was fed by a nasogastric tube as she had a very poor swallowing reflex. She could not suckle on Lisa's breasts, so she continued to express milk to feed her. Over time she did grow but not as much as she should have. 'it became increasingly obvious that she must have had a stroke because one side of her body was very much weaker than the other. Nevertheless, Lisa loved her with all her heart.

Lisa and Janet walked together back to the dorm. Mel and Kim were already there, dressed in their night garments and chatting away. Mel was doing some knitting. She was making baby clothes for Lisa's little one. Kim was busy writing; she was keeping a journal and made a point of writing in it every day. It was part of her therapy. Over the next week, Janet fell into a routine of therapy, gym, and craft room. She had moved from the starters therapy group to a longer-term one that had ten people in it. She thought she might be in with the girls, but they had been moved to the leaver's group.

In therapy, Janet learnt that part of the program was giving people the skills or tools to cope, so each person had their individual toolbox to use when times felt hard. This made good sense to Janet; she was quick to learn how to use her tools. Despite her active engagement with the regime, not that she had a lot of choice about that, she felt unable to really unburden herself. Her previous experiences of using the mental health system had undoubtedly scarred her, and she saw too many parallels between that and the Mind Complex in Second Chance. She felt it was a paternalistic nanny state with people deciding what is best for her.

She felt powerless, and still, that anger bubbled around inside her. The abdication that you needed to reach a stage of acceptance to be truly ready to move forward was proving problematic. She had been fighting this fight most of the time while in mental health care facilities. There, she felt staff jumped too quickly to deliver medication to settle someone in distress. Janet was never too sure if it was in the patient's best interest or to give the staff a quiet life. She always thought there had to be another way. Maybe the toolbox skills were what she had been seeking.

Janet missed her previous life. No, it was far from perfect, but she missed the people she knew and wondered how they were and if they still remembered her. She felt unable to bring these thoughts to the group environment. Janet had the feeling that bringing this up is taboo, though that was only a thought. She learnt techniques to distract herself from lingering on bad thoughts when she indulged in misery for too long to be healthy. She picked up tips from her peers on ways to manage painful memories. All in all, it was a steep learning curve for Janet, and it turned into a positive experience. There was a group of people who spent a bit of time each day tending the garden. Janet happily joined them, finding pleasure in nurturing the plants. In no time, she had a busy schedule for the week, with a mix of things to do as well as therapy groups. She found all of them useful in helping her to re-focus, be calm and stay in control. Her three friends were great at getting her out of the blues. In fact, they supported each other fantastically. They amused themselves as women do; by gossiping, speculating and bitching.

Janet had been in the Mind Complex for five weeks and was having a good day. The good days were beginning to outweigh the bad days, which was good. The therapy group sessions were productive as she had had several eureka moments when she came away with a new insight or when something made sense. On this particular day, she came out of the group feeling energized; she felt like the Janet she used to know, pre-Bipolar. She made her way from the session to the canteen when she saw Mel ahead of her.

"Hi, Mel," she called out. Mel stopped and turned round to face Janet. When Janet saw her face, she instantly felt that something was wrong. She caught up with Mel, who tugged the sleeve on her arm in a manner owned by her.

"Have you heard?" she said to Janet.

"What?" replied Janet.

"Kim, it's Kim. She flipped out during the session. She's been taken to a single room on a one-to-one."

"What happened?" Janet asked her.

"I don't know, not for sure. But she is in a bad way."

Kim was in her early 40's when her life ended. Before that, she worked for a firm that sold kitchen units. Not the most exciting of jobs, but it paid the bills, and her work colleagues were good for a laugh. She had been there for ten years in the finance department, working her way up from general clerk. She was a good worker, reliable, polite and, well, bored. She would have changed jobs if she had the mind to.

Her employers treated her well, and the fact that she did not want to let them down were the main reason she stayed put. Better the devil, you know, as the saying goes. Her husband Dave used to tell her to give up her job to be a stay-at-home mum, but she didn't want to give up working. The income was handy, and it meant she was not reliant just on her husband's wage. Her two boys, Richard and Kevin, were very much like their father, who didn't always treat her good. The boys copied his behaviour which left her seriously outnumbered and left feeling put upon. At times he would get aggressive with her. He would hit her in the face, often leaving her with a black eye.

She got very good at telling stories to her work colleagues when she went to work with bruises on her face. She worked, cleaned, cooked and tidied up; that was her life. Until Steve started work at the kitchen firm in the warehouse, he had a twinkle in his eye, and his eyes lingered on Kim. Kim felt flattered and blossomed from his attention. She found herself wearing colourful clothes to go to work. She undid a second button on her blouse, giving a hint of bosom; she wore her hair differently and discovered a spring in her step on her way to work. Hubby did not notice the change in Kim as his needs were being met, though he thought the changes in her appearance were for him, especially as she seemed more attentive in the bedroom.

Kim and Steve started meeting at the water cooler and at the printer. They chatted and flirted with each other when they sat in the restroom having their sandwiches. Kim felt young again. Attractive. Steve noticed the difference in Kim; he saw her blossom in confidence. He couldn't understand how her husband could not 'see' Kim. His feelings towards her changed over time from friendship to love. Kim felt the same even though neither told the other. It was something left unsaid; it didn't need saying. The body language and facial expressions said it all.

Kim and Steve talked about their future together. They explored the idea of Kim leaving her family and moving in with him. She felt terribly excited by that but was worried about telling her husband and her boys. She decided not to tell him, to just go. So, they set a date for the next Monday. On Monday, she was at work as usual. She had bought a suitcase with her filled with clothes, toiletries, cosmetics and precious items. At the end of the working day, Kim and Steve left together. She packed her suitcase into Steve's car, then sat in the passenger seat of his Toyota Yaris. A mix of nerves and excitement filled her body. She had already typed a message meant for her husband on her phone but was yet to press Send. She would send it once she was in Steve's home, their home. She wished it could have been different; maybe if she had not been taken for granted, it would not have come to this, maybe. She took a deep breath, brushing her thoughts of her family out of her mind as they set off to her new life. They chatted as Steve drove distracted. He did not see the car coming out of the road on his left. Kim took the impact; she was impaled by debris from the crash as metal tangled with metal skin and bones. She died before the emergency services could get her out. Steve survived with life-limiting injuries.

Kim missed her life, like everyone else there in Second Chance; the sense of loss was palpable. The loss was visible in the eyes of all those who dwelled there; for some, no amount of therapy could eradicate the emotion. It stayed like a scar. Kim stayed in the single room for a couple of days; she was very low in mood. When she was permitted visitors, the girls rallied around her and tried to ease her thoughts with humour and chat, anything that would distract her. It seemed to help her, and in no time, she was back in a dorm with her friends.

Janet felt cushioned by this part of Second Chance, safe in a supportive environment. She felt the emotional healing on her body like gentle caresses, soothing, caring. She had not felt so good for a long time. Nothing was being pushed; individuals could opt out of a therapy session for something else as everything else had a therapeutic value, whether doing art or sport or gentle contemplation in the chapel. People took responsibility for knowing themselves, and the whole set-up was geared for inmates to come to terms with their past and future life as a dead person. Kim's meltdown was not uncommon; over the time Janet was in this zone, half a dozen or so people broke down.

The one-to-one support helped to keep them safe and offered the opportunity for the inmate to talk and explore their feelings. Kim recovered quickly, helped, no doubt, by the care of her friends, who knew what it felt like to be dead. Despite the therapeutic environment seemingly supporting recovery, Janet felt the same unease about the Big Brother scenario of Second Chance. She saw all the residents on a type of conveyor belt, spending time to be mended physically and mentally. Then, once successfully rehabilitated, they live out the rest of their lives in Second Chance until Graduation, whatever that was. Yes, it was all done nicely, with disabilities and disfigurements, together with suicides and inner body damage.

All types of death were welcome here, with no hierarchy of conditions or cause of death. No obvious racism, sexism, nothing discriminative. Some may consider this as Utopia, but Janet considered it to be against human nature, sinister. Of course, people fell out; there were cliches, and some naturally gravitated to people who shared a trait. Exclusive relationships were not forbidden, couples had the use of single rooms for intercourse if they wanted, but the dead could not produce babies. Janet had been approached by a few men looking to have a relationship with her which Janet declined, and she was not ready to date.

Life in Second Chance rolled on, and Janet felt healed. She was not sure of what would happen next, her limited understanding coming from induction way back on her first day. She decided to attend a seminar held every three months for people getting ready to leave the Mind Complex. She sat in the room with half a dozen others. Lisa sat next to Janet; she felt ready to be reunited with her baby in the next stage; at least she knew what her purpose was, thought Janet. The seminar helped her to determine her next steps; she was thinking about her enjoyment in the garden and her experiences on earth as a nurse; maybe she could make good as a Fetcher? Lots to consider.

Moving on from the Mind Complex was not down to Janet; discharge involved input from Rose and group facilitators, as leaving too early or for the wrong reasons could be damaging. Feedback from the others indicated her discharge to be reconsidered in a month's time as they felt she could benefit from further therapy, particularly as she did not contribute much in the group therapy sessions. It was true; she was always a listener; she thought she gained as much therapy by quiet contemplation, and she felt that speaking would open herself up to scrutiny. That level of self-exposure would render her vulnerable in a pandora's box scenario.

Keep it down, swallow it down; openness works for some and keeping emotions under lock and key worked for Janet, or that was what she believed. Maybe the feedback from the others hit on that spot; maybe she should let go a bit. Could she trust people to contain her and keep her safe? What if the memories tumble out with their emotions just keep coming more and more, start to take out her insides, leaving her naked inside, all of it out there in a black, wriggling, stinking pile?

There, visible to all, everyone looking at the mess, no one looking at Janet, ashamed of her nudity. That's why Janet kept the lid on; she feared any exposure. This is what she said in one of the groups. People nodded, touched her hand, and empathized. She did not fall in a heap. She spoke about her fear; they seemed to understand. Maybe progress has been made. Another eureka moment. Janet celebrated her breakthrough by doing an extra quatre of an hour on the treadmill in the gym. She was happy to do that as opposed to hosting a party where she would be the centre of attention. Janet was a hide-in-shadow kind of person. She did share it with the girls, who were all proud of her. Janet thought it couldn't get any better. The week passed quickly, spending time with each of her friends, whether in the craft room or the gym. Soon they would be moving on to the main complex, and she would be behind them again. About a week later, the girls were having a girly evening in their dorm, celebrating Lisa's moving on and being reunited with her baby.

She had supervised contact with her daily to help with the bonding process, but from tomorrow, she would become her mother with ongoing support from the nannies if she required it. Mel, Janet and Kim had spent time in the craft room making soft toys for the infant, which made Lisa cry; she felt touched by their kindness. They were all on the cusp of leaving the Mind Complex, and the next step would be about using their past skills, interests and experiences for the benefit of Second Chance, being now physically and emotionally healed.

Chapter 6
Moving On

Mel left after Lisa; she was given two days' notice and plenty of time to organize a party. Mel said that she felt ready to go to the main Second Chance. She had found out from Rose what it was like, which she shared with the others. On the day she was due to leave, they all said au revoir knowing they would be back together shortly. Kim was next; she felt very nervous about going, even to the point of trying to see if there was somewhere she could hide to avoid detection. Rose spent a lot of time talking to Kim, and she was able to reassure her somewhat. On the day she left, they didn't tell her they were coming for her. Instead, they sprung it on her, which gave her less chance of getting hysterical.

Janet felt very alone, she continued with her routine, but the table she sat at mealtimes was empty of friends. She went to the craft room and got out of the project she was working on. She was making a rug for her room when she moved. It was nearly three quatres of the way done; she just hoped she would have enough time to finish it. As it was, she didn't have a chance to complete it; she wondered if they had the facilities for her to complete it on the final complex.

Rose broke the news to Janet that she was ready to move on that day. Janet felt ok with this decision. She asked Rose if she had time to pick up the rug. Rose told her she had a few hours before someone would come to collect her. This gave Janet the time to eat a fried breakfast and pop into the gym for a very quick workout. On the way back from the gym, she picked up the nearly completed rug. Satisfied she had everything she needed there, she went back to the dorm to pack up her belongings. She decided to grab a quick shower, so she got together her wash bits and then took her shower. When she had finished, she went into the bedroom to change into her clothes. At that point, she noticed that Rose had left her some clothes. They were brown in colour and comprised of a tunic and trousers. Janet assumed Rose had put them there, so she would put them on. She dressed quickly, unsure of how much time she had left before this person would come and get her. Janet saw Rose at that point as she walked down the hall. Janet called out to her to double-check the arrangements.

"Shouldn't be too long now; why don't you go to her day room and wait for her."

"I'm going to miss you, Rose; you have been so nice," Janet said, looking earnestly at Rose.

"Awh, thank you. You will do just fine," Rose said, smiling at her. Knowing she was not good with goodbyes, Janet averted her gaze and allowed Rose to continue on her way. She was expecting two new Greenies that day and wanted to make sure everything was ready for them. Janet gathered up her belongings and put them in a cotton bag that Kim had made for her. She had embroidered a picture of a cat on it, which looked a bit like Charlie, the black cat she used to have back on earth. Then she sat in the day room as instructed, waiting to be taken to the largest complex where people work and/or learn.

Janet had given some thought to what she wanted to do; she would not mind working to manage the gardens or learning how to facilitate a therapy group in the Mind Complex. She felt excited about moving forward. It would be a positive move. She began to feel impatient as she waited for this person. She wondered if she had time to make herself a coffee. She decided to wait for five minutes, and if no one came, she would make herself a brew.

After five minutes had gone, she got to her feet and went to the small kitchen and filled the kettle with water. Once boiled, she made herself a drink and took it back into the day room. She wondered if perhaps she had got the wrong information about the meeting place;

she was sure Rose said eleven o'clock in the day room; maybe she was in the wrong place. She began to feel a bit stupid sitting in a chair nursing her coffee while keeping on looking over at the door to see if he or she was coming. She thought about going back to the dorm to see if Rose could throw some light on the non-appearance of this person. She toyed with that idea and set herself a time limit before she went to the dorm. She looked at the clock again, thinking she would give it fifteen minutes, and if he or she had not come by, then she would go back to the dorm.

Fifteen minutes later, she stared at the clock and wondered what to do. Maybe she had gotten the time wrong; maybe the person had gotten lost; perhaps someone had been picked up instead of her. All sorts of scenarios filled her thoughts. A short while later, a middle-aged woman carrying the inevitable clipboard walked into the room. She asked Janet if she was Janet and Janet said yes, she was Janet.

The woman walked with a walking stick with a pronounced limp her face was mashed up with her eyes were barely visible from the scar tissue causing disfigurement. Janet was unsure where to look; she did not want the woman to think she was staring at her, even though she was. The woman held out her hand, or what was left of her hand, to shake as a welcome; Janet took a breath before reaching out her right hand to shake. The woman introduced herself as Edna and invited Janet to follow her. They walked past the therapy rooms and the craft rooms, then through a whoosh door which opened with a key fob Edna had around her neck. The route was very complicated, Janet thought. She would not be able to get back if she needed to.

They left the Mind Complex through a double whoosh door. From there, they walked down a very long corridor. Janet attempted small talk, but Edna was not particularly chatty. She tried once more to break the quiet with only the sounds of their steps and the slight rustling of their clothes. They must have walked half a mile down the corridor; it certainly felt like it for Janet. Edna was going at quite a pace; she was very focused on the route. The corridor was painted white with a black floor. There were no windows, no artwork, nothing to break the monotony of the blank walls.

After a while, Janet's initial excitement evaporated into nervousness; she became aware of her heartbeat and breath, something she does when she's anxious. With rising panic, she stopped walking, attempting to ground herself. She just needed a few seconds then she would be ready. Edna stopped walking and looked back at Janet. "Come along, dear, not much further to go. Do you need a sit-down?" She indicated a door in the corridor, but Janet could not recall seeing a door. "Just through there, dear, if you need to rest."

Edna opened the door gesturing to Janet to enter. Janet went through the door into a small meeting room; she selected a chair, then sat down and tried to smooth down her unease. "it's lovely there, dear; you will get on fine. Now you are healed and sorted, you can really start your Second Chance," said Edna, who sat down with difficulty. Janet felt like she was holding Edna up, and after a few minutes, Janet indicated her readiness to continue. It took Edna a couple of attempts before she got back on her feet.

Janet wondered if she should have offered her a hand to get up but thought it wouldn't go down very well. They both walked down the corridor for a further ten or so minutes to double whoosh doors. The door opened up into a hallway with several openings leading to who knows where. Edna pointed to one of the doorways which led to the outdoors. Janet went through the open door to the outside. Edna followed her and then called her over. Janet turned round to listen to Edna; Edna pointed to a vehicle that was parked nearby. She told her that she needed to get on the minibus as the tour would be starting soon. Janet was at a loss as to what to say. She settled for mumbling a thank you and then looked over at the bus. Janet thought the fresh air never felt too good after the staleness of the corridor. "Good luck, dear; it will all be OK." Said Edna, which caused Janet to turn around to face her,

"Thank you," Janet said. Then Edna hobbled off into the hall and disappeared through one of the doors. It was hard to get your head around being surrounded by deformed or disabled people all the time; it was not normal, not to Janet, who, despite her own limitations, had a hidden disability. Maybe, she thought, she was not disabled enough. Not like Edna, who looked like she had been through a fire. She did not consider herself disabled, and she wondered how people saw her.

Hopefully, they liked her. Her default was expecting people to dislike her, and she needed time to be convinced friendship was genuine. She knew she was hard work; experiences had made her know she was hard work. Janet shook herself free from the brain wandering off down avenues and looked over at the minibus. There were two people already on, one person in a wheelchair and the other ambulant.

Janet climbed in and took a seat near the back. At that point, another person in a wheelchair came over and went up the ramp into the vehicle. Finally, a few more people joined her in the vehicle, and she smiled that smile reserved for total strangers, noting that the vehicle had more spaces for wheelchair users than walkers. It was good to see on Earth, access to transport for disabled people was far from perfect. The minibus door closed, bringing Janet's attention back to the here and now. "Hi De Hi campers, I am Don, your driver and tour guide; sit down and enjoy the view. No need for seat belts. We are already dead. Everyone ready?"

There was a muttering of yes from a few of the passengers as the bus engine turned over and chugged to life. A young woman had sat next to Janet in her wheelchair. She had one leg and one arm; it was hard to see how she managed here on Second Chance. The woman noticed Janet stealing glances at her and introduced herself as Barbara.

Barbara had lost her limbs in a motorway accident where she had been trapped and crushed under the wheels of a lorry. They had to amputate her limbs to get her out of the wreckage. Unfortunately, she was injured so badly that she died before they could get her out. Janet was astonished at her story. She had been through hell and still had a smile on her face. Janet told Barbara a potted history of how she ended up there. She always felt awkward mentioning mental illness even though people generally were accepting.

The tour showed the pure size of Second Chance, acres of parkland, fields of crops, and buildings for this and that, too much to take in in one go. They passed no end of brown-clad Second Chancers going about their daily activities. They all waved politely; those who could wave back. The tour took about half an hour arriving back at the departure point where Don pointed out one last building with architecture resembling a religious building, "that" said Don "is the nerve centre, the beating heart of Second Chance."

It was certainly majestic, with three gold-coloured spires and painted gargoyles with stained glass windows, a real mismatch of styles. Janet wanted to know more about what went on in there, but Don didn't have time. He said that the career officer could probably give her more info. Janet disembarked, thanking Don for his tour. They were met by a brown-clad man who led them back inside. He called each person in turn, handing them a package of clothes. They were a second lot of the outfits with two towels and some underwear; thankfully, that wasn't brown. Barbara was struggling to carry the luggage, so Janet offered to help her. Barbara took her up on it, and they went along together to the next item on the agenda. Next, the new brownies were taken to their temporary homes, the living quarters for new arrivals until they moved into their permanent suites. Barbara was the first to be dropped off at number two.

She invited her in for a drink which Janet happily agreed to. Janet was above Barbara in room thirteen. She had some trepidation about being in an unlucky room but dared not speak up. Barbara and Janet explored the suite; there was a monkey bar over her bed for her to use to get in and out of bed, the lounge had furniture the right height for her to get in and out of, and the kitchen had lower surfaces to cope with her wheelchair. Barbara checked out the kitchen; there was tea and coffee in some canisters and a small amount of milk in the fridge. She put the kettle on to make them both coffee. Barbara took something else out of the fridge; it was a large slice of cake. It had cream and jam inside and white icing on the top. Both women laughed at this and wondered if Janet had the same thing in hers. Barbara cut the slice in two with a knife from one of the drawers and then found a couple of plates to put the cake on. They both chatted as they consumed the food, getting lost in telling their stories.

Once they had finished their coffee and chat had come to a natural end, Janet said her goodbyes and then headed off to find her rooms. Number thirteen was easy to find; she used the fob key she had been given to open the door, then went in to put her belongings and the bundle she had been given down. The suites were clean and functional, with a bedroom, a small gallery kitchen, a toilet with a shower and a lounge. It was nice to get some privacy back after the dorm. Janet sat down on the bed feeling very overwhelmed and extremely tired. She knew she had a few hours to pass before the next thing on the list. She decided to use the time to rest; she lay on the bed staring up at the ceiling. She stared up at the ceiling, thinking that everything here on Second Chance was well thought out, neat and tidy and sterile. With that, she fell asleep, waking up with a start two hours later, taking a few moments to remember where she was. She got up and made her way to the kitchen feeling hungry. She checked in her fridge to see if she had a slice of cake but found it full of food. She saw vegetables and salad stuff, cheese and bread and fruit. She put together a quick meal and then went into the lounge to consume her food. Her thoughts were, as usual, trying to make sense of this world.

She did not want to be here; she missed her past life terribly. She wondered what was said about her at her funeral, did people weep, did they play the right music, did they still remember her and talked about her. She felt uneasy in this place. She could not grasp the point of it all. Why bother saving these souls if, indeed, it was saving or something more sinister? She dragged her thoughts out of the ditch and considered what was happening in the here and now. She had been told to meet at the main door of the housing block to be shown some key places they would need to know. Janet got there early and wondered if to go to see if Barbara was OK. The brownie they had seen earlier came over to her and asked her how her room was. Janet said it was OK but decided to ask him how come she had food in her kitchen while Barbara just had cake.

The man looked at her, then scratched a spot on top of his head, and then leaned towards Janet.

"She probably won't be here long," he said, then went over to a couple of other people that were with her on tour. Barbara didn't join them; Janet assumed she was resting. The group went off and was shown the canteen, social club, arts and craft studios and the gym. There were a good number of people around using the facilities. Janet was impressed with it all. On the way back to the starting point, Janet noticed a room off the corridor; she asked the Brownie what the space was for, and he said it was the multiple faith chapel. She had a quick look in there, seeing a dark room with prayer mats on the floor and some seating in front of an altar.

Like all religious buildings she had experienced, the room was calm and peaceful. Janet made a mental note of the location as she thought she might well make use of it at times. She wasn't a member of any religion, but she classed herself as spiritual. Once back, Janet thanked the man whose name she could not remember and headed back to her suite. She was done in. It had been an informative day, but she had had enough. Janet undressed, washed and cleaned her teeth, and then went to bed. She turned off the light and thought about her day. This place seemed too large; it would take ages to explore it all. Still, she had the rest of her life to get used to this place. She wondered where Mel and co were. She hoped she would see them soon.

Janet and the other new brownies were given a day to settle in; in that time, she paid a visit to the gym and went out to explore the grounds. She found the way to the park and had a walk around the beautiful landscape. There was a large lake near enough the centre of the park with a small island in the middle. Janet noticed that sand had been placed at one point at the edge of the lake, which at that point was on the same level. Janet could not work out what it was for then it came to her in a flash. It was a space for people to enter the lake. Janet was pleased that that was an option and one she would explore one day. There were a load of Brownies working on some of the extensive flower beds; in one area, it looked like they were letting it just grow; there were loads of wildflowers and a mix of grasses. Janet made her way over there, thinking that to make it all work beautifully, they needed bees. The lack of insects was so noticeable around flowers; it also meant that the workers had to pollinate everything to keep them going; that was a huge task when there were so many flowers in this park alone. In the afternoon, Janet made her way to the indoor gym. The gym was well equipped with resistance machines and free weights, plus cardio equipment, treadmills and rowers. Janet stood in the doorway looking at all the equipment when she heard a voice. The person had startled her, making her jump.

"Sorry about that. Are you OK," said a gorgeous redhead. Janet looked at her and then told her she was new and wanted to use the gym.

"Have you been to one before?" the lady asked.

"Yes, I know what to do," Janet replied.

"Do you have gym clothes?" she replied.

"No," said Janet.

"What size are you?" she asked. Janet gave her her dress and foot size then she disappeared into a room next to the gym. A few minutes later, she came out with a selection of t-shirts and leggings and some trainers.

"What do you fancy? The orange or pink. She held up each outfit in turn, letting Janet examine them.

"The orange, I think," said Janet holding the outfit up against her body. She then tried on the trainers, which fitted her nicely.

"Do you need any underwear or a gym bra?" the lady asked her. Janet nodded yes then the lady went back inside the room and came out with a bra. Janet thought to ask her if there was a swimming pool. The lady said yes, but it was out of action at the moment. She then went on to say, "Some people swim in the lake. Would you want to do that?"

"Oh yes, I would. But I don't have anything I can swim in. Can you help?" the lady went into the room for the third time and, this time, came out with a swimming costume.

"I think this should fit you, OK," she said, handing the garment over to Janet. Janet thanked her for her help and then left the gym, mentally vowing to come back tomorrow. She went to her room to put the clothes down and then sat on the bed for a while. She was quite excited about being here on Second Chance. There were lots of things to do to occupy her time, she thought.

Later on, in the late afternoon, she found her way to the canteen to have her dinner. It was a huge place with an extensive serving area and a large seating area. Half of the tables were already occupied; Janet had a look around to see if she could see anyone she knew. She joined the shortest queue to be served, and when it was her time, she ordered veggie shepherd's pie with green vegetables. She opted for a banana for her dessert and then walked, carrying her tray, to an unoccupied table. She set down the tray and then started to eat her food. She thought about calling on Barbara on her way back to see if she was OK. Janet had been informed on her first day here that she had an appointment booked to see a job advisor the next day, so Janet put her mind on what she wanted to do. She had a few ideas but really needed to talk them through with someone. When she had finished her meal, she took the tray to the parking area and then walked out of the hall. She set off back to her room, knocking on Barbara's door on the way. She knocked a couple of times, but there was no answer. Never mind, Janet thought, she would try again tomorrow.

The next day apart from her appointment, the rest of her day was hers to fill. She had a little while before she was due to see the job advisor, so she changed into her gym clothes and went to the gym to have a workout. She did OK; she was pleased with how well she had done. She had set herself goals for each piece of equipment she used and managed to achieve them all. After an hour, she cooled down and then started to walk back to her room to shower and change. She turned a corner on the way back and saw a black woman ahead of her. She was tall and slim and walked with long strides. Janet called out "Mel" and then expected the woman to turn around. She did turn around, but it wasn't Mel who looked back at her.

"Sorry, wrong person," Janet said, then she carried on with her walk. After her shower, she had about half an hour to kill before lunch. Her appointment was after lunch at one thirty, so with a bit of spare time, she went out into the park and then walked to a bench overlooking the lake. There was something about seeing a body of water that made you think about stripping off and going in, Janet thought, then laughed at herself. There was a swimmer in the lake. He was swimming laps of the island at a steady but fast front crawl.

Janet enjoyed swimming, but her stamina was poor. She thought of how if she went to the gym each day, her stamina would improve. It sounded like a plan, she thought to herself. She strolled back to the canteen and then went in to see what delights they had prepared for her. She was going to keep an eye on her weight with all of this good food. She thought so virtuously and ordered an egg salad and a bowl of mixed fruit. Her mind said it wanted the nut roast with roast potatoes and sticky toffee pudding with custard, but she stuck with her first choice and then found a table at the back where she could see who came in. Straight after lunch, she went to the place she had been informed, where the job advisor's office was. She got there a little bit early, but that was better than being late, Janet thought. She knocked on the office door and then heard a 'come in' come from somewhere on the opposite side. Janet pushed the door that opened easily, which led into a small space with a row of chairs on one side. The back of the room was dedicated to a large desk and filing cabinets. The other wall had a door. There were files and paper all over the desk and the tops of the cabinets. One man sat on one of the chairs and said hello to her when Janet went to sit down.

"You new here," he said with a profound Scottish accent.

"Yes, what about you?" Janet asked.

"Been here before. Trying out a new job; that's why I'm here." He replied.

"Have you been waiting long?" Janet said, continuing the small talk.

"Not long; the person is in there; they should be done soon," he replied. That seemed to mark the end of the conversation, and each of them sat still in their own thoughts. Just then, the inner door opened, and a lady came out in her wheelchair clutching a couple of sheets of paper.

"Won't be long?" the job advisor said to Janet when she popped her head out of the doorway. She invited the man into her office and then closed the door. With time on her hands, she could not help herself but go up to the desk to look at some of the strewn papers. Most seemed to be lists of jobs with dates on the top. Janet picked up one of the sheets and looked at the various openings. Janet assumed she would get one of these lists when she saw the advisor. Janet was looking at some of the other papers on the desk when she heard the inner door open. Janet quickly went back to her chair after putting down the papers in her hand. She sat down just as the man exited the room. He looked at Janet and wished her good luck; then, he ambled out of the seating area through the door. The job adviser looked at Janet and then invited her into her office. She introduced herself as Sally and invited Janet to sit down on a chair by her desk. Sally sat behind the desk and then looked over the rim of her glasses at Janet.

"Nice to meet you," she said, then looked at a piece of paper, "Janet," she said, looking up.

Sally was a large lady with flyaway hair and an infectious laugh,

"Are you settling in OK?" she asked

"Yes, thank you," was the stock reply.

"Excellent. You have had a bit of time to think about what you can do to make Second Chance the place it is, but before we look at that, we need to let you know that most people here take turns in some of the menial jobs, even me, once a fortnight I clean the toilets in the social club, that way everyone is responsible for the upkeep and can do a more interesting job as their main one. I have a list here of vacancies that we can go through. There is one sweeping the floor along a selection of corridors; what do you reckon? Or how about washing up once a week in the canteen. Tuesday evenings, how about that one, or they need a cleaner to clean the gym." Sally said, not giving Janet a chance to say a word. Janet thought for a moment before saying that she wouldn't mind doing the washing up.

"Great," said Sally writing something down on a piece of paper on her desk. "Now, what about your main job? What do you think? You used to be a nurse; is that a no-no job or something to put on the list of possibilities? Always need Fetchers or nursery nurses for the little ones." Janet tried to get a word in edgeways, but Sally rarely drew breath.

"Well," said Janet, "Excellent, ha ha ha, now, I don't need an answer from you right now; we like our new brownies to settle in; I can see you again in two days' time, nice to see you," said Sally who stood up ushering Janet out of the door. "Next, please," her voice boomed out. Janet left the room and nodded to the person waiting in the outer office. Janet walked slowly back to her room; Sally had given her a list of current vacancies to look at before they met again later in the week. She decided to knock on Barbara's door again to see if she was in. She walked up to her door then, knocked a couple of times then waited. This time the door opened, but it wasn't Barbara at the door. Janet double-checked the room number to make sure she was at the right place, then looked at the person behind the door.

"Is Barbara in?" Janet asked the young woman.

"No, I don't know who Barbara is," she said.

"Sorry, but how long have you been here? Barbara was living here," Janet asked.

"I came today, and it's my first day here," the woman said.

"I'm sorry to disturb you; she must have been moved elsewhere," Janet said, taking her leave. Janet didn't know what to make of that. The only thing she could think was that Barbara had been moved to her permanent home. Janet went to her room, sat down in the small lounge, and studied the papers from Sally. She really was not sure what she wanted to do. There were definitely some possibilities here. She wondered if she could move around trying out some of the roles. She thought about asking Sally that when she next saw her.

Janet checked the time on the wall clock. It was three thirty in the afternoon. She decided to go and rest for an hour or two before dinner time, so she went into her bedroom and onto the bed. She slept soundly for three hours and then woke up with a start. She felt confused for a moment or two until she recognized where she was. She got up, used the toilet then brushed her hair. She grabbed her fob key and headed off to go to the canteen for food.

She had hit the busy time with long queues at each of the serving hatches, but she joined one of them and just waited for her turn, hoping that they had some of the macaroni cheese left when she got there. Macaroni cheese was still available when she got to the head of the queue. Janet requested garlic bread to go with it, then settled for bread-and-butter pudding for dessert. She carried her tray to a spare table and then started to eat her food. She searched the faces of people coming and going to see if she recognized any one from the Mind Complex. There were one or two who looked familiar but not one of the girls. After dinner, she thought about what she may do to fill her time, then decided to explore the place. She went outside to wander around parts of the complex to get familiar with the lay out. The social club had been mentioned to her several times, but she didn't know where it was, so that was her target today. She found it without any problem; she just followed the sound of the music. There seemed to be a party or something going on in there, but she didn't feel brave enough to go up close to see what was happening. She turned around to head back pass the Nerve Centre building. Janet found the building intriguing; externally, it was quite beautiful with all the various styles and the large stained-glass windows. She wondered around the outside of it, trying to fathom out how to get in. There were no obvious doors; the windows were stained to such an extent that nothing could be seen inside. She had a look for an entrance into connected and surrounding buildings with no joy. She stood looking at the building, wondering what to do now. Just then, she saw a tall, lanky man walking along the path near her.

"Excuse me," Janet shouted out, startling the man. He turned to face her. Janet forgot her quest for a moment when she saw his face. There was part of an axe embedded in his skull; his face was otherwise perfect with blue eyes and a kind smile. Janet was unsure if her reaction was a shock at his injury or an instant attraction. Either way, she lost her words for a moment. Stuttering like a schoolgirl, she asked him how to access the Nerve Centre.

"You need a pass to get in there," he replied.

"How do I get a pass, sorry what is your name," she said

"Gary, my name is Gary; passes are issued to people who work there," he replied.

"Gary, thank you, what goes on in there?"

"they monitor and problem solve, you know, as a Newbie, the yellow mist? Well, that is managed by the Nerve Centre. Hard to get into work there. Also, they are excused from menial tasks."

"What about you? What do you do?" Asked Janet.

"Me, oh, I am mainly overseeing the horticultural areas as my main job; before I was killed, I was a keen gardener and loved working with my hands."

"Lovely hands," Janet thought, not too sure if she had said it out aloud.

"Sorry, what was that?" he asked.

Janet inwardly cringed; she had said that out loud.

"Sorry, I said you have good hands for a gardener.

"Yes, and you, what do you do?" he asked.

"I only came here a few days ago, not sure what my job will be."

"Try something new, stretch yourself; very satisfying."

"Yours is rather satisfying," thought Janet, this time definitely out loud. She felt herself going red, trying to hide it by distracting him. "What did you used to do?" Janet asked Gary

"I drove a taxi for a living; I got caught up in gang warfare when giving three youths a lift; that's how I got this axe in my head. Silly young people squabbling over territory, anyway; I am glad I am out of that way of life. It's far from perfect here, but life can be good if you want it to be. Anyway, I must get on; the main kitchen needs to be cleaned; got to go; sorry, what's your name?"

"Janet, my name is Janet," she responded as Gary waved as he strode off with long strides and an axe in his head. She looked after him until he was out of sight, admiring what she saw. She set off walking at a fare pace back towards her room when she heard footsteps behind her. The she heard a familiar voice.'

"Janet's in love, Janet's in love," sang Mel, who appeared from nowhere. "How are you? Who was he?" So many questions. Janet was delighted to see Mel; they hugged tightly.

"Have you seen the others?" enquired Janet.

"I saw Kim the other day; Lisa is at the crèche with her baby. I have started working as a teaching assistant with the kids. Really good, though tough seeing them injured and deformed. My other job is dusting the conference room twice a week. There are loads of ornaments on the window sills, which takes ages. Anyway, no one has just a boring job; it seems a good system. No hierarchy except those deemed worthy of being in the Nerve Centre," said Mel. "I don't reckon much to the brown," she lifted the hem of her tunic, "so drab."

"Do they wear brown at the Nerve Centre?" asked Janet.

"They wear grey, except for the top people; they wear silver; they live in a separate building over there." Kim pointed to a cluster of the building near the Nerve Centre.

"Don't you find it odd that the Nerve Centre looks like a mix-match of religious buildings?" enquired Janet.

"Never really thought about that, but yes, I can see that now; anyway, I have got to go. See you in the social club a bit later on a bit of a social going on; the others are coming" Mel shrugged her shoulders before waving goodbye as she skipped off towards the canteen.

Janet thought she would take up the offer of going out. At least she didn't have to worry about what clothes to wear; that was already decided. She had a look at herself in the mirror, wondering if she could style her hair any differently. It was quite long now; it hadn't been cut for a good four months. She thought about asking Mel if there was a hairdresser somewhere around. She brushed her hair off her face, then dampened down the hair, hoping it would set. Then she brushed it out into her normal style. Why was she feeling nervous, she thought. She was only going out with her friends. She was so pleased she had made contact with them. Mel looked good;

her face had healed more, and there was still a hole in her face, but it was much smaller. In time all she will have is a scar. Janet set off for the social club at eight o clock. She took hold of her nerves as she approached, searching the faces of familiar people.

In no time at all, she spotted Kim and called out to her. Kim squealed when she saw Janet and came rushing over to hug her. Kim took her by the hand to take her over to where Mel and Lisa stood near the back of the room. The music was loud, and the patrons were louder. Janet found it hard to work out what people were saying; she just hoped she was nodding at the right time. Mel offered to go to the bar to get her a drink. Janet asked what they served, the answer being either wine or beer. No spirits, nothing fancy, but it was alcohol.

Janet asked her for a glass of wine then Mel disappeared into the crowds to go and get her order. Janet took a bit of time to study the room. It was a fair size with a stage at one end and chairs piled up on one side. The bar was in one corner of the room, and the music came from the other. There were proper DJ decks with someone playing dance tracks. Mel came back with a large glass of wine for Janet. Janet took a sip and then nodded, saying that it was good. It didn't take long for Janet to get hit by the alcohol; she felt a wave of warmth radiate out of her stomach, and then she felt like dancing. Now Janet, once upon a time, used to do a lot of dancing.

She always had enthusiasm but lacked the skill, but that didn't stop her. Janet felt her body move with the music; Lisa took her by hand onto the dance floor, where Janet had the time of her life. She knew she would live to regret having a drink, but for now, she was happy. It was lovely being with the girls; Janet had missed them.

She looked at Mel dancing away and felt almost maternal. She felt so proud of her for what she had been through. Her story was horrific. Let alone the injury she had obtained. She was very disfigured, and Janet knew that Mel had not seen the damage caused by the bullet, so she avoided looking in a mirror. Kim was doing OK, and Lisa had a rare evening off from looking after baby Linda. Janet saw that something was distracting Mel; she kept on looking towards the entranceway, "Are you expecting someone? Is it a fella?" teased Kim.

"Nosey, yes. I invited someone to join us, ahh here he is," she turned to face the door beckoning a tall man with an axe in his head to join them. Janet felt herself blushing and talking rubbish. Language seemed to desert her, and she felt like a silly schoolgirl. Kim, Lisa and Mel tactfully withdrew, leaving Gary and Janet to chat and dance. Gary was quite a good mover, and they moved in sync with the hypnotic music.

The talking was easy, but Janet knew if things were too awkward, the silent agreement between the female sex would mean they would find reasons as to why she needed to rejoin them. After the dancing, Gary offered to get her another glass of wine. She accepted his offer then he disappeared into the crowd heading towards the bar.

The evening passed quickly; Gary was a good companion; he seemed kind, accepting and as levelheaded as a man with an axe in the head could be. Janet could see pass the injury to see the man. And he certainly was a man; maybe, just maybe, he would be the man, she thought as he held her for the last dance. Gary offered to walk her home, but she declined. She thought she might ask him to join her for lunch the next day. He was agreeable to that, and he kissed her on her cheek before she set off for her rooms. A little later, she lay on her bed thinking about the fun that she had had that evening. It had been a good day.

The next morning, her head was rather tender, but she did not have the great hangover that she thought she would have. She had a look in her cupboards for something to eat but really didn't fancy cornflakes. She got herself dressed and then brushed her hair before leaving to go to the canteen for breakfast.

She got herself a cooked meal and sat on a free table at the back of the canteen. She watched people come and go and wondered about their tragic stories that brought them to be at Second Chance. Then she thought about Gary and about if he and she would or could ever be an item. Janet had not had a fella for quite a long time. Her last serious relationship happened about ten years ago. As soon as long-term commitment came up in their conversations, he disappeared into thin air.

He was not as into her as she was into him. Janet smiled at that memory; Phil was a lovely person; she thought about what he was doing now; had he found the love, she wondered. Knowing she had some time to kill before meeting Gary for lunch, she decided she would be active and go for a swim. Back in her room, she tried on the swimming costume she had been given to see if it fitted and if it hid what needed to be hidden. She had some stray pubic hair that needed to be tamed, so she found her razer to eliminate them. She then grabbed one of her towels and wrapped it around her. She had no suitable alternative footwear, so she wore her trainers. Dressed and ready, she left her room and headed off for the short walk to the park.

The park looked lovely, the grass seemed almost luminous, and the flowers were so bright in colour that they took her breath away. When she arrived at the lake, she took off the towel and her trainers. She put her fob key in one of the shoes, then, finally ready, she walked into the lake using the sand slope. The water was cold enough for her to hold her breath as she entered. She ducked under the water when she was in deep enough and then started swimming. The water felt like silk caressing her body; it was so smooth and steady.

There were tiny little ripples where the breeze tickled the surface, which Janet noticed with glee. She set herself a goal to swim once around the island in the middle of the lake and then to see how she felt after that.

She began to tire on the way back to the starting point. Her stamina had been stretched to its limit. When she was level with the sand slope, she made her way out of the water and to the place she had left her belongings. She wrapped the towel around herself and then started to dry the naked areas of her body. She rubbed her hair to get the worst of the moisture off, then sat down to pull on her trainers. Once she was done, she stood up and headed back.

Once in her room, she showered and changed already for lunchtime. She had a little while to fill before she was due to meet Gary, so she went off in search of the craft room. She headed towards the canteen, pretty sure she had seen a sign for it on her way there. Her memory served her well. She easily found the studio. The door opened with her fob key then Janet went in. The room was about the size of a good-sized lounge with cupboards and shelves containing masses of materials.

Janet rummaged around to see if anything tickled her interest, then settled on making a stuffed dog. It came in kit form and didn't look too complicated. She thought she could make it for baby Linda. It didn't have anything a young baby could swallow or get caught in. She sat down at one of the tables in the centre of the room and laid out the material, and started to tack the edges of the dog together. The felt material was easy to sew, and she made good headway into making the toy.

She lost herself in her work, and she didn't notice the time. She missed not wearing a watch, but no one she knew had one. There was a clock in the craft studio, which, when she thought about checking, she found to her dismay, that she was already late for her lunch invitation. She quickly gathered up the material and threads and stuffed them into one of the pigeonhole shelving. She left the room and marched as quickly as she could to the canteen. She was not terribly late when she checked, but the queue to be served was long. She looked out onto the diners to see if she could see Gary. He was not hard to miss with his injury and his height, but he was not there. She checked again, but still, he wasn't there. Just then,

"Are you looking for a handsome, rich and well-endowed man?" someone said. Janet looked around, spotting Gary in the queue behind her.

"I can't see anyone matching that description here?" she teased.

"I'm a bit late, sorry about that; we had an emergency in the polytunnel," Gary said, grabbing a tray. Janet was next in line to be served, so she had a look at the menu to see what she would like to eat. She chose veggie sausage, chips and garden peas for her main meal and Crème caramel for dessert. Once served, she went to a table where there was only one person; all the rest of the tables were nearly full enough. Gary followed her then once he had sat down, they both began to eat and chat. They found the conversation between them easy; Gary was a very interesting person who had a good knowledge about near enough everything. Janet asked him about what she should do the next day when she was due to see Sally.

"You used to be a nurse; I guess you could train to be a Fetcher or work with the children. Or you strike out to do something you have never done before but thought you might like to do. I only had a bit of experience of growing plants, and I had a garden at home that I used to look after. It was not too big a step to go bigger. I am now managing a team and a section of the horticulture."

Gary spoke sense; he was right; she could strike out to do something new. She made a mental note to go back through the list of vacancies when she got back to her room.

"There are vacancies where I work; you could join my team," he said between mouthfuls of sausage. Now, I would not mind that, thought Janet. She always admired the work they did with the flowers; she could be one of them. After lunch, Gary asked if she was going to the social club that night. It was quiz night, and they had one short in his team. Janet said yes, but she was not sure if she would be a help or a hindrance. Her general knowledge was not brilliant.

Gary left Janet nursing a mug of tea. He had to get back to the nursery, and Janet had another free afternoon. She thought she would have a bit more of an exploration but would have a rest first. Her body was aching from the swimming earlier that day. She went to her room and went over to the bed to have a rest. She drifted off to sleep for over an hour before waking up gently. She stretched out her limbs, then swung her legs to one side of the bed, sitting upwards.

She yawned and then got out of bed to check the time. It was three thirty; time for a coffee and an exploration, she thought. She made herself a drink in her kitchen. She saw the ordering form for groceries and found a pen to tick off some items. They had a post box at the end of the corridor to put the grocery lists; it was a quick turnaround, and they would be left in a paper bag by the next day. Janet thought it was strange not having or handling any money, but it was all part of the service. She couldn't criticize. The service was good, the food excellent, and although there were only two types of alcoholic beverages, it wasn't rationed.

She wondered if they had problems with people becoming alcoholics; she thought or hoped that people would be sensible. Janet finished her coffee, picked up her fob key and the grocery list, and then left her room to go and explore. She went past the social club to have another look at the Nerve Centre. She planned to go past it to see what was beyond it. She had been told that there was part of the park which had a waterfall in it which opened up around that area.

She found it with no problem; the sound of falling water was a good giveaway. She sat on a fallen tree trunk, just looking at the water, twisting this way and that. There were droplets suspended in the air for tiny periods of time before they dropped back into the pool of water under the fall. It was beautiful. Janet sat there for a good while before setting off on a path which she thought would take her back to the park area she was at earlier in the day.

She walked slowly, enjoying the sun on her back as she continued along the path alongside the river. The pathway was lined with shrubs and trees, which cast shadows onto the water then the path turned to the left, opening up into the main park. Janet sat down on one of the benches for a moment or two. It had been a good find; she was glad she had done it.

Gary had told her about the waterfall. He said there was a working mill further up which captured the power of the water to make flour to feed everyone on Second Chance. He had told them that where food was concerned, they were self-sufficient with farmland further out and more nurseries and polytunnels. She could really see his passion for his work which was infective; it made her want to be part of it. She guessed she had made her decision about what work she wanted to do; she would tell Sally, the job advisor, tomorrow.

That night, Janet did OK on the quiz. She was able to give several right answers. However, they were beaten by the mechanics by two points. To celebrate coming second, Janet tried out the local beer. She had never been much of a beer drinker, and after tasting, it was thought that she was still not a beer drinker. The girls were not there at the quiz night. She expected to see them and kept looking out for Mel, who stood out in a room. At the end of the evening, Gary walked Janet back to her room. They chatted along the way; she found out quite a lot about him in that short time.

Gary was born in Wales to a single mother with two siblings, girls. He was well cared for by the three females in his life and experienced a brilliant childhood. Money was tight right from the start, but as time went on, his mother got better and better-paid jobs. They lived comfortably in a lovely house in a nice area. Life really couldn't get much better.

Gary was a keen scholar but not blessed with a brilliant brain. He tried so hard to get his work noticed in class, but he was stuck in the middle large group of those who were left to their own devices. He left school with a couple of o levels at the age of sixteen and entered the world of work. At the age of eighteen, just after his birthday, his mum had a heart attack and died. It hit him hard, his sisters were distraught, but the family pulled together to manage the best they could without her.

Two months later, the elder of his sisters, Grace, was rushed to the hospital with appendicitis which turned into sepsis. She died two days later of organ failure. Gary really struggled after her death. His one remaining sister tried to do what she could to support him, but he went off the rails. He was arrested by the police on a couple of occasions after damaging vehicles by chucking bricks through the windscreen.

He was put on probation by the court and told to attend an anger management program. This he did then he found a new job with better prospects. He met his wife a few months later. They were well-suited and made a great couple. He had two children with her, a boy and a girl and always vowed to keep them safe. The children grew up with two loving parents who made sure they always had food on the table and a roof over their heads.

Gary worked hard in the government office; he was promoted several times and commanded a good wage. He balanced out his work commitments by tending to his garden. It took a bit of time to get it how he wanted it then; once that was done, he was at a loss as to what to do next. His wife suggested he put his name down to get a council allotment. This he did and was offered one a few months later.

Work was demanding more and more of his time. He often came home wiped out and stressed. One day after a particularly heavy day, he came home complaining of pain down his right arm and a tightness in his chest. Concerned, his wife phoned for an ambulance who blue-lit him to the hospital with a suspected heart attack. This was confirmed by a doctor who admitted him to the general ward.

Gary spent seven days in the hospital, which gave him time to reevaluate his life. He had to do something different; he was killing himself. He decided to give notice at work and become his own boss by becoming a taxi driver. He loved it. He got to meet loads of interesting people and work the hours of his choosing. The wage was less than he earnt at his last job with the DVLA, but by cutting back here and there, they managed OK.

One night he was taking a man down to Swansea town centre to meet up with some friends. Gary dropped him off and then started to go back to his home. He was done for the day. Just then, someone knocked on his window. Gary wound it down to see what the man wanted; the man told Gary that he had someone injured whom he needed to get to the hospital. Gary tried to explain that he couldn't take rides off the street as he was a minicab driver, not a taxi. The man drew out from his pocket a flick knife and held it to Gary's throat. Gary tried to fathom out what to do, he didn't want to get hurt, but he didn't want to get involved in some dodgy dealings. Gary nodded his head towards the rear door, which the man opened. Just then, someone came out from an alleyway holding up a third man who had been injured. The two able-bodied men helped the injured one to get in the car then one of them went to Gary's open window, telling him to take him to the hospital. The two men run off down the alleyway. Gary looked over his shoulders at the injured man; he didn't look very comfortable, so he got out of the car, went to the back door he reached in to see if he could get him in a more comfortable position. At his touch, the man jumped, yelling at Gary to leave him alone. Gary turned around then suddenly, he heard a noise then fell to the ground. The man had withdrawn an axe he had hidden down a trouser leg and had embedded the weapon in Gary's head. Gary died instantly.

The man panicked, left the back seat, then moved Gary's body aside so he could get in the driving seat where he sat and drove the car away from the area. Gary's body stayed on the ground as people came out of the pubs and bars with people walking around him. Eventually, someone stopped to see what the matter was; she saw the axe and then went to call for an ambulance and the police. The man who had murdered Gary was caught when he admitted himself to the local Accident and Emergency department. He was questioned, fingerprinted then arrested for his murder.

Janet woke early in the morning; the clock said it was seven-thirty. She was not due to see Sally until eleven, so she had a good few hours to kill. She decided to go for a swim first thing thinking how nice it would be to start her day that way. She walked out of her accommodation block and down to the park. The place was deserted. Generally, things seemed to sprint to life around eight, so she had a short time in her own company. The water was lovely, she thought, as she swam two laps of the island. She decided to swim to the island and started to look for a good place to land. She saw the right spot easily, then swam there and got out of the water. She sat looking at the scene for a few minutes. She could see some people jogging around the park using the path that ran around the outer edge of the space. She then thought she saw Mel; she looked again, deciding it was Mel.

Janet stood up to wave at her. Mel thought she saw things with Janet standing on an island like that. Mel carried on running after waving back at her, and Janet decided it was time to head back. She went up out of the lake on the sand and grabbed her towel to start drying herself. She pulled on her trainers, wrapped the towel around her middle then walked back to her room to shower and dress. There were loads of people around, in stark contrast to half an hour ago. People on their way to work, soon, she thought, that would be her. She was quite excited by the idea; she had had a good few days to find her way around, and she was ready to start doing her bit for Second Chance.

Janet found her way back to Sally's office at eleven, feeling pretty prepared for the discussion. She waited in the outer office when she arrived and looked at some of the posters on the walls. The desk looked just as congested as before, with paper everywhere. If she had worked there, she would have gotten on top of the filing in no time. At five past eleven, the door opened, and a man came out clutching a sheet of paper. Janet smiled at him, and he nodded back; then, without saying a word, he left the outer office. Sally stood in the doorway, summoning Janet. She went in and sat down behind the desk as Sally closed the door.

"Well, Janet, have you thought about what you would like to do?"

"Yes, well, yes, I think so," Janet said, feeling awkward.

"Yes," said Sally.

"I, erh, well, I would like to work in the Nerve Centre, I know there were no jobs listed in the paper you gave me, but I think I could do good there," Janet said, looking at the floor.

"It isn't as easy as that, and I can't place people there; generally, people are headhunted to go there. What I can do is make them aware of your interest. Is there anything else?"

"Well, I wouldn't mind working in the garden department, you know, the nursery," said Janet looking at Sally.

"Excellent choice. Could you start tomorrow?" Sally said.

"Yes, no problem; what time?" Janet asked.

"Nine o'clock," Sally replied

"OK," said Janet, then took her leave.

She thought about the discussion on her way to her room. She was going to go to the canteen for lunch a little later, once she had put some papers that Sally had given her down. She made herself a coffee and then let the feeling of excitement ripple over her; that was a pretty easy job interview, she thought.

She met Kim and Mel at the canteen, and she told them her news. Mel teased her by saying that she only wanted to work in the gardens because of Gary. Janet agreed, she had but also for a new challenge. The girls had to go back to work, so Janet wondered how she could spend her time. She had already done a lot that day; maybe she could explore some more or walk down to the waterfall. She decided to sleep and then go out for a walk. Janet slept soundly and then woke feeling out of sorts. She had slept too long, she thought. Nevertheless, she got up, made a coffee and brushed her hair.

After she had drunk her coffee, she set off for a walk. As she walked, she thought about the set-up here on Second Chance. She got the impression there were a lot of Brownies taking care of

Second Chance, whether as a cook, teachers or Fetchers, which kept work hours low and everyone doing menial work once or twice a week. They were right; it was a good system.

Chapter 7
Being a Brownie

Janet's first day working in the garden was something she was eager to do. She felt ready, after her swim the previous day, to take on a new challenge. Sally, the employment advisor, had given her the name of the person she would report to, Jim. Jim was aware that Janet was starting today and had made himself available. He came over to Janet when he saw her walking nervously towards him. He took several long strides to get to her, then offered his hand to shake as he introduced himself.

"Hi, you must be Janet? Good to meet you. I am Jim, the manager here; I'm in charge of the nurseries. My job is to support you in doing your work." Janet smiled at him, not too sure if she needed to say anything.

"Your injuries, do you think it, will impact your work here? It's a lot of standing, but we have perching chairs you can use if you think it will help."

"Thanks, yes, a perching chair would help. I'm pretty good on my legs but standing for long periods of time I find difficult."

"No problem, let's get you one, then I will give you a tour of the nursery. Janet was astounded by the depth of his knowledge about not only plants but how Second Chance works. She learnt that there were five gardens like this one as well as the farm. The set weather optimized the growing of food crops, and all the food served in the canteens is grown on-site. She really wanted to hear more of this as he showed her around, but she felt too shy to say anything. After the tour, he took her to her workplace, explaining as they walked what her role would be. She would be pricking out the young plants into flowerpots. Janet felt comfortable doing this as she used to work with her dad in his greenhouse when she was a child and often pricked out plants.

Leaving her to it, she set to work moving the fragile young plants one by one out of plant trays into individual flowerpots. She had not set any target for the day but tried to work steadily so as not to harm the plants. Every now and then, she stood up to stretch and get a drink of cordial. At lunchtime, once excused, she headed to the canteen, feeling in need of carbohydrates. She had an hour for lunch, half an hour to eat, and then a half hour to walk in the park. Time went past too quickly, she thought as she sauntered back to the grow tunnel. She returned to her workstation and then tenderly continued with her task. She took a bit of time looking around her, seeing the other workers and what they were doing. Most were doing the same as she was, though much quicker, she noticed. It was not the most glamorous of tasks; Janet hoped the work would be more varied. At three-thirty, Jim came over to her carrying a basket.

"How did you get on. I know it's a bit boring but vital for Second Chance. It does get better.

Here, this is for you," he said, handing her the basket. She looked inside it, finding an array of different fruits, including peaches, apples and strawberries. Looking up at Jim, she said

"My, oh, thank you, that's great; all for me?"

'Yes, one of the perks of the job. I will see you tomorrow."

With that, he turned away, striding into his office near the end of the polytunnel. Janet made her way home with the basket. She vowed not to eat anything until she was back in the room but just had to have a strawberry. It tasted like heaven. Back home, she changed out of her work clothes into her gym clothes and went to have a workout. There were a couple of people there using the equipment, and they both wished Janet a good day; people here were so polite, thought Janet.

She spent ten minutes on the treadmill fast walking to get her heart rate up. Then she worked on individual muscle groups on the resistance machines. She would never be a gym bunny; it wasn't very interesting, but she enjoyed the good feeling of having exercised, you know, that righteous feeling. After the gym, she went to her room for a shower and rest, then went for dinner at the canteen. She felt pleased with how the day had gone and was eager to share her experience with her friends.

Kim and Lisa were already in the canteen sitting at one of the tables at the back. After being served, Janet made her way to the table and sat down with the girls. Kim asked her how it had gone; Janet was happy to share. Kim asked Janet if she was going to the social club that evening. Janet decided to give it a rest and not go to the social club that night; she fancied a quiet night to catch up on some reading. She heads off there, picking up her grocery order in a box outside her door. She checked the contents to see if they had packed everything she had ordered; generally, it was OK, but occasionally she had things substituted. She got into her nightclothes and then sat in her lounge area to munch on fruit while reading a book she had picked up from the shelves at the back of the social club.

She had had a full day and was getting tired. She was no longer a spring chicken with boundless energy. She would soon be sixty, getting old. Reading seemed to be sending her to sleep, so she went to bed and turned out the light. She fell to sleep quickly and deeply and rested until the early hours. She woke up at six o'clock in the morning; she had run out of sleep, so she got up and made herself a mug of tea. It was too soon to go and get breakfast at the canteen, so she decided to go for a walk to the waterfall. There were a few people around, those on an early shift who were too preoccupied with their own lives to collide with hers. When she arrived, she sat on the tree stump to look at the water twist and turn and delighted at the bits of mist heading her way. It would have been even nicer if the water was shared with fish and birds; she missed the natural world terribly. She retraced her steps from the other day and walked in the park for a while. She guessed it must be time for breakfast because everyone she saw looked as if they were heading to the canteen.

So, she joined forces with them and walked along, guessing what would be on offer at the canteen, what she would like to eat and what she should eat. The food was so good here that she was worried about gaining extra pounds. True, she was pretty active exercising every day, sometimes twice a day, but at her age, it was easy to gain weight. Her eyes said cooked breakfast while her body said muesli. She opted for the middle ground, ordering scrambled eggs on toast with a mug of tea. She felt pleased with herself for her choice and ate the food quickly while it was still hot. It was still a bit early to see her friends, but she did see Gary in the queue; she waited until he looked her way and then waved. He didn't see her, so she gave up on that idea focusing on her food instead of him. What she didn't see was Gary waving at her. After he had been served, he came to the table she was sitting at,

"Any room for a little one?" his voice made Janet jump. She quickly collected herself and then pointed to a free chair. She had a mouth full of the egg, so she was not able to greet him apart from her body language. He sat down and then said that he had heard positive things from Jim about her first day at work.

'Really?" said Janet once her mouth was empty. "I was so worried about harming the plants by being too rough."

"No, he said you were very gentle with them," Gary said. "Mm, this food is delicious; I'm so glad I opted for the full English," he said, tasting the fried tomatoes. Janet and Gary passed the morning in amiable chatter then Janet looked at the clock. For someone who hated to be late for anything, recently, she had been cutting it fine to get to appointments. She saw she had five minutes before the start of her shift. She needed to go to the loo as well, so she said goodbye to Gary and hot-footed it to the bathroom a few doors down. After a quick long wee, she washed her hands and then fast walked her way to the polytunnel. Jim was already there talking to another one of the workers. Jim had introduced her to the others, but their names had not stuck in her memory. She tried to recall the man's name, but it had gone. Janet walked to her workstation, wondering if she would be doing the same job as she had the day before. When he had finished with the other man, Jim came over to Janet.

"How do you fancy going along with Ted to tidy up some of the flower beds in the park?" Jim said.

That was it, thought Janet, Ted, his name was Ted.

"Yes, of course," Janet said, getting up off her perching stool. Ted came over to Janet with some hand tools and a trug to put the rubbish in. Then he invited her to come with him to sort out one of the larger beds on the other side of the park. When they got there, Janet could see that some of the flowers were past their best. These were the ones that would be removed, and then in the afternoon, they would fill the gaps with new plants. Janet enjoyed doing that, and she could see the benefit of her labour immediately. They worked steadily, getting into a rhythm mainly in quiet. Janet did try to break the silence, but Ted was not very communicative, so Janet stopped trying.

After an hour or so, they stopped for a break going back to base to make tea and enjoy some biscuits. Jim popped over to where they were sitting near the place where they kept the kettle and asked them how it was going. Janet chewed the chocolate biscuit in her mouth, nodding wildly while Ted said that everything was fine. They went back to the bed they were working on and continued to tidy it up. Janet had an hour for lunch, so she did what she had done the previous day, eating in the canteen and then going for a walk. She saw Mel in the canteen; they shared a table and some natter before

Janet got up to go back to work. In the afternoon, they planted some mature plants into the space left by the dead flowers. Ted went back to the nursery to get some watering cans so they could soak the plants in the ground. Their work was nearly done; Janet hoped that Jim would say she could go once they had finished the watering, and indeed, this is what he did after thanking her for her work.

Janet enjoyed her work in the gardens; she took to it quickly and benefitted from the delight of working with her hands. The work was not heavy; she spent a lot of her working days in the polytunnel handling various plants. Some of them were flowers for the gardens, many of them for the vegetable area, tomato plants and the like. The things she learnt about plant management were great, but the information Jim gave her about Second Chance really got her attention. She learnt that it only rained at nighttime, and the temperature remained at a comfortable twenty degrees Celsius during the day. And apparently, the Nerve Centre controlled the atmosphere and hours of night and day.

Furthermore, the lack of insects and other wildlife meant the gardeners had to pollinate every growing plant. It felt odd not hearing the dawn chorus or seeing the maps of spider webs on the grass on a bright Autumn day. The greenhouses were extensive, with plants in various stages of growth. Outside behind the greenhouses were fields resembling old-time feudal farming with areas of land separated by narrow walkways. The diet at Second Chance was vegetable based, which was made very palatable by the chefs. She found her work rewarding, and it gave her time to think, heal and consider her life. She began to make friends and saw Gary quite often as he was Jim's boss. She enjoyed the banter with her work colleagues and the gentle teasing of the way Janet managed to drop tools when Gary came in sight. She could not deny the fact that she was attracted to him; she hoped the feeling was mutual.

The one part of life in Second Chance that she had an itch that could not be scratched was her growing interest in the Nerve Centre; it seemed people were discouraging her from talking about what went on in the celestial place. You know what it is like when people say no; it makes you want it more.

She spent some of her spare time exploring the rooms and walkways near the Nerve Centre. Most of them led to dusty rooms or storage cupboards filled with paper, stationary and other office stuff. Nothing really interested her except for the fact they looked like they had not been used in ages. One day she went to the chapel and sat down on a chair, just contemplating life. When she was ready, she went down a particularly dull corridor and turned left down a short corridor ending with a doorway. Beyond the door, looking through the dusty glass, Janet thought it looked like a library. She could see bookshelves and a couple of desks with ornate, heavy-looking chairs by them. Janet was surprised the room had not been made known to her during her tour with Don, as she was a keen reader. She had asked Don at the time if there was a library; he was the one who let her know about the store of reading books at the social club.

Janet entered the room with her breath held, worried that breathing out would blow away the precious words in the books. Everything was layered with dust; she carefully swept it away from one of the tables with her hand. She looked along the shelves at the books and then walked the length of the case. There were quite a lot of medical-type books and reference books. She took one out and flicked through the pages noticing the dust tumbling out and being carried in the air in the room. At the back of the library, she saw a whole load of papers. When she looked closer, she could see there were files of papers with writing on them.

There were filing drawers overflowing with paper; she picked up a couple of sheets noticing that they were notes and minutes of a meeting. She read a few sentences feeling as if she was trespassing. Nevertheless, she took a few of the ledgers and placed them on one of the tables. She sat down on one of the heavy chairs and then flicked through one of them. It looked like, on this particular occasion, it was a boring meeting, and the notes made would not win any prizes for stimulating reading. She got up and went to the second bookshelf, where she uncovered journals and diaries stretching back over twenty years. All of them were handwritten. She placed a few diaries on top of the ledgers, then sat back down on an old dark wood chair to flick through the documents. The library was all non-fiction by the look of it. Storytelling was left to the storytellers, who regularly narrated their yarns to spellbound audiences in the leisure rooms. Janet picked up one of the diaries. It had a cartoon character on the front, similar to what parents would give a child. The handwriting inside was very precise and neat. Janet immediately thought the diary belonged to a female. The pages revealed the story of the author's journey in Second Chance, focusing on her time as a Newbie. It was difficult to determine when it was written. The pages were yellowing a bit, and the ink faded in places. Janet assumed that it must have been written quite a while ago.

The words the author used to create a picture of her experiences added nothing to detect the age of the woman. Janet flicked through a few pages skim reading. She then started to read it in more detail. She did not know what to make of it, so she turned to the other journal picking it up to read. This journal was written by a flamboyant person, deducted from the sweeps of the handwriting and eloquent use of language. The first half of the journal was full of his/her life; it drastically stopped, with nothing written down to account for the abrupt change. Janet flicked back to see if she could find anything to explain it. Failing at this, she put the journal on top of the other one and picked up stapled sheets of paper of notes from the meeting of the heads of hospitality in May 1974. Reading it, it was typical drab notes of a rambling collection of people talking about everything and amounting to nothing.

Janet was not so idiotic to assume this world ran on its own without corporate direction and scrutiny; it just suddenly felt like she was back on earth again. She stood up and returned the papers and journals back onto the shelves in their dust-outlined places. She moved to leave the room, turned back around, picked up the flamboyant author's journal and hid it under her tunic. She had no real reason for doing that but did it anyway; then she left the room to retrace her steps back to her room, where she hid the journal under her pillow. She decided to go through it in more detail later on, but for now, she needed to shower and then go for food. Gary had invited her to join him down at the social club later; she was looking forward to that; she just wished that she had some makeup to put on. She could not recall seeing anyone wearing make up on Second Chance; maybe they just don't supply it. Instead of eye shadow and mascara, she tried some new styles for her shoulder-length hair. She could see her grey roots coming through; again, she didn't think they could get her some hair dye; she would just have to accept it and enjoy being natural. But she just felt old, even though she behaved like a silly schoolgirl when she was around Gary.

She did end up saying really stupid stuff and seemed to be more accident-prone in his company. Janet took one final look in the mirror and then set off to the canteen. She ate carefully, not really wanting to spill anything down her; the rest of her brown clothes were in the wash. She had an overall to wear when she was working in the garden, but with only two changes of clothes, she could not afford to eat messily. She avoided food like spaghetti, like the plague. Even soup was a no-no; she knew how backhanded she could be.

After food, she went just to sit in the park for a short while. She was meeting Gary at eight; she had time to kill, so she sat and watched the people using the park. When she thought the time was right, she ambled her way to the social club. For once, she thought, she did not have to hurry. She got there ridiculously early, so she sat at one of the tables outside the front of the club, looking out for him. She was beginning to think she had been stood up when she noticed his gangly gait coming towards her.

When he got to her, he bent down to plant a kiss on her cheek then they went into the club together, hand in hand. She had a good evening singing songs from the movies. Gary, like her, was not very melodic, but they both gave it their all. They had to keep drinking to keep their vocal cords working, or at least that was the excuse, and in no time, lightweight Janet was suffering from a dizzy head. She was getting pickled and was at the point where she didn't care how much she drank.

Gary was a bit behind her in the drinking stakes, but with him, it made him sing louder and more off-key. They must have been funny to watch and listen to. It was a good night, and at kicking out time, Gary walked her back to her room, leaving her with a kiss on the lips. Janet felt she was in heaven. She really had struck gold with him. He was so nice, kind and thoughtful. Janet undressed for bed, cleaned her teeth, and then climbed into her bed with her head whirling.

Eventually, sleep took hold with vivid dreams and lasted until the morning. She was not needed at work that day, which is just as well, as she had one hell of a hangover. She woke up at eight but stayed in bed until nine. She had some food in she could use for breakfast because she had missed eating at the canteen. She was a little worried that she had done something to embarrass herself the night before and that people would mock her. She was sensitive that way.

Still, she did have a good evening. He had asked her to go out with him that night, so she couldn't have done anything too bad.

When she felt a little more human, she got up, had something to eat and drink then got ready for a swim. The water was wonderfully refreshing, and she managed to add another circuit to her tally. She could now swim four times around the island. Janet went early for lunch at the canteen. She saw Mel ahead of her in the queue, who turned around when she heard Janet call her name. Once sat at their table, Janet filled her in on the evening before telling her she was never going to drink again. She was feeling a bit sheepish and was not sure how she was going to get on meeting Gary later that day. Mel had to zoom off back to work, so Janet went to her room to have another look at the journal. Once back, she read it carefully, trying to imagine the author; it sounded as if she had real problems adjusting to Second Chance.

That evening, Janet painted a smile, ready for when Gary came to pick her up. When there was a knock on her door at three minutes and thirty seconds to seven, not that she was checking, she opened the door. All she could see was a massive bunch of beautiful flowers. Below them, she could see legs that went on and on and above them was an axe. Janet invited Gary in and thanked him for the bouquet. After a bit of small talk, they set off to the social club. It was another quiz night, agricultural department versus repairs and hospitality. It was a bit of a stretch for Janet to consider this a date as she was in the team with other work colleagues. They lost miserably and jeered the winning team celebrating their victory with beer. Janet tried a beer, they brewed it in Second Chance, and as beer goes, it was not too bad. She felt her head begin to spin after a few sips.

"How strong is this stuff?" she asked.

"I have no idea," replied Gary.

"I think I need to go home, if you don't mind," Janet said, swaying to her feet. She really didn't want to get too drunk again. She had barely recovered from the night before.

"Let me take you," Gary offered, standing up by her side. She accepted his offer and his arm and walked out of the social club amid cries of "Light weights." She smiled and did a 'V' sign as they went through the door. The journey back took next to no time. He was the perfect gentleman opening doors for her and guiding her back. At her door, he took both of her hands in his and said, "Thank you for this evening. I know we were thrashed, but it's all about the team. I'm glad to be in the team with you." With that, he raised his right hand, which had her hand in it, and raised it to his lips, kissing it before letting her hand go.

"Thank you, and I had fun," Janet stumbled out the words; why oh why, she thought, do I mess up every time we talk? She wondered if she should invite him in for coffee but felt that was too forward. She smiled at him,

"I'll see you tomorrow at work," she said as she let herself into her room with the fob key.

"Nighty night," Gary said as he turned around to leave the accommodation block to go to his own quarters, wherever that may be. Janet sat down on her bed, running over the evening in her head. She wondered if she had read too much into the date. Maybe it was more of a work thing than a possible relationship. At least she had managed not to embarrass herself, she said out loud. With that, she changed into her pyjamas, cleaned her teeth, and then went to bed, worried she might have a bad head in the morning.

Janet's head was surprisingly clear the next morning. She turned up for work, determined to hold it all together if she saw Gary. He came into the polytunnel a couple of times to speak with Jim; on the second visit, he came over to Janet's workstation, asking her how she was.

"I'm OK, thanks; busy with the plants," she said lamely. Is that really the best she could do? After work, she sat in the park for a while before heading off home. She was due to work in the canteen washing up that night. She was oddly looking forward to it. She had some time to kill, so she went to the craft studio to work on the toy dog she had started. There was another woman in there doing some lace-making. Janet watched her as she wove the fine thread to create the design. It looked very complicated. Janet was impressed; it made her own project look juvenile.

They struck up a conversation, and during their chat, Janet learnt that the woman, Kate, was making a veil for a bride-to-be. Janet had heard that people could marry on Second Chance, but this was the first one she had come across during her stay. After a while, Janet came to a natural end to her work for that day, so she said goodbye to Kate. She heads back to her room for a coffee with a choccy biccy and to have another look at the journal. Janet had time to study the journal in more detail this time; having a clear head was definitely a bonus.

She had a few hours before she was due to do her turn in the kitchen washing dishes. She picked up the diary to study it, firstly to see if there was a year it was written. She saw that the author had written the date of the entry and, on occasion, the time if there was more than one entry per day. It was clear that the diary was written in 2016. That Janet started at the beginning of the journal and soon came to the conclusion the writer was female and a bit of a rebel. She seemed to fight about everything; Janet felt sorry for The Fetcher assigned to her during her time as a Newbie; it looked like she was hard work. She stayed outside after 5.00 pm, breaking the curfew. She, at times, refused to eat, and she lashed out at others. Janet could understand why people would rebel and kick-off at any opportunity. Living in Second Chance was a huge change from Earth, let alone trying to live with a serious injury and disability.

No wonder some people resort to anger. It takes time to adjust to their new reality. But, this lady, Janet discovered from her perspective, seemed to see everything as antagonistic. There was one entry made by the lady whom Janet decided to call Zoe, where she reported being "up against the board." There was nothing on the page making it clearer what this meant except a short entry the next day saying, "strike 1." Janet stopped reading for a moment, digesting this information. She guessed it was a warning and recalled back to the induction that they operate a three-strike system. Despite the warning, it appeared this did little to moderate her behaviour. A week or so later, Zoe mentions an incident when she attacked her Fetcher after he spoke to her in a "disrespectful manner." This, again, went before the board, which issued her with a second strike.

At this point, Janet stopped reading and closed the book after putting in a bookmark made from a scrap of paper. She placed the journal back under her pillow. She had read enough that day and needed a coffee before she went for her stint at the canteen. After drinking her coffee, she checked her appearance, left her room and made her way to the canteen. The washing up was piling up for Janet to clean. She rolled up her sleeves, put on the marigolds and an apron and got stuck in. She not only had to wash up but had to load the dishwasher and put it on to wash. She worked diligently clearing the soiled cutlery and crockery until the work ended. She had been there for a couple of hours, and it had felt good. She was working alongside two other people, each of them doing the work as their add-on. They had been helping out a lot longer than Janet but helpfully showed her the ropes.

One perk of the job was a cup of tea and a slice of cake at the end of the shift. Janet felt ready for that; she had more than used up the calories to counteract the cake. The ginger cake was lovely with the treacle and spices. It had butter icing on top and tasted wonderful. Janet chatted with the others before they turned off all the lights and locked the door. Someone would be in in the morning bright and early to clean the place and get it ready for the breakfast run. All through her shift, she went over what she had read in Zoe's diary. Zoe was becoming real to Janet; she began to imagine her as a redhead, maybe a stereotype for someone with a quick temper and a slim athletic build. She knew she had died in a fire, so she imagined her to be deformed and disfigured. She was an angry person but probably sweet underneath the bravado. Once back in her room, she toyed with the idea of reading some more, but the light in her room was not that bright and not good to read by, so Janet had to leave the compelling story of Zoe's Second Chance life to the next day.

After work and a swim, Janet continued reading Zoe's story. She learnt that Zoe had to have her wounds from the fire dressed daily, which with the walls emitting pain relief, would have at least been painless. Zoe found this process difficult, a sharp reminder of the traumatic event she experienced and the loss of her two children. She did not mention the children much; Janet guessed it was too raw. As Janet got to know Zoe, she felt sure that, with time, she would settle down. The pages said something different; her inner rage bubbled over, leading to Zoe attacking two more people who were calling her names, according to the author. Zoe was summoned to the board again, which is described in the journal. This was the last entry in the journal. Janet felt coldness prickle up the hairs on her arms. She repeatedly flicked back and forth between the pages to see if she had missed anything. What had happened to Zoe?

Janet was at the canteen queuing up for her evening meal. Choosing a sandwich and sticky toffee pudding with custard, she turned round to see where she could sit. She spotted Gary sitting at a table towards the back of the room. Once served, Janet weaved her way through the floor of tables and chairs to join him. They were not viewed as a couple at this point, but Janet was hopeful one day soon, that would change. She sat down and started pushing her food around her plate with her mind busy with thoughts.

"A penny for them," said Gary as he gently nudged her with his shoulder.

"Sorry, I'm in my own world," Janet replied, looking at him. "Do you know what happens to people with three strikes?"

"That's a bit random; why do you want to know" asked Gary.

"Just interested; I've found out about a girl who got three strikes here, that's all. What's the pie like?"

Janet changed the direction of the conversation; for some reason, it felt wrong to talk to him about it. She needed to find out more about Zoe and thought that maybe the library would give her the information she needed. The next day after work pricking out delicate young plants, Janet headed back to the library. The dust had begun to settle on the desk where she had cleared it to go through the papers. It looked as if no one had been in there; she found it strange that no one had used it. She started searching for papers dated 2016 which may relate to Zoe.

It did not take long for Janet to come across a whole load of notes from 2016 in one of the dusty drawers. She picked them up and carried them to the wooden desk. There were far too many pages to take back to her room, so she skimmed through, trying to pick out possible helpful ones. She felt uneasy as if she was doing something wrong being in the library. Any noise seemed to echo through muffling dust, Janet was worried about being disturbed, but there was not a soul around.

Eureka, she thought when she found a folder named 'Disciplinary'. She flicked through the pages to see if it would be helpful to her. Deciding it was worth proper scrutiny, she put the documents back into the drawer except for the folder of interest, which she hid under her tunic. She left the room and did a fast walk to her room, then put the folder under her pillow. She had arranged to see Mel that day, so she left her room to meet her outside the social club. Mel seemed OK; like other inmates of Second Chance, Mel had a haunted look in her eyes from the loss of loved ones, their lives and themselves. Some people reinvented themselves by taking on different occupations and mixing with people they would have avoided on Earth. Others were stuck.

A few refused to accept their new reality, finding opportunities to kick off, which only made things harder for themselves though they could not see that. Janet would find it too easy to be angry about the way she had been rescued after her suicide. She died because there was nothing on Earth that made a living a choice. She was rescued for a second chance in Second Chance, but she had not asked for this; she had no say in the matter; somehow, for some reason, someone made the decision to save her. It was difficult for Janet to get her head around that. She was nothing special. She had not lived a saintly life or been a particularly charitable person. But someone saw something in her to give her this opportunity. She did not want to mess it up. She just needed to find her place and live her life made bearable, knowing that someone saved her. She was valuable. Janet's thoughts distracted her so much that she was unaware of Mel speaking to her.

"Janet, Janet, come on, let's go out and play rounders, come on." Janet came back down to earth with a bump. She looked at Mel bouncing around enthusiastically, smiling at her, Janet grabbed her hand, and they went together to take part in the game. Janet was amazed that Mel was so upbeat, seeing she had such a severe facial disfigurement. The remainder of her face was so pretty; maybe that was enough for Mel; Janet was in awe.

They had laid out the rounders pitch in the park on a flat piece of land. There was a good number of players of both sexes, which made it possible to opt to play girls against boys. They divided into their teams except for Marie, who identified as a boy who opted to go on both teams as a fielder.

The match started off well, with the girls hitting a good number of rounders. They got a good score at the end of their innings; they were happy that it was a winning number as the boys went to bat. That's when the rules of the game were dropped, and it went to a free for all. It became a bit messy as fielders, the girls, impeded the progress of the batter running around the pitch after hitting the ball. Girls lurched at them, drawing them onto the ground and stopping them from doing a round. Janet, who was on second base, joined in by moving the cone further and further away just as a runner approached. She was really enjoying herself laughing until her sides ached.

She had not had so much fun in ages. Mel, the instigator, insisted the boys kissed her on her hand before they batted, then distracted them when the pitcher threw the ball. She raised her tunic flashing her boobs at them, then ran around in a tight circle yelling out. It worked well as a distraction; some of the men really didn't know quite where to look. It was a good, fun time with plenty of silliness from both teams. They decided to call it a draw as the night fell and the light faded. The teams headed off to the social club for a celebratory drink. It had been ages; in fact, when she was at school when she last played Rounders, it felt good being invited to join in. Janet expected Gary to have taken part in the game, but he was nowhere to be seen. She wondered how he managed with the axe in his head. How did he sleep? Or wash his hair? Did it cut his brain in half?

So many odd questions that Janet did not yet feel able to ask Gary; it was too early in the relationship for those types of questions. Janet had gotten off lightly with her injuries; she often felt people must look at her and wonder how she died with no visible scars or disability. Her legs had healed well. The bones had knitted as they should, and the internal injuries gave her a few problems with digestion but not too bad to moan about. Some of the inmates were so badly injured they needed care and attention from a Fetcher. Even in Second Chance. One bloke, Harry, had been a victim of a bomb explosion. He had lost both his legs and had his left arm and shoulder removed. Somehow, he managed to get by despite his obvious disability with the help of his Fetcher.

There was a small department in the complex where a team of experts made aids and adaptions for individuals. It was amazing to see what they created. They really needed people like this on Earth, but here in Second Chance, there was a heavy focus on ability, not disability. The next morning was her day off; she decided to have a bit of a lie in then go for a swim. She felt a sense of nervous excitement today as if something was going to happen. Something did happen; she had a note delivered by posting it through the bottom of her door. It said that she had been allocated a new suite in A block. The room number was 99, corridor 2. This must be her permanent home; she thought as she mentally changed her plans with the aim of moving today. She gathered up her clothes and possessions after breakfast in the canteen, checking out A block on her way. In no time, she had found her new home and fob key and moved her belongings in. The flat was lovely.

It had a large bedroom, good sized lounge and a luxurious bathroom which had a bath as well as a shower. The windows overlooked the park, and to her joy, she found a small balcony from the lounge with space to sit and maybe a few plants. There was already a small table and chair out there, which she sat in, feeling how far she had come from being a Newbie. After lunch, she had a swim, stopping off at the island before swimming around it. Her stamina was improving so much she felt toned and sunkissed. She was in a really good place mentally. She did not see any of her friends in the canteen or the park they were working today, but Janet was OK in her own company and liked having the time to herself. Later in the afternoon, she looked at the document she had secreted from the library. She sat on the balcony of her new home in preparation to see if she could find out any more about Zoe.

The notes from the Disciplinary meetings in 2016 were pretty easy to understand. It looked as if they sat monthly as the records were dated with the month and date. She found a match with dates and entries from the document and the diary. She quickly learned that Zoe was, in fact, Wendy. Janet cross-referenced the dates from Wendy's diary as to when she was in front of the board against dates in the document. The file named Disciplinary gave accounts of the events resulting in Wendy getting strikes. They also listed the consequences of her actions. The third strike event went into meticulous detail, describing the incident of Wendy assaulting two members of staff, one of whom was Mark. Janet stopped reading for a moment to digest that piece of information. Janet could not understand how anyone would want to hurt Mark; he was such a gentle soul. The entry made it clear that she was violent and unpredictable, but the consequence of her actions was less clear and left Janet with more questions than answers.

According to the Disciplinary notes, Wendy was facing Graduation. Janet was intrigued and confused about what Graduation was or meant. She hoped she could find some answers. She thought that people retired and went to Graduation, but it seemed that Wendy was not that old, maybe in her thirties.

Wendy was a loving mother to her son, who had a learning disability. He went to a school suitable for his needs which he enjoyed attending. She worked as a waitress and did a good job. She always came home with lots of money from satisfied customers. Life was not rich, but it totted along nicely. One day, she was on her way to pick up her son, Ben, from school. She pulled into a suitable parking bay near the school and then got out of the car to walk a short distance to the school. She got chatting with some of the other mums and dads waiting for school to end and spew out their offspring. Wendy spotted Ben being led out of the school by his form teacher. He waved at her, and she blew him kisses back. His smile was so large it filled his face; he really was a treasure. Wendy started to walk towards them, and as they approached each other, Ben ran to his mother, waving a sheet of paper where he had drawn her a picture.

Wendy bent down to kiss the top of his head and then had a look at the picture. It was an image of Ben with mum with another person who looked like he was going to chop her head off. Wendy dismissed it as Ben had a lively imagination then she got hold of his hand to go back to the car. Wendy opened the car and then began to put Ben in the child's seat. Just then, before it had time to register, a white van man ploughed into her, knocking the door off its hinges and flattening Wendy on the ground. Ben started crying inconsolably, clearly panicked. Just then, there was the smell of fire. The white van struck the back side of the car, causing the petrol to ignite. The flames covered Wendy's body quickly. Ben instinctively moved backward into the arms of his teacher.

Ben eventually stopped crying and allowed the nurse at the hospital to tend to him. The social worker was on her way to find him temporary accommodation until any living relatives could be tracked down to see if they could take the young boy. Everyone seemed to think that Wendy could not have suffered and that she would have been dead straight away. The truth was, Wendy saw the van coming towards her when she was in the road strapping Ben into his child seat. She looked the person driving the van in the eyes as he hit the door. The rest of it, she could only guess what had happened. All of this was written in her diary, which Janet was going through. Janet could only imagine what she must have been going through; it kind of made sense why she was so angry at Second Chance. She must have been so worried about Ben and his future. Janet wondered if she shared this with Mark or anyone else who would listen.

A couple of days later, armed with her secreted document and a plan of action, she returned to the library. There were still no signs of anyone else visiting it because the dust disturbances were down to her. Janet quickly went to the meeting records archives searching through 2016 for anything else relevant to Wendy's strikes. It took a bit of time, but she found a whole pile of papers about the Health Complexes, including daily records of the inmates and weekly Fetcher's meetings. Janet took these to the desk, sat down, took a deep breath then set about finding out more about Wendy. Worried that she would end up reading every entry, she focused again on dates from Wendy's journal. The last entry on the documents she read ended the date Wendy got her last strike. It read, 'Wendy has the inability to compile with the rules in the Health Complex. She exhibits severe and debilitating distress and frequently lashes out at others. Her behaviour remains unchanged despite two warnings, so the board have had to make the difficult decision to send her for Graduation.'

Janet read and then re-read the word, clueless as to what it meant. She knew from her induction in the Physical Complex that everyone graduated at retirement; she could not understand it being used as a punishment. She realised she had opened Pandora's box; her mind was alive with questions. She sat stock still as a fever of emotions washed over her. She felt she had uncovered something but was not sure what. She returned the papers back to the filing drawer and rifled through the rest for anything that may help.

There were numerous interesting-sounding corporate committees and groups, along with the less glamorous ones. Janet went back to the desk, stretched and picked up Wendy's journal. She hid it under her tunic and then walked back to her room, oblivious to the route and those she passed. Once back in her room, she changed to go to the gym, still with her thoughts lost in Wendy's life. She worked out hard, trying to wipe the image of Wendy's death out of her brain. She wondered how Ben was; he must have seen all of it. She finished her workout, then took a shower and started to prepare for the night ahead. That evening Gary and Janet were pairing up for a game of outdoor table tennis against two of her workmates. The table had been put right outside the entrance to the social club, so their play was punctuated with drinks of alcohol. Janet was not really in the zone to play ping pong as her concentration was elsewhere. She apologized to Gary as she bungled up shot after shot. Gary was encouraging and, fortunately, not too competitive. After the game, both teams went into the social club and had a drink at the bar.

"Are you OK?" Asked Gary as they moved to a table just vacated. Gary pulled back the chair for Janet being the gentleman he most definitely was.

"I'm fine; sorry about the game; I have something on my mind."

"Can I help?" He asked, placing his hand on hers. "I'm a good listener."

Janet smiled at him; he really was a lovely person it would be very easy to fall in love with him.

"I am thinking about Graduation. Do you know what it is?"

"No, not really; why do you want to know?"

"Oh, nothing really; I just heard someone talking about someone graduating after getting three strikes."

"That can't be right?" Gary stated, "Graduation is at retirement; you must be mistaken."

"Yes, that's what I thought, anyway; fancy a dance?" She quickly changed the subject, worried about giving too much away. She grabbed his hand to pull him up as the house band played something big from the '70s. The night was good, with plenty of song and wine. She felt less intoxicated than on prior boozy nights. She thought that she must be getting used to it. She was not much of a drinker on Earth; she had been drunk on a few occasions that resulted in a hangover which was enough of a deterrent to doing it again.

At ten o'clock, she got up to leave. It was a working day tomorrow, and she was feeling drained. She gave her apologies to the others and then left before Gary had a chance to offer to walk her home. Somehow tonight, she really did not want that to happen. She needed to think. Once home, she sat on her balcony with a mug of tea with thoughts rolling around in her mind, still seeking an explanation for Wendy's situation.

Once she had finished her drink, she put the half-full mug on the draining board in the kitchen. She got dressed for bed and then retired, hoping she could sleep. She fell asleep preoccupied and woke up preoccupied. She was due at work in the afternoon, working the late shift. She spent the morning taking it easy at first; then, when she was fed up with being in her mind, she went over to the craft studio with the aim of finishing the stuffed dog for Lisa's baby. There was the lace maker hard at work when she arrived. There was also another woman working on a cross-stitch design. All three of them chatted together as they worked, passing the time.

At half past twelve, Janet had given up on the idea of finishing the toy that day. She put it away in the cubbyhole and then went to get some food at the canteen. She was due to start work at one, so she had enough time to eat her meal at a civilized speed. Kim was in the canteen, just about to finish her meal, when she saw Janet. Janet went over to where she was sitting, and they talked for a couple of minutes until Kim had to go.

Janet ate her meal and then got ready to go to work. At work, pollinating trays of flowers in pots, she relaxed her mind with the rhythms of gentle concentration of her job and the time she worked; she also planned what her next steps were in finding out more about Wendy. Janet was sent home when she had finished working on all the plants. It was six o'clock in the late afternoon, and she had a bit of time to kill before dinner, so she made her way back to the library. She was on a mission; this time, her search was to check if there were other cases like Wendy's. Now she knew where to look. It did not take too long to uncover others. Andrew and Ian graduated earlier than Wendy in 2015 and Elizabeth in 2013. Andrew and Elizabeth graduated due to adverse behaviour with violence a feature. In Ian's case, it was less clear; there were no strikes against him; in fact, it was hard to understand what the reasons could be for him to be Graduated. She did not have enough time to see if she could see a paper trail for Ian but vowed to do that on her next visit. Armed with her handwritten notes, including references, she sat at the desk, thinking through what she had discovered. Three individuals who did not fit in one way or another were sent somewhere, she surmised, as a punishment. Ian had no reason to be punished; what was the link? They were removed from Second Chance, but how? Why? What about the older folk facing retirement and Graduation? Was it the same place they were sent to?

Chapter 8
Sherlock Holmes

Janet visited the library daily, searching through loads of records stretching back for years. She had to try to restrict her search to the past five years because of the pure volume of documents. Working in an organized way was easy for Janet as her past life was spent developing projects which required her to be methodical.

These skills helped her no end her current mission. Janet's research dominated her mind not only in the library but also in her room and work. She tried to plan her work, doing what she could in the library and what she could do from her room. She continued to secrete documents under her clothes and hiding them in her room. She kept handwritten notes in a notebook she found in the library and worked hard to keep her writing legible and in lay language. She was now familiar with the language and workings of the various committee and records.

It speeded up her work though she was worried about missing something. She came across other people who had apparently disappeared who were not old and not facing disciplinary hearings like Ian. It was initially difficult to understand why they were graduated but cross-referencing with notes from meetings the fetchers attended; the missing people appeared to have one thing in common: severe, life-limiting disability or injuries like loss of multiple limbs or multiple injuries... This knowledge sent a feeling of unease through her body. It was becoming absolutely clear to her that Graduation was some sort of euthanasia, the old, ill and bad removed from a Second Chance.

As she came to this conclusion and double-checked her facts, she felt sick and claustrophobic and needed air. She left the library quickly, having gathered up her notes. She slowed down once outside and breathed in the cool early evening air. Her head was pounding with the sound of embalming fluid being pushed by arteries in her body. She felt sweat dampen her clothes under her arms, and she was aware that she was still breathing deeply. She deliberately slowed down her breathing, managing to control it quite quickly. She began to notice things around her and started to walk back to her room. As she walked, she looked around her; she saw things with new eyes. It was all tarnished.

Janet debated with herself whether she should or should not share her findings with someone. She ran through each friend in turn, finally deciding that the one person she could tell was Gary. She felt sure the knowledge would be safe in his hands. But she needed to construct the conversation beforehand; she had to divulge the information in a factual manner. It would take a bit of time to prepare. Janet felt a nervous energy which, from past experience, meant that she would struggle to sleep. She decided to go for an evening swim in the lake. Once home, she changed into her swimming costume and grabbed a towel. She made her way down to the lake in bare feet, she had forgotten to put her trainers on, but the sensation on her feet from the different surfaces was nice. As she walked, she felt less agitated in anticipation of her swim. She dropped her towel and fob key on the bench and then walked down the sand slope into the water. Her swim was good. There was something very therapeutic about reconnecting with nature. The water felt lovely. She did her usual laps of the island, then went again. She really wanted to get it all out in a positive way. At the end of her swim, she got out of the water and wiped her face with the towel. It was still light though she had no idea of the time. What's more, she had been so preoccupied she had not only forgotten her shoes, but she had also forgotten to eat. She could not really go into the canteen dressed as she was, she was sure there were rules about that. She made her way back to her room, collecting a bag of groceries outside her door. She hoped she had ordered something she could eat now as she was feeling ravenous. Before pulling together a meal, she had a shower and got into her jimjams. She checked in the bag to see what she had ordered, selecting bread rolls and cheese. Brilliant, a meal in an instant. She sat on the chair on her balcony, enjoying the cool evening air as she ate her food. Finally, one cup of coffee later, she felt ready to go to bed. She parked the conversation she needed to have with Gary as she sunk into slumber.

Janet tried to find the right time to talk to Gary about her findings. She left it the next day as she really needed to get down in writing her plan of action. She really worked best with a pen and paper in front of her and planned to do it that evening. She was due to do the washing up at the canteen earlier in the evening; she thought she could use that time to think.

Janet was washing up at the canteen, and as usual, it was cathartic for her as she cleaned the dishes. Her mind wandered down many avenues all of them came to the conclusion that she needed to have that chat with Gary. She decided to do so at the weekend and would ask him to meet with her at work the next day. She had had time to plan what she needed to say and had the necessary documents 'borrowed' from the library to support her claims. She had no idea what she wanted from Gary, but for some reason, she needed to share it with someone levelheaded (despite the axe in his head).

At work the next day, Janet was moving trays of young plants to the ready for the planting area. She did not notice Gary coming into the polytunnel. She jumped out of her skin when he stood right behind her, saying her name.

"Don't do that?" she said, turning round to face him. "You made me jump."

"Sorry about that; I couldn't resist. You looked like you were a million miles away."

"I was," said Janet; she thought to herself that now was the time to ask him to meet up. She felt very awkward; he may take it the wrong way. A battle went on in her mind while her mouth engaged in social conversation with Gary. When talk had come to a natural end, it looked like Gary was going to turn away so she could get on with her work. Quickly she found her voice,

"Gary, there's something I want to talk to you about. Are you free to come over to my room tonight?'

"That sounds interesting, yes I could do that; what time were you thinking?" he replied

"How about eight?" Janet suggested.

"That's good with me, OK? See you later." With that, he turned away and started to walk away while whistling a nameless tune. Janet felt pleased with herself for asking him; it was one part of her plan completed, and now she just needed to be so sure of what she was going to say to him later that day. She planned to get some cakes from the canteen at the end of her shift in the nursery and serve them with tea or coffee. After work, Janet had a swim and then got ready to host; she had got the cakes and had filled the kettle with water. She had been through all of her papers, making sure they were in the right order, and she had found a second chair to put on her balcony so they both could enjoy the night air. At eight o'clock on the dot, there was a knock on Janet's door. She took a deep breath to steady herself before opening the door to let Gary in.

"Hi Gary, thanks for coming," she said, waving him in.

"How could I not come" he replied, handing her a beautiful bunch of flowers.

"Oh, they are beautiful, thank you so much, let me put them in water," she said, holding the bouquet carefully. She found a jug in the kitchen, which she put next to the flowers she had placed on the kitchen work surface. With her back to him, she tried to work out the best way to approach the subject of Graduation. All the plans she had thought through prior to his arrival seemed to be gone.

"Well, I'm dying to know what all of this is about. You have been acting very strange these last few days," Gary said, moving over to her in the kitchen.

"Well, I've been doing some thinking about Second Chance; I've come across some information that worries me," said Janet, touching the stems of the flowers gently. She went back into the lounge, sat down and invited him to do the same. Gary sat down next to her on the sofa and then stretched his arm nearest her around her in a hug. She allowed herself to sink into the embrace, which turned into a cuddle. She felt lost for words; it was so nice to be held, safe. The cuddle turned into a kiss, and all her plans went right out of the window. Janet got up to make coffee sitting down back on the sofa while the kettle boiled. She really didn't plan for this despite how lovely and natural it felt. Once the kettle had boiled, she made them both coffees; then she sat back down after handing Gary's his. They chatted about this and that while they drank, and once they had finished drinking, Gary put his arm around her again. They kissed gently, then passionately. At one point, she pulled away and tugged at his hand to come to the bedroom. She decided to love him instead of telling him because sex was more straightforward. Gary allowed himself to go with her into her bedroom and then laid on the bed next to her. Gently and slowly, they undressed each other kissing each other passionately between the discarding of each garment. Janet was worried that the scaring on her legs would put him off, but it didn't appear to, so she put those concerns aside. Their lovemaking was done with care and tenderness; Janet could not recall the last time she had had sex. In her past life, she had only had a few sexual partners, so she felt naive in the bedroom. Afterwards, they lay together and talked. He shared his journey to Second Chance with her and told her about aspects of his life on Earth. Janet shared some of her experiences as appropriate. She did not feel as if she could bring herself to talk about her research, well, not this night, anyway. After a bit, Janet got out of bed to make them both coffee bringing in the cakes she had taken from the canteen. They laughed together as the cakes crumbled, dropping down onto the sheets of the bed.

Janet invited Gary to stay the night as it was late, and she really liked being held. She really didn't want to let him go.

"I'm sorry, pumpkin, I am on an early shift in the morning. I don't want to disturb you when I go," he said

"Oh, OK, shall I see you at work then?" Janet asked.

"Yes, I've got a meeting with all the heads of the agricultural department. We have one three times a year to see if everything people do is meeting Second Chances needs. They serve a cooked breakfast as we meet, just something that seemed to happen. I will be back in the nurseries after that. Do you want to meet up after dinner?"

"Yes, that would be nice, thanks," she said, getting up off the bed. She pulled on her pyjamas and then went into the kitchen to put the flowers in the water. She really was not sure if she would be able to sleep tonight.

"Bugger the meeting. If you don't mind me leaving early, I would love to stay with you," he said, coming into the kitchen to stand behind her. He wrapped his arms around her waist, snuggling his head into her neck. Janet stopped messing with the flowers and turned around, so she faced him. Then they kissed passionately before returning to the bedroom. Janet woke in the morning with a man's arm wrapped around her shoulders. She smiled with the memory of the night before, then gently spoke to Gary, encouraging him to wake. He stretched his long limbs and then looked at Janet with his blue eyes. Yes, he looked handsome to Janet, but he had not long cherished her body. Janet as a middle-aged lady did not imagine ever being with a man again. She imagined all of that had withered away. The axe had not really gotten in the way, and she thought and giggled.

"What's tickling you?" Gary smiled, tickling her.

"I feel like a teenager again, half expecting my mum to come in through the door," she replied, placing a kiss on his lips. They kissed again and again until Janet broke the embrace. Gary was due at work soon; he had to go, and then she would have to get herself ready. Gary pulled on his clothes after using her shower and headed off to his business meeting. Janet made herself tea before following suit with the shower and getting dressed. She set off to the canteen for breakfast, feeling as if she was smiling from the inside. She was working an early shift that day; she started at nine and finished at three. She was dying to share her news with the girls, but unfortunately, they were not in the canteen. Instead, she ate her food on her own, thinking back on the night before. She really had not expected it to go that way; part of her wondered if Gary thought that that was why she invited him over; whatever, she was pleased it had happened.

He really was a lovely lover. At eight-fifty-five, she arrived at the nursery and started to prick out some strawberry plants. They were already showing signs of blooming, with the white flowers beginning to emerge. She lost herself in her work until Jim reminded her that it was time for a break. She joined her workmates around the tea-making area having coffee with biscuits. The next task on her list was to pollinate some pansies, so she set to work doing that until lunchtime. She kept stopping to look around for Gary, but he was nowhere to be found. Still, Janet had no idea how long his meeting generally lasted. Gary finished his meeting just around lunchtime and popped into the greenhouse several times over the course of the afternoon. He did not come to her workstation; he just blew her kisses to her when their eyes met. This made Janet smile and giggle. Her mind wandered back to their lovemaking and just how gentle he was.

Oh, if only she could stop smiling; her face was aching, and what's more, she broke into song twice. Yes, she had it bad. After work, she went into the canteen to get a drink before heading off home. She saw Kim and Mel at their table at the back. They waved Janet over, and once she had picked up her drink from the serving hatch, she went to sit with them. It didn't take the girls long to guess why Janet was behaving the way she was. They both wanted to know all the gory details about the night she spent with Gary; Janet was coy and very embarrassed. They chatted about this and that until Mel said, "you know that bloke with the arm, he seems to have disappeared; he may be back in the Mind Complex; he was finding things hard, nice bloke." This brought Janet back to earth with a bump.

"What's his name," she asked

"Was it Brian, yes Brian, one-armed Brian?" Mel replied. "You all right? You've gone pale."

"I'm fine; when did you last see him, Brian," Janet asked.

"A couple of days ago. He was the one with the Fetcher," replied Mel.

Brian had lost three of his limbs fighting in Iraq with the British army. He had been blown up by a landmine. He, as you can imagine, could do very little for himself with only one leg and had two Fetchers assigned to work with him over a twenty-four-hour period of time. He was very good at general knowledge, and everyone wanted him on their team at quiz nights.

"Kim, are you coming to the social tonight? You're coming, aren't you, Janet?"

"I'm going with Gary," Janet said distractedly.

The moment had gone, and the subject moved on, but Janet was left behind with the words 'Brian disappeared' in her mind. She made her excuses to leave the table and went to her room to change out of her overalls and thoroughly wash her hands. At work, she had the option of wearing gloves, but she liked the feel of the earth on her hands even though getting the dirt out from under her fingernails was a pain. She left her room shortly after and headed to the library despite knowing that the papers in the library didn't go back any further than in 2019. She had no idea where the latest ones were stored.

Nevertheless, and with no plan in mind, she just wandered around the room, picking up this and that. She knew something was going on, but something that did not make sense was that if the people she uncovered were subject to euthanasia, they would not be able to die. The dead can't die. She didn't find anything to provide her with any answers, but she gave the place a good go-over to see if there were any helpful documents. After about half an hour, she gave up and went back to her room. She needed to exercise, so pit pitted either going to the gym or going swimming.

She opted for the gym and changed into her exercise gear once she got home. She was distracted as she exercised, but in many ways, it did her good because she worked out hard and was powerful. She was the only one in there, so she felt free to talk out loud, going over recent events, including her night of passion. When she had lost her excess energy, she stretched out before going home. She sat on her balcony with a mug of tea until it was time to think about eating. She decided to dine in after having her second shower of the day.

After a toast with butter and fruit yoghurt, she checked the clock to see if it was about the right time to go and meet Gary, it was still a little early, but if she went now, she would have time to go to the waterfall. She sat on the tree stump, watching the water feeling excited about meeting Gary. She didn't have a watch, so she could only roughly guess what the time was and when she felt it was right, she walked down the river to the park. The grass-cutting machines were out on the lawns. It smelt lovely with the cut grass. Janet stopped walking to sniff the air. Then she remembered that she needed to eat, so she got a move on to go to the canteen. She sat at their table, tucking into her spag bol, trying hard not to spill anything down her. She was known to drop things down her front; sometimes, she didn't know exactly where her mouth was. It was a poor choice of food; the sauce dribbled down her chin and then fell down in spots on her tunic. She should get herself a bib, she thought as she dabbed it with a cotton napkin. Just then, she saw Gary coming into the room, her heart jumped when she saw him, and once he had been served, he came over to sit at her table. Mel came over as well, Janet had not noticed her in the queue, but she sat at the table smirking at Janet.

"Maybe I should just go to a different table; let you love birds be alone," she chided.

"No, you can stay; just avert your eyes now and then," Gary replied, laughing. The meal was completed with lighthearted banter then Gary offered to carry Janet's tray to the drop-off point at the front of the room. Janet thanked him, then bid Mel goodbye. They were all going down to the social club for a night of eighties music. Dancing was on the cards. They danced their socks off with bravery on the dance floor, fueled by beer and wine. Janet and Gary were both up for dancing and tried to recall some moves of the day. For someone as young as Mel, she may be familiar with some of the music; the dance moves were something else. Even Mohammed, the DJ, got in the spirit of things dressed as he was as Boy George. Janet did not have to work the next day, so she was not too worried about how much she had to drink. She didn't go silly but consumed enough wine to make the evening go well. Kim came along a little later; Lisa had Linda with her that night, so she was unable to join them. A couple of people from the nurseries came to partner Mel and Kim, which made it all a very good night. At the kicking-out time, Janet and Gary walked hand in hand to her room. He did not stay, but they kissed goodnight before she went into her flat floating on air.

The evening had gone well, and Gary had asked her to join him the next night as well at the social club. She was not sure what was on; she would have to ask Mel, Janet thought. She took herself off to bed and slept soundly. She had a few plans for the next day, but she didn't have to rush for anything. As it was, for her, she woke late and felt out of sorts. She took her time to get up, enjoying a mug of tea on the balcony before getting something for her breakfast. She really wanted to finish that dog for baby Linda. She had not been down to the craft studio for a few days, so she was making that a must-do on her mental list.

Also, she wanted to go back to the library, but this time with a plan of action. The third thing on her invisible list was to have a swim. She considered her list, trying to work out which one to do first. She opted to have a swim and to go once her breakfast had settled in her stomach. She was content just sitting looking out onto the park, where she saw some people jogging. An hour later, she felt ready to go for a swim. She put on her costume, then put her night clothes in the laundry bag and put it outside her front door. She walked down to the lake with a towel around her waist.

Once there, she dropped the towel and took off her shoes to go into the water. She had a good session doing circuits of the island. She was pleased with how her stamina was improving; she was finding it easier to go further and recovered after the exercise quickly. She spent about half an hour in the water before climbing out on the sand bank to collect her things. She put the fob key around her neck and roughly dried her body with the towel before putting it back around her waist to make the walk back to her flat. Once back, she showered and dressed, then made herself a coffee to enjoy sitting outside. Next, she was going to finish the toy for Lisa's little one in the craft studio and hopefully finish it before lunch. She made really good progress on it but ran out of time to do the finishing touches. She wondered if she should come back after lunch to finish it off. She thought she would because it was so nearly done. At lunch, she saw no one she knew, so she settled down to eat on her own. At least the meal would pass quickly without the distractions then she could get back to sewing the nose of the dog. She managed to finish the dog quite quickly and was pleased with the results.

It was now two-thirty in the afternoon, and she decided to go back to her room for a drink. She sat on her balcony and wondered why she might be putting off going to the library. She figured that it was probably down to the fact she had no clear sense of direction in her search. She needed a plan. She sat and let her mind wander; at first, she considered what she already knew and what the questions were that she needed to be answered. She kept imagining awful endings to people's lives, her mind going wild with thoughts of what-ifs. She sat on the chair on the balcony, nursing a coffee on the table. She slid it back and forth as her thoughts flowed.

She looked without seeing the view of the park. Getting nowhere with her deliberations, she focused on really seeing the park. The lake looked perfect in the landscaped gardens. Everything looked perfect. It would be very easy to go along and believe in the goodness of Second Chance, but it just left Janet cold. Despite the fact she had a lovely home and good solid friends, she felt like she was only visiting, that this was not permanent. She was sure that she would be here until she retired, but what after that? If people Graduated at the age of sixty-five, was graduation like going to a retirement home? Surely there must be different forms of

Graduations as naughty people went there as seriously debilitated ones. She really seemed to be making a bit of progress with her thoughts, so she found a pen and paper and jotted down some of what she had been thinking.

Janet thought that she should keep a journal and thought about finding out where she could get a ledger from. She wrote that down as an action point then her thoughts dried up. Janet felt a little peckish as she walked to the canteen for tea and cakes. Seeing no one she knew there, she sat down at the table she usually sits at, still deep in her thoughts. She became unaware of time as she pondered until that is she heard Mel's distinctive voice. Janet turned around, spotting her friend at the counter. Janet realized that it was now time for dinner; the afternoon had drifted away. Mel, with a tray in her hand with what looked like sweet and sour vegetables with rice on a plate. It smelt good, Janet thought as Mel approached.

"Hi Janet," Mel said, setting down her tray on the table where she normally stopped.

"Hi Mel, have you had a good day?" Janet asked her.

"Yes, not too bad. Are you coming to the social club tonight?" she asked.

"Yes, Gary has asked me; I have had enough of being in my own company today; I could do with seeing everyone," Janet replied. "I think I will get myself some of that," Janet said, pointing to the food on Mel's plate

"It's delicious; get up there before they run out," Mel said between mouthfuls. Janet got up to join the growing queue when she spotted Lisa coming through the door of the canteen. Janet called out her name, and when Lisa heard, she waved to her. Lisa joined Janet at the back of the queue, where they patiently waited their turn,

"Are you OK, Lisa? You look a bit stressed, is baby Linda doing OK?"

"She isn't doing very well; the nursery nurses and the doctor are having a meeting about her in the next couple of days. I asked if I could go, but they said it was not possible."

"Really, I hope it works out OK for her." Said Janet.

"Yes, me too." With that, they ordered their food, both opting for sweet and sour vegetables with rice and a cold dessert that looked very calorific. They went over to join Mel and started eating their food. Everyone agreed it tasted great.

"So, what's happening tonight at the Social?" Asked Janet to Mel.

"It's a dance class, Salsa. Apparently, Mario used to be a dancer; he is teaching us." Mel answered.

"Oh, that sounds good," Lisa said, "I might give that a go. I used to do ballet when I was small; I love dancing."

"I've got two left feet," Janet said laughing, "But I'll give it a go. When they had finished eating, they arranged to meet at the social club in an hour. This gave Janet more than enough time to make herself beautiful for Gary. Not that there is a lot you can do with drab brown clothes and unruly wavy hair. She sat on her balcony to kill some time, then walked over to the club room where Lisa and Kim were waiting for the others outside.

"Has Mario started yet?" Asked Janet when she arrived.

"No, not yet," Kim said as they waved to Mel, who arrived with Gary. They all went in and found a free table. Gary and Mel grabbed some chairs, pulling them up to the table so they could all sit down. Once seated, they speculated about the up-and-coming Latino class working out who was going to dance with whom. They all agreed, except Gary, that they should all take turns in dancing with him. They all laughed at Gary's reluctance claiming that he had two left feet. Just then, Mario arrived and looked super cool in his dancing attire. He went into the centre of the dance floor and went through some basic movements before asking people to step up and do the movements. It looked pretty simple looking at him, but Janet found it hard to know which foot to put her weight though; it was a lot more complicated than he made it look. Once people had mastered some of the basic steps, Mario elaborated on them by adding turns.

Now, that caused chaos on the dance floor as people collided with each other. Janet nearly ended up on the floor when two people banged into her. Fortunately, Gary was there to help her out, but Janet was so creased up with laughter that she felt like she was going to pee herself. She hurried off to the loo, leaving Gary with Mel and the others. When she came back, she sat down to watch Mel and Gary perform on the dance floor. Mel had rhythm, whereas Gary did not though he valiantly tried to dance to her standard. When he tripped up on his own feet, he gave up leaving Lisa to partner with Mel. Gary sat down with Janet and then offered to go up to the bar to get her another glass of wine. He came back with the refreshments then they sat chatting as they watched the girls dance. Lisa was pretty good; she seemed to pick it up quickly. Kim had found herself a male dance partner and was kicking up a storm on the other side of the room.

"Who is that whom Kim is dancing with? Do you know?" Janet asked Gary.

"I don't recognize him; perhaps he's new," he replied as they watched them effortlessly dance. Mario called a break, saying they were going to do something a little more complicated in ten minutes' time. Mel and Lisa came to sit down with Gary and Janet. They both looked a little flush from the exercise but had big smiles.

"That was fun," said Mel grabbing hold of her glass.

"You were doing well, both of you," said Janet.

"Will you get up and join in this half, Janet?" Asked Lisa. Janet nodded yes then they sat listening to the Latin beats and watched Mario and his dance partner demonstrate how it should be done. The second half was about as difficult as the first. They not only had turned to deal with some more complicated footsteps and dips. Janet and Gary did their best, gave up, and then started doing their own thing, which involved dips and lifts and a lot of swirling. Janet thought it was great. How she imagined how she was looking was far removed from reality, but she was enjoying herself. By the end of the evening, Janet was shattered. Her feet were hurting from dancing, and her head pounded from the loud music.

Gary had disappeared somewhere; Janet assumed he had gone to the little boys' room and waited outside of the entrance for him. Lisa and Kim said their goodbyes then they went off to their rooms. There was still no sign of Gary, so Janet debated about waiting some more but decided to go back to her home. Maybe he had left earlier, she thought. She reflected on a fun evening as she walked, thinking how lucky she was. She had, however, forgotten to take the stuffed toy to give to Lisa, so she put it somewhere obvious for her to give it to her the next day. She got ready for bed and then sat on the balcony for a little while, waiting for sleep to come. It finally arrived an hour later, so she took herself off to bed. She slept well despite the wine and woke up at eight in the morning, ready to face the day. She was working the late shift that day, so she had a bit of time to kill before she was needed.

After breakfast in the canteen, Janet did some more exploring. She was now familiar with key parts of the complex but was on the hunt for an area for the people who had retired. She could not find anything obvious; perhaps, she thought, they were taken down another long corridor to another complex which could be accessed through no end of doors. Taking that thought forward, she went to the main hallway, which had numerous doors leading off it, including the one back to the Mind Complex. When no one was looking, she walked towards the first door, which opened with a whoosh. The noise attracted the attention of a Brownie cleaning the main corridor with a broom. He raised his head to look at Janet. "Sorry," she said, moving away.

Satisfied with knowing that there might be an avenue for her to explore when she had more time, she walked to the nurseries to start her afternoon shift. As she walked, she mentally worked out her plan of action. She was so lost in her thoughts she bumped into another Brownie. "Sorry," she said, moving to the side to avoid him.

"Janet," the Brownie said, "Janet, how good to see you," this time, Janet looked up to see who knew her and immediately let out a whoop when she realized that the Brownie was Mark in off-shift clothes.

"Mark, Mark, oh, it's great to see you; how are you?" she said.

"I'm OK, what about you? You seem so much better," he said, grasping her hands with his. "We must meet up"!

"Yes, what about tonight? If you're not working, there is something I need to talk to you about," she immediately replied.

"I can't see tonight; my Newbie is quite poorly; I need to do a sleepover. I have tomorrow off if that's any good?"

"Yes, how about lunch in the canteen?" she asked.

"I will look forward to it; see you later." Mark carried on with his walk while Janet did virtual summersaults. She could not believe her luck; now she just needed to work out what to say to him and what to ask him about Wendy. She hurried to start her shift; today, she would be planting in the gardens and tidying up the beds.

Janet was hard at work humming a tuneless tune while she removed the debris in a beautiful yellow bed when she spotted the long legs of a man with an axe in his head. Her fella that sounds good, she thought, as he strode over and then dropped down to his haunches.

"You missed one," he teased, brushing some wayward hairs from her face. "Need a hand."

"Yes, do join me," said Janet as he leant in for a kiss. They chatted amiably as they weeded the flower beds; time became immaterial until Gary dismissed her off her shift while he went to check the other gardeners. She knew he attended a team manager meeting once a week. She was keen to find out where the notes of the meetings were stored in the hope that other meeting notes were stored there. She thought she would find up-to-date notes from the committee meeting that gave her so much useful information about Wendy and the others. Janet felt uncomfortable about asking Gary as he would want to know more details which, at present, she didn't want to disclose.

Janet had a sense that all inmates were under scrutiny, a big brother scenario. it was hard to know what was genuine, or maybe she was paranoid, she thought. Gary was in a position of authority; she was unsure how much control and power he held. She hated this way of thinking; her mind gets to an explosive point as thoughts expand and meander. She knew she was in the realm of mental illness, but not everything could be explained that way. Despite the fact she had uncovered something abhorrent, she lacked the confidence to believe it was so, and she felt vulnerable being on edge. She did not want to attract attention to herself, and she thought it would be too easy for her to be disciplined if knowledge of her knowledge got into the wrong hands.

What to do. Who would believe her suspicions? Maybe Mark can through some light on the matter when she meets him the next day.

Janet rehearsed her meeting with her ex-Fetcher Mark until her head hurt. She worked in the nursery in the morning, which was a helpful distraction. She enjoyed the monotony of her work; it was uncomplicated. She handled the young plants with care, teasing out the roots before potting them on into bigger pots. There were several people working there today; the chat and intermittent peels of laughter lightened Janet's mood. She felt herself tune in with the banter joining in from time to time. Janet was a shy social person. She found it hard to make friends but made good friends with those who made the grade. Janet always felt uneasy in situations where lots of people gather chatter turning into the rat-tat of gunfire in her mind.

She knew she was socially awkward and prone to say something silly, which embarrassed her; thankfully, her comments were laughed off, leaving Janet mortified. She was not the kind of person to confront others; she hated the prospect of upsetting anyone and taking it out on herself. She feared criticism believing words said in anger were the truth laid bare, the end of any friendship or relationship. She was a kind caring person who did empathy in buckets but, once hurt, remained hurt and plotted revenge, though rarely activated. Janet would stand up for the underdog and the voiceless finding her own voice driven by the sense of injustice and powerlessness. She was a complex soul who was prone to depression, a lot of it caused by her complex soul.

Just before lunch, she took off her apron and washed her hands, informing the others that she was off to lunch. She walked quickly and with purpose, still going over the conversation she had planned. Arriving at the canteen, she looked around the room for Mark. Not seeing him, she picked up some sandwiches, fruit and juice for her lunch. She selected a table with the best view of the door to the canteen and sat down. She ate her food slowly, constantly distracted by the movement of people, but no sign of Mark. She sighed to herself and then took a bite of her apple; it was then she spotted the familiar shape of Mark moving towards her. He carried a tray of food; non-shepherd's pie by the look of it thought Janet. Why she thought that? Who knows? As he approached, she drew back a chair at the table for him, which he took after putting down the tray.

"You look tired; bad night?" Janet asked.

"Yes, she really is unwell and needs constant care," he replied. He exhaled then looked at her with his lovely eyes then smiled.

"You look good; Second Chance is working well for you. I'm pleased," he said.

"Was there ever a time you thought I would not make it then?" She replied, placing her glass on her tray.

"What, no, no, not really," Mark said, shaking his head with each "no."

"What do you mean not really? I remember the teas you made me."

"Yes, well, I could not let you get upset; not so nice part of my job," Mark explained. Janet was not sure where to go with this, her rehearsed questions having gone out of the window.

"Do you remember Wendy; you were her Fetcher?" She plunged in; so much for teasing information out of him. Mark looked at her holding his gaze for a few seconds.

"Who told you that? It was a while ago, poor Wendy."

"What happened to her," Janet asked, looking slowly up at him; she was tense and acutely aware of every movement in her body, any invisible sound.

"She was very disturbed." He replied, then took a sip of his drink "where did you find this out?"

"In the library, I found her journal. She mentioned about three strikes. What happened to her? She Graduated; what is that." She realized she was talking quite loud at this point as she shot questions at Mark.

"Woah, hold on there. Not a great idea talking about this here; also, I am not sure we should be talking about this at all." Mark said while looking around and observing the others in the room.

"Where can we meet?" Asked Janet, not really wanting to let the subject go "come to my room; how about this evening? This is important."

"OK, though not sure what I can do to help. This evening about seven?"

"Great, thank you. You look great, by the way," Janet was unsure why she added that in; sometimes, her mind and mouth work to different scripts. She told him her room and block number then, with the conversation coming to a natural end, she stood up, taking her tray back to the drop-off point. She returned to work, falling quickly into the rhythm of the task stuck in her own mind. She was oblivious to the other people working in the polytunnel and did not hear Jim come up to her. She leapt out of her skin when he called her name.

"Janet, Janet, are you going home today?" Joe said when he had gotten her attention. Janet couldn't believe that the time had gone that quickly. She tidied her workstation and then took off her apron before leaving. She went to her flat, where she changed out of her work overalls, then made sure the place was tidy for when Mark came. Janet thought it was easier talking with Mark than with Gary; he was a good listener. She was in her room cleaning and tidying up, ready for Mark's visit.

He was due in half an hour which gave her enough time to do a deep clean and radical tidy-up. She always went into cleaner mode when she was stressed. Just as she was wiping the inside of the kitchen cabinets, she heard a knock on her door. She shouted, "come in" then turned around to greet the person entering her room. It was Mel.

"Are you coming to watch the performance? You know the drama group's interpretation of Romeo and Juliette should be a laugh?" Mel asked Janet.

"Oh yes, I forgot that was on; you go ahead; I have something I need to do first," replied Janet, keen to usher her out but to try not to show it.

"OK, I wonder if you can help me with something."

"What's that, Mel?"

"I want to look at my face in the mirror but want you to be there when I do it. I'm not sure how I will be; it's the first time since my accident."

"Of course, I will," said Janet honoured to be asked. "When?"

"Tomorrow?" asked Mel.

"I'm on a late shift; I'll be finished at seven. Do you want to come to mine?" asked Janet

"No, come to me. Great, thanks for that. Anyway, I will see you a bit later; I'll save you a seat." Mel said, retreating through the door. Janet was relieved she had gone; she felt a pang of guilt at that, but Mel's visit had interrupted her thoughts. A few minutes later, there was a hesitant unconfident knock on her door; Janet knew that it was Mark, having remembered his knock from when he was her Fetcher. She opened the door and gestured with her arm for him to enter. Janet looked both ways up the corridor; why, even though she was unsure. But she had a growing feeling of unease that she could not shake off. Mark came in bringing two bottles of the lethal Second Chance home brew. He set them down on the table,

"Where do you keep your glasses," he asked.

"Middle cupboard in the kitchen," Janet said, shutting the door, satisfied that all was how it was meant to be outside.

"What a lovely flat. I love the balcony. Could we sit out there? Wow, you have a great view," he said, looking through the glass in the door leading to the balcony. Janet got hold of one of the kitchen chairs, taking it outside on the balcony. Mark expertly opened the bottles of beer and decanted the contents into the glasses. You could see he was not an expert at this as the top foam threatened to overflow out of the glasses. He tilted the vessel to pour the beer at a slope which worked better. Once seated on the chairs they engaged in the usual trivial conversation with, Janet prepared to leap in with her questions about Wendy. She opened her mouth to speak when Mark said.

"What do you need to know about Wendy and why?" He took a sip of the beer, which gave Janet the space to think.

"I'm not too sure, but there are a few things I am unclear about'" with that, as an opener, she went on to tell him her concerns about Graduation and her supporting evidence. Mark listened intently, just asking a few questions for clarity here and there.

"Where do the retired people live? Where are they?" She finished her solo.

"Janet, does anyone else know about this?"

"No, you are the only one."

"Keep it that way, you know you can trust me, but there are a lot of people out there who would make your life very hard," Mark replied, reaching out to hold her hands with his. "There have been quite a few Wendy's. Those who do not fit in, who rebel, who cannot contribute to the running of Second Chance. They are told that they are going somewhere more suitable for their needs. As for the elderly, I don't know where they go. There is no one I know who can provide an answer; I guess people who are part of the Inner Circle know. The chairman surely must, but no Brownie can get access to him or her. They live very differently from us in the Nerve Centre. They could cause trouble for you if they find out what you know."

Janet felt the hairs on her arms prickle up, and she became aware she was holding her breath. She felt fearful, switching between being glad she had talked to Mark and then wondering what she had uncovered. Mark looked into her eyes, cupping her head with his hands. "Keep this to yourself; promise me, Janet." Janet nodded; she felt drained. "They have people placed here who report things back to the Nerve Centre. Be careful." With that, he gave Janet a hug making a move to leave. "What are you going to do now, Janet."

"I'm off to watch the am drams ruining Shakespeare. Do you want to come?" Janet said, moving over to him "what about you?"

"Me, sleep. It was a busy night with my Newby."

"Lots of tea," Janet smiled at him

"Either that or Graduation" the full impact of what he said knocked the breath out of her. It could have been her. Mark left her with a kiss, asking her to take care. Janet felt cold; she was feeling quite worried for herself after the chat with Mark. She sat back down on the balcony finishing her beer. She really didn't feel like going out; what if someone was following her? What if they knew what she knew about the way vulnerable people are treated? She tried to ease her thoughts by chanting a mantra she had learnt in the Mind Complex.

She drew her attention totally onto the words until she didn't have to force it. She relaxed her body bit by bit, becoming aware of just how tense she was. She decided that she really didn't fancy watching the show. Instead, she would take herself off for a swim. She changed, then walked the short distance to the sandy area by the lake. It was beginning to get dark; the light was fading gently, sloping down to complete darkness. Her swim had the desired effect. The silky water caressed her body, and her muscles, used now to working this way, did not complain even when she moved from breaststroke to front crawl and then finally backstroke. It was dark by the time she had finished. It took her a moment or two to find her towel and fob. She looked up at the sky of stars; it really was quite wonderful.

Nature, in all its expanse, was beautiful; the stars told their own stories. She waited to see if she could see signs of aeroplanes flying over, now such a feature of the sky, but none crossed her vision. Janet, having gathered up her bits, wrapped the towel around her and then headed back to her flat. She felt ready for bed now; tomorrow, who knows what is going to happen. She slept deeply but had dramatic dreams which woke her up on the brink of danger. Her dreams were vivid and featured people she cared for. One particular dream about her sister ended when she woke up covered in sweat. She got up feeling uncomfortable and had a glass of water. Then she felt ready to go back to bed, so she got in and covered herself with her sheet and blanket. She fell asleep quickly and fortunately had no more violent dreams.

She woke up at eight-thirty, washed, dressed and cleaned her teeth. She ran the hairbrush over her waves, noticing the grey in her hair. She wondered if the hairdresser could do tints, she would have to ask him, she thought. Once she was ready, she walked to the canteen for breakfast. She chose muesli and fruit and tea, then carefully carried the tray of food to the table. Lisa was there eating her breakfast, looking like she was miles away. Janet felt bad about disturbing her, but she knew that her baby, Linda, was not doing well. Janet sat down next to Lisa and said Hi. Lisa looked up at her sitting with a tiny bit of a smile on her face though it looked as if she had been crying. Janet wanted to give her the space to talk, so she did not through many questions at her. Her first question was so obvious,

"How are you, Lisa?" Janet said, looking at her gently.

"I don't really know," Lisa said in response.

"Are you seeing Linda this morning?" Janet asked.

"Yes, I'm going over to the nursery after I've eaten." Said Lisa before she took a sip of her tea.

"I've made Linda a present; when would be best for me to give it to you?" Janet asked.

"Oh, that's kind of you. Could we meet up for lunch, or are you working? Lisa said with a more melodic tone.

"I'm working a late shift; I start at one. I could be here at twelve-thirty. Is that good for you?" Janet said.

"Yes, that's fine, thank you. Anyway, I had better go; I have a demanding baby to feed," Lisa said. Then she pushed back her chair then stood up to take her to leave.

"Take care, Lisa," said Janet with care. Lisa left looking like she had the world on her shoulders. Once Janet had eaten, she thought about what she should do now. She didn't feel like going to the library but thought she would try to find the corridor that goes to where she thought the old folk would go. She still thought that they were graduated from the day-to-day stuff to a life of leisure in another complex. If she found it, that would be great, but if she couldn't, then she would have to rule in instead of out that older people went the same way as the ill and bad. Janet got up out of her chair then, dropped her tray off then went back to her room. She still had time on her side, so she decided to go for a swim.

She got her nearly-dried swimming costume from the back of the chair on the balcony. She had a look around the space out there, thinking how nice it would look with some plants in containers. She thought about asking Gary if she could have some later that day on her shift. Back to the here and now, Janet wrapped the towel around her and then took herself off to the lake. She sat on the bank when she got there for a while, enjoying the warmth of the sun. She really didn't feel in the mood for a swim. She felt more like going to her home, where she felt safe. Out here, in her cozzie, she felt vulnerable even though no one had ever approached her when she was dressed as she was.

Eventually, she talked herself out of going for a swim and walked back to her flat. She changed into her day gear and then put the kettle on to make coffee. She dug out some biscuits, putting a pile on a plate on the table on the balcony. She was so lost in her thoughts she didn't hear the kettle boiling but heard it click off. She made her drink and then sat on the balcony, looking out at the park. She could make out two women stripping off to go swimming. It looked like they had no costumes on under their clothes, but from that distance, she could not be too sure.

They looked older than her, with both sporting grey haircuts. Janet couldn't stop looking at them standing on the bank, and she was sure they were naked! The ladies entered the water and started to swim. They were both doing breaststroke side by side, probably gossiping as they swam. Janet's attention then went to some other people using the park. She could see someone de heading roses. She could not tell which of her workmates was doing that it was just too far away. She watched a couple walking hand in hand down the path towards the lake. They sat on Janet's bench, watching the swimmers and each other. It was lovely to see young people in love; they seemed to be infatuated with each other. Just then, the two swimmers exited the water. Janet saw the young woman with the man and immediately put her hand in front of his eyes. He squirmed a bit and used his hands to pull hers away. Then they both stood up and walked quickly back up the path away from the naked ladies. Janet felt herself smile at the scene.

It took a lot of guts to go skinny dipping in the daytime, she thought. After a while, she got her act together, thinking it must be lunchtime. She checked the clock, which said twelve fifteen, which meant she should go now to get ahead of the crowd. She remembered to pick up the toy dog she had made for the baby and set off to the canteen. The queue was long when she got there. Janet joined it, shuffling along with everyone else until she was at the head of the queue. She had not thought about what she wanted to eat and took a short amount of time to make her choice. The person behind her started moaning about Janet taking ages to choose, which made her fluster. She collected her order and then made her way around people at tables to the back where Lisa was waiting for her. Once Janet had sat down, she gave the toy to Lisa. Lisa seemed to really like it and thought that little Linda would love it. Despite being happy to see the toy, Janet saw sad tears roll down her face. Janet moved her chair over to hers a bit closer so she could put her arms around her friend. Lisa cried silently, her body heaving with the effort of crying. Janet tried to soothe her but stayed quiet as the situation didn't warrant talk. After a minute or two, Lisa stopped crying but was very apologetic,

"I'm so sorry," she said.

"You don't need to apologize; you have a lot to deal with," said Janet looking at her.

"I know, but I've not long been reunited with Linda; now she might have to go somewhere else; what about me? What happens to me?" Lisa said, breaking down again. Janet rubbed her shoulders as she held her, allowing her to cry. Some people were looking over at them but stopped staring when Janet gave them the evil eye. Just then, Mel came over to join them at the table.

"Is it baby Linda?" Mel asked. "Is she, you know, dead?"

"No, she is not meeting her milestones; she is very disabled mentally and physically," said Lisa taking the offered napkin to blow her nose. Janet moved her arms away from holding Lisa and started to eat her now cold food. They ate in silence, only punctuated now and then with the odd comment. Janet gave Lisa a kiss on the forehead before standing up to take her tray away and go to the loo. She left the canteen to use the toilet next door. When she had finished, she had another hour to kill until she started work at two. She went back to her room, where she noticed something down by her door. Janet went over to see what it was, and to her surprise, she saw a notepad and pen.

She wondered where it had come from but picked it up and took it inside, and put it on the table in the lounge. She decided to write her journey in the book and use it as a diary. She sat out on her balcony for a little longer, then dressed in her overalls and set off for work. Gary was in the polytunnel when Janet arrived. He waved to her in greeting, then came over when he next could. Janet was pricking out delicate young plants that day. She had to be so careful because they were easily bruised. She stopped to chat with Gary, and she remembered to ask him about having some plants for her balcony. He said that that was no problem and to help herself to the adult plants. He asked her if she enjoyed the play the other day; Janet told him that she hadn't gone as she was too tired.

"Are you alright?" He asked her. "Do you need to see a doctor?"

"No, I'm fine; I'm just getting lost in my thoughts," she said.

"Isn't that a sign that you are getting unwell?" He said, looking concerned at her.

"No, well yes, it is, though otherwise, I feel fine. I will keep my eye on it in case my mood goes haywire," she said, turning back to her work in effect dismissing him. Gary walked away to go to have a word with Jim about something. A little later, Jim came over and asked her if she was OK.

"What Gary been saying? I am OK. Just a bit stressed, that's all."

"Do you need some time off?" Jim asked her.

"No, I'm better working," said Janet looking up at him.

"Let me know if you need anything," he said, then walked away to go about his business. Janet carried on working but tried to keep her brain focused on what she was doing. She didn't feel as if she was getting ill, she had been obsessing about her research into Graduation, but she thought she had control of it. Janet's shift seemed to drag, but Jim sent her home early with some plants he had searched out for her.

"Here, these should do nicely on your balcony. Can you manage to carry three? If you need any more, just let me know, and I will see if I have some decorative pots to put them in." Janet thanked Jim and then gathered up the plants. They were on the verge of blooming, and all looked healthy and well cared for. She managed to carry all three, then headed off home to put them on her balcony. She decided not to go to the canteen that night. She would throw something together with what she had in her cupboard and fridge. After eating, it was getting dark outside, so she sat in her lounge and started to write in her journal. She started by writing about today's events, then wrote down her plan to find the old folk. She found writing things down seemed to settle her mind; there is something very therapeutic about writing. She took herself off to bed at nine, feeling tired and achy. She fell into a restless sleep waking up once to go to the loo.

Chapter 9
Big Brother

Janet slept badly that night despite feeling tired. She tossed and turned most of the night; she even got up once or twice to divert her attention off her inability to sleep. The next day she got herself ready for work, eating her breakfast while sitting on her balcony. She tried to think about what she should do now. Should she continue with her investigations or give up? Especially if there was a chance, she would be in trouble. Mark's word of warning was prominent in her mind; she didn't want to stir the pot, or at least not until she had all the information. She made her way to work, looking at the people around her, wondering if any of them were not what they looked like. Anyone of them could be a spy. At the nursery, she worked quietly and diligently putting flowers into plant pots. She found it quite therapeutic as it took enough concentration to keep her mind on the work.

Her colleagues seemed to pick up on her mood; one of them, Frank, brought her over a mug of tea and a chocolate biscuit smiling at her as he handed it to her. She stopped working to take it from him, thanking him as she took hold of the mug. It was just the right bit of kindness she needed. She stopped for lunch, having food at the canteen. She sat alone at her table, still stuck in her thoughts. Everything was coming out for her to think through. She was finding no answers, so it was futile. After eating, she sat for a while in the park before returning to her workstation. She continued with her task working quietly and speedily handling the tender plants and repotting them in bigger plant pots. Jim came over once or twice to see how she was doing. He dismissed her early with no reason offered. Janet thanked him and then headed back home.

Entering, she immediately realized her room had been disturbed. She quickly went to the place she had hidden the documents taken from the library. Relieved that they were still there, she checked to see if anything else was missing. There was nothing to say something had been taken, and just the room ransacked; she still felt violated. She put right an upturned chair and smoothed back the bed sheets. Nausea swept over her as the reality of what had happened struck home. She rushed to the toilet in her en suite, vomiting up her last meal. She vomited until her sides hurt, and all she brought up was water.

She felt in her bones that she wanted to get out of her room but was scared whoever did this could be outside somewhere, watching her, wanting to hurt her. She decided to stay, locked the door then got to work tidying up her living space. Once the room was straight and thoroughly cleaned, she sat down with a mug of tea. She sat in her lounge, worried about sitting on the balcony where she would be visible. She wondered who had been in there, let alone how they got in without her fob key, which was hanging around her neck. She put the kettle on again to make coffee, but she really fancied something stronger and debated whether to go to the social club to get a glass of wine. It was at that point she remembered that she had made arrangements with Mel. Mel had invited her over to support her in looking at herself in the mirror. She could not let her down; it was a big deal for her. Janet checked the clock on the kitchen wall, realizing that she could make it in time if she hurried. Really hating to be late, she grabbed her jumper and left her flat, making doubly sure she had locked the door. She got to Mel's room in D block quickly as she powerwalked most of the way. There were not many people around as most people would be in the canteen at that time. She knocked on Mel's door, which was opened promptly. Mel invited her in with a smile, then pointed to a bottle of house red.

"Do you want some," she asked.

"Absolutely, Yes, yes, please," Janet replied.

"Are you OK? You look a bit flushed," Mel asked.

"Yes, I got held up by something, I didn't want to be late, so I hurried," said Janet, taking hold of the bottle of wine; she poured out two glasses. Once poured and sat down, they both took sips of wine and engaged in casual chat.

"Right," said Mel. "I've got to do this, I've been nervous all day, but today, I will do it; thanks for being here with me. I have felt my face; I know it's got a lot of scare tissue there. I just hope it is not too bad."

"How do you want to do it?" Asked Janet, putting down her glass. The alcohol had worked well in relaxing her.

"Well, if you could stand next to me and remove the cover over the mirror in my bedroom. Can you do that?"

"Sure, come on, let's do it now, so you don't have time to change your mind. You can do this." Said Janet as she got to her feet. They went into her bedroom, where there was a full-length mirror attached to the wall. It was covered in a bit of an old sheet with the edges tucked behind the mirror. Mel and Janet stood in front of the mirror. Janet took her hand as they counted down from three to nil. On nil, Mel closed her eyes, and Janet dislodged the material over the mirror. As it fell to the floor, Mel slowly opened her eyes. She looked, looked away, and then looked again. Her face had healed pretty well from the injury she had sustained. Janet tried to imagine what was going through her head. Mel was silent for a while. She studied her face, tilting her head in various positions so should get a really good look.

"Are you OK?" Asked Janet, still holding her hand.

"You know what, yes, yes, I am OK. I will never win any beauty competitions, but it's not as bad as it was in my mind. I dread to think what it was like at the time'.

"It was pretty gruesome; there is a big change. I know you lost sight in your eye, but you don't let that hold you back. You are beautiful; you know that, right?" said Janet giving Mel a hug.

"Thank you, Janet, thanks so much for this; I knew you were the right person to ask."

"That's no problem, Mel; I think you are so brave." They went back into the lounge and resumed sipping the wine. They chatted and laughed and drank all the wine before Janet decided she needed to face going home. She did feel fearful about it, but after Mel's bravery, she knew she could face it; it was nothing compared to what she had been through. She stood up to leave, saying she had an early shift the next day. She did not feel it would be right to share what had happened with Mel, at least not until she knew what was going on. Janet walked quickly from Mel's flat to her own. Once inside, she had a quick look round to see if anyone had been in; satisfied that it was the same as when she left, she put down her fob key on the coffee table. She sat outside on her balcony for a while until she felt that she might be able to sleep. The wine, no doubt, is helping with that. She went to bed in her day clothes; she thought if anyone came in, she would be less vulnerable, being fully dressed.

In the morning, she got out of bed, feeling somewhat grubby; she felt too exposed to take a shower, and nudity would render her powerless was her reasoning. Instead, she brushed her hair for the second time, worried about leaving her room, scared about staying put. Forcing a smile on her face, she opened her door, crossed the threshold, closed her door, and then set off to the canteen for breakfast. She was not hungry but had to go through the motions. Mel was already there with Gary; they waved a small wave to each other as Janet joined the small queue at the buffet. Selecting fruit, coffee and a croissant, she joined her friends. She felt better in a larger space, and sitting at the back of the room offered a good vantage point for observation. She imagined everyone in the room as potential criminals.

After all, bad people can die traumatic deaths, so who knows the history of everyone here? Janet listened to the chat as Mel and Gary put the world to right while sitting at their table. She was happy just to listen, enjoying the throwing of talk between the both of them. Mel's laughter sounded like snowbells; she had an infectious laugh which made others smile. Janet always considered her own laugh to sound like a horse. She did a lot of snorting when she laughed. When Janet had finished eating, she said goodbye to both of them and then stood up with her tray. She dropped the tray off at the drop-off point and then walked to work. She felt ready for the day ahead and had plans to go for a swim after work. She needed to get back to her routine.

Janet's day of work passed slowly; she was preoccupied with being aware of Gary standing behind her watching her. "Are you alright, Jan?" He asked, placing his hand on her shoulder. She jumped from the contact and looked up at Gary smiling her smile of pretence, well practised from having a mental illness and struggling to appear normal.

"Oh Gary, you made me jump; I was miles away."

"Are you due a break? Come on, let's get a coffee, I need a break, and I'm the boss," he said, then gently took her arm, helping her up from her perching stool. He slipped his hand around hers then they walked hand in hand together to the canteen. Once seated, he asked her again if she was alright; Janet avoided the subject by asking him about his biopsy of the karaoke performances the night before. Gary avoided that question posing his own, "I get the feeling something is wrong; you seem absent. Can I help? I'm a good listener."

Janet smiled a true smile this time and took a sip of coffee before telling him about the state of her room last evening. She mentioned it looked like whoever did it was searching for something. Gary mentioned that he knew several others who had that done, but they were not around now and moved onto something more suitable to their needs. They were trouble. Janet stopped breathing for a few heart beats. She was curious to find out more from Gary. She asked him what they had done for all this to happen. Gary explained that they fought against the authority, were rebels and, made no effort to fit in, were always asking questions.

"Am I like that then?" Janet asked, holding his gaze "am I like them?"

"No," he said, dropping his gaze, unable to look her in the eye. Janet had cold shivers running up and down her spine. She had heard enough to know she could not share her concerns with Gary; in fact, it may be wise and safer if she kept a bit of distance from him. Draining the coffee from the mug, Janet stood up and headed back to the nursery to finish her shift. She was due to do her job in the kitchen that evening. She was glad for the distractions. As it was, it was a busy shift washing up at the canteen. One of the dishwashers had broken, so Janet had a lot more to do by hand.

She got stuck in with fellow washer Jane, and between them, they made good with the dirty dishes and containers. Because of the broken dishwasher, it took longer than usual to clear up, so Janet got away later than normal. After her shift, she sat down with a drink and a slice of rather a lovely carrot cake with Jane at one of the tables. They had earnt it that day. The noise of the kitchen had blocked out Janet's annoying inner voice, and the work gave her a real lift. Janet and Jane finished their cake then both headed off back to their rooms. Janet felt a little nervous about going into her flat; she opened the door cautiously and then put on the light immediately. The room was how she had left it, relieved she locked the door, checking it twice to make sure.

She sat on her bed in her jimjams; fresh from the shower, she felt refreshed and clear-minded. She knew she had to either be more discrete in the search for her answers or drop it. Janet knew she had nothing to lose. She was a suicidal dead person who did not ask to come to Second Chance who, for all its good points, had a feel of eugenics about it. She reckoned the people Gary mentioned were probably removed from Second Chance by Graduation; maybe, just maybe, Graduation was about transferring those who were outside the norm to go to another form of Second Chance, like a Third Chance.

Her train of thought relaxed her as she fell to sleep imagining her utopia. She thought someone or something created their own utopia when they created Second Chance. Perhaps there was no provision for non-conformists or elderly and severely disabled in this world which is where Graduation came in. Residents of Second Chance should be grateful for what they have; all their needs met in a simpler, stressless environment. Janet pulled the blankets up high under her chin as she drifted off to sleep.

Tomorrow, she would return to the library to put back the documents she had secreted and to see if there was anything else that would be helpful, maybe another diary. She felt she had nothing to lose. She woke up early and then got up to start her day. She pulled on some clothes and prepared herself to go to the canteen for breakfast. She hoped that she would see some of the girls but knew that their own work patterns made it hard to know when they would be there. As it was, only Lisa was there, nearly finished her meal.

As Janet went to the table, she was getting ready to leave. Linda, her baby, was being assessed that day to decide her future. Lisa wanted to spend as much time as possible with her, so she hurried away without stopping to chat. After breakfast, Janet went to her room to pick up the documents she had taken from the library. She intended to return them along with Wendy's diary. She walked down the various corridors to the library. She pushed the door only to find that it would not open. It was locked. It was then, in the corner of her eye, she spotted the tell-tale red blink of a security camera. Janet immediately stopped what she was doing, turned round and walked briskly back down the corridor. She hoped it had not captured her; maybe it was just a dummy one, she thought. She needed air, so she headed out into the park. She spotted a free bench and sat down on it at once, feeling the warmth of the fabricated sun on her face and arms. Her mind was jumbled with thoughts. Fear was the emerging emotion with panic hot on its tail.

Janet tried to control her breathing to abate the panic, but it was proving ineffective, so she got up to walk around the landscaped garden, trying to allow nature to sooth her. No rabbits, she thought as she walked. No birds, no insects, nothing. Today was her day off; she had nothing really planned and actually felt like doing very little. She sat on the bench until she could focus on the movements in the park instead of her fear. After a while, she felt much calmer, ready to go back to her room and try to find a place to hide the documents. Really, she thought, she should destroy them, but that was easier said than done. She had no matches or a lighter to burn them, which left her with the option of tearing them up and then putting them in the various litter bins around the area. But, she thought, if she was being watched, then that behaviour would look quite dodgy.

Or maybe she could eat them, she thought, trying to keep a hat on hysteria. She got up and started to walk around the park, coming out near the waterfall. She sat down in her usual spot, watching the water. The documents were still tight against her under her tunic, but she really needed to get back to her room to hide them until she came up with a solution, so she headed back to her room. She hid them in one of the cupboards under her clothes, not that original, but she thought that if they had already searched her rooms and had not found anything, then they were not likely to come back unless they wanted her to think that way. Maybe they had found the papers and deliberately left them to scare her into thinking they had not found them. Stop, she thought, stop doing this. She commanded her mind to think about making some tea which she took out to the balcony.

She sat down and gradually settled down. She was not a brave person. All of this was freaking her out. She thought about what to do now and came up with the idea of going for a swim. She changed into her swimsuit, grabbed her towel and made her way to the lake. The water was lovely; she swam well and managed to increase her lap count, adding one extra to the tally. She stopped to rest on the island, enjoying watching people come and go. At one point, she saw Gary walk along one of the paths. She assumed that he was checking the work done on the flower beds, but he passed one of them without looking. Then she saw Mel walking slowly on the grass by the large rose bed where Gary was heading. They saw each other and stopped to talk. Janet hoped that Gary wasn't telling Mel about her odd behaviour. She was sure he thought she was ill and was worried about her. Janet didn't think she was ill, but bipolar disorder is a psychotic illness where there is no insight, so she would not necessarily know she was ill. She watched as they talked; Janet wished she could be a fly on the wall now.

A short time later, they parted company, with Mel going back along the path she came from and Gary striding on, looking like he was heading towards the polytunnel. Feeling a little chilly, Janet got back into the water and swam around the island again before getting out and towelling herself dry. Back in her flat, she took a shower before dressing and sitting on her balcony to let her wet hair dry. She tried to make it business as usual that day, thinking it would be best to keep a low profile. She decided to go to the bingo that evening with Mel and Kim, but she still had lots of time to kill before that. Janet found her book and took it out onto the balcony, where she started reading. She didn't get very far until her mind started wandering. She tried again to focus, but her thoughts were just too noisy. She gave up on that idea and decided to go to the craft studio and found something there to do. She saw some printed tapestry kits that interested her the last time she was there. Janet left her room to go to the studio, passing Lisa on the way.

Janet asked her if she had any news about her baby; Lisa said that she hadn't heard anything yet and continued on her way. There was the lace lady working steadily in the studio who looked up from her work when Janet entered. Janet greeted her and asked her how her work was going. Lace lady showed her work which Janet admired. Then she went over to the place where she saw the tapestry kits, selected one then sat down to make a start on it. She had completed several of these when she was on Earth, so she soon settled down to do the sewing. The change in environment helped Janet's inner voice to settle. She sewed for a good hour and a half, then decided to go for lunch.

The lace lady was packing up to go; she took her work away with her in a hessian bag. Janet left hers in one of the cubbyholes in the unit and then headed off towards the canteen. It was one fifteen by the time she got there, most of the people had eaten, so she had no queue at the serving hatch. She selected curry with rice and rhubarb crumble and custard. She went to sit down at the usual table but saw four people sitting there. They were no one she knew, and she felt a bit out of sorts, so she went to a nearly empty table nearby. Her occupants nodded towards her, which Janet mirrored then she sat down to eat her food. After lunch, she went back to do some more work on the tapestry she had started working there until four o'clock. She popped into the canteen to pick up a cake to go back to her room.

Once back, she made herself tea and then took the mug and the cake onto the balcony. She decided to go rest for an hour, so she laid on her bed, hoping that sleep would come. It was quiet hard having a day off with no one else around, she thought, but still, she had kept herself going. Sleep did come, but she slept quite a bit longer than she anticipated.

When Janet checked the time, she realized that she had left it too late to go and eat at the canteen, so she grabbed a bread roll and cheese from her fridge to eat before going off to the bingo session with her friends. Janet rolled up at the social club in good time for the first bingo session that evening. Mel, Kim and Lisa were already there and had picked up some cards for them all. Janet very nearly won by one number a bag of sweets. Poor Mel was not having a lucky evening; the numbers did not go her way. As for Kim, she won twice. One of her prizes was a bottle of wine which they consumed between them. It was a fun evening, and Mel was full of joy.

Janet admired her sense of fun and apparent lack of self-consciousness despite her appalling injuries. She wondered if she was so upbeat when alone, then it could be an entirely different kettle of fish. At the end of the bingo, they parted ways, and Janet headed back home feeling a bit tipsy. She really should not drink, she thought as she swayed as she walked. As she walked, she thought about Mel with her injury and Kim, like her, who had a hidden disability. Janet wondered if there was a hierarchy of disability, then played with that thought for a little while before opening the door to her flat.

She checked she had had no unwanted guests, then took off her shoes and sat on the sofa in the lounge. She felt tired from deep thoughts, so she went to bed feeling less stressed than the night before and less fearful. She needed to meet up with Mark again. She needed to find out as much as she could about the Nerve Centre, the beating heart of Second Chance. Janet was not a brave person, but she was blessed with a good brain. She realized her way forward was to use her intelligence to get intelligence. She went to work on the morning shift the next day but didn't see Gary. Jim said he was off that day and that he was in charge. Janet was out in the park preparing beds for the flowers; she was digging the soil and then raking it flat. Then, in the afternoon, she planted some geraniums.

It was good working like that; she could see her work coming together to produce colourful beds. At the end of her shift, she quickly changed and then went for a swim. She was pleased with her progress, adding another lap to her total. Her brain had settled down, and she felt more in control than she had. Whatever was going on with her seemed to have rectified itself. Even Mel and Kim commented on how well she was looking.

The next day, Janet was at work de-heading roses in the park, when someone approached her. She jumped a mile when someone said her name. Looking around, she faced the person talking to her; it was a man wearing a grey tunic and trousers, the dress colour of people who work at the Nerve Centre. Janet stopped working and asked if he needed anything.

"Do you like doing this, then?" He asked, "by the way, I'm Andrew; how do you do" he put out his hand for Janet to shake, which she did with her dirty hand. His handshake was rather limp, with his hands hot and a bit sweaty. Janet took a chance to look at him; he was probably around her age with a bit of a belly. He was tall with greying hair at the sides of his black hair. He had slim lips and brilliant blue eyes, which looked a bit wrong with his colouring. His speech was that of what Janet would consider a posh voice, clear and precise. "Can you and I talk?" he said, motioning for her to walk with him. Janet tried to clear her mind thinking she needed her wits about her but set off walking alongside him, thinking he was probably some kind of a nutter.

"Sorry, why do you need to talk to me?" She asked, then stopped walking for a moment until he had answered her.

"Let's get somewhere where we can sit and chat. I have a dodgy leg, can't stand or walk for too long," Andrew said as they walked. They sat down on a bench in the park. Janet was at one end, and Andrew, just a bit too close for comfort, was sat at the other end. She looked out ahead, seeing the immaculate beds with the flowers facing the pleasant sun. "Now, I have been asked to see you and find out how you're settling in; how are you doing?" he turned his head to observe her as she mulled this over with a view to come up with the right answer, whatever that was.

"It was hard at first. I struggled, but I think I have settled in now. I have made some friends, and I enjoy my work here," she gestured, taking in the gardens with a sweep of her hand.

"Good, good, it is hard when you first get here; the adjustment takes time, anyway I have heard good things about you; my boss asked me to ask you if you would like a new job," he said, brushing an invisible piece of dirt from his very clean tunic.

"I am happy here," Janet responded, "what would this job entail?"

"It will be in the Nerve Centre, working for one of the teams, I don't know exactly. It means leaving your job here and moving to a room in the centre. What do you think?" Janet did not know what to think; she was somewhat flattered, intrigued and well out of her depth. She thought he was there to drag her to a room to be Graduated for being too close to the truth.

"Can I think about it?" She asked.

"Certainly. I will meet you tomorrow in the library after your evening meal. How does that sound?" Andrew looked at her trying to read her face. Janet felt it was time to get out of there; she stood up, looked at Andrew, and then took her leave without answering his question. She felt weird, buzzy, anxious, inquisitive; you name it, she felt it. She found it strange that he wanted to meet her at the library. She must have been caught by the security camera. Maybe they are after the documents, she thought. She returned to work tidying up the beds until it was lunchtime. She stopped working on the bed and walked to the canteen, hoping that one, two or three of the girls were there so she could tell them her news. As it was, no one was there. She debated going back to her room to see if it was still intact and eating there but made the decision to eat at the canteen. Gary came over to sit with her, she had not spotted him in the queue for food, but she was rather distracted. She had to be to not notice a tall man with an axe in his head. Janet smiled at him and then launched at him.

"Gary, did someone ask you where I was working this morning?" she asked.

"Yes, someone from the Nerve Centre; why, what's going on?"

"He offered me a job at the Nerve Centre," she replied, then went on an attack on her food. She stabbed a roast parsnip with her fork, then took it to her mouth to eat. Gary looked at her for a moment, then said.

"Oh, do you know why? It's quite an honour to be asked." He spoke.

"Is it?" Said Janet feeling rather good after hearing that. Maybe she has nothing to fear. Janet finished off her shift, working hard to complete the task she had been given. Jim dismissed her a little bit early, so she went home to think. Her mind buzzed around the meeting with Andrew. Maybe, she thought they selected her because she expressed an interest in working at the Nerve Centre when she was with Sally, the job advisor. Or maybe they have been watching her and head-hunted her because of the hard work she did, or maybe they want her to be somewhere where they can keep an eye on her.

Janet hoped that, in time, she would find out which version was true. She mused about what it would be like living at the Nerve

Centre instead of here. She sat on the chair on her balcony with a busy brain. Time passed, and still, she sat. A knock on her door made her leap and called out. It was Mel knocking her on the way to dinner. Janet joined the others in the canteen, deciding she needed carbohydrates; stodgy food galore. Once seated at their table, she quietly ate her meal, not really engaging in the conversations around her. She was really not too sure if to talk about her encounter with Andrew. Gary remarked on her quietness and asked her if everything was ok. Janet looked at him, nodding affirmative, then blurted out about the event earlier that day. Mel placed her hand on Janet's arm, saying, "That's how they recruit new staff. They have probably been getting information about you; that's what they do. What are you going to do?"

"I don't know; I just don't know. Can I say no?" Janet said.

Gary poured some water into her glass, motioning her to take a drink.

"Generally speaking, people do not say no when they are asked," he said, "now eat up; you have barely touched your food.

"But what about you lot? I won't know anyone there," Janet said, close to tears.

"We will still be here, and you will make new friends; it might help you to settle in more; you have been all over the place mentally recently," Mel said. Their kindness was overwhelming; Janet gave in her tears, and they made lines as they ran down her face. She was immediately apologetic, as people are at times like that; it is part of the social language of humans.

Janet did not sleep that night. She was up and down all night long. She sat on her balcony until she felt rain, then moved indoors to sit in her living room. She left her room in the early hours to walk outside. She wondered if the stars were real or just another man-created phenomenon. She thought she might find that out when she was in the Nerve Centre. She walked a little further when she noticed someone ahead of her sitting hunched up on a bench. Janet approached the person, who turned around when hearing the footsteps. It was Lisa; she was crying, her face looked so miserable, and her cries were guttural.

"Oh my, Lisa, what is it? What's wrong" Janet placed her arms around the weeping women rocking them both gently in an attempt to soothe her.

"It's Linda," Lisa cried.

"What about her? Is she ok?" Janet asked while holding her. Lisa's baby Linda died from having the umbilical cord around her neck. She sustained brain damage causing mental and physical disabilities. She was not making any progress and certainly not meeting her milestones.

"They want to send her somewhere more suitable for her needs without me," Lisa cried, stuttering over some of the words with her distress.

"Can you say no?" Asked Janet.

"They say it's best for her. She will do better there; it would be wrong for me to stand in the way." She replied.

"Why can't you go?" Asked Janet.

"They said it would be best for me to stay here; they can't take parents of the babies. They said she would be well cared for; they said to forget her and move on," replied Lisa, looking up in a state of despair. Janet did not dare share her thought on this matter with Lisa; it would not help her. Instead, she cuddled her as she gently sobbed on her shoulder. Janet accompanied Lisa back to her room then, settled her down in bed then quietly left. The babies are cared for by a nurse in the crèche at night-time, meaning the mums can rest. Janet returned to her own room, still not ready for sleep.

Instead, she took out her secreted documents, including Wendy's journal, sat and read and reread the words, sentences and paragraphs until tiredness knocked on the door. She climbed into her bed, pulled up the covers and drifted into sleep. The chatter in her brain finally abated. She had her decision made; she would take up the offer of working in the Nerve Centre for the sake of those who had graduated. She needed to know the truth.

Chapter 10
Wearing Grey

All throughout the next day, Janet was jittery. She fumbled through her work in the nurseries and accidentally dropped her coffee mug twice. The first time it bounced but shattered on the second drop. She felt like a butterfly flitting here and there, feeling nervous and on edge. She forgot to take a tea break with the others, only stopping her work when reminded by Jim. Word had gotten around about Janet being invited to work at the Nerve Centre. It was viewed as a privilege by Second Chancers, especially if someone was plucked out of the masses to join them. Janet rarely saw anyone from the Nerve Centre socializing with brownies. Maybe it is frowned upon, she thought. At lunchtime, she trotted along to the canteen with Jim, who had had to remind her to eat; such was her distraction. Mel and Kim were already in the dining room eating their food. Janet went to join them while Jim sat with some of his mates at another table.

Mel was quick to ask her how she was; Janet thought for a moment before saying, "I am all over the place," then set about devouring her non-shepherd's pie with veg. It tasted lovely, she thought, almost feeling like she was having her own final meal. Kim asked her if she had made her mind up and what she was going to do; Janet told her she was nowhere nearer making a decision and that she didn't really want to leave her life here and her friends even though she was curious about life in the Nerve Centre. After lunch, she returned to her workstation, where she was putting small plants in bigger pots to give them room to grow. She was enjoying her work; it was satisfying that much was true, but it was hardly brain surgery; she probably would do well with a fresh challenge. Her friends found reasons to be around her offering moral support in the afternoon. Mel was not working that day. She came over asking

Janet if there were any houseplants she could have for her flat. Janet pointed her to Jim, who could help, but she found another reason to be there, which Janet found puzzling.

Gary came over to say hello he seemed a bit distracted as he stood next to her. He put his arm around her to give her a hug, then ambled off to the other side of the polytunnel to have a word with Jim. At some point later that afternoon, Janet noticed Mel and Gary chatting and giggling together just outside of the nursery. Janet looked at them and the way they naturally fit together. Their body language mirrored each other, she realized. Then the penny dropped, and Janet realized that there was a bit more going on between Mel and Gary than just friendship. Thinking about it, she recalled several incidences when they had been together. What a couple they would make with their two odd heads. The axe in Gary's head compensates for the missing part of Mel's face. Janet came to the conclusion she had been so wrapped up in her stuff she had not noticed what was going on with her friends.

There were things she wanted to ask them, stuff to clear up. Now the time was precious; she decided to spend time with each of them as a way to say goodbye. Janet realized she had made a decision not only about seeing her friends but about her own future. She was going to say yes to Andrew when she saw him that night. She took an opportunity a short time later, having abandoned her work. She saw Mel was on her own at the edge of the park, warming up before her daily run. "Hi Mel, how far are you going to go today," Janet asked her.

"Oh, three circuits should do; wanna come with me?" Asked Mel

"No, it would kill me," joked Janet. "Mel, how do you manage? You are so full of life despite your injury; how do you manage?"

"Positive mental attitude is the main thing I picked up in the Mind Complex, that and the fact that by avoiding mirrors, I don't see how ugly I am." Mel laughed as she said that. Janet did a small smile back, hoping that she was doing the right thing. She would hate it if Mel thought she was being unkind.

"Oh, Mel, you are far from ugly. You have an amazing smile; you are lovely," Janet replied, holding Mel's hands. "How do you cope here? You just seem to accept all of it, this place, losing everything on earth."

"This place is tons better than what I had on Earth; I feel freer, not focusing on how I look. I'm not being a slave to my iPhone. Also, I have a better class of friends than I used to have." Mel said, gesturing with her arms as she spoke.

"Talking of which, Mel, is there something going on with you and Gary?"

"That depends; if you two are an item, we just get on well together," she said, clumsily tripping over her words.

"Not sure if Gary and I are an item, you can have him with my blessings; he is a good guy. He won't get you shot," Janet laughed as she mimicked the shooting of a gun. She felt stupid saying that; it was far from OK. "Sorry about that. Do you know what I mean?"

"Yes, Gary is nice; I like him a lot. Now, if you are done, I must get on with my run. See you later. My room is at six, OK." With that, she waved her hand and broke into a run, settling her pace into a fast jog. Janet watched her leave; glad she had had a chat and the confirmation of a developing relationship between her and Gary, she was pleased.

Janet returned to the nursery to see if she could rescue the delicate plants she had mishandled earlier. Focusing on her task, she was at first ignorant of a man's hands circling her waist.

"Gary," Janet said, slapping his hands, "Are you checking up on me."

"I had a 999 call about some half-murdered plants, I thought I would come to the rescue, but you beat me to it."

"What's this about you and Mel?" She asked him as he joined her in potting on the young plants.

"What about it," he teased.

"You know what I mean, you two getting pally; she really likes you; you two should get together."

"You alright with that?" Gary asked.

"Of course, if I am in the Nerve Centre, we will be apart, so you and Mel should be together." Janet was struggling with her words as a wave of excited nervousness swamped her body. Did she know what she was getting into?

"See you later at Mel's," Gary said as he sauntered off with long strides from his long legs. The axe bobbed up and down in time with his steps and the movement of his body. Jim called Janet over to the tea stand, where he offered her tea and a cake. He had got one for all the workers who crowded around. Once everyone had been served, he called a toast to Janet, who was going on to bigger and better things. All the other workers wished her good luck and then chatted among themselves as they ate cake and drank tea. Jim had got Janet her favourite, carrot cake; it made her feel overwhelmed. Jim gave her a quick awkward hug and then sent her on her way. She left the nursery and then walked back to her room, wondering what to do next.

Should she pack a bag? Should she put the laundry out and find somewhere for her plants on her balcony to go? Instead of doing any of these, she put the kettle on to make coffee, then sat with her mug on her balcony and watched the people go about their business. She would miss this, she thought. She could still stay, she thought, then thought it might be worthwhile finding out what Andrew had to say. She was worried about meeting him at the library, though, a bit raw. Then she thought about what to do with her notes and the documents.

She could hardly put them back when she went to the library, and she may be searched when she went into the Nerve Centre, then they would be uncovered. She decided she needed to destroy them, but how? If she had matches, she could burn them outside somewhere, but she didn't have matches. Where could she get some? Then she remembered there was a box of matches in the drawer in the polytunnel from when they had bonfires. She could go over and get them, then go somewhere to burn the documents. She decided there and then to give that idea a go, so she left her flat with the documents under her tunic and walked back to the nursery. No one was around, and as nothing was ever locked up, she had no problem going to the drawer that contained the matches.

After a little routing around, she located them and then thought about her next steps. They usually had the bonfires at the rear of the nurseries; it was quiet there and not overlooked. It seemed to make sense for her to destroy the papers there. She walked around the polytunnel and then went through the gap between the nursery and the polytunnel to the area at the back. She deftly screwed up some pages of the document and then got ready to set them alight. The first match she struck broke, so she added it to the pile to be burned, then tried a second match. This one fizzled but did not alight, so she discarded that one, third time lucky, she thought. The third one lit without a problem, and she lowered her hand with the match to light the screwed-up paper.

The flame took and grew to make short work of the screwed-up paper. Janet put more onto the growing fire, tearing them into strips. The heat forced her back for a moment, but it didn't take long for all of the paper to be consumed by the flames. Janet wondered if she should distinguish the fire or let it burn itself out. She decided to stay until it had burnt down in case the flames spread. In time the flames died, leaving only a small whisper of smoke curling upwards. She was pleased with having disposed of the documents; she had kept the diary, thinking it was too personal to leave to the flames. Once the fire had died, she went back to her room. She stank of bonfire smoke and needed to shower and change her clothes before going to Mel's room.

She had a feeling that she had arranged a fair well do for her though Janet really didn't feel like going. She was no good at goodbyes; she would much prefer to fade away from their lives. It was the fact that she would not be part of their journeys that they would grow on without her. That made her feel sad. She would miss them though no doubt would meet new people who may become friends once she was there. Six o'clock took a long time to come, or so it seemed to Janet. She was due to meet Andrew at seven. Arriving at Mel's room, she gently knocked on the door, hearing an array of shhhh's from inside the room. Mel opened the door, followed by a noisy shout of 'surprise' from a room full of friends and acquaintances.

Janet mocked surprise and delighted as she stepped into the room. Several bottles of Second Chance brew were thrust at her, which she declined. The beer was powerful, and she needed a clear head. She accepted a glass of fruit juice and then joined a group of people reminiscing about life in the Physical Complex and the Mind Complex.

She was asked several times what she would be doing in the Nerve Centre; she explained she had no idea, probably washing up in the kitchen and dusting public rooms. It was lovely and thoughtful of Mel to arrange this; it had been a long time since she had true friends. She spotted Lisa sitting on Mel's bed; Janet went over to her, mouthing, "Are you alright." Lisa nodded, then shrugged. That was enough for Janet to understand how things were for Lisa.

Kim was also there; she now worked at the Mind Complex, helping to organize the programme and run some sessions. She seemed to have settled in well, though Kim, as had others, had the haunted looks in the eyes of memories of other places and other times. Janet was wondering whether she could just creep out as she felt rather overwhelmed. At that point, Mel came up to her carrying a crudely wrapped package in her hand. She gave it to Janet without saying a word.

"What is it? Is it for me?" Asked Janet.

"I hope you like it; I didn't have a lot of time to get you something." She said. Janet pulled off the wrapping paper revealing a sketch of Janet sitting in the park near the lake. Janet knew Mel was gifted; she had no idea she could draw.

"Did you do this, Mel?" Asked Janet looking at Mel.

"Yes, is it OK?" Mel said.

"It's just perfect, thank you so much," at that point, the tears began to prickle in her eyes and then spill down her face. Mel gathered her in her arms, which made Janet cry even more. At that point, Kim came up carrying a mug that she had decorated when she was in the Mind Complex pottery group. Kim was very proud of her achievement at the time, so Janet knew what it meant to her. Janet accepted the gift but could not find any words to thank her, so she touched her on the arm as a way of acknowledging the mug. At that point, Gary handed her a basket of fruit from the garden and then kissed her gently on her cheek.

"This is what was meant to happen; you are always destined to go far in this place. I know you will go and do well. Anyway, we can still see you; it's not as if it's the other side of the world." He kissed her again as she took the basket; she felt overwhelmed and still lost for words. Concerned about the time, she asked Mel if she knew what it was; she didn't want to be late for meeting Andrew.

She had about five minutes, so she had to leave the party to be able to get to the library on time. She wanted to pop into her room to drop off the gifts as they were too heavy to carry around. She assumed that she would be leaving in the morning, so she had so far only packed a few things. It was hard for Janet to say goodbye. These people accepted her warts and all. She never imagined she could be in the position of having such lovely friends. She left the gathering with all her goodies and made her way to the library via her room. She arrived at the library on the dot of seven, and Andrew arrived shortly after. He used his fob key to open the door to the library. Immediately Janet realized there was something different about the room. It took her a bit of time to fathom out what it was, and then she knew; the place had been dusted. The air was clean, and all the surfaces had been polished. Janet was still concerned that this was a way they were going to get her to be Graduated. She kept looking to see if Andrew had brought anyone else as she was sure, if necessary, she could overpower Andrew; he was not a very robust man. She was under no illusion that she had been selected to work in the Nerve Centre because of her skills and that it was because she had uncovered the truth about Graduation. It was safer to keep her close than allow her to poison people in Second Chance. Whatever the outcome was, she felt ready now. If not for herself, then baby Linda, one-armed Brian, Wendy and all those others who had disappeared.

Despite arriving on time, she apologized for keeping him waiting, one of the odd habits of humans. He looked at her smiling warmly and invited her to sit down. "Hello Janet, I'm glad you came; I gather your friends put something on for you."

"How did you know that?" Janet asked incredulously.

"We know everything," he said in a made-up spooky voice, "one of the cleaners heard. Is it Mel arranging it? It looks like they were planning to surprise you," he said. Janet was not convinced but decided not to pursue it. She wanted to keep all her wits about her, especially if this was the last minute of dead life.

"Now, have you given any thought to the plan of you joining us in the Nerve Centre?"

"I just need to know what you mean by that - what is it you want me to do?" Janet responded.

"You are bright; you don't accept things without getting to the truth; you have a good heart as well as a good mind. You are wasted as a Brownie. Your potential will be better realized in the Nerve Centre. Second Chance must work for all; you're better off with us," Andrew said, mindlessly rotating the ring on the middle finger of his right hand.

"What about those that Second Chance does not work for" Janet blurted out. Andrew looked at her, nodding before he spoke. "I have heard all the rumours, too. Those decisions are made by the Inner Ring of the Nerve Centre."

"What colour do they wear," Janet asked flippantly.

"Silver," he replied quickly; for some reason, they both started laughing, which broke through the atmosphere. "Now, you have questions, no doubt. They can all be answered in the morning because now if you want to, I will take you to your new suite in the Nerve Centre; Debbie is ready and waiting for us; she is your maid. She oversees the wing where your rooms are. Now, are you ready?"

"What about my things in my flat?" Janet asked.

"That's been sorted; I sent someone down to pick up your stuff. It will all be in your new place when you arrive. So, are you ready?"

He stood up, waiting for either a verbal or physical response. Janet smiled at him,

"I have nothing to lose, do I?" she stood up and took a look around the library, then indicated her readiness to move. It felt like a walk to doom. Her body felt ultra-alert and aware; every footstep seemed to echo on the tiled floor. They walked to the end of the corridor beyond where her explorations had taken her, down several flights of ramps until they reached a heavy-set door. She was surprised when it turned out to be a whoosh door; she had imagined bolts and chains. Andrew showed her a fob he had attached to his tunic discreetly placed, which allowed access to the Nerve Centre. She followed him through the door down a brightly lit corridor, then deeper and deeper into the heart of the impressive-looking building. Finally, they passed through another whoosh door to a long corridor with many doors on either side.

"Here we are; this is the one," he said, then knocked on one of the doors calling out for Debbie. A young woman with no legs came out in a wheelchair and held out her hand for Janet to shake.

"Hello, Janet; lovely to meet you. I am the maid for this corridor and will help you get on your feet" Janet instantly knew she and Debbie were going to get on well. "Thank you, Andrew," she said, dismissing him. Andrew waved goodbye and made his way back down the corridor. "We call him the bear; he is so nice and cuddly. You will be working with him. Now let me show you your rooms. Someone brought up your things from your flat and put them on your bed. Your new tunic and trousers are there as well. Here we are," she stopped outside door number sixty-seven, pressed a fob against a panel to open the door then handed Janet the fob key. Janet expressed her thanks and then peered into the darkness of the room. "King Charles On," said Debbie; the light in the room came on. "I've written all the code names down for you and how to change them. They do all the electronics, and we are quite high tech here," she paused as Janet had a quick look around her room, wondering where the bed was, noticing this Debbie pointed to two more doors, "in there is your bedroom, there, that's the bathroom, did you notice your garden? It is a bit of a mess, but I'm sure you can work your magic there. I was told you made good use of your balcony when you were there, so I made it possible to have a garden. It's not very big, but I am sure you can make it your own," Debbie said, showing Janet the outside space.

She then showed her the kitchen, which was stocked with essentials and a big box of chocolates. "You don't get that as a Brownie; we have a limited stock, Andrew was insistent. Enjoy. Now, I will leave you to settle in; then, in the morning, I will give you the guided tour." Debbie turned round to exit the room smiling at Janet. Janet realized she had not spoken since arriving in the Nerve Centre and found a croaked response and said thank you as the door closed, leaving her alone in her new space. She opened the door to the bedroom, and the light was off, so she reached for the codes Debbie had given her. Finding the entry she needed, she said the magic words 'Elvis Presley On'.

The light immediately came on, illuminating the space within. She checked her belongings, noticing that the secreted journal was not part of her belongings. She did a thorough check which failed to uncover Wendy's diary. Janet moved the hamper of fruit from Gary into the kitchen, as well as the mug from Kim. She had a look at the rest of her belongings; the pile of her stuff comprised a few written mantras from her days in the Mind Complex and some pottery figurines given to her by Kim, who had a creativity that Janet could only hope for. She quickly found space for them and then wondered what to do with her time.

Her rooms were a vast improvement from the ones she had had before. They were bright, with windows emitting the evening light, a comfy chair, and space for books. Her bed was made up and a selection of grey uniforms hung in the wardrobe. Not much to call her own but possessions were not really necessary in Second Chance as everything was provided. No currency exchanged hands as food, entertainment and board were provided free of charge. Janet was surprised at how this difference from her past life had reduced her stress level. The few things she had came with a story, a history; they were precious.

She found a place on one of the walls in her lounge to put up her new picture and took a pear from the basket of fruit. She went into the lounge to the double door that led out to her garden. It was more of a courtyard, but Janet was pleased with what she had found. She mentally made plans as to how she could make it her own, feeling sure that Gary would not mind if she had a few plants to put there. She sat down on a rickety chair next to a wobbly table, but she did not notice this; she was busy enjoying watching the sunset. She made herself a hot drink, sat down outside, and contemplated her situation. Janet was in no doubt that she had been moved here for them to keep an eye on her. Why else?

She wondered if her maid, Debbie, had been briefed to observe her, follow her, and record her every action. Janet laughed at her ridiculous thoughts. Yes, she had been selected to turn to the grey side in time, the reason why will come out, she was hardly a danger to them. Having explored her suite, she opened her door on the corridor and peeked out to see if anyone was about. It was deathly quiet; venturing out, she walked as quietly as she could. Each step sounded loud to her, but she heard no sounds apart from her steps. She walked along the corridor, noting the door numbers. At the end of the corridor, she found a dining area, a large lounge, and a small gym. She was impressed with the quality of the furnishings, half expecting to see a television in the lounge, but no, there was a piano. She imagined singing songs around the piano, a Sound of Music-type scenario, and again she laughed out loud.

"Hi Janet, can I get anything for you? Are you hungry?" Asked Debbie making Janet jump out of her skin. Debbie's wheels had been silent, her presence a surprise. Janet felt mortified and embarrassed at having been caught laughing out loud; it seemed such a wrong thing to do in this place. She felt a sense of sadness about leaving her life as a Brownie.

"No, I'm fine, thank you, just getting used to my surroundings. Where is everyone?"

"On-shift. They are working until nine; the place is very different with everyone around. They are all lovely; you will fit in fine. They, like you, were all selected to work here. We spend a lot of time in these rooms; last night, we had a sing-song around the piano," said Debbie. Janet was not sure if Debbie was taking the piss, but unless she could read her mind, she could not have known her mockery. Janet smiled and then asked Debbie to show her where the stuff was for making a coffee.

"How do you like it? Would you like a slice of cake to go with it?" Debbie replied, instantly turning around and heading for the kitchen in the dining area. She emerged a short time later holding in one hand a steaming mug of coffee and on her lap a plate with a slice of ginger cake. Janet could not stop salivating at the prospect of cake and tried to be polite in her consumption of the desert. She sat down in one of the armchairs enjoying her snack. Debbie left her to it, returning to the kitchen to prepare food for the others due to finish their shift very shortly. The cake was delicious, and the coffee perfectly accompanied it; Janet felt relaxed in the chair. A short time after, she heard a babble of voices and the sound of a dozen or so footsteps on the corridor heading towards her. Or so it seemed to Janet truth was they were heading down for beverages and cake, not her.

The next couple of hours Janet spent mixing with the other residents of Blue Wing. She found it hard to take it all in; they all seemed noisy and larger than life. A few of them were placed in the environment section where Janet was going to work. She asked them several times what it was like, but the movement of the conversation swept her questions away. Three residents were in wheelchairs; two used crutches with lower limbs missing, one was blind, one had a facial disfigurement, two had upper limbs missing, and the rest, like Janet, had hidden disabilities.

Debbie was busy fetching and carrying for her charges. Janet offered to help her, which was declined. Eventually, feeling drained, Janet bowed out of the gathering and made her way back into her suite. Commanding the light to come on in her seating area, she decided sleep was needed, took off her brown uniform for the last time, put on her nightwear then went through the pre-bed rituals of washing and cleaning. She fell to sleep eventually, feeling like the odd kid at a new school. She woke up to the morning sunlight in the land of eternal late spring weather.

She felt well-rested and eager for the day ahead. After having a shower, she put on her grey tunic and trousers, then put on a pair of black lace-up shoes. They looked new; Janet could not imagine how they managed to get her correct shoe size. Tossing that thought away, she left her suite and headed towards the dining room. Debbie was there switching on the kettle and making toast. The entire kitchen was at her height to accommodate her wheelchair; it really was her place and space. Debbie asked Janet for her breakfast order and then set about preparing her food. There were only a couple of people sitting in the dining room; they were deep in discussion. Janet did not want to disturb them, so she selected a table near the other end, feeling it to be too intrusive to sit anywhere else. She was concerned that she might intrude on someone's space by sitting somewhere. Janet was not very bold; her shyness often kept her at the edge of a gathering than at heart. It did not take Debbie long to prepare tea and toast, delivering it to Janet with a smile.

"Andrew is coming to get you at eight-thirty. He will be showing you around and introducing you to members of the environment team. Enjoy your breakfast, just yell if you need anything else." She spun around on her wheels, heading back to the kitchen. Janet thought that maybe those on the late shift enjoyed a morning lie-in; she had expected to see more people than this. She took her time eating her breakfast as she had about an hour to kill before Andrew was due to come.

When she had finished, she had a look at the books on the shelf to see if there was anything she wanted to read. She found one that sounded OK, so she read the synopsis to see if she would want to read it. She was happy with her find and then left the dining room to go to her room. She had decided to sit in her garden for a while and took the book with her. She struggled to read the words; it was all blurry. Janet had noticed that her sight was better looking at things in the distance; she was coming to the conclusion she needed glasses but had no idea if there was anywhere to get some.

She thought she might ask Debbie the next time she saw her. She made herself a drink and started to consume it, then noticed the time. The big hand was edging towards eight-thirty. She left her room carrying her mug of tea and walked down the corridor to the dining room. At eight-thirty exactly, Andrew peered into the dining room, wishing Debbie well.

He spotted Janet at the table and headed towards her. He smiled warmly, enquiring how she had slept. He did not wait for an answer; instead encouraged her to finish her tea and sat down on the chair opposite her. Janet drank quickly, not really wanting to keep him waiting. When she had indicated finishing her beverage, they both stood up and headed down the corridor. He activated the whoosh door and then headed right along one corridor to the end; through that door was a hallway with multiple doors leading off, similar to Janet's dormitory. Andrew explained that this area is where all the suites are, with a maid managing each one. Leaving the hub, they headed off down some slopes, up in a lift, and along numerous corridors, thankfully with signs on the walls and directions to various sections.

Finally, they arrived at a floor dedicated to the environment team. Andrew used his fob key to enter through a door into Janet's new place of work in the heart of the Nerve Centre. There was the general sound of talk and intermittent laughter, giving the place a friendly feel. The room was vast, with many windows lighting up the space. Apart from the glass offices, it was an open plan with workstations lining the walls of the room. The natural light was enough to see by, so there were no lights on.

Many of the desks had computer monitors on them with corresponding mice and keyboards. They looked rather antiquated and had seen better days. Janet saw some all-purpose printers in the centre part of the room, along with supplies and wastepaper bins. The majority of the workstations had people working there, but there were some spaces here and there. In one corner of the room was a large filing cabinet, with another one at the opposite corner. Janet took it all in to get her bearings, and then Andrew, still in the doorway, called out.

'Everyone, can I have your attention" Andrew addressed the room. The sound of chatter dropped away, "thank you, now, this is Janet; she is starting here today; she's our new GDB. Please make her feel welcome and help her out if she needs it." There were a few murmurs of hello from the workers then people turned around to continue with their work. Janet was underwhelmed by the response, but in truth, she didn't really know what to expect.

Andrew took Janet around to each workstation in turn introducing the worker and giving her their name and role. Janet quickly gave up trying to remember names and settled on their job titles instead. In between introductions, Janet looked around the room. She was missing the park, the flowers and all her friends, she really wanted to go back but had a feeling it was too late for that. She had to be brave and embrace her new world. Andrew took Janet over to one of the free workspaces. He told her that was where she would be working alongside Jane, another GDB. Jane was a young woman with distinctive red hair. It was a beautiful colour which worked brilliantly with her pale complexion. It looked like she was wearing a touch of makeup which enhanced the green of her eyes. Janet felt immediately intimidated by her, by her appearance and the stance of her body.

"Sorry, what is a GBD," asked Janet to Andrew.

"GDB stands for General Dogs Body. It's a way to get used to working for this team; we all started off as GDB, even me. Oh, I've just realized we have Janet and Jane. That's funny." Andrew laughed at this. Behind his back, Jane shrugged her shoulders which Janet took to mean that he was always like this. "Anyway, I'm sure Jane has some work for you to do; she is going to show you the ropes." With that, he turned away, heading off to his glass office, which looked deep into paper and files. Just as Janet was about to sit at her desk, Andrew came back out, making his way over to her.

"I forgot to say. I will meet up with you at lunch time to go over a few things. Is that OK?" He didn't wait for a reply, just headed back to his office.

"Is he always like that?" Janet asked Jane.

"Yes, he is sweet, but I wouldn't like to get on his bad side. By the way, people here, apart from Andrew, call me Jazz."

"Jazz, OK." Replied Janet. Jazz explained what they needed to do, which was to prepare documents for one of the bosses. The documents had graphs on them showing the ambient internal and external temperatures. The graphs showed little change; it felt like the work and time used to compile them was rather wasted with so little change. Janet knew the corporate desire to measure and analyze everything, most of it not necessary. But it kept the wolf from the door and made people think they were clever and necessary. While Jazz printed, Janet stapled the papers in order to be ready for a meeting later that day. They finished quite quickly, then headed to the small rest room in one corner of the department for a break.

"Can you tell me where the ladies are?" Janet asked Jazz.

"Yes, sure, it's on the left outside of the entrance; you can't miss it," she said as she put water in the kettle. Janet took her leave and went to use the toilet; she hated feeling like the new girl, and she knew that the first day was aways the worst. She came back into the department and made her way to where Jazz was pouring hot water into mugs with coffee in them.

Do you want a biscuit? I think we have some chocolate ones," asked Jazz.

"Thank you, that's great. How come you are here? I don't remember seeing you in Second Chance." Asked Janet.

'I was headhunted, probably like you. I always wanted to know about what happens in the Nerve Centre and found it hard to settle in as a Brownie. I left Second Chance about three months ago. It was the best thing I could've done. I like being here; it makes somethings make sense, replied Jazz in between mouthfuls of biscuits.

"What does a GDB do," Janet asked, inclining her head to the left.

"A bit of everything, it's a way to learn what each person does, you know, Jenny, over there, oversees keeping the oxygen levels right. She has to go to various stations around Second Chance twice a day to get readings; often, that's something I do. Paul is keeping an eye on the weather. He checks that the temperature is OK and that the rain falls properly." Jazz replied. Janet thought it was very strange to have to monitor this kind of thing; surely, they cannot totally predict the weather. She asked Jazz that who replied, "Yes, it's all automatic now; they have to make sure that the pumps are working, you know, the ones that pump the oxygen and the water to make the nighttime rain. Why did you think that it was all natural?" she teased.

"Well, yes, I had no idea that someone was behind all of that." Janet felt a little blown over finding this out; maybe she will find out a lot more while working here. For the weather to be set by man was amazing. Taking Jazz's lead, they both left the restroom, returning to their desks to compile more data. This time drawing graphs of nighttime rain quantities. Which, again, showed very little change and was another waste of time. It was of use to someone though a simple sentence of analysis would have done, or at least that's what Janet thought. Jazz took Janet through the daily and weekly procedures and explained what the Environment Team was responsible for. As well as ensuring the sun shone for 12 hours a day, rain fell for 4 hours at night, and the mix of medication was infused through the porous walls of the physical complex for seven hours a day. This information blew Janet's head off, figuratively speaking. She had not thought about the sun being able to be controlled by man.

"How do they do that? Jazz, they can regulate the sun and rainfall?."

"It isn't a real sun; it's held up there by atmospheric pressures and a huge blinking rope; they have to be precise, or the sun will fall out of the sky, or that's what we say to Brownies who ask, in reality, it is held up by rope."

"Rope?" said Janet checking Jazz's features to see if she was joking.

"Yes, a long piece of strong rope. At the end of the day, as dusk falls, the sun is physically lowered slowly like it is setting, and the LED lights go to fade into orange to make it look real. When the sun comes down, we can maintain it, and of course, it marks nighttime. There is a dirty great big winch that we use to move the sun up and down. You're looking like you don't believe me?"

Janet could not believe what she was hearing. In a disbelieving tone, she said,

"You have me on. Is this what they say to all new people, some kind of initiation?"

"No, it's all true; you will see it for yourself soon; some of the bulbs look like they are dying. We may need to replace them, then you'll see." Janet considered this, still not too sure if she was telling porky pies. If it was true, they were duping a whole load of workers in Second Chance and the two complexes.

"I don't think I've seen a moon; is there not one?" Janet asked, finishing putting some data on a graph.

Jazz replied, "There is one, but it is out of action; they are waiting for a part to arrive." At this, they returned to their work and made sure they had all the data they needed for the bosses. Jazz looked in a folder and pulled out a table. It showed some data about the sun and how much heat came off from the bulbs. The less heat meant that some bulbs were dead and needed to be replaced. The minute changes in the graphs showed the number of spent bulbs. Janet began to get ideas about what the Environmental Team were about; she felt excited to be part of this and had a better understanding of the need for statistics and graphs.

Jazz went onto explain that ecosystem in Second Chance was finally balanced to maximize food crops grown to feed inmates and to send to other Second Chance structures. The news that there was more than one Second Chance was incredulous to Janet; she had not even imagined multiples. Her immediate world at that second expanded, making her feel very small. The time between coffee break and lunch time went by quickly as they amassed all of the paper for the manager's meeting after lunch. Jazz would be attending to take notes while Janet familiarized herself with the file of the rules and procedures that the workforce needed to be guided by. Right at one o'clock, Andrew came over to Janet and invited her into his office. She went in and waited to be invited to sit by Andrew. He sat down at his desk and then motioned for Janet to sit. He asked her how she had found the morning.

"Interesting, especially by learning that the sun is a load of lightbulbs and that there are other Second Chances out there."

"Yes, a bit of an eye-opener. This is a good team to work with. I think it is the most interesting one. I guess you have realized that we are responsible for the smooth running of the place and help out with the Newbie's pain management in the Physical Complex. We work alongside the medical team on that one, anyway. Before you go off for lunch, I need you to read this and then sign at the bottom if you are happy to."

"What is it," she said as she took the offered sheet of paper.

"Read it," Andrew said. Janet skimmed and read the paper to get an idea of what it was about. It was a confidentiality agreement to not talk about the work of the team and the running of the Nerve Centre to anyone outside of the Nerve Centre. Janet went through it twice before taking hold of a pen handed to her by Andrew. She signed the sheet at the bottom and then handed the pen back to Andrew.

"Brilliant, now off you go for lunch. Jane will show you the way to the canteen." Andrew got up, opening the door of his office to dismiss Janet, who got up and left the glass office. Jazz was waiting for her to go to the canteen. Janet could smell the canteen before she saw it. It was not far away from the department building, just down a couple of corridors. There was quite a queue made up of some people in grey and others in grey and blue. Janet had seen people dressed in grey and blue as a brownie but was not too sure where they fit in the scheme of things. She decided to ask Jazz.

"Jazz, do you know who they are," she said, pointing at a couple of men.

"What, the ones in grey and blue? They work for the Nerve Centre, you know, do the physical stuff. Does that help?" Jazz said.

"Yes, thanks," Janet said as they got to the head of the queue. She selected a hot meal, veggie toad in the hole with veg and gravy. She opted for a fruit salad for dessert and then carried her food to the table Jazz sat at. There were a couple of her work colleagues sitting there, so Janet assumed it was their table. These sorts of things are important to know, especially on the first day. The two men asked Janet a few questions, which she happily answered. One of them, the quieter one, looked at her and asked her if she was there because she was in trouble.

"I don't think so. Why is that how they select who comes to work here?"

"It's one of the reasons. Just beware, there are eyes everywhere," with that, he focused his gaze on his food, leaving Janet feeling a bit shaken. She chose to change the subject and asked them if there was a social club there. Jazz said yes, there was, but it was not that good. Most people stay on their wing. There is a gym and a swimming pool, though.

"Oh, really, where is that, then?" Janet asked.

"Ask Debbie to take you; it's a bit complicated to try to explain," Jazz said, then changed the subject. Janet really didn't know what to make of Jazz; she was not going out of her way to be friendly.

"There is so much to take in. My head is spinning," Janet said as they ate their desserts.

"It will take time. I'm still finding out new things. It really makes you look at things differently, especially all the care they took to make this place." Jazz said as they ate. After lunch, they returned to the department and set about preparing notes for an interdepartmental meeting the next day. Jazz run up the agenda before going to minute take in the manager's meeting. She left Janet sorting out piles of documents ready for the meeting tomorrow. By the end of her first shift, she had a numb brain from absorbing so much information. Returning to her suite, she flung herself on her bed and fell quickly into a deep slumber with no time to remove her shoes. What felt like a few minutes later, she heard someone knocking on her door. Feeling disorientated, she got up to open the door; Debbie smiled up at her, enquiring if she wanted to eat. Janet followed Debbie down the corridor to the dining room, where she collected her meal. She asked two people sharing a table if she could join them, and they both nodded, making space at the table. "Hi, I'm Janet, I'm new here, and you are…" she said, looking at the man on her left.

"Fred, and this is Stephen," he replied, gesturing towards Stephen. I've been here just short of two years. I manage all the waste, you know, packaging, that type of thing."

"And you, Stephen?" She asked, facing the other man.

"Me, I am a GDB like you. I'm on the night shift this week, so this is my breakfast. I've been here for about a month or so." He said, holding out his hand to shake hers. Introductions over the conversation rumbled on, sometimes flying, then dipping. They were funny guys; they had her laughing at their awful jokes. Then Stephen took his leave to go to work. The dining room was getting busy. Fred introduced Janet to the others one by one, adding anecdotes which made for light banter. Debbie was kept busy feeding the masses; she joined in the teasing in good spirits, and it was clear she was valued by the team.

The food was good. After dinner, someone suggested playing Dominoes, others used the gym equipment, and some sat down to read quietly. Janet felt like going to bed but thought it was important to stay and join in in order to really be part of the team. She joined those reading in some comfortable chairs. There were a few books on the mantel sill from which Janet selected one with a good-sounding title. She tried to read it, but the words were jumbled and illogical, or that is what her brain made of it; she really was tired. She was on the morning shift the next day, so she decided to take her leave to go to her suite and wind down to sleep. Before going to bed, she sat out in her little garden and looked up at the sky; now, after today, she had to come to terms with the fact that the night sky was probably false. She got up, stretched then went into her bedroom to get ready for bed. It had been a strange but exciting day.

Chapter 11
Grey on Grey

Janet woke up with a start from a dream where she was being chased down a road on earth by a frog. In the few seconds from the time of waking, she tried to recall all the dreams, but her memory of them faded away. She got up, washed and dressed, and then went down to the dining room for breakfast. Debbie was already there anticipating her arrival. She prided herself on thinking about her lot and what their preferences were. Debbie had put the kettle on to make Janet's tea as soon as she saw her walking down the corridor.

She double-checked if she wanted toast then once that was confirmed by Janet, she set about cutting the bread into slices. Debbie plonked the meal down on the table where Janet was sitting, then went back into the kitchen to get her coffee. She came back out and then parked her wheelchair opposite Janet. Debbie was keen to find out how she was doing at work and to ask her if her room was OK. Janet filled her in on her day and her room, which she was very happy with.

"I have put a laundry bag aside for you to put your dirty washing in. Just leave it outside your door in the morning, you will have nice clean clothes in the afternoon. Is that OK?" Debbie asked Janet.

"Yes, thank you," she replied. "Where is the bag now?"

"I've got it in my office. Let me get it for you," she said, wheeling off to her room accessed through the kitchen. She came out carrying the sack and gave it to Janet with a smile.

"Thanks," said Janet. "Debbie, I'm not too sure of the way to work. Could you draw me a map or something?"

"Yes, of course, let me get a paper and pen," with that, she went back into her office. She came out with both paper and pen on her lap, which she put on the table once she was back in her original position. She drew a concise map which was easy to understand.

"What about the canteen? Do you think you can find it for your lunch?" Debbie asked her as she marked the department with a large cross on the map.

"I'm OK with that; it is well signposted," Janet replied. Janet carefully folded the map and put it in her pocket; she just hoped she could read it; that reminded her,

"Debbie, do you know if there is somewhere I could have my eyes checked? I've noticed that my close sight is not what it was," Janet asked.

"Yes, we have an optician; I could make you an appointment if you like. It's quite hard to find in the medical centre; he only has a tiny room to work out of. Do you want to go today?"

"That would be great; I finish work at two. Can they really do it that quickly?"

"I know; it's much better than the NHS back home," Debbie said. "I will do that for you and let you know the time of your appointment when you come back after your shift'.

"That's great, thank you." With that, Janet quickly checked the clock on the wall and saw she had ten minutes before the start of her shift. She took out the folded map and then said goodbye to Debbie before setting off for work. Debbie's map did the trick. She made no wrong turns and arrived at the department right on time. Jazz was also on the early shift; they would be working together again.

The shift went by quickly. They were collating data on one of the computers of the information gathered from the oxygen and carbon dioxide monitoring stations. And going through paperwork to get it ready for filing. There seemed no end to the paper, and Janet failed to understand why they didn't use the computers more. They could email the survey results to the manager without having to print them out. Janet didn't like to see waste, she thought about asking Jazz why they still use paper, but that thought drifted away as she piled up the papers for filing. At the end of her shift at two o'clock, she used the map to guide her back to her ward. Once back, she went down the corridor to where Debbie normally stayed to see if she was in. She couldn't see her in the kitchen, so she went into the doorway of her office to see if she was there. She couldn't see her but spotted her upturned power wheelchair lying on its side at the other side of the desk. Janet quickly went into the room and then around the desk. She immediately saw Debbie on the floor, trapped by her chair. Janet got down to her level.

"Debbie, are you OK? Are you hurt?" Janet asked her while assessing the scene.

"I think I'm OK, just need to get the chair off me, don't you try; it's very heavy," Debbie said with a false lilt in her speech.

"Let me see if I can get you help. Any idea whom I could call?" she asked, seeing the telephone on her desk.

"Try security; they have strong people there, the numbers on the wall."

Janet stood up and moved to the desk picking up the phone. There was a list on the wall, and in no time at all, she spotted the extension number for security. She picked up the phone receiver and punched in the numbers. It had hardly started to ring on the other side when someone answered the phone. Janet quickly asked them for help and told them where they were, then put down the phone. She was not sure if she needed to let them in through the whoosh door or if they had passed.

Within five minutes of making the call, three men turned up. They wore navy blue trousers and tops, and all looked like they regularly worked out. Janet got up from holding Debbie's hand and then stepped away, allowing the guards to look at the scene. Two of them moved the desk out of the way; then all three got hold of the chair and, on the count of three, lifted the chair off from resting on its side, pinning Debbie down on the ground and setting it back on its wheels next to Debbie.

"Debbie, are you happy about going to get checked up by a doctor in case you're hurt?" asked one of the guards after one of them gently lifted her back into her chair.

"I feel OK, thanks; I will see how I go; if anything hurts, I will go down there', said Debbie.

"Thank you for your help," Janet and Debbie said in unison. The guards took their leave after they had put the heavy desk back where it belonged. Janet went into the kitchen to make them both tea while Debbie composed herself.

"Janet, what about your appointment? It's at half past three; you don't know the way. Shall I come with you?" She gabbled. Janet bought the tea and then sat in the chair in her office. Debbie kept everything neat and tidy in her room. Janet noticed some ledger-type paper with what looked like a budget. Janet didn't even think that she had to make the book balance. She found a new respect for Debbie. Her job was a lot more than the smooth running of the wing. Debbie felt absolutely fine and had no injuries from her fall and accompanied Janet to the medical centre.

This one catered for Brownies and those from the Nerve Centre; both complexes had their own specialist staff. Janet had not been there before and had no prior notice of it being there. They went into the reception area, where Janet told the receptionist that she had an appointment. At dead on three thirty, a slim little man came out of a door and up to the reception area. He wore white trousers and a tunic and sported a pair of very thick-lensed glasses.

He went over to Janet and invited her to go with him. They went through the door he had just exited from, then walked down a short corridor, taking the second door on the right. He ushered her into the room, where she saw the ophthalmic equipment and charts. He took down a brief history before he examined her eyes and her sight. She heard him tut-tutting here and there, which made Janet feel on edge. At the end of the exam, he turned on the room light and told her that she needed glasses. Janet thought as much as he showed her a somewhat limited style of spectacle frames. Janet selected one and then got ready to leave. He said to make an appointment with the receptionist for the next afternoon when they are ready.

"Really? As quick as that," said Janet, stunned at the efficiency. He took her out of the room and back to reception, where she booked another appointment at five thirty, after her shift. Janet and Debbie made their way back to the wing. Janet was still speechless with what had just transpired. Apparently, according to Debbie, the optician ground the lenses himself, so he would probably be doing that now. Janet and Debbie had another drink and sat in the dayroom. One other person was in there doing some sketching.

Janet asked him if she could see what he was doing; he lowered his sketch pad so she could see an image of Debbie in her chair. It was very good, she thought, then told him what she thought. He continued with his work now and then and took a sip of tea Debbie had made him. His sketching was even more impressive because he had only a thumb and index finger on one hand and no fingers on his other. He sketched using soft nibbed pencils lodged in between his fingers; Janet was impressed with how he managed to do it.

She really had seen people who have horrific injuries have amazing talents. She was yet to find her talent. She did enjoy doing upcycling when she was on Earth, there was something good about changing the purpose of an item. After dinner, Janet took herself off to her room for a bit of quiet time before bed. She sat outside in her garden enjoying the evening regulated and filtered air. Just like the lights in the sky were not stars, they were lights hung on a huge net. Despite knowing that everything had been created by man, she still found it mind-blowing.

Maybe she would be able to come up with an idea to make Second Chance more like earth. Liking the idea of that, she left her mind wandering, exploring possibilities. She thought of various things but had to discard them because it was too complicated. She thought about the times of the day; they had the sunrise and sunset sorted, but, then it came to her, one thing that was missing was the dawn chorus. Surely it would not be too difficult to play a recording over a tannoy system. That was a good thought; she held onto that one as she went to bed, hoping that she would remember it in the morning. She could have written it down in her journal but could not be bothered. It would mean getting up and finding a pen and all that. She slept well and woke up early. She was not due at work until nine-thirty, and it was only seven. What would she do with her time, she thought. She lay in bed for a bit longer, dozing, then when it was a sensible time, she got up and started her day.

Debbie cooked her scrambled eggs on toast, her favourite, which she ate quickly. There was nothing worse than cold-cooked eggs, she thought. After breakfast, she made her way to the department. She didn't need the map this time. She found her way easily. Jazz was already there; she was working an early shift; today was the first day Janet would be on her own later in the day. Today they had to go out to take the readings of the oxygen and carbon dioxide levels. Janet and Jazz left the office with a book and pen to go to the various places over Second Chance where the monitoring stations were.

They firstly went to the garage forecourt just down from the main entrance; they were being transported around in one of the buggies with a worker from the garage driving them. Janet felt quite excited by her field trip and hopped on board the small buggy with Jazz. There were eight stations in all to visit. Some of them were in the open and looked like you would expect them to look. Jazz showed Janet how to take the reading. It was pretty simple; it was just a case of writing down some numbers. Janet asked Jazz if she knew what they meant. Jazz said she didn't have a clue, and at that, they both laughed. Some of the stations were disguised as lampposts, and some of them were in the gardens of the Physical Complex and the Mind Complex.

All in all, it took just under two hours to gather all the readings before heading back to the department. Once back, Jazz showed Janet how to enter the data on the computer, which somehow turned the numbers into a graph. She could see where the oxygen levels were above or below a line of what it should be. It was the same for the carbon dioxide readings. Jazz saved the readings and then suggested they grab a coffee.

During their break, Janet told Jazz her idea of having a morning bird song. She didn't seem to think people would go for it, then changed the subject. After coffee, Janet started assembling paperwork for the manager's meeting while Jazz did some work on the computer. Janet asked her if they had internet there. Jazz replied that anything online had to be agreed upon by the Inner Circle. They would grant some things, but it was strictly monitored. She explained that people might be tempted to go on social media or send emails to loved ones which could cause a whole lot of problems. It would be better if people made a clean break from family and friends. Janet thought that through and could understand why they made it not possible.

At lunch time, Janet didn't feel like going to the canteen; instead, she stayed at work eating chocolate biscuits and drinking tea. When she felt chocolated out, she went to her desk and continued getting the documents together. Now that she had been out gathering the information that morning, she could see somethings making sense to her. They would really benefit from sharing things on the computer than printing everything out, but if they had no means to share information, she guessed they had no choice.

Jazz left at two-thirty, leaving Janet flying solo in the office. She completed her task quickly and then wondered what to do with herself. There were a couple of people working in the office, so she went up to one of them, Sheila, to see if she had anything that she could do. She found some filing to do, which Janet jumped to do. It did not take her long then she sat down at her desk with a file full of procedures and rules to read up. She made that last until the end of her shift at three thirty. She went back home, saying hello to Debbie when she arrived. She had time to kill before she went to pick up her new glasses, so she sat in the day room of the wing and watched Debbie wipe down tables and tidy up.

Janet asked her if she needed a hand with anything, but Debbie had no work for her. Getting bored, she got up and went to her room to get her reading book. She sat outside on the rickety chair, straining to see the words. Her arms weren't long enough for her to see the type clearly. She really needed those glasses. At five fifteen, Debbie knocked on her door for them to go to Janet's appointment with the optician. Debbie needed to get something done to her wheelchair and had made her appointment at the same time so they could go together. When they arrived at the Medical Centre, Debbie went downstairs to the store, where they had various types of equipment.

One of her tires needed to be replaced as it had worn out. While Debbie was being seen, Janet was called into the optician's office, where she had her new glasses fitted. She checked out her reflection in a hand mirror and thought she looked OK. What's more, she could read the second from the bottom line of letters on the chart. Pleased with her new glasses, she thanked the optician and then went into the reception area to wait for Debbie. Debbie came along a few minutes later, sporting a new tire.

They walked together back to the Nerve Centre, passing the social club. Janet knew it was too early for anyone she knew to be at the social club, but it made her realize just how much she missed her friends. Debbie was great, but the girls were too. She tried not to let her sadness show, but Debbie picked up on it and asked her about her time as a Brownie. Janet told her about her work, her friends and her swims in the lake.

Debbie told her that they had a large pool in the Nerve Centre, which she should give a try. Janet agreed that it would be a good idea and made a mental plan to check it out the next day she had off or had an early shift. Once back on the wing, Debbie went off to start preparations for dinner, and Janet went to her room. She got her book and sat outside, finally being able to read the words instead of having to try and guess. After a while, she checked the time and saw that the food should be ready. She went out and headed to the dining room, where Debbie was busy feeding the masses. Janet sat at one of the tables with space, and within a few moments, Debbie had placed a plate of food in front of her. It was a non-fish pie with green vegetables. It was delicious; she really was a good cook.

Janet ate quickly, savouring the taste and texture of the food. For desserts, Debbie had made apple crumble with custard. Janet hoped there might be seconds, but someone got there ahead of her. She needed to be quicker, she thought. Janet helped Debbie to wash the dishes and tidy up so she could end her shift early. She was due a day off even if she really didn't have anything to do. Janet felt the same on her time off; it felt like she was just waiting to eat. She was not sure what her current weight was; she must be piling on the pounds with all the good food she had been eating. Her clothes didn't feel any tighter, though, she thought, tugging the material on her stomach. Janet went to her room after dinner and got out her diary to make an entry for the day.

She looked back on what she had written the day before to remind her of yesterday, then wrote down what she had done during the day and how she was feeling. It was getting a bit monotonous, but really very little interest had happened. She wasn't going out anywhere; she had no gossip and no dramas. Janet wondered if she had made a mistake coming to work here. She had given up so much in pursuit of what, to get answers to questions, power, and to change things. Her search for the truth about Graduation seemed to have come to a halt. She had no idea where to go for that. She had to decide if she wanted to get back stuck in with that or leave it be. She wrote this down in her diary, finally pleased she had found something more interesting to write.

As usual, she hid her diary in her knicker drawer and put the pen on the table in her lounge. She looked around her main room, thinking about what she could do to put her stamp on it, to personalize it. She had put Mels drawing of Janet by the lake up on the wall, held in place with sticky tape. She had also put one of her most used mantras on the wall in the lounge and one by her bed. Apart from that, she had nothing else to decorate the place with. Maybe there are rules about what you can and cannot do, she thought.

She decided to ask Debbie in the morning about it and if she had any ideas of how to make it hers. The garden was relatively easy; she just needed plants. Maybe a small tree in a container and some colourful shrubs. She tried to imagine what it would look like and then came up with the idea of making a wind chime. There was always a light breeze generated by electricity harnessed from the waterfall near the park (another interesting fact she had found out from Jazz). She could easily make something light that could be blown around by the wind. She thought about using foil or some other reflective material, then thought that she would make something next time she had time off. She was pleased she had made a plan, and with that, she took out her diary again and updated it so she would not forget. Then, she took herself off to bed and fell asleep after twenty-two sheep.

The next few shifts passed quickly. Janet got to grips with the daily routine and saw how the various jobs within the team worked, especially while shadowing some of the workers. Jazz was her main go-to person who always had time for her, and a friendship began to grow inside and outside of work. Janet missed not being a Brownie. She had been part of a good solid group of friends and hoped in time. She would get to like her new role. It was interesting to understand the pure logistics of creating a living and working environment from the correct amount of rain fall to maximize plant development to the right level of brightness of the artificial stars in the artificial sky. It was sad to think that this place, Second Chance, was fabricated and built up around the needs of disabled and deformed dead humans.

The smallest of touches to create a homely feel was some one's brainwave. Janet learned that one of the team had an idea to recreate the dawn chorus, the most delightful sound prevalent on Earth. Janet thought someone had had her idea when she learnt that Jazz had put it forward to Andrew. Janet felt slighted at this, especially when Jazz took the accolade. Janet thought that she should talk to Jazz about it but decided to leave it the way it was. She was not confrontational and didn't dare upset Jazz. Janet asked Andrew if she could be part of the small team to get this project up and running.

Andrew agreed to this and told her there was a meeting that day to bounce around some ideas that Janet should go along with them. She was excited about being part of something from the start and happily went along to the meeting. Andrew was there too, which was nice. At the meeting, she was brimming with ideas but had less idea of what was feasible or possible. Maybe one day, Janet thought, they could find a way to introduce wildlife, but, she mused, would the wildlife have to be dead to survive in Second Chance? She felt sure that the common garden wasp would be just as menacing dead as they were alive. Janet did not feel confident about raising these thoughts with the team as she felt they would think her silly or ridiculous what's more, they were very focused on the project at hand. The meeting ended with the small team given roles and a date set for the next meeting. Janet had to research the morning bird songs, especially the order of the singing. She knew the little Robin was the first to kick it off, but she didn't know what other birds were involved. She had a look at her work schedule, helpfully compiled by Jazz, to see when she could do the research needed.

Janet was bemused that the Nerve Centre had access to computers and the internet. There was nothing like that in Second Chance for the brownies. She had no access at all to her computer; really, all she could do was manage data. However, Andrew was in the position to request access to the internet for Janet so she could do her research. It would only be for specific sites, though. He requested access directly to the Inner Circle, who, within a couple of days, agreed.

Janet's work with the Environment Team was going well. She was settling in good, and now, she would be doing her first night shift with Jazz. Janet tried to get her body and brain used to working nights by having a sleep in the afternoon the day before. She dually went to bed at two in the afternoon, but her mind was too busy to allow sleep to happen. At three, she gave the idea up and got out of bed to make herself a mug of tea. She sat in her garden with her book and did a spot of reading up until the time when she should eat. She had a medium-sized meal at five thirty in the dining room prepared for her by Debbie.

Janet ate her macaroni cheese and trifle while Debbie prepared a packed meal for her to take when she was on the night shift. She set off with her food to the environmental team department just as Jazz arrived with a similar-sized package. There was nothing much to hand over to the three of them on the night shift; their main job on nights was to deal effectively with any emergencies and the maintenance of structures. On her first night, Jazz informed Janet that they had to replace some blown bulbs in the sun. Janet thought this sounded very exciting and was keen to get started. Jazz had to run some logistics first, so Janet found something to do until Jazz was ready.

Finally, after what seemed an age, Jazz was ready to repair the sun. They left the department and took the lift to the ground floor. Jazz told Janet to stay where she was while she went to the stores to collect the spare bulbs. After a while, Jazz emerged with a canvas bag containing several what looked like regular household bulbs. To say Janet was underwhelmed was an understatement. They walked a short way to the garage to a two-person buggy on the forecourt of the garage. Jazz got into the driver's side of the battery-powered buggy, inviting Janet to get in next to her. Jazz drove with skill and care along roads and past places Janet simply did not recognize. They drove past polytunnels and fields and what looked like a farm beyond areas Janet had explored as a Brownie. Eventually, Janet saw a tall wall ahead of her; it stretched beyond her vision on both sides. In the wall, she saw two large gates blocking access to whatever lay beyond the wall. Jazz slowed down the buggy to a stop and disembarked. She went up to the gate and then knocked on one of them using a large metal ring. To Janet's surprise, a very dirty window in the wall opened, and a man's face filled the space.

"Hi John, how are you?" asked Jazz.

"I'm doing OK," said the man with a very strong Welsh accent. "You doing the sun tonight? It's all ready," said John. He disappeared back from the window then Janet saw the gates begin to swing open. John stood in the opening gap, writing down something on some paper on a clipboard.

"So, who's this with you then," He asked, indicating Janet.

"This is Janet, our new GDB," Jazz said as she got back in the buggy.

"The work team is there waiting for you," he said, walking to the side of the road to let them pass. The gates opened into a huge yard surrounded by out buildings. The buildings looked old and well-used. But the thing that got Janet's immediate attention was the structure in the centre of the yard. It was a Sun. It was quite a bit smaller than Janet imagined; it had a radius of ten and a half meters. In fact, it was disappointingly small. Janet tried to work out how it looked so big outside, Jazz, used to people's reactions when seeing the sun for the first time, explained that it is all down to people's perception from their experiences of seeing the sun when on Earth, to put it bluntly, people expect the sun to be big, so they see a big sun.

This psychology made sense to Janet though she felt it was cheating. Due to the size of the sun, the work team took no time to find the defective bulbs and replace them with new ones. However, there were a number of bulbs around the edge of the structure that were dead, which they did not replace. When asked why Jazz explained that the sun was having to shrink because it was very hard to get hold of the bulbs, which were in short supply. So, a decision was made at the senior level to make the sun smaller.

Janet laughed out loud at the thought of the sun being rationed. She also suggested that the nighttime rain was the Environment Team members watering all the plants with watering cans, which in turn made Jazz laugh. Janet did not feel too bad about the actual size of the sun and found the use of psychology to convince Second Chancers that the sun was the sun interesting. After all, if people are susceptible to this mind game, what other ones are they falling for? After overviewing the mending of the sun, they got back in the buggy and left the area. Janet had so many questions to ask Jazz that she struggled to select one to ask. She settled on one question:

"Do you know the place that old people go to?"

"Sorry," said Jazz," What do you mean?"

"Is there a place for them outside of this Second Chance, you know, like a retirement home?" Janet elaborated.

"I don't know; I know they go somewhere; I have not really thought about it that way," Jazz said, looking at Janet.

On the short journey back, they chatted away, finding out what they had in common. Jazz loved swimming. Apparently, she told Janet that there was a heated pool in the Nerve Centre she could have access to. Janet realized that she knew so little about what the Nerve Centre had to offer. She knew it had a fully-fledged gym somewhere. She asked Jazz if she knew where it was, and she happily gave her directions from the canteen. Janet was pleased she had found a friend in Jazz. She seemed so nice and bouncy. Janet had no idea of her age. She was probably older than she looked. Her hair was a beautiful red with no sign of grey, and her complexion was perfect. Janet asked her about her story, interested in finding out how she ended up in Second Chance.

Apparently, Jazz was working a late shift in a call centre on the Friday before Christmas last year. She was tired but looking forward to the holidays. She said bye to her workmates and then went out of the building where she had left her bike. It was locked with a chain to a drainpipe, and she was relieved, still intact. So many bikes around there had been vandalized or stolen. It was pouring with rain, the large drops hitting her body, rolling to the ground as water on the ground met them as they fell. It was getting dark, and the temperature was reading cold. Jazz felt just as miserable as the weather. She had had a tough day at work, which left her feeling that she had not really achieved anything. Still, she was looking forward to being met by her lovely dog, Snoopy, and her son Conor, who was being looked after by her mum.

The rain was relentless, being driven by a north blustery wind; Jazz just wanted to be home. Some cars passed her at speed, going through the puddles at the side of the road where the drains were blocked with rotting leaves. She got drenched as the thoughtless drivers hurried on their way to their homes. The smug drivers sitting in the warm and dry interiors of their cars appeared to mock her, or so it appeared to Jazz. She was approaching a bridge over the rail track when the traffic slowed to a halt for no apparent reason that Jazz could see. Then she spotted the reason for the hold-up. A twit was driving his car erratically, followed by two police cars with blues and twos.

The driver seemed oblivious to the weather, focused instead on escaping the police. He dodged in and out of the traffic lanes, not giving a damm whom he cut up. He then veered directly towards Jazz. She had no space to take evasive action, and the car ran into her bike, crushing her against the wall of the bridge. The last thing she recalled was the noise of her crushing bones. She felt the warmth of blood as it gushed and then trickled out of her body, fading as she died. She arrived at Second Chance with a broken body and felt the loss of her son and family. It had taken her a while to leave the Physical Complex because she needed a lot of healing; also, mentally, she was struggling. In the Mind Complex, she took a while to get to grips with what they could do there; her mind was ravaged by her experiences and her loss. All in all, she had been part of Second Chance for nearly two years, then was offered a place at the Nerve Centre. Janet was keen to find out why she was selected but felt it was not appropriate so soon into their friendship.

After righting the sun, they returned to the office to see if there was anything they had to attend to. As both of them were quite new and GDB's there was always one of the managers on call. Though Jazz assured Janet they seldom had to call one out. Things generally run quite smoothly if everyone does their jobs. With no outstanding work, the night began to drag, and no amount of coffee could stop Janet's eyes from closing. Jazz left her to slumber while she attempted the daily crossword devised by a rather clever member of the Publications Team. Morning came with the sun being hoisted slowly to position, convincing the hapless Second Chancers that dawn was dawn. Dawn brought the end of the night shift for Jazz and Janet, who made their way to their suites to rest. Back in her room, Janet debated whether to go for breakfast or just go to bed. She decided to go to the kitchen and see what there was to eat.

Once there, she said hello to the others and sat down with tea and toast. She reflected on her first night shift, glad that it was over. She was off the next day and had planned to do some exploring, seeing if she could find the swimming pool and the other leisure facilities. Someone had told her there was someone who did wonderful massages. Janet wanted to see if maybe she could book in but was not so sure of where to go. She asked Debbie if she knew where to go, but she did not know, so Janet parked that one until she had more information.

She set off after breakfast, hoping that she would not get lost. It was a vast place with at least six floors and a honeycomb of rooms and departments. It had taken Janet a little while to do her exploring because she was sure she was being watched. She was pretty sure she had been selected to work in the Nerve Centre in order to keep tabs on her. She was sure her boss was reporting to someone higher up about her, but she had no idea how to prove it. Or, maybe, she thought, it could just be paranoia. So, she decided to change into her grey gym clothes that Debbie had kindly found for her. She thought she would have a workout when she found the gym and decided to start at the bottom of the building and work her way up.

The ground floor and first floor were the accommodation block, so she could bypass them. They were unlikely to offer anything useful for her. She took the ramps down to the lower ground floor, which is where she and jazz had taken the buggy from. Janet immediately spotted a door with steps going down to a basement. She was sure that was where Jazz went to get the light bulbs; she rattled the door finding it locked and not responding to her fob key.

She made a mental note to ask Jazz about it at some opportune moment in case she ever needed to get supplies. She took the next door, which went into the garage. There was a mix of vehicles there, including a couple of buggies and what looked like the open-top minibus that was used to give the guided door back when she was a new brownie. There were a few medium-sized vehicles, one of which looked very smart and expensive. She guessed it would be used for special occasions. There didn't seem to be anyone around. She called out to check, but with no response, she walked from the carport to the inside of the garage.

There were three doors off the garage, one big enough for the vehicles to enter and leave, the second, a smaller door which was open with an office on the other side. The office had keys and clipboards and a selection of hand tools, and no end of a loose sheets of paper piled up on the table. The third door, when she looked, led to steps going up and down. The steps going down were blocked by a metal gate with a large, heavy-duty padlock stopping access. The steps going up were free of obstacles, so Janet climbed up the concrete steps.

At the top, there was another door which, despite multiple attempts, Janet could not open. Giving up, she decided that she really wanted to see what was in the basement; the curiosity of a locked gate gnawed at her. She went back down to ground level and then looked to see if anyone was around. Satisfied that she was alone, she popped into the room with keys in it and quickly and furtively scouted around to see if she could find a key small enough to fit a padlock. It did not take long. It was hanging on a peg on the wall with a label on it saying Carport Padlock. Not believing her luck, she grabbed the key, looked around her again then headed to the door leading to the steps.

Her feet sounded so noisy on the concrete stairs, so she tried to go down quietly, stopping only when she got to the locked gate. She held the padlock in one hand and used the other one to use the key to unlock the padlock. The padlock opened with a couple of clicks, and the gate screamed as the hinges moved on little-used pivots. Glancing around, Janet descended the steps; each footstep echoed loudly. Ten steps later, she came to a door. Fearing it would be locked, she considered her time might be wasted. She tentatively pushed the door. It opened easily and quietly. She entered the space, which was in complete darkness. It took a short while for her eyes to adjust to the gloom. She could make out numerous shapes from their outlines.

Janet considered what to do; speaking out loud to herself, she grumbled about finding a torch and about finding where the light switch was. Then an idea came to her, thinking about how the lights in her room and office were voice-controlled. Maybe, just maybe, it was the same here. In which case, what could it be? She tried a few random names with no joy; she stopped to think it through, coming to no conclusion. Thinking she had come to a dead-end and feeling pissed off, she said, "Oh Fuck it, what the hell could it be."

To her delight, the lights switched on! Janet giggled at the thought of the person who had set it up to respond to expletives; she looked around her. She felt a sense of being let down when she saw the room. It was vast, with things on pallets, hundreds of cardboard boxes and several large, locked metal storage containers. There were some gas canisters in one corner of the vast room and an area storing bottles of alcohol. Looking around as she walked, one pallet with some boxes piled high interested her; they were stamped with what looked like the font and colour of NHS National Health Service.

Interested, she went over to see if she could see anything in the boxes, but they were well sealed up, so she gave up on that idea. She was very surprised to see that, so she thought there were connections here with Earth; maybe there was a way back there. She kept that thought in her mind as she continued exploring. At the back of her mind was the awareness of time and the possibility of being caught. She sped up her examination of the space. It was a huge warehouse; she would have expected people to be in and out of there all the time. Having concluded that the space was used for supply storage, she had expected something … what, what had she expected. She wandered around reading labels, checking the contents, trying to fathom out what use they had in Second Chance and how did they get there.

Second Chance was its own complex; she now knew there were others out there, but how did they relate? Are there roads connecting them? So many questions swamped her brain. Maybe in time, her job in the Environment Team will answer some of them. She continued her search for whatever she might find; she spotted some large containers near the middle of the space and went over to see if she could work out what was in them. When she got there, she checked one of the labels to see what it contained. One of the barrels looked like it contained cooking oil, and one contained fat. A couple of used ones were blocking a metal cabinet that had two locks on it. The cabinet was taller than her and looked pretty heavy. Janet's curiosity was heightened again, so she moved one of the part used barrel so she could have a better look. There were two padlocks on the cabinet, one for the top door and one for the larger lower one. She tested the upper lock, which held tight, then tried the lower one.

When she looked at it, she found that the padlock was not locked. She took it off and tried the handles of the door. To her surprise, they opened with ease. Someone had not locked it. Janet couldn't believe her luck. She crouched down to get on the same level as the lower part of the cabinet, which was about two meters high. She looked inside, spotting some dark glass bottles immediately.

They looked like the ones they have in hospitals to hold medicine, she thought, surely, they would not leave medication here unlocked. What if they were dangerous? She picked up one of the bottles and gently shook it, then read the label. The contents said that it was Fentanyl which Janet knew was a controlled drug. With her interest growing, she made a mental count of the number of bottles, twenty-one. She checked the labels of some of the other bottles, which all said the same. Janet found it incredulous that they would store a strong opiate in an open cabinet. She took stock of this, thinking that maybe they infused this drug through the walls of the Physical Complex.

The management of the infusions lay jointly between the Environment Team and the Medical Team in the Nerve Centre. One of her workmates assumed responsibility for monitoring the levels and administering them. It felt weird to see the bottles of this highly potent drug in her hand. She was tempted to take one of them for her own recreational use, considered it, put the bottle back, then quickly secreted a bottle under her tunic, deciding her exploring should probably end there. Then she noticed on the lower shelf some more bottles. It was less obvious to her what it was, but then she saw one of those information sheets that come with medications. She took one to read and skimmed through the medical language. She gathered the drug was an enzyme that caused the defection of a protein, causing instability of a protein blah blah blah. She gave up after that and was none the wiser, and in fear of being caught, she took the leaflet and stuffed it in the pocket of her trousers. She closed the door of the cabinet, replaced the canisters, and made her way back to the door. She tried to turn off the light using the password of expletives with no joy. Janet decided to leave it, started to climb the concrete stairs, and passed through the gate. She locked the gate and took the remaining few steps to the door of the carport. To her dismay, she spotted a couple of women heading from the key room to one of the buggies.

A third person was opening the two large doors by pressing a button on one of the doors. They opened silently and quickly, showing the emerging picture of the late spring day. The lady driver and passenger started up the vehicle, selected first gear then released the hand brake. The buggy left the forecourt, and then the man dressed in a dark grey top and blue bottoms closed the door using a button outside. Janet spotted the man who closed the door jump on board the vehicle settling to sit on the back seat of the buggy. While this was happening, Janet froze, hoping to merge with the walls.

She held her breath, fearful they would hear the mechanics of respiration. With the coast clear, she quickly replaced the key and then made her way back to her room. Fortunately, she did not see anyone on her journey, and she felt as if her heart was beating in her ears. She hurried back, locking the door behind her when she got in. Janet sat down on her bed and tried to settle her breath and fast heart rate. She removed her ill-gotten gains from their hiding places and put them first on the bed. She wondered where there would be a good place to secrete the bottle and leaflet, finally deciding to put them in the cupboard on the wall in the bathroom until she could locate a better hiding place. She made herself a cup of tea and took it out to the garden. She looked around it, thinking about how she could put her stamp on it, flowers would look nice, but she had no idea how to go about getting some. Maybe she could go out to the nursery where she used to work and ask for some. She decided she would ask Debbie about it. She drank her tea quickly, then checked the clock in the kitchen as she had lost touch with the time. She felt hungry, with the clock confirming that, indeed, it was time for food. She needed to behave as normal, so she left her room and made her way to the kitchen and dining room to see what was on offer.

Debbie greeted her with a smile, telling Janet what was on the menu. It all sounded nice to Janet it was hard to make a decision. She hummed and harred until finally settling on a mushroom omelette with salad. Once she sat down at one of the tables, she tried to engage in conversation with the others in the room. She decided to see if they could tell her where the gym was; Stephen told her that it was on the fourth floor, along with the swimming pool. Janet decided to go along there later that day after lunch had settled.

Janet was unclear about her morning's expedition when she gave it some thought. She felt uneasy having taken the bottle of Fentanyl and realized that was probably a mistake. The powers that be must have a way to monitor the storage of such a strong drug. Perhaps complacency had set in. Whatever, she was sure it would be missed. But could she dare take a chance and return it?

After all, it was there to help damaged people cope when they first entered Second Chance in the Physical Complex. Battling with her conscience, she left the dining room and went back to her room. Janet changed into her gym clothes, grabbed a towel and her swimming costume then set off in search of the gym and pool. As soon as she came out of the lift on the fourth floor, she found it easily. The lift door opened slowly, giving Janet a chance to enter the hall space that had stained glass windows on two sides. They gave a great but distorted view of Second Chance. Looking, she spotted the nursery she used to work in, and there, there was the social club entrance. She missed all of that, the work, her friends and her life as a brownie. She saw signs in the room to the gym and swimming pool with arrows, so she had no problem finding them.

Once she had found the gym and said hello to the other people there, she put down her luggage heading towards the treadmill. The treadmill had one of those screens that showed your progress on a route. She played around with speed and slope happily, surprised that at a walking pace, she did OK. Getting off the treadmill, she did some stretches before lifting free weights. She really did not have much idea of what she was doing, so she tried to make it look like she did it for the benefit of the other people using the gym. She used some of the resistance machines to work her arm and leg muscles and then completed her workout on the recumbent bike. She wiped the sweat off her face with a towel and left the gym with her head held high; she had not embarrassed herself.

While in the gym, she saw a door at the far end of the gym opposite the door she had come in. It was signed as the 'swimming pool', so she headed towards it. She went to the door, opened it then walked through. On the other side, the first thing she noticed was a row of changing cubicles then on her left was the pool. There was no one else there; she would have the pool to herself. She quickly changed into her costume and then approached the pool. She tested the temperature with her hand and then walked back down the steps into the pool.

Once in, she bobbed under the water to get her whole body immersed, then set off for the far side with a breaststroke. She found it very easy to swim in this water; it certainly tasted better than the lake that had a vegetation smell about it. She set herself a goal of doing ten lengths, figuring that would be good on top of her gym workout. She completed her lengths, got out of the pool then headed back into the same cubicle to dry and dress into her gym clothes. She felt proud of her achievements; she had really challenged herself and succeeded. With her head held high, she left the pool and crossed through the gym to start the walk back to her dorm. She was walking back towards the lift when two men stopped her passage. They were tall, dressed in dark blue and looked like they lived in the gym. One of them looked down at her five-foot-two height, saying, "Janet, yes?"

"Yes," replied Janet, really unsure of herself.

"We've been asked to talk to you. Rumour has it that you are delving into things that don't concern you. Any more, you will get a strike against you. Do you understand?"

"I'm not sure what you mean, but thank you for bringing it to my attention" Janet mumbled as she pushed past them. Breathless, she hurried to her room, brushing past a couple of people in the corridor. She closed the door of her suite, finally feeling able to breathe. She was right. She was being watched. What else could it be? She thought. Janet spent the remainder of the day in her garden drinking a mug of tea after tea after tea. She felt afraid to go out and get food but rather worried about staying in case her room was unsafe. She figured a safe place was the garden, though, without a doubt, they could even be spying on her there. She was going back into her kitchen to get another drink when it occurred to her to check on her ill-gotten gains in the bathroom cabinet. She walked into the room and opened the cabinet door.

Looking inside, she was assured that the bottle and leaflet were still where she had put them. She picked them up and took them into the bedroom. She unfolded the information sheet she had 'borrowed' and tried to decode the heavy use of medical terminology. Her translation did little to understand the use of the drug; it appeared to be a genotoxic chemical that interferes with the cell nucleus causing the ends of chromosomes to atrophy, causing premature ageing, whatever all that meant. She could not imagine why this would relate to life on Second Chance. Janet folded it back up and put it aside.

Janet wished she was back with the Brownies and her friends. Life was simple there, tending the plants, playing games, and drinking the very rough beer made locally. Janet wondered if they ever thought of her; she really wanted to go back. She did not feel safe. Bar Jazz and Debbie had not made friends, and the place felt unfriendly despite all the smiley faces. She missed not walking around the grounds and swimming in the lake, and there was little chance for that in the Nerve Centre.

Boy, was Janet on a downer. She reached for the Fentanyl, wondering how concentrated it was. She struggled to remove the seal on the bottle by hand, and in the end, with no joy and two broken fingernails, she went into the kitchen to get a knife. With a bit of twisting, the seal broke, and the bottle opened easily. Janet first sniffed the mixture and then poured a tiny bit into a cup. She resealed the bottle, added a quantity of water into the cup with the Fentanyl then took a deep breath. She raised the china vessel to her mouth and took a small sip. It tasted fowl; her mouth felt like it was burning.

She rushed to the kitchen tap running cold water and drunk and drunk to stop the sensation. It was at this point she remembered that Fentanyl is a topical pain killer; it was infused, and this bottle was a concentrate. she poured the remainder of the Fentanyl and water down the drain and downed more fresh water. Eventually, the burning eased, but then she felt the effects of the swallowed drug. Oh boy. When it hit her system, she initially felt a rush of warmth followed by nausea followed by weird sensations over her body. She went into her bedroom and lay down to keep herself safe, ironic really as she was doing something entirely unsafe.

If she got high on opium, for Janet, it was hard to tell. She felt the rush of the drug sweep over her body again and again. Her head felt muzzy, in a nice way; her thoughts were drifting here, there and everywhere. In time, she fell asleep and entered a weird night world with dreams that made no sense at all.

She felt partly human the next morning. She was on the night shift, so she had time to get back to the whole human. She felt absolutely drained. Janet took a shower which helped to remove some of the lethargy; she dressed, tidied her bed, brushed her hair then ventured out of her room and down the corridor to the dining room.

"You look rough. Are you going down with something?" Asked Debbie, "What do you fancy eating? Toast? Cooked?"

"Cooked," Janet replied, feeling sure that a fry-up would help, give her something for her stomach to work on, or that was what is said the morning after a bender. She helped herself to a mug of tea and sat down at a table offering a good view of the room and corridor. A few minutes later, Debbie scooted over with a tray on her lap containing Janet's breakfast.

"There you go, that will help," she said as she placed the tray on the table; she turned around and wheeled her way back into the kitchen. Nice as Debbie was, Janet could not trust anyone; who knows whose reported whom or what. Janet felt very uneasy as she looked around the room. There were a couple of other diners in the room who smiled and waved at her comradely. Janet smiled back without feeling it; she was on high alert. When she had finished her meal which did not help her feeling of lethargy, she waited until Debbie was free. Janet called her over and asked her about getting plants for her garden.

"Yes, I can order them for you, that's no problem; tell me what you want, and I will get on with it. I'm glad you are settling in; it can take a while here. It is so different to the other areas of Second Chance." With that, she wheeled back into her kitchen to start washing the dishes. Janet wondered if Debbie had ever had a bad day. She seemed to be always smiling, and for Debbie, that was a true smile, not the false ones that she got from people she did not know. For the rest of the morning, Janet stayed in the communal area of the dorm. She settled down to read a very old and worn magazine. When she looked at the date it was published, it said 2016; she was surprised it was still intact at that age. Still, the magazine had some good stories in it, and even the adverts were interesting as they reminded her of home. At lunchtime, she opted for something light and then took herself off to bed for a sleep before the start of her shift.

That night she was in the office checking over various papers, sorting data and compiling reports for the team meeting the next day. Janet felt exhausted, not so much from working the night shift, which is a battle against nature, but from worry and stress and a hangover. She knew she had to be careful but also knew she was close to something that the dark blue shirts didn't want her to be nearby. She was a tough cookie who felt she had nothing really to fear as she was already dead and did not really want to be in Second Chance. She had given time to think that Second Chance had links with other similar complexes and Earth. After all, all Newbies come from Earth, so there must be a way to transport broken bodies here.

Maybe, just maybe, she mused, she could find a way back to Earth. That thought thrilled her to think that only several months ago, she had killed herself as she could not bear to be alive; now, being alive or dead was acceptable to her. She felt sure if she kept a low profile, they would see that she took heed of the warning while putting out her feelers. It seemed like a plan. She carried on with shuffling papers and then checked on her 'to-do' list what else had to be done.

The next item written down was to do a stock take of the stationary cabinet and Alan's cupboard. Alan was one of her work colleagues who had joint responsibility for managing the Fentanyl infusions. It seemed odd that there were tight controls over the infusions but none with the storage of the drug. Anyway, she decided to prioritise that task over the stock take. She sat down on Alan's chair next to the cupboard. It was unlocked, funny that thought Janet as she opened the two doors displaying three shelves, one containing Fentanyl bottles, one with books, ledgers and files, and the third was empty.

It did not seem necessary to do a stock take when there was so little there, but she went through the motions. Just then, she stopped. She thought about the task she had been told to do and wondered if someone was laying down a trap. But what? Why? Who? She pulled herself up to stop herself from going down that thought train, exhaled and told herself out loud that she was paranoid and stupid. Janet returned to her stock check, cross-referencing the last few items in the cupboard against the number she had on her list. Just then, the title of one of the books caught her attention.

She picked it up to study it and then dropped it by mistake. Her fingers were temporally not engaged with her brain. The book fell to the floor and opened with a table of names, dates, weights and dosages. Janet picked it up to take a closer look. It seemed an odd thing to find, which is why it attracted her attention. She quickly scanned the names when she came across a familiar name, Wendy Faright. Could it be Marks Wendy? Janet reread the data. The date was about right. She looked down the list of names with increased scrutiny to see if there were any others she knew. Around a couple of months ago, Janet saw the name Barbara Sunnit.

Janet thought that that must be the Barbara she knew from the minibus back when she was first a Brownie. Janet opened the book to the next page of data. Towards the end of the entries, she saw another familiar name, Linda, Lisa's baby. Janet's eyes misted over; she wiped her eyes with the back of her hand and re-focused. What did this mean? Janet was no further forward to working out what this Graduation was. The list was sure of those who had Graduated. Then she saw another name of someone she knew, Ron, or one-armed Ron as they used to know him; he had just disappeared one day. He had two Fetchers assigned to him, but he was very dependent on them as he had lost both legs and his right arm, hence his nickname.

Did they go on to a better place? Maybe they returned to Earth, or maybe they were killed. Janet was aware she was holding her breath; she forced herself to exhale, stood up, walked around a bit, and then sat back on the chair that happily took her weight. She closed the book, replaced it on the shelf with the others, closed the two doors, and stood up again. She decided it was time for a coffee break and set about the mechanics of making that happen. So many thoughts whizzed around her head it was like an itch she could not scratch. The rest of her shift went quickly as she was so distracted. Somehow, she had managed to complete her to-do list and hand it over to the morning shift. Janet could not recall her walking back to her suite or eating her morning meal.

She became consciously aware when she went back into her room with the door firmly closed behind her. Only then she began to relax. Debbie knocked on her door a little later to get the list of plants Janet wanted. She had not gotten around to writing it down yet, so Janet did it while Debbie was there. Debbie asked Janet if she was OK, and she seemed quite distracted. Janet did her best to reassure her that she was fine, just missing home.

This is something the majority of inmates of Second Chance could relate to. Debbie left her to start preparations for lunch while Janet sat in her garden thinking. She was trying to get it together to go for a swim, but really, she would have preferred to swim in the lake than the pool upstairs. A bit later, she talked herself into moving; she picked up her swimming costume and a towel and made her way to the swimming pool. She was fully aware of all the people around her on her way to the pool; she felt as if everyone was staring at her or following her. Janet realized her paranoid thoughts were unhealthy and tried to focus her mind on the journey instead. She had the pool to herself again that day. She swam fifteen lengths before stopping and sitting on the side of the pool with her legs in the water. She got her breath and then noticed that the hairs on her arms were standing up; she looked around her and then caught sight of someone by the door to the pool from the gym. Janet turned around a bit to get a better view, but whoever it was, they had gone. Janet's brain did summersaults thinking through who was there and what they wanted until her voice of reason came through the murk. Maybe, just maybe, it was someone new looking for the pool.

Yes, that had to be it, she thought, then got back in the water to swim out her tension. Six lengths later, she stopped swimming until she got her breath back and then decided to get out of the water. She grabbed her towel that had been left in a pile near the steps going down into the pool. She wiped her face and arms, then went off into the changing cubicle. Janet didn't really understand why more people didn't use the swimming pool. It must cost a fortune to keep it running, what with chlorination and heat. Still, she was happy to use it on her own. Once she had dressed, she walked back to her wing to see if she could find Debbie. Debbie was in her office filling in supply from her head down, focusing on her task. She looked up when she heard Janet walk across the kitchen's tiled floor. Janet stood in the doorway, looking at Debbie hard at work. "Sorry to disturb you, Debbie," Janet said.

"No problem. Do you need something?" Debbie said, putting down her pen.

"Do you know if there are security cameras around the public area?" she said.

"Oh my, that's a loaded question; the answer is the Inner Circle. Look in at everything, and always think to yourself that someone is watching you; why, has something happened?" Debbie asked, looking concerned.

"No, but, well, I'm not sure; I think I saw someone checking up on me when I was in the swimming pool, though I can't be sure," Janet said.

"There is a good chance he or she was. After all, you were brought here, so they knew where you were," Debbie said.

"How do you know that? Did they tell you?" asked Janet feeling distinctively uneasy.

"No, but that's the usual reason when coming over is done within hours instead of planned over a period of time. I, like you, was brought over quickly. I don't know if they are still watching me or if they have accepted me now," Debbie said. Janet sat down on the chair by the wall, feeling suddenly giddy. She thought as much but had no idea that Debbie had a history like that.

"Now, do you fancy some cake? It's your favourite, carrot cake," Debbie said, moving her chair with her joystick away from the desk. She went into the kitchen and put a plate on her lap with a cake on it. It looked delicious, thought Janet, who got hold of a couple of plates and a knife to slice it. They ate cake with mugs of tea and enjoyed some light banter. A couple of other residents came into the dining room, and Debbie cut them both a slice. The cake tasted amazing; the balance of spices was done brilliantly. Debbie had even made little carrots made of icing as decoration.

Debbie had to go back to work, so Janet went into her flat. She sat out in the garden with her diary and planned what to write. She now had an idea that it wasn't in her imagination about being followed; she would just have to keep her head low for a little while until they got bored. She then thought about the book she had read with the names of people whom she knew had disappeared, presumed graduated. She recalled her emotions when she read the names of people she knew, even tiny little baby Linda. She knew things that sounded strange, but as yet, she couldn't link it all together. Her attention then went to the bottle of Fentanyl she had taken.

She needed to get rid of the bottle, but if she was being watched, that would prove to be difficult. She decided to leave it where it was for now until she came up with a solution. Having written her diary and having had a swim, she had done all there was to do on her day off. She decided to see if any of her wingmates were doing something she could join in, a game of cards or something like that. She walked down the corridor into the day room, but there was only one person in there. It was Don; he worked as a Nerve Centre worker wearing grey and blue. He knew nearly enough everyone who worked at the Nerve Centre and was a great source of gossip. Janet asked him about his day, and he took his cue to tell her all that was going on.

About who was sleeping with whom and who had been promoted or demoted. He certainly saw a lot as he went around the centre mending this and that. Janet smelt the smell of cooking food and made a bet with Don about what it was for dinner. Janet thought it smelt like a casserole or a stew. Don put his money on it being veg chilli. When Debbie came into the room, they quizzed her about what she was cooking to see who had won, as it was neither of them got it right; Debbie had prepared a pasta bake. She let them know that it would be ready in half an hour, then left them to lay the table. Janet went over to give her a hand with the table bringing in glasses and jugs of water.

Dinner was delicious; Debbie certainly made them eat well. She had not only baked the pasta, but she had also found time to make an upside-down pineapple pudding with custard. After eating, Janet did the washing up for Debbie while she finished off her paperwork. She had budget sheets to work out, trying to stretch the costs as far as she could. Janet put down her t-towel when she had finished and dried her hands on a towel. She went to Debbies office to bid her goodnight, then went to her room. She sat to read for a while until she had had enough, then undressed for bed. She closed the curtains in the lounge and bedroom, then went to her bed and lay down.

She was not really feeling sleepy, but she was trying to sleep because of boredom. She had gotten used to going down the social club as a Brownie; they didn't seem to have anything like that here, she thought. She turned off the bedside light and lay there waiting for sleep to come, but it didn't. She was finding it hard to adjust to working nights. It upset everything. At around twelve o'clock, she got out of bed and went to sit outside. It was raining, but she didn't care; she could not bare being in her bed any longer. She felt like going outside for a walk but knew that security guards were patrolling around. She had gotten used to seeing them when she was a Brownie. But her room was doing her head in, so she thought she would get herself dressed to go outside for a short while. The break might help her to sleep, she reckoned. Once dressed, she put her fob key around her neck and then left her room, trying not to make any noise.

There were no signs of lights around the doors, so she assumed everyone was asleep. As her room was on the ground floor, it didn't take long for her to get to the door leading outside. The whoosh door opened, and Janet stepped through into the evening. The rain was wonderfully refreshing, she thought as she walked away from the Nerve Centre. She saw she was near the garage, but there was no sign of life. She couldn't hear any noise except for the gentle fall of rain and her own steps and breathing. She slowed down to get the full effect of the rain caressing her body. Her clothes began to stick to her, and drops were falling off her hair into her face. She carried on walking past the garage with the aim of going up to the social club. It was unlikely she would see anyone there, it would have closed by now, but she just wanted to see something familiar. Just ahead of her, she saw a beam of light. She looked up to see the source and then followed her gaze up until she saw the face of a security guard. She approached Janet and asked her what she was doing out this time of night.

"I couldn't sleep, so I thought I would get some air," Janet explained.

"What's your name, and which wing are you on?" demanded the lady. Janet gave her the information she wanted and then waited for the security guard to speak. "Don't you know about the dangers around at nighttime? Not everyone on Second Chance is nice; you should go back to your wing." Janet agreed and then turned around to start the walk back. To her annoyance, the guard followed her until Janet entered the building using the door she had used earlier. At that point, the guard moved away, sweeping the area with her torch to see if there was anyone else around. Janet made the short walk to her wing and let her in with her fob key. She unlocked her own flat and ordered the light to come on. She sat on her sofa in her lounge and thought about what had just happened. The guard was right. Janet had assumed that everyone on Second Chance was nice, that it was safe there. She undressed and dried her hair with a towel, then got ready for bed. She felt a bit tired and hoped that this time she would fall asleep.

Chapter 12
Changes

The next day she was working an afternoon shift with Jazz. Jazz was a breath of fresh air, and she seemed to have boundless energy and a positive view of life. Janet always felt better around her. They were supervising some maintenance jobs outside of the Nerve Centre, taking readings of the water pressure, re-painting of two of the stars and checking the irrigation system in three of the nurseries with the head of each of the buildings. Janet did wosnder if one of them would be where Gary worked, but she knew there were loads of polytunnels and greenhouses on Second Chance. As it was, she did not see Gary, which she felt was a shame. Janet felt odd being around the Brownies during the day. Somehow, she felt as if she was above them, which in some ways was actually true. She was not too pleased coming to that conclusion. But despite seeing quite a few faces of those she recognized, there was no Mel, Lisa or Kim. Still, it was lovely being outside despite knowing that all the features of the outside, the air, sun, moon and stars, were fabricated; in fact, Second Chance was just one very large stage. It felt strange to think that it was not cracked up as others would believe. The work was boring, the company boring the dormitories and living spaces lonely. Very few workers in the Nerve Centre found love, and friendship was the best you could hope for. She felt a little sad at that as she remembered her nights with Gary.

"Janet, back to earth," said Jazz, nudging Janet, "you are miles away."

"Sorry, I miss not working here," she said, indicating with a sweep of her hands the nurseries.

"Yes, the Nerve Centre is very different; I worked as a teacher when I was a Brownie." I liked working with the little ones; they were always so optimistic. They carried on collecting information about the irrigation system. They needed to make sure the water pressure was right, and the hoses were not damaged or blocked. Once they had finished all their jobs, they made their way back to the department to log everything on the data base. She had been given permission to use a few websites for her research into bird songs. The Inner Circle always restricted the search to specific sites so people would not be tempted to look at things which may link to their past. There was no social media on Second Chance. In fact, Janet thought, she really does not miss having her iPhone and other gadgets. She was happy to read or sew in her spare time, and now Debbie was going to order her some plants to go in her garden; she would be able to enjoy that space and caring for them.

Back in the office, Janet approached Andrew. She said, "Hi, Andrew. Do you mind if we have a chat sometime?"

"Yes, of course, Janet, I will be free straight after tea. Is that good for you?" he replied.

"That would be great, thank you," Janet said, then turned away to go back to her workstation. It was not long until teatime. She had time to plan out what she wanted to say. She ate light at tea. Sandwiches and a lemon meringue pie. She really loved her sweet things. Once she had finished, she grabbed another tea in a recyclable cup to take back to the office with her. She sipped it en route, still going over and over what she wanted to say to Andrew. When she got back, she saw he was in deep conversation with Jazz, so she went to her desk and started preparing printouts for the team meeting the next day. After about ten minutes, Jazz returned. Janet was not sure if she should go over to Andrews's office or wait for him to come and get her. She often struggled with situations like that. It was part of office etiquette that eluded her. As it was, Andrew came over to her desk and invited her to follow him into his office. He closed the door and invited Janet to sit.

"What can I do for you, Janet," he asked, dropping his head towards his left shoulder.

"Well, I have been giving this a lot of thought, well, what I want to say, well, umm, I really want to go back," she garbled.

"Sorry, go back where," he asked, picking up a pen mindlessly.

"I really want to go back to being a Brownie and work as a gardener. Can you help me?" She said in a rush. Andrew moved about in his chair a bit, then looked at her in the eye.

"It takes a bit of time to get used to working here; you will settle in. How are you finding the work?" he asked.

"It's interesting, but not really my cup of tea. I prefer more hands-on work, you know, physically demanding ones." Janet replied now she was the one shifting in her seat. She could not meet his eye, so she set her gaze on the upper part of his grey tunic.

"You are doing well here, but if you like, I could ask around to see where there may be other vacancies and get back to you."

"Really," said Janet, moving forward in her chair, "that would be great, thanks."

Janet was not sure what it was she wanted, but maybe working for another team would give her job satisfaction. But despite that, she needed to stay under the radar for a while. Janet was the kind of person who felt directionless. She had no goals or ambitions to work towards, happily drifting as she thought life was unexciting. Being someone who rode hard on emotions, with the extremes being chaotic and dangerous, her Bipolar had put her in perilous conditions. Yet she felt no fear, no regrets, nothing about it. The change was hard for Janet; like most people, she could see the positives and negatives, the pros and cons, all of making any hard decision work. The only decisions she felt sure about were around ending her own life. She was a middle-aged woman with no children, no pets, no really close friends, no partner, and no aims, just plodding through life until she woke up smelling the roses. Whatever it was, she was on the cusp of, and she was sure her life would be much different. She sat down and turned on the computer to do her research. She needed a list of birds who join the morning choir and, ideally, recordings of the birds. She found the three sites that had been vetted by the Inner Circle for her to use and opened up one of them. As she read the information about the dawn chorus, she realized it was a bit more complicated than she first thought. There were regional variations of the singing by the birds, which Janet didn't know about. As Janet was in a fabricated world, she had the power to select from the examples the one she liked best. She selected the one she thought was more melodic and found out the types of birds that contributed to the sound.

She then downloaded the chorus and saved it on the computer in a folder accessible through the home screen. She then looked at the other two sites to see if they had anything to add to her research, but they near enough confirmed what the first site had said and had sound examples of listening to. Janet, having finished her work on the computer, closed it down and then looked at her to-do list to see what was next. Just then, the phone rang, that was something that rarely happened, and several people got up to answer it. Andrew was the most senior, so he took the phone call while the others milled around. He started to write things down on a pad of paper next to the phone and said a number of 'yesses' and 'no's' before putting the receiver down and confronting the crowd. Apparently, someone who was drunk had knocked over and damaged the weather station placed at the far end of Second Chance. He asked for someone to go and check it out and to take Janet along with them.

Tom volunteered and asked Andrew if any of the workforces were going there. Andrew confirmed that they were on their way and would meet them there. Janet was asked to use the phone to call the garage to book a buggy which she did, stating that it was needed immediately. Tom and Janet left the department and walked together to the garage forecourt. There was already a three-seater buggy waiting for them, complete with a driver. Luckily Tom knew where they were going and ordered the driver to go to the far wall. He seemed to know where it was and started up the buggy. Janet enjoyed the journey watching as the Brownies left their workplaces at the end of their working day. It always surprised her just how many people lived on Second Chance and the range of work available.

Janet looked out on the crop fields on either side with the road in a valley. She saw an area with what looked like vines with grapes, a heavy burden on the thin stalks. She saw a group of people digging up potatoes from a long strip of soil; they turned over the ground with a garden fork and then bent over to pick up the white vegetable. Janet saw the long high wall in the distance. Apparently, it ran all the way around Second Chance marking the boundary with access only for people who worked for the Nerve Centre. She had not been to this particular part of the wall, but as before, there were large gates that enabled access and someone manning the entrance gate. She came out when the buggy drew near. Seeing Tom and Janet, she turned around and manually opened both gates allowing passage. In this area, there was housing for the Nerve Centre workers, some outbuildings and what looked like a farmhouse.

The building looked old and decrepit. It was hard to imagine anyone actually living there. In the courtyard by the gate, Tom pointed out the weather station to Janet, and the buggy driver stopped nearby. The passengers alighted and walked over to the station. It looked like it had been pushed over. The casing had buckled, and the structure had fallen on its side. Tom knelt down to see if he could unlock the door to see the equipment inside. Failing that, he asked Janet to give him a hand to stand the structure up. The buggy driver offered to help Tom, so Janet stood back and watched the men righten the station.

Once it was up, it leaned heavily to one side, but Tom was able to unlock the door. The innards were not intact; the mechanical parts were twisted out of recognition. Tom got into the buggy to where he had placed some tools and took out a large screwdriver to take out the screws securing the station to the concrete floor. It took a little while, but in the end, they were able to lift the station up and over to the back of the buggy. Tom put the screwdriver and screws into his bag and then encouraged Janet to get in the buggy to take the weather station to the workshop to see if it could be repaired. Tom, Janet and the driver headed back to the centre of Second Chance to the Nerve Centre. There, Tom dropped Janet off as it was the end of her shift while he took the weather station to the workshop with the help of the buggy driver. Janet was on her way to her room when she spotted Andrew walking ahead of her down a corridor. She called out to him, which he heard and turned round. He stopped and then started to walk back to her. Andrew asked Janet what had happened on her excursion, and she told him. He nodded, then wished her good night and set off on his way. Senior members of staff like Andrew didn't live on a wing like Janet but had bungalows for their own use at the back of the Nerve Centre. They had a maid who worked for two or three of them. Janet imagined that it must be even lonelier being there than she experienced where she was.

Andrew's life was so much different now from the life he had on Earth. A happily married man with two girls and a dog named Rosie, he worked six days a week running a pub. He loved his life and his work and being a very social kind of person. He always gave the patrons his full attention. It was kicking out time in May last year that his life ended. It still was not entirely dark outside; certainly, visibility was good with all the lights of the pub shining forth.

Andrew ushered two young men towards the door, so he could lock up and then he could do a tidy-up before bed. He felt tired that night; it had been hectic with the Friday work crowd. His wife, Melissa, was behind the bar putting empty bottles in the crate for recycling. At that point, a man came out of the area where the toilets were situated. He was weaving around, looking like he had had one drink to many.

Andrew unlocked one of the doors for him to exit, but instead of leaving, he lurched towards Andrew. "Gimme another beer, then I will go," he asked.

"No, it's chucking out time, time to go home." Said Andrew, trying to guide the drunken man towards the open door.

"I'll be the one to decide that, not you" he slurred.

Andrew took hold of the man's arm to lead him out; the man pulled his arm upwards so Andrew could not get hold of it. Melissa, aware of the commotion left her spot behind the bar, came over to give Andrew a hand with the inebriated man.

"Billy, it's time to go," she said, standing next to Andrew.

"Melissa, one more, please. Then I'll go home." The man argued.

"No, you've had enough" Melissa replied.

"You can't tell me that; I know when I've had enough," he raised his voice while saying that, clearly, his hackles were raised. Then he lurched towards Melissa, almost falling on her, shouting and swearing about his rights, whatever there were. Melissa lost her footing and fell to the ground. She did not make a sound as she fell. Andrew went towards her to give her a hand up when he realized she had a growing red stain on her blouse. He looked at it as the blood spilt out of her aorta. Finally, he realized what had happened; he looked up from his crouched position only to see Melissa's attacker standing over him with a large knife dripping with blood, Melissa's blood.

Billy struck Andrew with the knife. Andrew put his hands up to block his face, but Billy aimed lower, cut his jugular vein with the weapon then just stared at Andrew as his lifeblood left his body. Andrew died next to his wife, but only he ended up at Second Chance; it was Melissa's time to die but not his. How these decisions are made is complicated and made by a higher order. He came to Second Chance in a state of anger and confusion. He spent a lot of time wandering around to see if he could find Melissa. When he finally concluded that she was not there, he settled in quite quickly. Once out of the Mind Complex, he took to working in the small department that made aids and adaptions. He did well there and enjoyed his work. He learnt lots of new skills and showed an aptitude for the work. His skills did not go unnoticed, and within a few months, he was head-hunted to work in the environment department working as GDB. Then he was promoted twice to end up being one of the managers of a team. He was prone to suffering from bouts of depression and, when low in mood, could lose his temper. People working with him got to know the signs and found them tiptoeing around him at certain times. So far, Janet had only seen him at his best. He was a good boss, one that actually listened.

Back in her flat, she sat in her garden thinking about her day. She was pleased that Andrew had sent her on the 'emergency'. It gave her another insight into the job. She made herself a coffee and then sat back down in her chair, admiring the pattern of froth on top of her coffee. It looked like Jesus Christ, she thought. Jesus got drunk quickly, with Janet realizing that it was nearly time to eat. She did not feel very hungry but went to the dining room, ready to see what delights Debbie had prepared. She produced a veggie con Carne with rice which smelt enticing. Janet asked for a small portion and ate it slowly, savouring every mouth full. The lady sat at the same table as she was new and started asking Janet some questions about the place.

Janet answered her questions and then asked her where she would be working. She said that she was going to be a cleaner at some of the rooms where members of the Inner Circle live. She was looking forward to starting the next day. After dinner, Janet thanked Debbie for the meal and then returned to her room to think about going to bed. She was tired today, she had thought about going to the gym, but now, she just wanted to rest. She sat outside in the garden with her diary. She wrote about her day nearly enough, writing a second to-do list which was now a done list.

Janet stretched, then stood up and walked the four steps to the wall of her garden. She wondered when her plants would arrive; the ones she had chosen would really lift the place. She tried to picture their bright colours along the walls hiding the ugly brick work. She had requested a fruit tree and some strawberry plants along with the shrubs. Hopefully, they would come soon, she thought, then she turned round and headed indoors, locking the door behind her. She drew the curtains and then went into her bedroom to undress and get ready for bed. She debated the idea of having a cup of tea, but she really felt too lazy to bother. She lay in her bed thinking about what Andrew would come up with as a new job for her, then felt herself relax and drop into sleep.

On the next shift, Andrew assigned her to work with Alan, the person who regulated the amount of Fentanyl infused through the walls of the Physical Complex. She thought it rather odd that this would happen, seeing her recent dallying with the drug and hoped it was not done deliberately to trip her up. Her suspicions were that it was a planned, thoughtful intervention, but nevertheless, she made her way to his workspace in the office. Alan started off by giving her a talk about the use of Fentanyl and the importance of accurate dosage depending on the number of Newbies in the complex requiring pain relief. He showed her the file where recordings were made and explained the data input to her. Once the briefing was over, they left the department and headed off towards the ground level.

To Janet's dismay, Alan took her to the underground warehouse where she had been exploring recently and took the bottle of Fentanyl. It was as clear as day to Janet where they were heading. She felt weird, with mixtures of dread and anxiety. Nevertheless, she fell into step with Alan as he navigated the way to the large cupboard containing the dangerous chemicals. This time though, there was a heavy-duty combination lock on it which certainly was not there before. Alan inserted the code and then opened the cupboard as Janet finally exhaled her long-held breath. Alan was saying stuff to her, none of which registered with her; she gave herself a virtual kick up the bum in order to let his words register; he mentioned a recent loss of a bottle which is being thoroughly investigated. Janet held those words in her mind. She felt frozen to the spot and aware, so aware of each and every breath she took. She mumbled something in response that seemed to satisfy Alan. Alan reached into the cabinet, taking out a bottle of Fentanyl; as he did that, he said, "who ever took it will get a strike and possibly enforced Graduation." "Why was the cabinet not locked before," asked Janet.

"How do you know it was not locked?" Alan responded, looking intently at her.

"I assumed, you know, if it was stolen, you know" she stumbled over her words.

"Well, yes, anyway, let's go," with that, he closed the cupboard and reset the combination lock. Janet felt worried about her slip-up; she hoped that Alan would not think too much about it. They made their way back to the ground floor, where a vehicle was parked. It was one of the little buggies. "Hop in," said Alan as he took the driving seat. Once she was on board, they set off to go to the

Physical Complex. They sat in silence as he drove, Janet taking in her surroundings with mock interest while trying to settle down her fast-beating heart. She chastised herself for her words and reaction, and she was really not too sure if she came across the right way. Fifteen minutes later, they came to two large gates. The one on the right was attended by a dark grey and blue clothed guard who waved to Alan in recognition. He opened the gate revealing a garden scape immediately familiar to Janet.

She recognized the area she used to sit when she was a Newbie when life was confusing but simple when she laughed and teased Mark, where she had attempted to take her life. She stroked the scar tissue on her wrist as she remembered that. Bringing herself to the here and now, Alan steered the buggy to a door that Janet could not recall seeing, but if you are not looking for a door, you may well not see it, she thought. Janet alighted from the vehicle and entered the door, which opened with a key. The space behind the door afforded little room for two adult-sized bodies forcing Janet to get a bit closer to Alan than she wished, especially as he had B.O. She watched as he opened a hatch, removed an upside-down spent bottle and placed the new bottle of Fentanyl in its place, and closed the hatch.

Alan typed something on a keypad under the place for the bottle, but he typed too quickly for Janet to see. Janet expecting to leave, turned around to go out of the door when she felt hands on her breasts. She pushed them off. Alan grabbed her hands, pinning her onto the wall. He used one hand to hold her and one hand to close the door, shutting them in. Janet was panicked. She tried to shout out but felt paralyzed with fear.

Alan fondled her breasts with his free hand while the other held her wrists. he forced his lips onto hers with acrid breath as he tried to French kiss her. She moved her head from left to right to fend him off. She then, in one movement, raised a knee quickly upwards to make contact with his testicles. He immediately doubled up, releasing his hold on her to hold his afflicted area. Janet took this opportunity to get out. She pushed the door open and exited the room, pleased to be in the relative safety of the grounds. She gulped in a few deep breaths wondering what to do. Maybe she could drive the buggy back without Alan or let him go back without her. She was familiar with the route to walk; then Alan could explain why Janet was not with him on his return. That seemed the preferred option. Janet was happy with the decision and looked over to where Alan stood, bent over at the doorway. He started swearing at her; he called her a slut and a tease. Janet ignored him and set off walking towards the gate, feeling relief with every step. She heard the sound of the buggy behind her, then to the side of her as Alan encouraged her to get on board, saying that he would keep quiet if she did. Janet ignored him and carried on walking, getting settled in her stride. Eventually, he got the message and drove on, leaving Janet to ponder her next steps. The guard at the gate stopped her and asked her why she was not in the buggy. Janet was not too sure how to respond and said, "We had a disagreement, so I decided to walk back. Can you let me through, please?"

"What did he do? He has a reputation with the ladies?" the guard asked her.

"No, nothing, no," she said, wondering why she couldn't tell the truth, she had nothing to hide, and it sounded as if Alan had a record. The guard let her through the gate, "Report it to your boss. He needs to get what's coming."

Janet mumbled a thanks, then set off at a steady pace heading towards the Nerve Centre. The route was pretty easy as there were few roads on Second Chance; it was basically a case of going straight ahead. Janet felt proud of how she had handled that. Now she needed to work out what to do back at the office. She desperately needed to go to her suite first and have a shower; she could smell his body odour on her. She felt disgusting. It took her about an hour to walk back. She reckoned it must be lunchtime, so she used that time to go and shower and change her clothes. After that, she went to find Debbie to get some food. She requested a sandwich and then sat down in the dining room to figure out what the hell she was going to do.

"Penny for them," Debbie said as she put the sandwich down in front of Janet.

"I've had a rough morning," Janet replied, pushing the food around her plate.

"You going to eat that or just exercise it?" Debbie asked; she placed a hand on Janet's shoulder; Janet immediately jumped, jerking the hand away from her.

"Has something happened?" she asked her.

"Well, not really, but yes, someone tried it on with me," Janet said, looking up at Debbie.

Debbie moved around, so she faced Janet. "What happened," she asked.

"He tried to kiss me and put his hands on me," replied Janet, very close to tears.

"Was it at work?" asked Debbie.

"Yes, we were out at the Physical Complex."

"Are you OK? Did he hurt you?"

"No, I'm OK, just a bit shocked, that's all; what should I do," Janet asked Debbie. Debbie held both of Janet's hands in hers. "You should report it. Could you go to Andrew?"

"Yes, I could. Do you think that would be alright?" Janet said as tears traced their way down her face.

"I could come with you," Debbie said, "A bit of moral support."

"Would you, thank you."

"Give me five minutes to see Stephen; then we will go together. With that, Debbie wheeled herself away to ask Stephen what he wanted. He was only after coffee and biscuits, which she quickly prepared and gave to him. That done, she took off her pinny, then holding Janet's left hand, they set off to go to the department, hopeful that Andrew was there and Alan was not. Janet was not sure how she would cope if she saw him. Janet felt satisfied that she had decided it would be best if she reported the incident thinking that he may have more to lose than her. Debbie and Janet entered the Environmental Department building to see if Andrew had time to speak to them. Andrew was not there; it was his day off, according to his secretary Nellie.

"Will he be back tomorrow?" asked Janet. Nellie nodded, then checked his diary, offering her a time to see him where they would not be interrupted. To Janet's relief, Alan was not at his desk; he was at lunch. Janet decided that she was not going to stay to work out her shift. She really was not in the right mind to work and didn't want to be around Alan. Instead, she was going to have a swim and go to the gym. That was a good release for her. Also, she would be able to shower again. She still felt like she had Alan's smell on her.

Debbie and Janet returned to the dorm. Debbie went off to do whatever Debbie did while Janet went to change into her gym clothes and pack up her cossie. She headed off to the gym, spending about an hour and a half at her exercise. It did the job; she came out of there feeling calmer and focused. She walked back to her room, opened the door with her fob key and walked in. Entering her room, she had a strange sensation; things appeared to be the same, but not quite. Her nightclothes had been left folded in a way she did not fold; her pillow was not quite as plumped as it was. Her initial thought was that Debbie had been cleaning, but it was not her day.

Janet checked around her rooms for changes; on her bed was her diary, open at the first entry.

Janet thought it was a kind of sign. She went to check in her bathroom to see if the empty bottle of Fentanyl was there. Too her dismay, it was missing. The information leaflet was still there; it looked like the only thing missing was the bottle. This was not a good day. Maybe, she thought, Alan had told someone that Janet may have taken the drug. But how could she be sure it was him? Either way, she guessed she was in trouble. Janet was really unsure of what to do next; feeling stressed and tired, she decided to get changed out of her gym clothes and into her night clothes. She needed to rest and really could not face Debbie and the others. Her brain felt overwhelmed and overstimulated; she needed to take control. She recited a mantra she learnt back in her days as a Greenie in the Mind Complex. It paid off, her thoughts settled, and she could give her body what it needed, rest.

Janet woke up a few hours later feeling revived and ready to go. She was no further forward in working out what to do but had made one decision, to take it as it came. Admit to anything, even if it means Graduation or strikes. Suddenly, a knock on her door made her jump. Nerves on edge, she called out, "yes, who is it?"

"It's just me, wanted to make sure you're OK," said a familiar voice. It was Debbie; she, no doubt, was the one who let them in to search her room.

"Oh, Debbie, yes, come in," Janet said as she opened the door. Debbie expertly steered her wheelchair in and motioned her to close the door.

"I expect you realized what had happened. I did try to tidy up the best I could; I hope I did the right thing," Debbie said, reaching out her hand for Janet to take.

"What will happen to me," asked Janet feeling tears prick in the corner of her eyes. "I was stupid."

"Chances are, if you explain, they will be lenient," she replied.

"I'm not even a drug addict, just took it because I could," Janet tried to explain, but even to her, it sounded weak.

"Anyway, come and have some food; I've done you a mushroom omelette, just how you like it."

"I'll be along in a minute or two," Janet said, indicating her tears and clothes.

"Of course," Debbie left her room, heading back to the kitchen. Janet changed back into some fresh work clothes and then went down to the dining room. Janet had little appetite, only managing to eat half of her eggs. She didn't even want dessert; Debbie could not tempt her with Eaton's mess. After food, she excused herself to go to her room. She had no idea of how to handle this mess; what on earth was she going to do, she thought. She heard a noise outside of her door followed by a knock, knock, knocks. Janet got up out of her bed and put on a dressing gown. She ordered the light to come on and then opened the door.

Outside the door were two men dressed in blue. They were security guards. One of them asked her her name, then when Janet gave it, he checked on something in his hand to make sure he had the right person. He handed Janet the thing he was holding which looked like a letter. Once she had it in her hand they bade her a good night then turned and moved away towards the wing door. Janet closed the door, making sure she had locked it then took the letter into her lounge where her pair of glasses sat. She put them on then opened the envelope revealing a letter. She unfolded it and began to read it. The bottom line was that she had been given a strike, her first, for theft. Janet balked at the word 'theft' she had not really thought of it that way. It made it sound so serious, but really, she thought, she guessed it was serious. She put down the letter on the low table and took of her glasses. She walked to her bedroom, took off her dressing gown then went back to bed. She would deal with it in the morning.

The next morning Janet turned up for her shift as usual. Andrew was already there, he summoned her to his office closing the door behind her. He invited her to sit, which she did on a swivel chair, avoiding the temptation to swivel. "I guess you know why you are here" he said, doing that thing pressing fingers together making an Apex shape, "well, I won't drag this out, firstly you have lost your job here in the Environmental Department, you will be on domestic duties, and secondly, you have had your first strike. I don't need to spell that out, but you have been warned. Now all the formal stuff has been done, let's have a good talk, fancy a coffee?" He stood up and went over to the kettle, shaking it to determine how full it was he plugged it in. Both of them ceased talking until they both had a mug of coffee in their hands acting as a social barrier. He asked her if she had a drug habit, Janet shook her head, feeling that that would probably be the best scenario.

"I took it because it was in an unlocked cupboard. Strong medication like that left for anyone to get hold of, that is negligence."

"What do you mean unlocked? It has a security combination lock on it, only known to a handful of people. Still, you should have reported it, not stolen a bottle."

"I know, it was stupid of me", Janet said slowly.

"I will have a word with Alan about that; it is his responsibility."

"There is something I have to tell you about Alan" said Janet who related her experience in the annex the day before. "He groped me and tried to kiss me, I tried to push him away but ended up kicking him in his balls." As she told him, Andrew's face paled, he took thoughtful sips of coffee absorbing every word.

"I'm sorry you had to put up with that. Thank you for telling me. Leave it with me, I will deal with it. You really have not had a good day have you.

'I've had better" Janet admitted.

Enough said. I have found a good place for you to work which is more physical. Down on ground level is where Stuart manages the garage and forecourt. I have made arrangements for you to work with him there. How does that sound?" he asked.

"That sounds good", she replied.

"You will have to wear the dark grey tunic and blue trousers of the work crew, but you can keep your room on the dorm with Debbie, I think she will be good for you to get some support. How does that sound?"

"Thank you, so much" Janet said near to tears.

"When you are ready, go down to the ground level, ask for Stuart, he will go through what needs to be done." He said gently touching her on the shoulder.

"Just be aware, there are eyes everywhere around here. Be careful." After issuing his warning he ushered her out of the room for her to say goodbye to Jazz. Jazz had no idea what was going on, but as she frequently had use of the buggy from the forecourt, she felt certain their paths would cross again. Maybe she would be able to tell her what happened then. Janet felt no qualms about throwing Alan under the bus, he really was a sleaze ball who had what he had coming. She somehow felt his days in the Environmental Team were numbered.

Janet left the department after saying a few goodbyes then made her way down to the ground floor. She popped into her rooms before going to the forecourt just to have a minute or two to compose herself. She had so many things she did not understand, for example, could she still use the canteen and facilities in the Nerve Centre, maybe Debbie could help her with that. She was not sure of the boundaries. She made herself a mug of tea and sat in her little garden, at least she didn't have to give that up. Debbie had told her her new plants would be arriving very soon, that was something to look forward to, it will be lovely having some colour out there. Once she finished her drink, she wondered along to the kitchen to see if Debbie was there. She was in the kitchen washing up singing a song with a beautiful singing voice, she looked very much in her own space. Janet was not sure if to disturb her but so wanted to talk to someone about all that was happening. Janet picked up a cup and put it noisily down on the worksurface to see if that would get her attention, but no. Debbie was so focused on her singing and work. Janet tried again with the cup, still no joy, she would have to try something else. Eventually she tapped Debbie on her shoulder which made Debbie react by jumping in her seat. She steered her power wheelchair backwards and swung around to face Janet.

"Oh, you made me jump. Have you finished work already? What happened. Are you OK?"

'whoah, where do you want me to start?" Janet asked.

"Did you see Andrew?" Debbie asked.

"Yes," said Janet, "I've been sacked. He was so nice about it but all is not lost, I'm going to be working as the work crew but still live here." Janet went on to relay all about the conversation between herself and Andrew. She also found breath to ask Debbie about the use of the facilities here in the Nerve Centre. Debbie went onto explain that because she lived here, she would have use of the canteen and leisure facilities. Janet was pleased about that, today was beginning to look a lot better. After their chat, Janet went over to the garage to introduce herself to Stuart. He was expecting her and once they had briefly had a get to know you, he gave her the guided tour of her new place of work. He asked her if she had been given a new uniform and made arrangements for Debbie to get hold of it for her for when she started work the next day. Janet returned to her room, going over and over the events in her mind. She thought everything that had happened was fair and reasonable. She was pleased with the outcome. After lunch she took herself off to the swimming pool with the aim of completing twenty length which she finished with still some energy going spare. She went back to the dorm where Debbie met her with some work clothes in her lap for Janet. They comprised of three blue polo shirts, three dark grey trousers two overalls and one pair of steel tapped boots. The garments would not win any fashion awards, but they were functional. She spent the rest of the afternoon in her room doing some sewing. Her new work trousers were made for a giant not a five-foot two inch of woman. She was taking up the hems so she would not trip over them. After that she made herself a coffee and sat in her garden with her reading book. She would have to find another one soon she had nearly finished this one. Her coffee was so nice, she made herself another one, just killing time until food. She decided to write in her diary today's events now, while everything was still so fresh. Janet wrote about what had happened and her imagination as to what would happen to Alan. He had been naughty having broken several rules, the chances are he would get a strike. She had no problem with having blown the whistle on him. At six, she left her rooms to go and get food. Debbie was busy in the kitchen creating wonderful smells that made Janet salivate. Debbie was a good cook, she made non fussy foods that would please all her wards, ten in all. She was fortunate that none of them required a special diet or were allergic to anything which would have given her even more work to do. She was always busy but had time for everyone.

Debbie was always a happy sort of a person. She was a natural nurturer even as a child she took care of animals and younger siblings. She came from a large family, seven children in all, she came along as number three. Her parents worked hard to put food on the table and despite not having much, they had enough to give them a good life. Debbies mother took in ironing, she could do that while watching her little ones but it didn't pay much. She tried being a Avon lady but was allergic to some of the products so found it hard to endorse them. She did sell some stuff but the commission was so low, she didn't make enough to be worth her while. Once the younger ones had started school, she was able to go out to work. She worked as a dinner lady at the same school some of her children went to, the hours were good and the pay OK. Debbie was nine when the youngest child left nursery to start at school. Debbie always went to check on her at play time to make sure she was OK. Debbie always offered to babysit to give her parents an evening off to go out, but her mum was concerned that Debbie was too young. Maybe when she was older. Debbie did well at school, she was quick to learn and was popular with her peers. She enjoyed her school days but had already decided what she wanted to do for a living. She wanted to be a social worker and work with children. She had done her homework finding out what qualifications she needed to do the training and worked hard in the key subjects to get the scores that she needed. When she was a secondary school, she worked as a babysitter at the weekends in the evenings to get some money. The little ones liked Debbie and she did a good job. As well as getting money, it was good experience for her. She stayed on at school to do her A levels, which did not go down well with her parents. They expected her to go out to work to bring home a wage to pay her way. Debbie tried to see what she could about that then negotiated with her parents about her finding work in the evenings. She found work as an office cleaner working not too far from where they lived. Debbie was fortunately young enough to have the energy to be a full-time student and to hold down a physical job. She left school with three good A levels and her ambition intact. She applied to the local university to do her training to be a social worker. She was accepted and was due to start studying the next term. Debbie was excited about this and had planned to live at home and to travel the short distance to the university. Her parents had other ideas. They didn't see her ambition they just saw Debbie as someone to bring home the bacon. Debbie thought about what she could do to earn some money but struggled to find anything that would pay her enough to cover her rent. She had been given a scholarship to cover the cost of her tuition at university, so she didn't have to worry about that. She eventually found a job working two nights a week working at a night club as a waitress. She had to wear a short black skirt with black tights and a tight white blouse. She felt very exposed, but she realized that she was wearing more than some of the females that turned up at the night club. Most of her job was going around picking up used glasses. She was taught how to serve behind the bar and once she had mastered that was often found behind the bar. She enjoyed her job, even the less savoury aspects like cleaning up vomit. She made a good number of friends there and often hang out with them after her shift. One night, Debbie was coming to the end of her shift when Melanie asked her if she wanted to stay for a drink. Debbie was not a drinker, she rarely drank alcohol, she just didn't like the taste. However, she said she would stay and once all the patrons had left, they tidied up then the bar man, Trevor started to make cocktails. Now, Debbie had never had a cocktail but agreed that she would try one. Trevor made her a Sex on the Beach cocktail that Debbie thought looked and smelled delightful. On tasting it, she could not detect the alcohol just a nice tasting drink, so she happily drank it down.

Trevor made her more and more cocktails which Debbie drank even though she was feeling the effects of the alcohol. Her 'friends' encouraged her to drink more and more until she started to feel sick. She couldn't make it in time to go to the toilets, she could barely walk so she ended up spewing up down her front and over the floor. Jon, one of the other men encouraged her to remove her top as it was soiled which she did. Then he suggested she took of her small skirt, which she did. She was in no position to refuse. Her friends encouraged her to remove her tights and her underwear and once she was naked, the males took advantage of her. She was feeling very dizzy and very sick, and she ended up vomiting over Jon who had mounted her. Jon lashed out and hit her across the face which made Debbie vomit more. He asked the others to hold her down while he finished the deed. Once he was spent, he got hold of a bottle of scotch and poured it down her throat while someone forced her mouth open. Debbie started to gag with the fluid. Most of the liquid went over her face but a good quantity went down her throat and into her lungs. Debbie started to feel like she couldn't breathe. She began to panic but still Jon poured the whiskey down into her mouth. She tried to push them off, but they were holding down her limbs tightly. Debbie was fading in and out of consciousness with the onslaught of alcohol. The scotch in her lungs sounded bubbly and gurgle as it filled the space. Debbie was fighting for breath during her lucid moments but that was short lived as her body began to close down. They continued to pour the alcohol down her even though she was no longer moving, and they released their hold on her limbs. One of them prodded her body to see if they would get a reaction. They were prodding a dead body. When it had sank in, they debated about what they were going to do with her. One of them came up with the idea of putting her in his car and dumping her body somewhere. This seemed to be OK with them and with that, Jon went to get his car and put it near the front door. The others lifted her up on to her feet and walked with her. To anyone it would look like she had had too much not that she was dead. They manhandled her into the back seat of the car then discussed what to do now. There was very little traffic around that time of night so there was no one around to see what they do. They took advantage of that and drove her onto the dual carriageway outside of the town. One of them opened the door at the back and two of them pushed Debbie out onto the carriageway. They then zoomed off to go back to their homes as if nothing had happened. Debbie's body laid on the road in a heap. At one point during the night a lorry was travelling up the dual carriageway. He didn't see her lying there until it was too late he ran over her legs. Debbie arrived at second chance in a mess. She had damaged lungs and two badly crushed legs which took her a long time to recover enough to leave the Physical Complex. She had to get used to the idea of being in a wheelchair and the fact that her body had been violated. However, she did adjust, and her personality came through. Debbie was asked to join the Nerve Centre shortly after she became a brownie. She was happy to go there, she felt ready to make a difference to some people's life.

After breakfast the next day, Janet set off to her deployment wearing her new uniform. It was a short walk from her suite, so it took next to know time. Stuart was by the office when she arrived, she went over to him ready and willing to get stuck in.

"Hi Janet, glad you are here. Just give me a minute and I'll give you the tour and go over your duties." He said going into the office. Janet stood there like a lemon waiting for him looking around at the garage and forecourt. She could see a couple of other people working there she supposed they would be her work colleagues. They were both quite young, one, it was hard to tell what his disability was, the other one had an arm missing and walked with a profound limp.

A short time later, Stuart came over to her with a key in his hand. They walked and chatted together as he introduced to her James and Nigel, her new work colleagues. After a little bit of a chat, Stuart pointed out things around the area so she would be familiar with the lay out and knew where things were that she needed. The tour done; he took her over to a four seated buggy.

"We wash the vehicles every day on the outside and hoover them every other day. We all get on and do that when we arrive in the morning. This one is yours. All the cleaning equipment is over there" he said pointing to an area in the forecourt with a tap and buckets. "Are you OK with that?"

"Yes, that's fine." She said definitely feeling in work mode. Once he had left her, she went over to the wash station to pick out some clothes, bucket and cleanser. She filled the bucket with water and soap, returned to the buggy and started to clean it. She made the vehicle shine. It was hard work, but it paid off. Even James and Nigel came over to view it. Janet felt proud of her achievement. Once finished Stuart came over with the keys to the buggy. He asked her to jump in the passenger seat as the buggy was needed. This she did as he got into the drivers side. With a gentle purr the car started, and he carefully steered it out of the forecourt and onto the road.

"Where are we going?" Janet asked.

"Got a couple of customers to pick up, both from the Inner Circle. They are doing a recky of the new moon they hope to get up and running soon. Did you hear, we are going to get early morning birdsong starting in a day or two. It's funny the things you miss being here, don't you think?"

"Yes, I'm pleased about the bird song, I helped with that."

"Did you, wow." Stuart steered the vehicle to the other side of the Nerve Centre to a door which was open with two people standing in front of it. He stopped the buggy right next to them, who, without saying a word got in and sat down in the back seats. Stuart drove the vehicle to the compound she had been to once when Jazz and her went to repair the sun. Janet felt a surge of excitement at the thought of seeing the moon but tried to contain it because of the high and mighty passengers. Stuart stopped the vehicle and the members of the Inner Circle alighted. Stuart moved the vehicle to the edge of the compound and turned it round so they both could see what was going on. It was interesting to watch them walk around a large figure resting on the floor. It was so clearly the moon with ridges and bunkers just as you would expect. The man and woman from the Inner Circle could be seen talking with members of the work force who had been constructing the moon. The previous one was broken beyond repair as the rope holding it in place had perished causing the moon to fall to the ground and shatter.

"It's good to be here, we are not important enough for them to care about what we see. You learn to keep quiet and be discreet."

"Yes, I can see that" Janet said. "On Earth once you reach middle age you might as well be invisible, do you find that, is it the same for men?"

"I guess so, must of mit I got to be fifty-nine here on Second Chance, I've been here since I was twenty. I sure have seen somethings in my time" Stuart said as they both looked forward watching the inspection.

"That's a long time, wow. Do you remember much about your time on Earth?" Janet asked.

"Bits and Bobs. I think about my parents who may well be dead now, I do go over in my head how I ended up here, but that's about all."

Stuart Gold was a smart arse twenty-year-old who struggled with authority. He did what he wanted, when he wanted and with who he wanted. He lived just on the wrong side of the law believing himself as inconvincible. One day him and his cronies were working on his rust bucket of a car trying to coax it back to life. Eventually their tinkering worked, and the engine turned over and started. Stuart put the bonnet of the car down and clicked into place high fiving his friends. They all piled into the car to give it a test run. Stuart sat in the drivers seat with Rob next to him with Fred and Ben in the back.

The car stuttered a bit before it finally moved forward once the handbrake had been released.

He drove the car around the neighbourhood for a while before opting to go on the dual carriage way to get some speed going. He pushed down on the accelerator put it up to top gear then steered it around slower vehicles. Whatever speed they were going, it certainly was not the legal speed limit for the road, Stuart really did not care about that. He headed off towards the motorway with the slip road about fifty meters away when he heard the call of a police car. Stuart looked into his mirror seeing a police car with flashing lights behind him. He floored the accelerator urging his car to go faster but the car was at its limit. It was then he spotted smoke escaping from the bonnet of the car as the engine rejected Stuarts desire for speed.

The police car was right behind him with the driver encouraging Stuart to pull over by using his turn signal lights. Stuart did not want to, but he was aware of his struggling car. He decided not to go on the motorway but to see if he could lose them in the narrow streets of suburbia. He turned off the dual carriageway at the next possible place, by now the car was slowing down significantly. Not only was there dark smoke coming out of the bonnet but you could see flames. Realising the end was coming for his car, Stuart stopped it so everyone could debunk. Fred, Ben and Rob got out easily, Stuart was less fleet, he was halfway out of the car when it exploded. Stuart suffered horrific burns on his body and legs, so bad that he died shortly after in hospital. However, his love of cars was satisfied with his work managing the garage, though now days he was happy going at a sedate speed.

When the two members of the Inner circle were satisfied with the moon one of them gestured for Stuart to bring the buggy nearer. This he did. The journey back was done in silence broken only when the two silver clad figures were returned to their base. Stuart chatted as they drove back to the garage.

"We have a diary with all the bookings for transport, mostly people come in person to book it, some are done every week. I will show you the diary when we get back." Stuart said, "I think you will do just fine here with us."

"Thank you, I think I will too" replied Janet.

Janet was happy with her new deployment, it was physical and simple, what she was good at, also it gave her the chance to learn. She was set to work in the vehicle forecourt cleaning buggies and minibuses, driving people around and taking the guided tour of new Brownies. She found her workmates friendly often ribbing her about her poor mechanical knowledge. Life felt definitely better, she felt she could move on and leave her dodgy behaviour behind her.

She started her working day washing down the vehicles, a job Janet particularly liked. She worked steadily, ringing out the cloth with vigor. One of her work colleagues, Nigel, was cleaning the buggy next to the one Janet was cleaning. He had the bonnet up fiddling with something or other, periodically turning over the engine. Nigel was quite young, he used to be in the army which is where he sustained his injuries. He managed surprisingly well the damage he sustained from treading on a land mine while in Iraq. He lost one and a half legs and his internal organs fell out of his body when his abdomen burst. They were held in by scar tissue and used crutches to get around. He used the body of the buggy he was working on to support him, he really did not let his injuries stop him from pulling his weight. Despite this, he was cheerful and enjoyed banter with his work colleagues. On one particular day during tea break in the morning he was filling Janet in on the gossip.

He said, "Did you not used to work with Alan from the Environment Team?

"Yes, yes I did, why?" asked Janet before taking a mouth full of hot tea.

"Well, he is going to be Graduated, seems he over stood the mark with the ladies. Did you hear anything when you were there?" Nigel said.

"Yes, I was one of the ladies. Tell me what Graduation is; lots of people have different ideas. I'm just confused." Asked Janet.

"My understanding is that they are sent to another place, another Second Chance" he replied.

"What, dumping those who don't fit in somewhere else for them to be dealt with" said Janet finishing her tea and reaching for another biscuit.

"I guess so."

"Do you reckon they are returned to Earth?" Janet enquired; Stuart looked at her putting down his mug looking as if he was calling time on this conversation.

"You know you can get into trouble with this kind of talk, someone might be listening, I know people who disappeared after asking too many questions. Do your work, blend in, keep your head down, you already have one strike" with that he returned to see if the buggy was working by twisting the key the ignition. Janet followed suit, put her mug down then returned to her cleaning. The minibus was due out in half an hour, she wanted it to be gleaming. As she worked she thought about what Nigel had said. She did not know if to be pleased or worried that her reporting Alans action was going to make him be Graduated. She still felt there was more she should know or do to get people thinking about what happens at Graduation. At the end of very day shift she would take herself off to the gym or the pool, likewise if she was no a late shift she went in the morning. She was still making improvements in her fitness from the exercise and could tell the difference in her body. Her muscle tone had taken over some fatty areas on her upper legs and upper arms. She had more stamina which helped her with her new job which was very physical. Janet was doing well, and even she would agree with that. She put the first strike at the back of her mind and felt somewhat better for doing so. She didn't miss her job with the environment team, she had learnt so much about the running of Second Chance working there. She saw Jazz now and then as she went out to collect data from the various stations around Second Chance and used one of the buggies. She also had been promoted from being a GDB to taking over Alan's old role. She was now the one to do the Fentanyl run on the Monday. Sometimes she had a new person with her who was learning the ropes, Janets replacement which felt weird.

Janet had managed to fill her days pretty well, but, she had very little going on in the evenings, except if she was on call. It was not that often that she was called, most of it was stuff that could have waited until morning. But Janet had settled down into the rhythm of work and within a week, it felt like she had always been there.

Chapter 13
Graduation

Janet was in her bedroom readying herself for bed, she stretched and yawned, pulled back her bed linen then climbed into the fresh sheets supplied and fitted by Debbie earlier in the day. Janet felt tired but before allowing sleep to engulf her she took her notebook out and turned to a fresh page to write the entry for that day. Most of it was a run through of the tasks she undertook, the rest her thoughts and feelings. Her recap of the daily events was proving to be a helpful task in her sleep hygiene. By writing it all down it acted as a way to remove it from her brain and onto the paper, thus enabling restful sleep. She was settling down in her bed when Janet heard a strange noise coming from her lounge. She could not identify the sound so reluctantly got out of her bed, crossed the room to her lounge.

Janet ordered the light on by saying Fuck Off, the room was immediately illuminated showing a piece of folded paper that had been pushed under her door to the corridor of the dormitory. She quickly unlocked and opened the door to see if she could spot the person who had put the note there. She was not fast enough so closed and locked the door. She opened up the folded note it read 'be careful, they are on to you, you are getting too close' it was not signed, and Janet could not identify the author by the handwriting, though it looked familiar. With sleep now out of the question, she made herself a coffee, grabbed a few biscuits then sat down in her lounge. Her heart was beating fast which she tried to steady with meditation, reciting her mantra over and over until all intrusive thoughts had gone. With her mind clear, she picked up her journal and pen. She allowed the pen to write in a slow methodical way recapping on past and recent events. She could not say she felt really any nearer to the truth. She knows that Graduation is used to control some sectors of Second Chance though she was no closer to what Graduation was. She hoped it did offer persons a more suitable environment though she felt sure it was more sinister than that, that theory only works if Graduation is something different for each person. She found it mind blowing to even think that Graduation was a way to manage people, it felt far too much like Eugenics, enough lessons had been learnt by that method to know not to go there, or maybe they hadn't. Maybe the Inner Circle of the Nerve Centre believed they were doing people good. Janet thought about her own place in all of his, she had already had one strike, pursuing this may put her life in jeopardy, though she could not let it go, it wasn't going away. Then back round her thinking went to the carefully worded note, she needed to find the author, but how?

The next day Janet got up and dressed to start her day. She felt as bad as she looked as someone who had barely slept the night before. Debbie was looking at her usual perky self. She came to greet her when Janet entered the day room. She asked her what she wanted for breakfast, and Janet requested porridge and tea. Debbie knew just how Janet liked her porridge, thick enough to stand a spoon in it with two teaspoons of sugar. She popped it down in front of Janet, who sat at one of the free tables.

"I've got news for you," said Debbie as she watched Janet take a mouthful of porridge. When she was able to speak without spraying everyone with porridge, Janet replied,

"Oh, what's that then?" She thought she might say something about the note, but that was not the case.

"Your order is arriving today, you know, the plants you wanted for the garden," Debbie said. "Shall I put them in your room for you for when you get home from work?"

"Yes, thank you, that would be great" Janet replied surprised at how short a time that took to come. She wondered if Gary had sorted them out for her, he would know what she likes.

"Are you OK, Janet?" Debbie asked her with genuine concern in her voice.

"Just weary, I didn't sleep to well last night."

"Poor you. Do you think you will manage at work?" Debbie said.

"It will be fine; I have a busy day ahead; I think the work will wake me up." Janet had finished her breakfast and excused herself from the table.

Once on the forecourt, she checked the rota to see whom she was working with and what her jobs were. Knowing the first job of the day was to clean the vehicles, she grabbed the cleaning kit to make a start on the first vehicle, the open-air minibus set aside to transport members of the Inner Circle to do some checks of the grounds. Janet looked up from her work and spotted some Brownies outside the forecourt; she thought one of them looked familiar, and he did; it was Gary still with the axe in his head. Janet put down her sponge and ran across the garage and onto the forecourt calling out his name.

"Gary, Gary, over here, Gary."

"Janet, it's you. What are you doing here" he said, opening up his long arms for an embrace. Janet ran into his arms, feeling a huge rush of love and missing him and her friends. Although she still worked in the Nerve Centre, the forecourt was in Brownie land, though quite a bit away from the gardens and nurseries. She could have, if it had even crossed her mind, made contact with her friends though generally, it would be disapproved of.

Nerve Centre workers were discouraged from mixing with Brownies. It was not the thing to do. Janet was not sure if it was something that would lead to a strike. Janet led Gary into the garage and picked up the sponge to continue with her work while firing questions at him about Lisa, Kim and Mel. He did his best to keep up with answering the questions, including the last one, which was why he was here.

"I'm leading a tour around the grounds for a couple of people from the Inner Circle, it's their annual inspection" he replied, Janet tapped the bus indicating the vehicle as the one commissioned for the tour.

Janet was keen to find out how things were going between Mel and Gary, she asked him and was delighted when he told her they are thinking of taking things to the next level and make it formal. Janet was thrilled when she found out their intentions to marry. It was not uncommon for couples to marry on Second Chance though no possibility of them being able to have children, the dead can't reproduce. But they may be able to adopt a dead baby from the nursery. She gave him a hug and asked him to give Mel one from her. Janet spotted her manager Stuart coming over to see what was going on.

"Hello Gary, long time no see. It looks as if you know our Janet." Stuart said as he shook hands with Gary. "Janet, we need to get moving. Could you move this bus out of the forecourt, please?" She did his bidding while Stuart and Gary talked like two people who were friends. Then Stuart came over with Gary and the other Brownie, whom Janet did not recognize. Gary introduced her to Ahmed then they all got on board the minibus, ready to pick up the people from the Inner Circle. "Janet, you go on back there and prepare the two-seater for the Fentanyl run. It should not be too long. Don't get into trouble while I'm gone." Janet was not entirely sure if he meant that seriously or not, but she let it ride.

Janet moved onto cleaning the small buggy and getting it ready for someone from the Environment Team. After that, which would take her to the afternoon, the four-seated buggy had been booked for a driver and two passengers to go to an outbuilding on the edge of Second Chance. Janet was down to drive this one later in her shift. Fred had done a dummy run with her the day before to make sure she was familiar with the route. Janet particularly liked doing the drive-outs. She got to see parts of Second Chance that were hidden from general view. It was Fred's day off, so Janet was left with Nigel. He was checking over some bicycles, which were a new addition to the fleet. Someone suggested people could cycle around Second Chance instead of using electric vehicles on short journeys. Janet went over to him to see if the bikes needed cleaning.

"I'm nearly done with them; yes, they could do with a wipe down. Tell you what, I'll do this one, and you do that one." Janet went off to get the washing kit, and they both started to wipe down the bikes. Janet was cleaning the spokes on the front wheel when suddenly she got hit by a wet, soapy sponge. She looked over at a laughing Nigel holding a wet cloth. As he got ready to chuck it at her, she retaliated by throwing her sponge back at him. It hit him right on the face; they both giggled as they did their best to soak each other. When the game came to a natural end, Janet suggested it was time for a tea break. He agreed and went over to the office to put the kettle on. Janet found the tea bags and the sugar and then started to prepare the mugs. Shortly after, Stuart returned with Ahmed and Gary in the minibus. Janet went over to meet them, asking if it went OK, which Gary acknowledged with a nod. Stuart went off to check the buggies leaving Janet and Gary a chance to talk. Ahmed went off with Nigel to have a look at the bikes, giving them a chance to talk.

"Why are you so wet?" Gary asked her.

"I had a fight with a wet sponge", she replied. Gary asked Janet to meet him at the garage at seven, so they could go and see the others.

"Am I allowed to do that?" Janet asked with alarm in her voice.

"Technically, yes, there is nothing written down about it. Do you still have the Brownie clothes you could wear?"

"Yes, I do; I could wear them under my clothes and then take them off when I get back here." Said Janet feeling thrilled with the idea of an adventure. Seeing Stuart returning, Gary kissed Janet on the cheek and said goodbye. He said goodbye to Stuart and called Ahmed to join him. Janet watched as he strode off with short-legged Ahmed, nearly running to keep up with him. Janet was delighted she had seen Gary; it was turning out to be a good day.

Over lunch, Stuart filled her in about the trip in the afternoon. Stuart said they were taking someone to be a Graduated and that it was a privilege to be part of someone's onward journey. She wondered who the person was, what he or she had done, and whether they were old or bad or too injured to manage. Stuart looked at his clipboard and said that there was no name of the person and that Janet had to keep quiet and just drive.

At 2 pm, Janet drove the buggy from the garage and onto the forecourt, ready to transport her passengers to the outbuilding. To her dismay, she saw a blue top and tail security guard and a silver-clad Inner Circle-suited person leading a man with his hands in handcuffs. The man was Alan. Janet felt a rush of panic but held it together as she led the men to the buggy. She could not make eye contact with Alan, who looked dishevelled. When he saw Janet, he stared at her at first, and then he started to shout at her, blaming Janet for what was going to happen to him. Janet recoiled at that and took a step backwards. The security guard whispered something to Alan, which made him shut up.

Janet was, in many ways, sorry for him. Whatever it was that they were going to do to him, she hoped he would find peace. Stuart came over to Janet, asking her if she was OK and told her to be professional. Shortly afterwards, the passengers got on board with the man from the Inner Circle sitting next to Janet. Janet drove steadily following the map route Fred had scrawled on a piece of paper for her. The journey took her to places she was not aware of, like large warehouses and barns, to areas that looked like houses; she passed people wearing the Brownie uniform going about their business, whatever that was.

Eventually they reached the area Stuart had marked on the map and applied the buggy breaks to stop the vehicle. The area was similar to what she had just passed; it looked industrial, with old heavy machinery parked to gather age and dust. There was a large furnace chimney behind a single-level building, which, she considered, had to be the place where Graduation happened. It was a more modern building than the ones that surrounded it. The white-clad woman stood outside the door of the building and raised her arm briefly as a welcome. She had a type of brief case with her by her feet. Janet's three passengers climbed down off the buggy; Alan was not so willing to get off the vehicle, so he was assisted down by the security guard dressed in blue. Once they had had alighted, Janet drove the buggy to park it off the thoroughfare, selecting a place that gave her a good view.

The silver-dressed man asked the guard to remove the handcuffs on Alan, which he did with a quick turn of a little key. The guard advised Alan to do as he was told or he would replace the cuffs. Alan looked over to Janet, then pointed at her, yelling, "You, this is your fault, you fucking bitch." Janet felt herself redden as the words hit her, but she kept the professional persona by keeping quiet. The party walked together towards the entrance. The door opened with a whoosh by the command of a fob key worn by the female Inner Circle worker.

Once inside, the door closed, and the women in White who had stayed outside walked to a second door. She unlocked it manually and entered the tiny room. Janet could not see what she was doing, so she stepped down from the driving seat of the buggy on the pretext of stretching her legs. She moved to a position offering a clearer but discreet view. The woman opened the bag she had with her withdrawing a bottle. She then pulled on some surgical gloves and a mask before opening the bottle and pouring the contents into a flip-down receptacle in the wall. The procedure mimicked the one she helped Alan with topping up the analgesia for the Newbies. Then the women turned around, prompting Janet to move as if exercising quickly. Despite this, she could not be sure the women had not spotted her.

Janet returned to the buggy as the woman entered the building through the main door, which was open. Janet felt anxious and intrigued; she dared herself to go to the entrance to see if she could see anything. She checked around her first to make sure the area was clear, then made her way to the entrance. Nervously Janet peered in through a crack in the door to see if there was anybody there, but the room was empty. She pushed the door further open, taking one or two steps inside the room. The entrance space was small, with a heavy door on the right and a small one at the end of the room. She could hear no sound, smell no smell, but she had a sickie feeling of trepidation. She took a couple of more steps and then spotted the bag the woman was carrying on a table near the heavy door. Janet quickly swooped on it, immediately finding the empty bottle. She looked around again, just to make sure she was alone, then studied the bottle. Janet recognised the name of the contents from the information leaflet she had taken from the unlocked store cupboard.

But what was it? Poison? A hallucinogenic? Whatever it was, it seemed like Graduation was the end product. Hearing a sound of chatting, Janet quickly retraced her steps leaping out of the door. She still had the bottle in her hand; peaking around, she wondered where she could hide it. No one came out of the door. Janet exhaled, trying to get her brain to find a solution to her predicament. She did a semi-run back to where the buggy was parked, chucked the bottle into the undergrowth, and then sat on the passenger seat, feigning sleep. Her senses were on super high alertness, and she could feel her hands shaking with the adrenalin rush. Janet heard no sounds coming from the entranceway. Daring to chance, she got off the buggy, retrieved the discarded bottle and ran to the building. She pushed the door open first checking for sounds and signs of people, then she quickly replaced the bottle in the bag, turned round to leave when,

"What on earth are you doing here?" The white-clad women stood in the doorway at the bottom of the room.

"I just needed the ladies. Is there one in here," Janet quickly piped up, doing the 'I've got a full bladder dance'.

"Yes, on the right through this door here; you know this area is out of bounds. I could get you a strike for coming in," she said as Janet thanked her for the directions and quickly went through the door, which led to a couple of more doors and one with the sign of 'toilet' on it. She quickly went in, closed, and then locked the door; what was she going to do, she thought.

She breathed deeply, not truly believing she had gotten away with it. She stayed there for the rough amount of time it took to wee, flushed the toilet, washed her hands and splashed her face, now sure her heart was not going to explode out of her chest. Janet opened the w c door, peered out left and right, and then made her way back to the hallway, through the main door and out into the fresh air. Her passenger and the woman were not there, so she had time to wait with the buggy for them. She had had enough excitement for one day now. She just wanted to be in her room to evaluate what she had found out this day.

Janet noticed smoke coming out of the chimney as two Brownies; one sat in a tractor, and one was tinkering with the engine stirring it into life, stirring it into work mode. There were a few other people around, one of whom kindly offered her a drink of fresh fruit juice. Janet happily accepted it and engaged in conversation. His name was Derek; he worked on the nearby farm and lived in one of the homes she had passed on the way there. "Are you part of this?" Derek asked, indicating the Graduation building with his thumb.

"No, just the driver. Do you know what goes on there?" Janet asked.

"We have our suspicions; no one comes out, you know," Derek said, "they say people go somewhere more suitable to their needs; that's what they say."

"Why, what do you think?"

"The furnace fires up when people go in, every time and no other time. Bit of a coincidence if you ask me," Derek said, wiping his floppy fringe off his face with a tattoo-clad hand. At that point, the security guard came out of the building and made his way to the buggy. Seeing him, Derek said, "Anyway, got to go, chicken to kill" with that, he took the drinking vessel from Janet, looked up at the smoke, scratched his head, and then strode off into the distance. Janet watched him leave. A cold, cold feeling flowed through her blood vessels; she felt nauseous. However, she had to snap herself out of her thoughts because the lady with the bag and the silver-clad male were walking towards the buggy in deep conversation. The guard got in the buggy next to Janet while the two workers from the Inner Circle boarded the buggy at the back.

One of them gave Janet the word to go, so she started up the vehicle and set off back to the garage forecourt. Both back seat passengers were quiet in contemplation during the journey, which pleased Janet. She had had information overload, which left her feeling drained and tired. The guard looked over at her once or twice, almost looking as if he was going to say something, but he remained quiet. The journey back took next to no time, and Janet, for one, was pleased to get back. Her shift was nearly over, and she desperately wanted to go to her suite. Once back at base, her passengers thanked her and then headed off to their respective homes. Janet steered the buggy back into the garage, stopped the engine then disembarked. She nodded to Stuart, her return which came over to ask her how it had gone.

"It went fine; I did not get lost. I got talking to some of the farmers; they gave me a drink."

"What, Derek? He usually gets me some apple juice when I do the run. Right old gossip he is," Stuart said. "Right off you go, you are over your shift time. Take half hour back tomorrow morning, OK?"

"Yes, thank you," Janet said, immediately turning round to start the walk home. It only took her a couple of minutes. Once there, she opened her door and flung herself onto her bed, mentally exhausted. She took off her overalls, making it a lot harder to do lying down. Then in the process of undressing, she saw the state of her hands. There was grime under her fingernails. She thoroughly washed her hands, scrubbing her nails with soap. She dried them and then went back to lie on her bed. After a little rest, she went in search of food which Debbie had lovingly prepared. Janet tucked her toad in the hole with relish. She really was hungry, which could only be relieved by carbohydrates. After her meal, she glanced at the clock; it said six forty-five, which gave her quatre of an hour to get herself ready for meeting the gang. She put on her Brownie outfit under her Nerve Centre clothes and brushed her hair in readiness for the evening ahead.

She felt excited but nervous about meeting up with the others, partly because she may be breaking an unwritten rule and partly because she had no idea what to say to them about her journey in the Nerve Centre. She painted on a smile when she arrived at the garage and saw Gary waiting for her. After greeting each other, she quickly took off her dark grey top and blue trousers revealing her Brownie uniform. She put her discarded clothes in a cupboard in the garage then they walked to the social club to meet up with the gang. They chatted amiably as they walked. Gary reached to hold her hand as they went. It did not take long to get there.

Janet looked out for her friends, who were at the entrance waiting for them. They all waved at her, and she returned the greeting. Once there, it was hugs all around, and then Janet noticed another man with them; she thought she recognized him from before but was not absolutely certain. Gary went over to the man and introduced him to Janet as Martin, Kim's boyfriend.

Janet felt chuffed that Kim had found someone special, he appeared to be attentive and caring, but there was something a little bit iffy about him. He kept looking nervously around as if expecting something or someone. But he stopped being so fidgety as they set off for a walk around the lake to chat and catch up on all the news. Janet did not need to worry about telling them what she had been up to. Mel and Kim had so much to tell her she could not really say anything except listen.

Since being part of the workforce in the Nerve Centre, much of what she had to do when around customers were to listen and keep quiet. The evening air was fresh and low and beheld, and the moon appeared in the night sky.

"Look, it's the moon," she said excitedly.

"Yes, it looks good, doesn't it? Better than the last one. Have you heard the bird song in the

mornings?" asked Lisa. Gary joked about Janet going into the lake for a swim that night, only to learn that that is something he has started to do. Their talk ebbed and flowed, and it got to feel like they had never been apart. Word had gotten around the Brownies about Janet's fall from grace, Gary asked her about it, but Mel interjected, saying that the night was for fun. They sat down on some picnic benches immediately. The mood changed when Martin looked at her and said, "did you get a note the other day?"

"What do you mean?" she replied as her breathing temporarily stopped. She made good eye contact with him and relayed her receipt of the note by nodding. Breathing again, she asked him if he had sent it,

"On my instructions. I gather you have been asking questions that have not gone down well," he asked Janet.

"What is this about? Who are you really?" she was feeling stressed and anxious.

"It's nothing to worry about. I am here to help. You see, I lead The Resistance. We are an underground organization exploring and examining what the Inner Circle are truthfully doing about Graduation." He explained, holding her stare. Janet feeling uncomfortable, dropped her gaze, saying, "wow, very cloak and dagger. Are these lots part of it?" She asked, gesturing towards Gary, Mel, Kim and Lisa.

"No, only to lead me to you. You are well known and much admired. I think you would be a great asset if you joined the team." Martin said,

"I need to keep my head down; I am already on their radar. It's too dangerous," Janet said, feeling insecure.

"Yes, but your knowledge would be helpful to us. We want to let people here know what Graduation really is; we have team members in the Nerve Centre as well as the Brownies; even if I link you with one of them, just make it look like your friends or something. What do you think?"

"I need a drink; let's go to the social club; what's on tonight? Karaoke?" she said, walking on ahead of the others. She just needed a bit of time to think. Was all this for real? She thought.

The five of them strolled to the bar chuckling at Mel's blue jokes and Kim's lack of understanding them; from the outside, they looked like a group of friends, not members of a secret army. The beer went down well. Janet was remorseful that she had not even thought about doing this before. There were no rules saying you could not mix. It's just an assumption. She got up to dance with the house band playing their version of Bad and Thriller. She did all the moves and more. Mel was the best dancer, with her shapely body gyrating to Michael Jackson's masterpieces. It felt so good to let her hair down; she had probably drunk a bit more than was sensible, and she knew she had to be careful as she was down to drive the next day; she did not want to be over the limit. It really would not be a good look.

Janet watched Mel dancing admiring her pure strength of character. The scar on her face was fading nicely through the hole where the bullet entered and blew up her face, still interfering with eating and drinking. She had to tilt her head to the side and use a straw to sip her beer, just a little at a time. She was pretty good at it, though as the effects of alcohol took hold, her skill waived, and streams of beer traced a path down her chin which drip dripped onto the floor. Martin was a good mover, and he grabbed Janet for a slow dance, whispering instead of sweet nothings, a strong message,

"See him by the bar over there," he nodded towards a bloke chatting to a rather beautiful buxom redhead. "Tony, he is retiring next week from working as a doctor; he will be Graduated a short time later."

"Oh god, have you spoken to him?" asked Janet pulling away from his hold.

"Yes, he is one of us. Please help us." Janet looked up at him and nodded her head up and down. She felt euphoria; finally, she was not alone. She was not bothered if she lived or died, but other people, well, that was different. They finished their beers and danced, and they all began the walk back to the outskirts of the Nerve Centre to the garage. The chatter was lovely, like ripples of bird song intermittently disturbed by laughter. Janet had had a good night. She felt reenergized and complete. It was a joyful hug of old and new friends with promises to do it again next week. Martin told Janet that someone would be in touch soon to give her information about the next meeting. Janet felt sad as she returned to her new life. She would do anything to get back to being a Brownie. They really were good days. Although things were definitely improving, and she was making friends, it did not feel on the same level as her old friends.

Perhaps it's because they had some shared history. Janet pulled on her grey and blue clothes to make the short journey to her room, just in case she met someone. As it was, the area was quiet, everyone asleep in their rooms in their wings. Janet tried to walk quietly, but to hear her footsteps sounded loud in the corridor to her wing. She used her fob to open the wing door and again her own door and entered her room. She ordered the light in the lounge to come on and flung herself on her sofa. She pulled off her two layers of clothes and then sat naked on her sofa, feeling rebellious. And for some reason, she felt like running naked down the corridor to the day room. She didn't do that but did fall asleep sitting on the sofa. She woke up about an hour later. Once she had her bearings, she took herself off to bed and pulled the covers over her up to her head.

Janet slept well that night. She hummed melodic tunes while dressing and rose with optimism and hope dominating her emotions.

She strode down the corridor towards the dining room, almost breaking out in song. She spotted Debbie ahead, serving some wingmates. Janet grabbed a chair at an empty table and asked Debbie to make her toast and tea. Debbie smiled at her, then went into the kitchen. She came out a few moments later

"Look at you. You look like you lost a pound and found a tenner, it's that, or you are in love," Debbie said as she put the teapot, milk and teacup and saucer on the table, "do tell" oh, if she only knew, but the idea of a boyfriend might be a good cover she decided to roll with it.

"Well, yes, I did meet someone," Janet said, acting coy.

"Do tell me, what's his name? Where did you meet him, was it love at first sight?" Debbie bombarded questions her, which offered Janet a bit of thinking time. She decided to be vague, giving Debbie enough information to appease her, "he is a Brownie, a doctor," Janet offered, then made her excuses to leave for work. She popped into her suite to pick up her overalls, noticing another note on the floor by the door. She closed the door, picked up the slip of paper and quickly read it. It said '7 pm, Social club tonight, poker'. Janet screwed up the paper and put it in her pocket, pulled on her work overalls, and then set off for work. Once there, she got stuck washing the posh car that was due out in an hour. She started off wiping the inside, then got a small vacuum cleaner to hoover out the debris on the floors. She cleaned all the windows inside and then checked over her work to make sure everything was clean.

Then it was a case of washing down the outside of the car and cleaning the wheels and windows. She was pleased with her handiwork when she stepped back to look at the clean car. Satisfied, she closed all the doors and put the car key back in the office, then went to check over the bikes. They had proved to be really popular, so they had increased the stock to ten. Janet's job was to maintain them and keep them clean. Two had been booked for use later in the morning, so she moved two of them outside of the office and gave them a check over. She checked the brakes and the tyre pressure before giving them a clean. When she was satisfied with her work, she checked the time to see if she had done enough to earn a tea break. She was the only one on the forecourt that day as Stuart was out with the large buggy giving a tour of the place with some new people from the Inner Circle. Janet made herself tea and dug out the biscuits before sitting down and resting. She found her job satisfying and much preferred it to the work she used to do with the environmental team.

She had just finished drinking when two brownies came along. Janet went up to them, suspecting that they were the ones who had reserved the bikes. Her hunch was right. She checked that the bikes were the right height for them before sending them on their way. They were doing a tour of the grounds in Second Chance; they were new, and Janet made sure to tell them about the waterfall near the park as a place to visit. Janet checked her list to see what else needed to be done. One of the buggies was out of action due to a puncture. She had not been shown how to change a wheel to do the work herself but made sure that all the equipment needed was ready for when Stuart came back.

He was due to return shortly; in fact, Janet thought he should have been back by now. Janet was driving the posh car today, taking some members of the Inner Circle to a function being held in the park in a large gazebo. Janet didn't know what the event was for, but the people she would be driving the short distance to the park were the star attraction. She checked the time; they were due very soon, but Janet was at a loss as to what to do.

During working hours, someone had to be at the garage at all times. If Janet was needed to drive the posh car and Stuart was not back, it was a dilemma. She thought about locking up the garage if he was not back, but that would make it difficult for the bike people.

Anyway, her concerns proved unfounded as, at that moment, Stuart came into the garage driving the buggy. He had already dropped off his passengers, so he parked the vehicle, got out and locked it before going up to Janet to see if there were any problems. Janet told him that the two people had taken the bikes and everything was ready for the tyre change. He thanked her and then told her to take a quick break before she needed to go out. She opted to pop back to her wing to get a sandwich and a drink. She had about twenty minutes before she was needed, so she hurried back. Debbie was serving one of her wing mates but turned to ask Janet what she wanted to eat. Janet requested a cheese sandwich and a mug of tea, then sat down on a seat by the table. She then checked her hands; they were filthy with oil. She asked Debbie if she could wash her hands in the sink in the kitchen, saying that she would clean up after herself. Debbie nodded her agreement, so Janet found the soap and lathered up her hands. She looked down at her overalls, and they looked really dirty. She would have to see when she could get them washed.

Debbie came out of the kitchen carrying her lunch on a tray on her lap. She handed it to Janet, who quickly tucked in, aware of her limited time and the ticking clock. She finished her sandwich and picked up her mug of tea when Debbie put a cupcake in front of her. Janet couldn't refuse; it looked delicious. She put down her mug and picked up the cake peeling away the paper cup. She sank her teeth in, enjoying the sugar rush. Janet really found it hard to refuse sweet food. It was her nemesis. The cake was consumed in record time. Janet had only a few minutes before the end of her break, so she shouted out a thanks to Debbie, who was in the kitchen, and then rushed back to the garage forecourt.

Her passengers had just arrived; it was good timing. Janet took off her overalls and led the two Inner Circle workers to the posh car opening the doors for them and closing them when they were inside. She got into the driver's seat, waved goodbye to Stuart, and then pressed on the switch before steering the vehicle out of the garage forecourt and onto the road.

It only took five minutes to get to the park. Janet could see the gazebo and rows of chairs on the green but was not too sure where she was supposed to stop. She turned around in her seat and asked her passengers where they needed to be dropped off. They said that where they were now would be fine. Janet turned off the engine and got out of the car to let out her passengers. They thanked her for her work and then headed off on foot to the function. It looked like a celebration of some sort, no doubt, in time, the gossip mongers would start, and it would be common knowledge of what it was. Janet drove the car back to the garage, got out then went over to see if Stuart needed a hand with the flat tyre.

He was doing OK but told her they had another booking for the bikes if she could get four ready for tomorrow morning. She took four aside and then put on her overalls to begin the process. It had been a full-on day, but every day was different. That is one reason why she enjoyed it. Her shift passed quickly; it was busy enough for time to pass but not so much that there was no time for coffee. During one break, Janet and Stuart stopped to eat biscuits and drink tea. They had their usual banter, but then the conversation turned when Stuart said that a couple of security guards had had a chat with him the other day about her. He warned her that they were sniffing around.

"Is there something I should know?" Asked Stuart.

"No, not really. I got into trouble a while back. It could be that." With that, they both simultaneously got up and returned to their workplaces. She was shaken and started to question her potential involvement with the underground team. She took her stress out on polishing the wing of the large posh car. There was a wedding the next day with the bride using the car, so Janet did her best to clean it thoroughly. She had an invite to attend, which was pending, but Janet was not sure. She barely knew the couple.

After work, Janet returned to the wing, had a shower then hunted out some food. Debbie was prepared for Janet's appetite and had a steaming dish of vegetarian curry and rice for her. She set herself at the table, joining Janet in the meal as they ate and gossiped, giggled and expressed dismay. Once she had finished her food, she thanked Debbie and turned down apple pie with custard, then returned to her room. She put on her Brownie outfit and then dressed in her work clothes. She had a little while until she needed to leave, so she spent the time in her garden admiring her new plants, which looked so nice against the brick wall. She was pleased with how it looked; she vowed to keep on top of the gardening jobs and wandered if perhaps she could get a rose bush for the corner plot. Getting her thoughts back on that evening, she felt rather nervous about what this underground movement did and knew. Janet changed out of her clothes before looking around to see if there was anybody around. Satisfied she was on her own, she headed off towards the social club.

The walk gave her time to think about the evening ahead. She kept her wits about her, just getting an unsettled feeling that she was being watched. But still, there was no sign of anybody around until she got to the social club. Once she arrived, she made her way to the bar after scanning the room for familiar faces. She ordered a beer and then sat on the bar stool sitting somewhere where she thought she could be seen. Shortly after, Martin joined her and led her to the back of the hall, where half a dozen people sat. It was not quite what Janet imagined, but she went with it.

Everyone introduced themselves to her and invited her to join them for 'poker'. It was quite a clever ruse than sneaking off to a small dark room somewhere where their absence would be obvious. Janet had no idea how to play poker, so one of the team went to get the dominoes. While playing, they discussed the situation as they saw it asking Janet to share as appropriate. Janet laid down a double six as she told them about her experience the other day driving Alan to his Graduation.

They were particularly interested in the bottle she had time to view, quizzing her on what it was. Janet, at this point, told them that she had an information leaflet relating to the drug, which was not taken when her room was searched. She agreed to give the pamphlet to Martin to pass it onto the doctor, who may be able to make sense of the professional language and terminology. They agreed the next time to meet for dominoes; as the game ended, the players dispersed. Janet finished her pint and stood up to make her way back to the Nerve Centre. Just then, she saw Lisa and Kim entering, so they called them over to where she was by the bar. The girls ordered wine then all three of them found a free table and sat down to gossip. Janet was delighted to see how well her friends were and how well they were succeeding in their jobs. Kim had been promoted, and Lisa had been given more complicated work. Janet asked them if they had seen Mel and Gary. It still sounded odd to hear those two names together; she always thought Janet and Gary sounded so good. But hey ho, it was not to be. Janet held no grudge against her friends. Her time with Gary was lovely and served a purpose, but she felt fine about letting him go.

After a while, Janet said her goodbyes and started the walk back to her suite in the Nerve Centre. As she walked, she grew increasingly aware that she was being followed. She stopped walking to see if she could hear anything. Hearing only her breath, she started walking quickly towards the garage. Then she heard two lots of footsteps behind her. Whomever they were marching quickly, walking faster than her. Janet really was not sure what to do, so they just focused on the path ahead. Just as she got to the garage, two men caught up with her and then passed her, stopping in front of her. She stopped and looked up to see a couple of blue-clad young men.

"What are you doing out here," one of them asked her,

"On my way back," she said, forcing a smile.

"It's dangerous to be out on your own", the other one added,

"I'm going back now," Janet said, "is there anything else?"

"What's your name? Where are you based?" he replied. Janet told him the information he had requested, and then one of them asked her why she was wearing Brownie clothes if she was based at the Nerve Centre. Janet was lost for words, so they mumbled something, hoping they would just move on. The guard did not ask her anything else, but they moved away; it was when they turned their backs to her she saw that one of them had no bum.

She thought it an odd injury; it must be hard to sit down. He seemed to be able to walk well. This, she thought as she sped up her walking, deciding not to change back into her work clothes but to retrieve them and then go to her home. She went to the cupboard in the forecourt where she had put her clothes, gathering them and holding them close to her body; she looked around once more before quickly walking to her suite. Once in her suite, she locked the door and then sat down in her armchair, going over the meeting in her head. She made herself a coffee and then went out into her garden. The moon was very prominent in the sky, she noticed, thinking that it was far too big. Janet felt very unsure of what the group wanted to achieve, what the goals were, and what they would do if they got an answer. She was not too convinced they were an activist kind of group or an endlessly playing dominoes mulling things over type. Whatever she was left feeling, she was happy to join them. The power of communities of interests interested her and gave her a sense of belonging.

She slept well, waking only once to check that the information leaflet was still in its hiding place. Once satisfied, she fell into a deep, restful sleep until dawn knocked on her windows, along with the artificial bird song heralding the start of the day. She got up stretching, enjoyed a leisurely mug of tea while sitting in her garden then started to mentally prepare for the day ahead. She hoped to go swimming after her shift, it had been a few days since she last went, and she really felt the need for exercise. Once she had dressed, she took herself off to the kitchen, where Debbie was preparing breakfast for the workers. Janet greeted her and requested scrambled eggs on toast with a mug of tea. Shortly after she had sat down in the dining room, Debbie put her food down in front of her on the table.

"Did you have a good night last night?" Debbie asked her.

"Yes, I met up with some friends," Janet replied, deliberately being vague.

"I'm glad you have made some friends. Are you going to the wedding?" Debbie enquired.

"I'm not too sure yet, and I don't know the couple. It would feel a bit strange going. It looks as if everyone is invited anyway. Maybe I'll go. I will decide nearer the time." Janet replied between mouth fulls of egg and toast. With breakfast done, Janet made her way to the garage for her shift. She had buggies to clean.

Chapter 14
Hurt

Janet, over time, had come to view Second Chance as a large stage with props and pretend everywhere. Nothing bar the people were real, even though they were dead. It was odd to see how the place operated and how having fit workers was important. She was appalled at how they culled the old and ill but guessed they could not cope with dead wood. Janet was in a philosophical frame of mind thinking of ethics and values maybe her way to rationalize Graduation.

She truly believed that the Inner Circle, who policed the public and acted as jury, judge and executioner, felt they were doing good; after all, killing the dead was a good way to keep the people under control. Janet wondered if her work mates polished vehicles with such deep thoughts as her. She looked across the forecourt at Stuart bent over like a surgeon undertaking abdominal surgery.

An arm covered in dirt and grease, the occasional swear word uttered as he dropped something or other. They generally worked the same shift together; he was nice enough, but not enough not to be wary of him; she often felt he was observing her more than a boss would. Janet kept those thoughts to herself but remained mindful of what she said to him. She felt she was looking at people with different eyes, getting suspicious at every word or look. She had always had the belief that she was being watched, and now she had been warned. She turned up for work, did what she needed to do that day then spent time in the gym or in the pool. Apart from Debbie, she had not made any friends while living in the Nerve Centre. Everyone kept themselves to themselves.

Stuart went out in the four-passenger buggy, leaving Janet to work on the posh car ahead of the wedding. She checked the tyre pressures, wiped down the leather interior and cleaned all the windows inside and out. The car looked good, she thought to herself. Janet had made up her mind not to attend the wedding as she really did not know the bride and groom. It felt odd that they had invited her, the link coming from Stuart, who was the best man. He had asked if Janet would be his plus one, but Janet had already made up her mind not to go. It did cross her mind that Stuart was using the occasion to ask her out, but Janet shoved that thought aside. She really didn't need the complication. She felt uneasy about being in a large crowd of people. She would much prefer just having her own company. She had a lot of stuff to think through.

Once the posh car was clean, to Janet's satisfaction, she looked about her. There was only she and Stuart working that morning, which worked in Janet's favour. She went over to the small buggy and got things ready to clean it. She set down the bucket and sponges and looked around again. Janet was following orders from Martin to hide the information leaflet about the drug used for Graduation in the pocket at the door of the buggy. Janet hid it the in the user manual of the vehicle and then checked around her again. This had all been arranged the night before. The buggy was going to be used to transport some less able Brownies to the wedding. The plan was for Martin to retrieve the paper when the buggy was parked waiting for its passengers. Janet did her bit; it felt quite exciting being part of this; she just hoped it went according to plan, there was no reason why it shouldn't, but if it failed, it would not take an expert to link it back to her. The risk was thrilling. She felt alive, buzzing.

She was aware of the nervous adrenaline rush as she tried to force herself to not keep looking at the buggy. Once she had secreted the document, she looked around again. There was no one around; Janet breathed out in relief then rolled up her sleeves to start cleaning the vehicle. As usual she took pride in her work polishing the paint work to a degree that satisfied her. After cleaning the buggy, she stopped for a tea break. Stuart would be back soon, there were no further vehicles being used that day. So, she thought, maybe she would get off early. Stuart finally arrived back at the garage with the four-seater. He checked over the posh car and the small buggy before letting her go. Once dismissed, Janet went to her suite to change out of her overall. Janet assumed the plan had not backfired as no blue clad security guards had stopped her or gone to her suite. Janet sat on her bed, waiting in anticipation for a loud knock or the door being forced open by the guards. After a while, she left her rooms in search of food. Debbie as usual, came up trumps with an all day breakfast and a steaming mug of tea. Janet ate slowly, savoring each mouthful, almost as if it was her last meal before execution. Debbie wheeled over with her own food and drink to join her.

"This is so good," Janet said to her between mouthfuls.

"Good, glad you like it. The eagle has landed," she replied.

"Sorry, what?" Janet asked.

"The eagle, it has landed," she repeated. Taking a sip of her coffee. She looked down at her lunch, then tucked in, spearing a sausage before biting it in two. The grease dripped off the remaining end, which made Janet's mouth salivate.

"You, the notes," said Janet, finally cottoning on to what she was saying.

"Yes, now do you want fruit crumble and custard for after?" Her change of direction of the subject matter was down to the arrival of two dorm mates who took a nearby table to play cards.

"Yes, crumble would be nice" Janet answered still uncertain if all of this was some kind of a code. They fell into an amiable chatter as friends do while enjoying their lunch. Debbie asked Janet for advice about wedding attire and for help to choose an outfit for the afternoon.

Janet agreed to help seeing it as a good time to talk to Debbie about the Resistance. Fruit crumble and custard went down a storm along with more girly chat about men and the sort. Sometimes with chat like this it felt like what it was like with the onset of puberty. When interest in boys raises its ugly head along with the endless wondering if he fancies you and all that, it really doesn't go away as you age, just the dance gets more complicated. When food had been consumed and Debbie was free, they headed to Debbie's rooms. She lived in the dorm in a small but tastefully decorated room at the end of the corridor. She had decorated it beautifully to represent her character. It was the first time Janet had been in there. Janet looked around with delight, she certainly had put her stamp on it as she had with her power wheelchair. She had decorated that with plastic flowers, ribbons and stickers. Debbie had put a selection of dresses on her sofa for them to go through. There was a supply of these made available for special occasions. They came from the dead Earth bodies.

They were cleaned and mended and stored in readiness for times like this. You have to be pretty quick off the mark to get a good one. Debbie had grabbed three, she was ace at hunting out bargains and seemed to know where to be at the right time. Debbie changed into a fetching red dress, she wore it well it filled all the darts and curves splendidly. She tried to get Janet to try on a blue skirt suit, but she refused feeling ill of wearing a dead person's clothes. What's more, what would it be like to see someone wearing your own final attire. While Janet brushed and braided Debbie's hair, they chatted away about something and nothing until the subject turned to the Resistance. Janet asked her how long she had been involved and how she got involved.

"Only a couple of months after I heard that a baby had been Graduated because it was badly disabled" she replied.

"Lisa's baby, Linda. Lisa's a friend of mine. It broke her losing her baby," Janet said, stopping momentarily from her task,

"That's it, I have two sons, I miss them terribly it never goes away. Richard and Samuel, twins. It took me ages to stop crying when I arrived here. They were great lads, very loving and gentle." She wiped a couple of tears from her eyes then, changed direction of the conversation by asked Janet to do her makeup. Janet quickly realized that asking her about her children would upset her further had a look in Debbies make up bag to see what she had. She applied the base and was starting on outlining her eyes when she admitted to Debbie that she had no idea of what she was doing. Debbie thought that she was talking about applying makeup but then it clicked as to what she was really talking about.

"Don't worry, and we will look after you. You are too much of a hot potato for them to get you," she said, which was meant to be reassuring.

"It seems to be common knowledge about what I have found, is that true?" asked Janet.

"Word has got out, we have a mole, we have a few ideas who it could be just need to find a way to prove it. That's not so easy. Anyway, you know you are being followed, just don't give them any reason to call you in." said Debbie. Janet felt far from reassured by her words. She was losing touch with what she was doing. She wasn't sure if she should dress as a Brownie when she went to the social club, she would stand out like a sore thumb in her uniform. Maybe she should just not go and stay in the Nerve Centre but then she would not be able to see her friends. The few months that she had not seen them had been hard.

Doing it again would break her. Janet took her time to do Debbie's make up, she didn't make too bad a job of it, anyway Debbie was pleased with the final result. Now with her dress, hair and makeup she was ready to go to the wedding. It was being held in the chapel with the wedding meal going ahead in a gazebo in the park, a bit like what happened the other day. Janet thought that maybe some people from the Inner Circle had got married, maybe. Janet went out of Debbie's room and went to her own. She looked in the garden at her plants wondering if they needed watering. She felt the soil for dampness on one of them and was satisfied that they were OK. She sat on the rickety chair looking at the wall now partly obscured by the climbers. As they matured, they would fill the wall with colour, she could only hope that she would be around to see it. With a lot of people going to the wedding the gym would be empty she thought, in fact most of the people in Second Chance would be going she mused. With that thought in mind, she changed into her gym kit, grabbed her key fob and headed to the gym. She would never consider herself as a gym bunny, but it was a good place to think while moving. She switched on the running machine and got into the stride of a fast walk. As an overweight middle-aged woman, she was beyond running as the impact hurt her knees, a good walk was less impact but still raised her heart rate. Her thoughts helped her process all the information that had come her way featuring the Resistance. She was surprised to learn that Debbie was part of the group, she had not seen that coming. Still, it felt good to know they were on the same side. Wiping the sweat from her brow Janet moved onto the weights. She was less sure of what she was doing with them but tried to copy what others did. She found this as equally strenuous as the tread mill but fathomed out it must be doing her good. She attempted a dead lift with small end weights then lowered her arms. She did a few more then she increased the weight on the bar and tried to lift that. She got so far before she heard something go in her back. Janet dropped the bar and yelled out loud in pain. She felt around her lower spine to see if she could determine any injury but apart from causing her more pain nothing felt out of place. Despite knowing it would hurt she kept prodding the area almost as if she wished to cause herself more and more pain. She had pins and needles up and down her right leg which frightened her. She sat down to see if that would help the pins and needles which helped but instead, she felt a numbness in her foot. Janet needed to get some help and the only thing she could think about was to go back to the wing. She grabbed her belongings then ungainly stood up then took a step to see how well she could walk to see if she could make her way back to her home. Tentatively she walked slowly along the corridors. She used the wall to support her bending forward to minimize the pain. Her breath was laboured with holding it in when a spasm radiated out from the injured area. She hoped someone was around who could help her but failing that she needed to get to her suite. With that target in mind, she slowly made her way. It took an age before she got to her rooms. She used her fob key to open the door, entered and made a beeline for her bed. Janet gingerly sat on the edge and spent a bit of time fathering out how to lay down without aggravating her sore back. She settled to lying on her side and felt relief as the pain and numbness abated allowing Janet to relax her breathing. She had no idea what to do next so settled to resting for a while to give Debbie the chance to return after the wedding celebrations. Janet reckoned she would know what to do. She fell into a semi sleep waking when her spine again started complaining. Janet concluded that she had to get up and get to the kitchen. There was a telephone there for the use of the maid, Debbie, but Janet reckoned this was an emergency. Getting up made Janet wince. She held her breath as she moved her feet and legs from the bed to the floor in a swift movement. She used the bedside table to lever herself up to a standing position. Then one step at a time, still in her gym outfit she made her way out of her bedroom and lounge into the corridor then slowly slow towards the kitchen. Finally, she got to the kitchen and grabbed the phone. Debbie had put a list of useful numbers on the wall near the phone, scrolling down the list Janet found the number for the medical centre. She tapped out the extension number to be put through to a lady receptionist who had all the attitude you expect from a gate keeper. "Yes" she growled, "how can I help?."

Janet carefully explained her predicament in great detail in order to give the receptionist all the information she could possibly need. She asked Janet if it could wait until the morning as the doctor was attending the wedding, it was his one day off and only death and death would warrant his attendance. Janet was on the point of caving in but held on with bated breath. It worked, after taking a deep breath and tutting the receptionist agreed to get the doctor to come to the dorm to see her. Janet thanked her, replaced the handset on its cradle and tried to figure out how she was going to make it back up the corridor to her suite. Slowly she retraced her steps back to her lounge where she semi sat semi laid on the sofa in a position that caused no more pain. About an hour later she heard a frantic knock on her door and Debbie's voice asking if she could come in. Janet shouted the affirmative and heard Debbie swiping herself into the room with her fob key. "Oh my, what happened, what did you do?" She asked wheeling her chair over to the sofa. "God, you look dreadful, the doctor is on his way, hopefully he will give you something for the pain" she reached over to touch Janet's hand, "can I get you anything. Do you want me to stay?" Just then there was a knock on the door, three short to the point raps. Debbie released her hold of Janet's hand to open the door to allow entrance for the doctor. Janet saw a rather dashing older gentleman with a kind face. Just what she needed. He asked her what she had been doing to cause the injury and to list her symptoms. He felt around the area of her lower back his head gently nodding as he probed and prodded. He stood upright, stroking an invisible beard.

"Your back is in spasm, that's what is causing your pain. It's the way the body acts to guard an injury. From what you were saying and your symptoms I think you have ripped a ligament. It can take time to heal. When the spasms settle down you will need physiotherapy. I recommend you return to the Physical Complex so you have the care you will need to recover plus access to pain relief. What do you think?" He said looking at her.

"Can't I stay here?" Janet asked, "Debbie can look after me." Debbie nodded her agreement.

The doctor scratched his head as he said "well, I guess I could arrange that, but it is not what we usually do. How about a compromise, you stay here but go to the physical complex for physiotherapy? I can make arrangements to get you antispasmodics and pain relief. Now, like any back injury, it is best to be as active as you can without causing you pain. How does that sound?"

"That's great" Janet replied. With that the doctor got ready to leave "oh by the way, thanks for that information leaflet. I will study it tonight" he headed for the door pulling it shut behind him.

"That's him? The one who's due to retire" Janet said as she pulled her body into a seated position.

"Yes, you would think Second Chance would value a good doctor; they owe him a proper retirement, not Graduation," Debbie said as she busied herself making tea. Debbie was brilliant; she fetched and carried for Janet, who struggled to carry things as she needed the wall for balance. Also, Debbie popped over to the medical centre to get Janet's prescribed medication. When she was there, she had a talk with the doctor about how best to help Janet and to touch base with the doctor about the Resistance business. Debbie headed back to the Nerve Centre with the medication, her mind preoccupied with everything she needed to do. She didn't notice a man and a woman ahead of her, who stood in her path. Debbie noticed at the last minute and stopped her wheelchair. She looked up at the blue-clad guards who stared at her.

"What's up?" Debbie said.

"Your what's up" one of them said.

"How can I help" she said feeling worried.

"You have been a naughty girl" the man said leaning down to her level and looking her in the eye. He was clearly trying and succeeding to intimidate her. "You have been meddling into something you shouldn't be involved with. What do you say about that?"

"I erh, I really need to get going, one of my wards has been injured. I have pain killers for her." Debbie said then reversed her chair with the joystick. She went around the pair who let her pass without another word. Then one of them, the woman came after her asking her to stop. Debbie did as she was asked and looked the woman in the eye defiantly.

"You now have two strikes. Don't do anything to get one more. You know what happens to people who get three" said the woman who stood up letting Debbie pass. Debbie went as fast as the chair could to get away from the guards. She was visibly shaking from the encounter and could not get to the wing fast enough. When she got to base she went to her room to compose herself before knocking on Janets door to give her the drugs. Janet yelled for her to come in which Debbie did closing the door behind her. She steered her chair into the bedroom where Janet was lying in a peculiar position after trying to find the most comfortable position she could. Janet looked at Debbie who clearly had a forced smile on her mouth.

"Debbie, is everything OK?" she asked her.

"I'm fine, you're the one needing care" Debbie asked but could not hold her gaze at Janet.

"No, there's something wrong, what's happened? Janet said sitting up in her bed. She could see Debbie better now and could see her fighting back tears. "Debbie what's happened?" Janet asked her again. This time Debbie drew a bit nearer to put the medication on the cabinet by the bed. She took the tablets in there bottles out of the bag and looked at the labels. She was clearly trying to find the words.

"Two guards gave me a warning. They have been watching me." Debbie said looking at Janet.

Janet could see she was frightened by the encounter. She knew what it felt like and reached out for Debbie's hand. Debbie held out her hand for Janet to hold, the human contact meaning so much at times like this.

"I'm so sorry you had to go through that. Did they give you a strike?" Janet asked.

"No, just a warning. I have already got two strikes. I have to be careful" Debbie said. Janet had no idea she had been given strikes. It was the first she had heard of it.

"Oh dear, I understand now why you are so upset. I think I would feel the same if I was in your shoes" Janet said. "Why don't you go and make some tea for us both while I take some of these tablets" Janet said knowing herself that sometimes doing a physical task can help when you are overwhelmed with emotion. It would give Debbie chance to compose herself. They needed to talk this through properly and come up with a plan to keep Debbie safe. Janet checked the dosage and frequency of taking each of the tablets then took some with some water by her bed side. She had been given pretty strong pain relief and she was concerned how they would affect her. Debbie came into the bedroom carrying two teas. She handed one to Janet and moved her chair as close as she could to the bed.

"You know what we need? Cake, give me two minutes to get it, I baked a ginger cake this afternoon, I think we deserve a slice. Won't be a moment." With that Debbie put down her tea next to Janet's glass of water and left the flat to go to the kitchen. She was back within a couple of minutes with two plates of ginger cake on her lap. She handed one to Janet then took hold of her mug of tea.

She held it up saying "cheers" then took a sip of the beverage. Janet followed suit then they ate both in their own thoughts. Eventually Janet asked Debbie what she was going to do.

"I really don't know Janet. I need to keep my head down; I probably shouldn't be part of the resistance. I don't want to be Graduated. The thought of it frightens me." Debbie said.

"Well, that sounds like a plan. I think your right. It is too risky being part of the group. I am not too bothered about being Graduated though will miss this place terribly. I have made some really good friends here, it's about the only place I have felt I can be myself.

"I know what you mean. I guess everyone is afraid of the unknown. What ever Graduation is it maybe something good, we simply don't know. The fact that it is used as a punishment kind of gets you thinking that its awful. That's the bit I don't get. Debbie said.

"Yes, you are right about that. I used to think there was another complex, one for the older folk who have retired. I tried to see if I could find it. But I think they go the same way as the sick and bad." Janet said picking up the crumbs of the cake with her index finger.

"Funny, I've never really thought of myself as bad," Debbie said, laughing.

"Me neither," said Janet joining in the merriment. Janet could feel the tablets begin to get into her system. She felt woozy, but it did feel as if the back spasms were relaxing. She got out of bed, and they both went into the lounge, where Janet sat in the armchair. She moved her stiff limbs in turn and did some neck exercises.

"Do you need anything else?" asked Debbie.

"No, I think I have everything I need; thanks, Debbie," Janet replied.

"Okey dokey, I will leave you to it. I will come to check on you in the morning. Hopefully, you will sleep OK." Debbie said, moving her chair towards the front door. "Thank you, Janet. You've been brilliant."

"No problem. You've been helping me with this bloody back" Janet said smiling. Debbie opened the door and exited the room. She closed the door behind her then Janet got to her feet to go and locked the door. Once the place was secure, she went into her garden to check that the plants were still alive and to enjoy the evening air. She wished it would snow, that there would be strong take your breath away breeze, thunder and lightning. Even if they had two seasons would be an improvement. If she had stayed in the Environment Team, she might have been able to make that happen. Surely people there would think about things like that. Yes, the weather was nice.

The temperature was lovely, and the artificial sun 'kept' things warm and growing. But, how nice would it be for it to rain during the day now and then. Ah, she mused if and buts get you know where. Maybe they had a suggestions box somewhere or maybe she needed to suggest a suggestions box. Yes, thought Janet, the medication was working. She took herself of to bed through the brain haze and loose limbs. Boy were those drugs strong. How was she going to manage everyday stuff taking these. But they had helped, her back felt less angry and the pain, well, the pain was still there but she wasn't bothered by it. It just goes to show that pain is felt in the brain not the site of injury. She fell into a drug induced sleep not waking until the morning when the pain hit her like a brick. She involuntary shouted out when she moved her body to get out of bed. She held her breath as she moved tensing the whole of her body. After a while she felt able to get up and went into the lounge to look at the clock. She had no idea of the time and was surprised when the clock said ten in the morning. "Shit' she thought then sat down on one of the chairs thinking about what she needed to do. A few moments later, she heard a knock on her door followed by the zing of a fob key. Debbie opened the door and came into the lounge where she saw Janet.

"Boy, you look pale" she said, "Have you had your tablets yet? Perhaps you need to eat before you take them, what do you think?"

"Yes, I need to eat. Could you get me something please." Said Janet.

"Sure, no problem, what do you fancy?"

"Hard boiled eggs with soldiers please," said Janet.

"OK, tea?" asked Debbie.

"Yes, with one sugar please." With that Debbie took her leave as Janet stood up and went into her bedroom to dress. She couldn't be bothered to wash; she had decided to do that later in the day. For now, she needed to heal and get used to the opiates she had been given. Talking of which, she re read the labels on the bottles to see how often she should take them. One of them was every four hours and six hourly for the anti-spasm tablets. She checked to see how much water she had left in the glass then seeing it was low, she picked it up and took it to the kitchen to fill it up so she could take her medication. Debbie came back fifteen minutes later with two boiled eggs, soldiers and sweetened tea. She came in after knocking on the door finding Janet dressed looking like she had been run over by a train. She looked disheveled and pale, getting dressed had taken it out of her. Janet ate her breakfast quietly trying to work out what she had to do that day. She would have to let Stuart know that she wouldn't be in, maybe, she thought, she could use the phone to call him.

"I've spoken to Stuart, I put him in the picture, he asked me to tell you he wishes you well" said Debbie who was drinking her tea.

"Oh, I was just thinking that, thank you Debs" said Janet looking at her. Debbie smiled back and asked her what she felt she could to today.

"Well, I was thinking about going to the day room for a while so I'm around people. Then I will take a rest after lunch. Then do the same in the afternoon. I am going to have to be careful with those tablets, they make me feel very strange. I can't understand how some people get addicted to them; it feels horrible." Said Janet, "I may need you to walk with me in case I get unsteady, is that OK?"

"Yes of course, whatever I can do to help." With that Debbie collected up the crockery and cutlery putting them on a tray then left Janet to take them back to the kitchen. "I'll be back in a moment, let me just put these away." While Debbie was away, Janet carefully stood up and went to get her meds. She checked the dosage then swallowed the tablets with some water. She then went in search of her hairbrush to try to do something with her wavy hair which at the best of times, did what it wanted to do. It could not be tamed. She picked up her reading book from the cabinet next to her bed then declared herself as ready. Debbie came back then they both went down the corridor slowly to go to the day room. Debbie had got a wing chair ready for her in a good position to be able to see what was going on. She thought that the arms would help Janet to move herself. Janet got gingerly into the chair then exhaled. She had held her breath while she was walking and could feel the rest of her body tensing up in anticipation of pain. She got a lot of sympathy from her wing mates who all offered to get her this and that in the hope of making things better. She was very appreciative of their kindness, and it gave her a lift to get so many offers of help. Debbie popped in to see her now and then and took her breaks with Janet. After lunch Debbie walked with Janet to her room so she could have a rest, she felt knackered. It took a while to find that comfortable position then she fell to sleep for a couple of hours. When she woke she carefully unraveled her body and moved her legs over the edge of the bed to a sitting position. She was due another dose of painkillers and the doctor was going to come in to see her at some point. Janet carried the bottles of tablets with her as she made her way down the corridor to the day room. She got there with no drama and sat down on the same chair as the morning. Debbie came in with a tea and some cake so she could take her meds. Janet was not sure how Debbie seemed to know what she needed. She would have made a brilliant nurse.

About an hour later, the doctor came by to check on her. He felt her back to see if it was still in spasm which it was. He increased the dosage of both medications telling Janet that it was a serious injury. She was still getting numbness in the left leg and pins and needles going down both legs to the knees. Janet expressed concern over taking more medication because of the wooziness. He reassured her that would diminish within a day or two but in the meantime make sure someone was with her when she moved. Debbie immediately said she would do that and that she would go to get the stronger prescription from the medical centre in a short while. After the doctor had gone, Debbie went over to Janet who was crying.

"Oh, Janet, what's wrong. You will be alright, you will see" Debbie said putting her arm around her shoulders. "In a day or two you will start to feel much better."

"Thank you Debbie, you've been wonderful, I never expect people to help me" said Janet still blubbering.

"You're my friend. I really don't mind helping you." Now, if anyone asks tell them I'm out, I won't be long, just going to get you those tablets," Debbie said as she spun around then went up the corridor to the door at the end. Janet sat wondering what she was going to do, she made a lousy patient. Two of her wing mates came down the corridor having finished work. Both of them wore the same uniform as her. One of them Oscar, worked with the hospitality team he managed the stocks and wing orders. The other, Sheila was new, she worked now with the environment team, as someone who maintained the equipment. They both sympathized with her then asked her if she knew where Debbie was. Janet told them that she wouldn't be long that she was running an errand. They both went into the kitchen to make tea and have cake then they came and sat with her. They told her about their workday. Janet listened intently nodding when she needed to nod and exclaiming when she needed to voice. Both of them had had particularly difficult days. The greys, talking about those who wear the all grey uniform of the Nerve Centre, had been on edge as if something was happening. They had asked people to be extra vigilant for what, they did not know. At that point in the conversation Debbie returned from the medical centre with the new drugs. She welcomed the two wing mates and asked them if they had all they needed. She told them it was chilli non carne for dinner, with that they both stood up, put their cups and plates in the kitchen then went to their suites. Debbie checked the time then went to get Janet some water so she could take her meds. Janet shook out the dosage of both tablets then when she had the water, she swallowed them down. About half an hour later she was feeling very spaced out. She asked Debbie if she could take her to her room as she felt she would be safer being in bed. Debbie wheeled her chair beside Janet as they made slow progress down the corridor. They made it to her rooms with no drama and Janet weaved her way to her bed where she set herself down while Debbie removed her shoes. Do you want to get undressed?" Debbie asked.

"Do you mind?" replied Janet.

"No, of course not, here let me help," said Debbie. With that she helped Janet to remove her day clothes and into her nightdress. Debbie then went into Janet's kitchen to make her some tea then when it was ready, she took it into the bedroom setting it down next to Janet. Debbie spoke to Janet as she set it down but did not get a reply. She looked at Janet realizing that she was now asleep. Debbie took away the tea and poured it down the sink then got her a glass full of water to put by her bedside for when she woke. With that done, she left her to rest, went down to start preparing the ingredients for tonight's dinner. Debbie popped into Janets flat three or four times to see if she was OK. She was still asleep so left her to rest for the night, worried that Janet had not eaten nor taken a dose of her meds. She did wonder if she should wake her and make her something light, but Janet looked so relaxed that she didn't dare disturb her. She went in one last time before she retired to bed.

Janet managed to find a position in bed where the pain was less aggressive. She had the added benefit of opiate pain killers and anti spasm tablets which made her nicely woozy. Debbie had been brilliant helping her to get in her night clothes and bringing food and drink, as she tended to her they chatted about the benefits of going to the gym and about the imminent retirement of the doctor. Apparently, no one knew his actual name everyone referred to him by his job title. He had been on Second Chance for nearly ten years following being killed by a blast when gas cylinders exploded in a fire near where he was cycling to work. He had a good reputation being known as kind and efficient. It must be odd mending and healing the dead, Janet wondered if it was different to being on Earth caring for the sick. Janet slept well despite her injury, just getting up once to wee then struggled to find that comfy position again. Eventually she fell back asleep, waking to a knock on her door. Debbie came in balancing two teas and toast on a tray on her lap. She helped to arrange the cushions in the armchair in the lounge to provide support when Janet transferred from the bed. They ate breakfast together planning out the day, Debbie had already contacted Stuart to let him know Janet was still out of action, he sent his best joking about the hazard of going to a gym, something Janet, would no doubt, get endless rib about. After taking her medication Janet aided by Debbie got dressed ready to take on the day. The doctor was coming to check on her later that day but to pass the time she sat back in the day room in a comfy armchair flicking through some novels Debbie had brought her until she found one that took her interest. She filled a few hours reading, getting up to walk up and down the corridor to keep the circulation going. She was definitely feeling better than she did, her lower back did not feel so inflamed. She still felt pretty spacy from the drugs, but at least the spasms had stopped.

Debbie popped out every so often with food and drinks and any gossip she could find. It was painful to laugh feeling like a mule had kicked her in the chest, Janet felt certain the area was bruised, something to tell the doctor when he called. Janet and Debbie worked together to prepare lunch for the work people. Debbie was catering for four today, as well as Janet; it was spag bol for lunch. Janet cut up the onions and chopped the tomatoes, anything to be useful. At lunch she had lots of jolly ribbing from the boys. It was done with affection, but Janet found it all a bit waring. After lunch Janet felt sleepy from the Morphine, so Debbie went with her to go back to her room for a rest. The doctor was doing his rounds in the afternoon so Janet asked Debbie if she could wake her at three if he had not been. This he did in the early afternoon, Debbie escorted him to Janet's room then went off to her duties preparing food for the masses. The doctor examined her, prodding here and there as he asked questions and nodded at her answers. He gave his verdict saying that the injury was severe and that it was going to take a good while to heal he checked the bruising on her chest agreeing that it was probably done at the time of her back injury. He upped her pain relief suggesting that she should get some fresh air as a change of scenery will make things seem better. He said he will ask one of the nurses to accompany her and to use a wheelchair because of the effects of the medication would make her unstable. Just as he was leaving Janet asked him about the medicine information leaflet she had secreted to him. He scratched his chin, sat down saying "I have looked at it. Some of it I could understand a lot of it is too specialized for me. By the look of it is not a medication but a genotoxic chemical. It damages the DNA chromosomes making them multiply with a fault. So I am none the wiser without finding more information about this subject how it is relevant to Graduation. It has given me a lot more questions than answers." He sat down putting his head in his hands, for one split minute he looked old and weary. With the clock ticking towards his retirement and Graduation it all seemed so wrong. Janet wandered what she could do to help, she felt absolutely useless.

"So, we need to find someone or something that knows about this. There must be someone here that used to work in this field of science, surely, or a book or something. What about the library, would that have something, it had loads of reference type books?" Janet said, immediately trying to work out how she could get in there.

"I guess it's worth a try. I am pretty sure I have a pass somewhere that gives me permission to use it." The doctor stood up, "could you use it? I am under surveillance" he said.

"I think I am being watched as well" Janet said. "What about asking Gary or Martin to check it out. If Debbie can get it to me maybe, we can go through them when you come to see me."

"Sounds like a plan. I will brief Martin; I see him more. I can give him some key words to look for when selecting books" with this the doctor stood up, "now, be gentle with yourself and don't be shy about using the pain relief. There is something about Second Life illness or injury either heal quickly or you end up being Graduated. Let's keep you going." He left her room and walked down the corridor leaving the wing. Janet felt tired and drained. She gingerly stood up making her way to her bed for a nap. A little later before supper the nurse came over to see her. She doubled up as a physiotherapist as Second Chance did not have one. She had received training through a book but her previous work as a nurse put her in good stead. The nurse agreed with the doctor's idea of her going out to get some air. She talked about getting her a wheelchair and the need to be accompanied because of the effects of the medication she was taking, pretty much what the doctor had said to her. When she left, she assured Janet that she would come daily for the mean time. Janet went out to her garden through the door in her lounge and gingerly settled herself down on the chair. It was good for her just to sit and look at the fruits of her labour. The garden looked lovely. The colour of the plants was uplifting but it could all be seriously improved if there was butterflies and bees dodging from plant to plant. Or ants following an invisible path, or having a robin watch when she tended the garden waiting for her to unearth a worm. But there were no worms. Janet felt saddened about that. She missed these kinds of things. She wondered how her cat was on Earth, how her family were managing. Janet realized she was travelling down a depression road, snapped her wondering thoughts back to the here and now. Debbie let herself into Janet's room baring coffee and cakes. She moved her wheelchair outside then placed the tray on the garden table. She moved Janets mug nearer to her along with a very tempting slice of ginger cake.

"Debbie you are so good. I can see why you got your job, you make amazing cakes" said Janet.

"Why thank you" Debbie replied. "How are you feeling?"

"The pain killers are doing their work, it feels a lot better than it did as long as I don't move," replied Janet.

"Poor you. We are going to see if we can get you a wheelchair so you can go out and about. Perhaps we can find a way for you to get to the social club for the next meeting." Debbie said before taking a bite out of her slice of cake.

"That sounds good, I am worried I am going to get bored. Debbie, I've been meaning to ask, how was the wedding?" Said Janet taking a sip of her steaming coffee.

"Oh, it was lovely, the bride looked stunning. I don't know where her dress came from, but it fitted her beautifully. The ceremony was lovely, they chose to not have religious music they settled on the Beatles, you know how they like singing them at Karaoke."

"And the reception. Did the cake you made go down OK" asked Janet.

"It seemed to, I enjoyed making that, I'm going to see if I can make more for special occasions, you know personal ones like steam trains and dogs" Debbie said. She had spent ages making and decorating the cake and Janet thought it looked amazing. Debbie left Janet still sitting in her garden promising to return later on. Janet sat out there for an hour then got up to walk around. If she held her body in a certain position, she could get round OK though it must have looked odd.

The next few days passed like a dream, the medication Janet had been prescribed caused a haze and brain fog. Debbie was fantastic fetching and carrying for her and she stopped to chat and find things for Janet to do. Debbie got word to Gary through Stuart about Janet's infirmity. Janet was delighted when Gary and Mel came over the same day to see her. Generally, Brownies were not allowed in the Nerve Centre, but Debbie had managed to persuade someone to let it happen. Mel and Gary came when they were off duty and promised to come every day which Janet looked forward to. The nurse had dropped off an attendant wheelchair which they used to take her out and about. They took her to the social club for a hot drink as she could not drink alcohol with the medication she was on. She really did not want to do anything to jeopardize her recovery by drinking with drugs. It felt good being in the fresh air and to have a change of scenery, it all looked so alive and vibrant. Janet was thankful for the distraction it was getting boring looking at her own four walls. Her friends did a tour of the gardens with Gary filling her in with all the developments in the plant nurseries. It felt a world ago that she attended the garden as a Brownie. A lot had happened since then and a lot of it bad. Janet breathed in the warmed air feeling the positive benefits as the scents from the flowers tickled her nose. She felt alive and wished she did not have to return to the Nerve Centre, everything felt grey there where in the gardens there was colour. Feeling invigorated she thanked Mel and Gary for taking her out as they returned to Janet's rooms. Debbie was there with a tray of teas which they all supped in the lounge. It was a lovely end to the afternoon but always at the back of her mind was the ticking clock of the Doctors impending retirement and Graduation. She deliberately avoided that subject with her friends to protect them. They had an idea of what The Resistance was about but that was about all. Somehow it felt safer not involving them as she felt sure she was under surveillance. The group were due to meet at a social dance the next day. Janet needed to arrange getting there, she did not have much upper body strength to propel the wheelchair so needed help with that. She asked Mel if she would take her which she agreed to before the discussion focused on what to wear, Debbie suggested that they have a girly time doing hair and make-up which sounded fun. With that and seeing Janet battle fatigued Gary and Mel said their goodbyes leaving Janet in the very capable hands of Debbie who encouraged her to rest. Janet did not need a lot of persuading headed off to her bedroom to sleep. Debbie left her, collected up the mugs for washing and wheeled down the corridor to the kitchen. She set about doing the washing up humming a nameless tune when she heard a sound behind her. She turned around expecting to see one of the people she catered for but instead was surprised to see two tall blue clad men standing in an identical stance with their arms crossed over the chest pose.

"You are to come with us. Someone from the Inner Circle wants to talk to you," said one of the men; the other nodded with each word he said, almost like a puppet.

"I have work to do, it's time for me to start preparing the evening meal" Debbie said busying herself moving crockery around to hide her fear.

"They will have to fend for themselves, this is more important than that" replied the first man while his colleague nodded his head. Debbie found this amusing and tried to suppress a giggle.

"This is no laughing matter, this is serious" he said though very unconvincing, "let's go" with that he grabbed the attendance handles on her power wheelchair and started to push her out of the kitchen and down the corridor towards the dorm door. He used his pass to get through numerous locked doors taking Debbie down corridors she did not know existed. Finally, the three of them went through a whoosh door which opened into a circular room with small rooms coming off it. There was a blue clad woman with a clipboard seated by a table just off centre of the circle.

She pointed to the door of one of the rooms which they entered with the pass, inside was a seat come bed that was molded to the wall with little else in the room. There were no windows just a half clear door. The guard wheeled Debbie into the room then let go of the chair handles then retreated out of the room backwards, not letting Debbie out of his sight. Finally, he shut the door closed leaving Debbie in an echoey room or cell, she was really not sure. She felt fear in her abdomen and chest. A tight ribbon of dread entwined with fear which impacted on her breathing. She was aware of the inhalations and exhalations rattling around the space. She stayed in the position she had been left in for a while until she moved her wheelchair around to face the door. The glass in the door was at such a height that Debbie could not see out of it sitting in her wheelchair but at least it let in light which made her feel better. She tried to imagine how scary it would be if it was dark. Debbie became aware of sounds from outside or may be the other cells. She stopped breathing so she could focus on the noise but was none the wiser for it, she tried to call out but the fear affected her vocal chords resulting in a gargle emerging instead of words. She gave up on that deciding to listen instead.

Debbie lost track of time she tried to count seconds and minutes, for some reason she felt this necessary but at least it kept her busy and her mind off the fear. A few hours or so later, she heard footsteps coming to the door and the whizz and clicking of the pass activating the lock which unlocked and opened to reveal the clipboard woman and another blue dressed man. He entered the cell , roughly grabbing the wheelchair handles and pushing her out into the circle beyond the door.

"Name" barked the woman, "What is your name."

"You know what my name is? It's on your clipboard," said Debbie looking at the board.

"Just tell me your name, no funny business" she responded abruptly.

"Debbie Munro, why am I here?" She asked desperately trying to keep her rising panic under control.

"You are no longer needed at Second Chance you are being sent somewhere more suitable. You will be leaving this evening. You can have one final meal, what do you want?" the woman words hit one by one to a fearful Debbie who felt unable to reply as her tongue felt too big for her mouth. She was aware of the quickening of her breath.

"But why? What have I done?" She stuttered as she spoke, her eyes pleading with her captor to let her go. "I do a good job; I've not heard of any complaints."

"You have been known to be plotting to overthrow the Inner Circle, you have been observed attending meetings and covering up for others. Now what do you want to eat?"

"Nothing, I don't want anything" Debbie said trying to keep her tears away. She looked up at the woman with pleading eyes "what can I do to make you change your mind? Do you want names?"

"We don't need your help. Anyway, it would make no difference. I will come for you about seven, if you change your mind about the meal, let the guard know. Don't worry, it's not as bad as all that, you will be going somewhere better, your time here on Second Chance has come to its end see this as an opportunity." She smiled kindly then nodded to the guard to move Debbie back into her room stroke cell. Debbie sat still and quietly digesting the conversation, she was scared.

She didn't know what to do. Someone will miss her when they have no evening meal because she was not there. Would they even suppose of her being in a cell? She was kicking herself for ever getting involved with the Resistance. None of them saw this coming, it was meant to be the Doctor next. What about Janet, she thought, surely, she is at risk as well, if only she could get a message to her, warn her. Debbie moved to the bed and maneuvered herself onto it and tried hard to relax. She was going to die tonight, the words rattled around her head. She began to sob and gently rocked her body to try to comfort herself.

"Please, please let me go. I won't do it again, please" she pleaded over and over again. She just heard the echo of her words in the air. The lady with the clipboard ignored her, she had probably heard everything coming from criminals like Debbie. It seemed strange that if Graduation was such a positive experience why would they hold people in cells? The irony didn't escape her as she wept tears of despair. Debbie had no idea what the time was as her remaining time clicked by. It felt like a short time before the door to her cell was opened with the fob key. The lady with the clipboard stood in the doorway.

"Do you want a drink? Tea? Coffee?" she asked Debbie.

"Yes, please. Tea, no sugars" replied Debbie unsure if she should have one or not, maybe they spiked the drinks, maybe it was all part of the Graduation process. Either way, she was going to die tonight, drinking a mug of tea was the least of her worries. Debbie thanked the woman when she handed her a drink as she rested on the bed. She sipped it slowly determined to make it last as long as she could, maybe it will put off her Graduation for a while to give the Resistance chance to rescue her. Despite clinging onto that hope, Debbie knew she was clutching at straws. At precisely seven o'clock, the woman with the clipboard opened the door of the cell and beckoned Debbie out. Debbie got into her power wheelchair and steered it towards the door.

"Do you know your weight?" the woman asked.

"I'm about nine stone, I think" Debbie answered handing the empty mug back to the woman.

"The guards and someone from the Inner Circle will be here shortly to take you to the Graduation Centre." She said taking the mug from her and putting it on a table next to her chair. Debbie took the opportunity to look around her. It looked like there were four cells like the one she was in but they were empty. One of them was nicely decorated with a proper bed in it, Debbie wondered if that was for those people who would not be a problem. Like those who believe in Graduation as a positive thing. Debbie had a look to see if there was a lock on that door, to her surprise she saw one. A short time later, two blue clad guards came into the round room through a fifth door in the wall. They were accompanied by a silver clad person from the Inner Circle. Debbie looked at them with defiance in her gaze. She wondered if she could charge them and let the weight of her chair to plough through them. As if she had said it out loud, one of the guards looked at her then moved round to the back of Debbies wheelchair and took hold of the handles. Manual use of the chair overrides the use of the batteries which enabled the user to move her. Debbie lowered her gaze, "please not this, I will do anything, I can give you names, just let me go to my home."

"It's too late for all of that," said the member of the Inner Circle."

"I need to feed my babies, please, please. What do I need to do?" Debbie begged, she had tears running uncontrolled down her cheeks. She felt her nose run and angrily wiped it away with her sleeve.

"No, Debbie, it is time for you to go to a more suitable place," answered the woman with the clipboard. "This is the best part of my job" she said proudly. With that the guard started to wheel Debbie out of the room and down a corridor. They went through some whoosh doors and down numerous corridors to the outside where the open top minibus was waiting for them. Debbie was wheeled up the ramp to one of the wheelchair spaces in the vehicle with a guard either side of her. The woman from the Inner Circle sat next to the driver who, Debbie instantly recognized as Stuart.

"Stuart, do something. Quick. I don't want to be Graduated, help me, please, help me." Debbie exclaimed in a panic. Stuart just shook his head to say no then turned the key in the lock of the minibus then proceed to drive it down the road to Debbie's death.

Chapter 15
Resistance

Janet woke up feeling rested and ready to face the day; her back was out of spasm, which felt good though moving was still limited. She gently stretched before getting out of bed and tried taking a few steps. Her gait was a lot better than the preceding day things were definitely improving. Janet dressed with care, attended to her toilette then left her room with a fried breakfast beckoning her. The smell of bacon enticed her down the corridor towards the kitchen and dining room. She shouted out a hello to Debbie before finding a seat. Janet sat down and then moved the chair closer to the table.

There were a couple of other residents in the dining room, both eating and looking as if they were enjoying their breakfast. Janet said hello to them both and asked about their breakfast. Both of them replied that the food was scrumptious. One of them lent forward towards Janet, saying, "no, Debbie, today, it's Joe." Before Janet could digest this, a tall older man with a pronounced stoop came out of the kitchen carrying a mug of tea and a plate of food. He put them down on the table in front of Janet, smiling nicely, "I hope this is OK for you."

"It looks great; where is Debbie? She didn't mention having a day off" she said this as she picked up her fork to stab the sausage.

"Don't know, I was called to cover last night," said Joe "lots of rumours going around, though," Joe spoke in his Brummie accent.

"Oh yes, what is being said?" Asked Janet between a mouthful of fried bread.

"That she has been Graduated, lucky girl, I can't wait until I retire" Joe replied, he walked back to the kitchen to get more tea for one of the residents. Janet stopped chewing. She suddenly felt cold, as if all her blood had left her body "what did you say?" she asked Joe, "she's Graduated, but why?"

She put down her knife and fork and then wiped her mouth with a paper napkin; a million thoughts entered her mind. She did not know what to say or what to do. One thing she was sure of, she had to attend the meeting of the Resistance; someone was targeting members, and they needed to escalate their plans. Janet left the dining room without finishing her meal. She felt nauseous and hurried as best as she could to her room, where she started retching. She threw up until there was nothing left for her to bring up. She then sat out in her garden, trying to work out what she should do. She was somewhat limited with her torn back, but she would do whatever she could in the memory of Debbie. Thinking about her brought Janet to tears. She tried to brush them away but gave up and let them fall.

Once that was out of her system, she would be able to plan; she thought as she wiped away some tears. She felt cold, so she grabbed a cardigan from her dresser. As she lifted it, a folded note fell out onto the floor. Janet manoeuvred to pick it up the best she could, then unfolded it.

It was the note Debbie had written to her only a few days ago. She put her arms through the cardigan then pulled it around her so she could do up the buttons. She still felt cold, Janet was sure that the coldness was not one that could be changed with layers of clothes, she needed to do something about this so-called Graduation. At the forefront of her thinking was that it was being sold to the residents of Second Chance as something wonderful, a place where their dreams become real, a utopia.

Janet grabbed her pass and fob key, left her dorm and walked stiffly down multiple corridors through many doors until she came to the library where her journey had started. She used her cardigan to cover the surveillance camera and her fob to unlock the door.

Once inside she took a deep breath then set about to find information, anything that would strengthen their cause. She scoured the shelves quickly to see if anything jumped out at her. She spotted a medical encyclopedia type book that she thought would help her with some of the professional terminology. She flicked through it quickly, not really being too sure what she was looking for. She put it down on the dust free table then moved to the back of the room where the files were stored. She quickly read the tabs on the files pulling out any that warranted scrutiny.

She carried them to a table and then started the laborious task of going through them page by page. It was time-consuming, with many entries taking her down paths with nothing of any use; she nevertheless persevered skim reading data. She did come across a list of names of residents who had Graduated and the reasons why for the dates between January 2005 to December 2010. Janet thought this would be valuable evidence, so she carefully folded it up and placed it under her tunic against her skin, then continued her search. The last file she had pulled was marked as 'confidential'; she quickly pulled out the papers inside it, wondering what she would find. The first five documents were minutes of meetings of the Inner Circle; Janet was surprised to see this in a semi-public library.

There was little of any use in these bar a couple of entries about residents who had received strikes and the reasons why, she noticed that one of these was the author of the journal, Wendy. Janet stopped to think about Wendy and how Janet's journey had started with her. After scouring the papers, she turned her attention to the book she had removed from the shelf. She flicked through looking for anything related to genotoxic but that provided a small amount of information but nothing revealing. Standing up and gently stretching Janet walked back to the area in the library that housed the books. She stopped to understand the filing system used to store the books, it didn't look as if there was one, so Janet took more time to read the titles to see if they gave any insights. She was looking at the third shelf, the third book along when Janet whispered the word 'bingo'. With a flourish she moved the book off the shelf and firmly into her hands. The book was titled 'DNA, The Impact of Enzymes on Cell Ageing' it was the only book that focused on genes and all of that, most of the book introduction was hard for her to understand but nevertheless went to the back of the book to the index, looked under G for Genotoxic finding several entries including a whole chapter devoted to this in the body of the book. Without hesitation she stuffed the book under her tunic with the other document. She made haste out of the library after she had replaced the files and encyclopaedia. She grabbed her cardigan from the camera moving the focus of the lens away from the corridor. Janet quickly put on her cardigan then made her way out of the building to the fresh air. She walked the way she used to go after visiting the library as a Brownie, when she reached the door that went to the outside, she went through it and made her way to the park. She went to her favourite garden bench feeling the warm air on her face and arms. She looked out at the lake, the water looked so inviting, so much so that Janet walked over to the lake dipping her hand in the water. She checked around her to see if anyone was around. That water does look inviting Janet thought. Next thing she did was to take off her cardigan, tunic and work trousers and carefully concealed the papers and book under them. She made her way to the waters edge by the sandy area then walked into the lake. She submerged herself gasping at the cold. She found it invigorating but swimming was rather painful so she walked out as far as she could then floated on her back looking up at the sky. Now and then she checked that her clothes were still there; but the water just felt so good to get out too soon. Time to get out came when she felt cold which was about fifteen minutes into her swim. Her back complained as her body took her weight. She felt like she had done something wrong, people just don't go skinny dipping in a lake in the daylight, more so if you are a middle-aged lady who should know better. She sat down letting the sun dry her body. She quickly removed her underwear then dressed in her tunic and trousers. She replaced the documents under her tunic then wrapped her underwear in the cardigan. She had an idea of what her next steps were, but for now, she needed to get back to her rooms so she could really study the documents and find a good hiding place for them. She had had the feeling of being followed for several weeks now, she was sure she spotted someone dart behind a building when she turned back after hearing a noise. She could not be sure though, so she continued her way back. Back in her dorm, she put her bra and knickers on the chair in her garden to dry then sat down with a coffee to look through the documents she had stolen. After a short while she noticed the time, she left her rooms to go to lunch. Joe was a good cook; he had assembled a nut roast with a selection of fresh vegetables which was delicious. There were a few other residents in the dining room who she sat with to eat her meal. At a suitable time, Janet 'accidently' dropped her fork onto the floor. She bent over to pick it up then dramatically yelled out clutching her back. She then fell to the floor writhing around in pain. Janet thought she had probably done enough to get everyone's attention. Joe rushed over to her to help.

"Janet, what have you done here? Let me help," he said, bending down.

"I need the doctor, please could you call him? My back is gone," Janet said in a small urgent voice. Joe ran to the phone to call the medical centre requesting a doctor to attend; the others supported Janet to walk to her room, where they carefully lowered her onto her sofa. She winced in pain and then thanked them for their concern and help. They checked to see if she needed anything else. Janet pointed to a drawer which contained her painkillers which one of them grabbed while the other one fetched water. Janet took two tablets and then excused her helpers to wait until the Doctor arrived. Very shortly after, Joe knocked on her door then opened it with his master key.

"The doctors here, Janet, shall I show him in?" Asked Joe.

"Thank you, yes, please let him in," Janet said through spasms of pretend pain. The doctor entered her room with a very concerned look on his face. He asked her what had happened as he checked her back. Janet whispered to him to look under her cardigan, which was on her bed, where she had hidden the book and the document. He went over there and then looked over his shoulder at her before lifting the garment to see what it was underneath. He read the book title and scanned the documents, then quickly put them in his doctor's bag, saying, "you need to rest, Janet."

"Have you heard about Debbie?"

"Yes, tragic, but you really need to take care, Janet; you're not safe." With that, he took his leave. Janet sat still for a while, digesting everything that had been said and not said; she felt afraid. The gardening days seemed like a long time ago when life seemed simpler and safe. She stayed in her room for the rest of the day with her thoughts getting intrusive, like a record stuck playing the same tune over and over. It was difficult to get her head away from her thoughts as they seemed to suck her in; this was not productive, she thought, then forced her attention on brushing her hair, using mindfulness to fully immerse herself in the task of pulling a comb through her hair in a rhythm. The bad monologue diminished, permitting Janet to attend to some nonessential tasks, deliberately avoiding her precarious situation. She knew she was under surveillance which made her feel anxious; she was increasingly aware of the people around her and modified her language as a result.

She was not sure who the bad people were, so it seemed better to treat everyone with a cautious approach. She was worried about Debbie; she hoped she really was taking a day off, but she had told Janet previously when she would not be in, but she had not said anything to Janet about today, and Janet had a bad feeling that the rumours of her Graduation were true. But why would the Inner Circle do that? Debbie was certainly not old enough to retire, she was contributing to the smooth running of Second Chance, and it made no sense. With all these questions whizzing around and around, she could feel her muscles tense. She averted her attention by moving into the garden to look at the flowers. They looked as if they needed watering, so she got up and found the vessel she used to water them. She then started pulling off the spent flowers and leaves, leaving the debris in a small pile to pick up later. This easy act helped kick start her mind off the questions that dominated her mind to the simpler things like tending her garden. After sorting out the flowers, she checked over her small apple tree. There were a few tiny apples on it. Hopefully, they will grow into lovely big fruits, but who knows if she will be there to enjoy them? She felt the soil around the tree to see if it was damp enough.

It seemed OK, then moved along to the next of her plants, a rather beautiful rose. The flowers smelt beautiful. They were a rich red colour and looked so lovely against the white brick wall. She removed a couple of dead heads and added them to the small pile of debris. Janet felt much calmer now; the wonders of nature, she thought as she moved to make herself a hot drink. She was just about to pour the hot water onto the teabag when she heard a knock on her door. She moved over to answer it, seeing that it was Joe making sure she was OK. She was able to assure him that she was fine and took up his offer of another slice of cake. He took off down the corridor returning with a generous slice of walnut and coffee cake. Janet thanked him, then closed the door to go and finish making her tea.

Once made, she took the plate and the mug out into the garden. She remembered at that point that she was due to take her tablets, so she got up to get them and then sat back down. She was pleased with how well she was doing. She had learnt quickly the way to move to minimize the pain, likewise, the best position to sleep. She knew when she was due to take pain relief because it hurt. She had gotten over the worst of the side effects, with her head feeling massively less foggy. Janet sat out there in her daydream world for an hour or so, then, as it was getting darker, decided to take herself off to bed. She took the plate and mug back into her kitchen, washed them up, then went to go to the loo and cleaned her teeth. Once finished, she took herself off to bed and moved into the comfortable position on her side with her knees up. It felt as if she was stretching her back. Whatever; it was comfortable.

The next day Janet got up and dressed and considered how she was going to fill her day. Joe made her scrambled eggs on toast and a mug of tea which Janet consumed quietly. She was the only one in the dining room; the rest of them were at work.

"Penny for them," said Joe standing by her table. She had not realized he was there. She looked up with a smile,

"It would cost more than a penny," she said. "I could really kill another tea, though." Joe smiled at her, then picked up her mug, "no problem", and then went into the kitchen to put the kettle on. She had planned to see if she could get to the garage today. Also, she needed more medication, so she had to get to the medical centre. Also, she had it in her mind to go for a legitimate swim; it certainly had helped her the previous day. Her plans were made; she gulped down her hot tea and then gingerly stood up to see how her back was.

The was quite a bit of complaining from her muscles which she attempted to stretch out. No, it was too painful; not going to happen, she thought. Janet went to her suite to check her hair, then walked the short distance to the garage forecourt. Stuart and Fred were there diligently cleaning two of the vehicles. Stuart was working on the posh car when he spotted Janet by the office. Somehow it felt wrong to see Stuart doing her work. Janet felt like she was not pulling her weight but knew at the present time, valeting the vehicles was out of the question. Her bad back was very stiff, and it was hard to bend. But she was missing, not working. On seeing Janet, Stuart put down the cloth he was using to polish the paintwork and walked over to her. "Are you OK? Nice to see you; you here to work?" He spoke.

"No, just stopped by to say hello", Janet replied, gently stretching her back which was starting to complain. "Nice to see you working, but you missed a bit," she teased, enjoying the banter. She stayed there for about an hour sitting in the small office tidying out a drawer. She could not stop herself from working. She was born with a strong work ethic, but at least she was being useful. Fred came over to talk to her during a coffee break. There always seemed to be more breaks than when she worked; maybe they see her as a taskmaster; either way, it was good to find out what was happening in Fred's world.

When the drawer looked tidier, she took her to leave; the pain in her back was excruciating. She slowly and carefully got up off the chair and started the walk to the medical centre, which was, at normal times, about a ten-minute walk. It took Janet a lot longer than that, as she had to keep stopping to rest. There were either steps or a ramp up to the building; she tried doing a step and then resorted to going up the ramp to the entrance. The building was two stories.

It was modern looking, with whoosh doors and a large cross on the wall. Once inside, she painfully made her way to the reception desk, which was halfway across the room. There was a beautiful long wooden desk where the receptionist sat. She had a computer in front of her with a phone next to that. The room itself was airy and light, with a very soft blue colouring the walls. There were several doors on all sides of the room, one of which went downstairs to the storeroom, the others to various reception rooms. The receptionist smiled a small smile when she saw Janet struggling to make her way to the desk.

"I need to see the doctor," Janet said, leaning on her side of the desk.

"I can see. Do you want to sit down," the receptionist replied, pointing to a row of four chairs along the wall just beyond the desk.

"Thank you," said Janet making her way to one of the chairs and then easing herself down. She realized that she had overdone it; probably, the swim the day before might not have been as beneficial as she first thought. The receptionist came over to her with her arms crossed over her enormous breasts. She had a piece of paper and a pen with her.

"Can you tell me your name?" she asked. Janet obliged by giving the woman the information she wanted. Once the receptionist had written that down, she gave Janet an amazing smile which lit up the room. She went to one of the doors with white paint on them and knocked once she entered before any permission had been granted. A few minutes later, she came back into the lobby with the doctor, who came over to Janet. "You look pale; how are you feeling?" He asked.

"I'm in pain; my back is in spasm. I need some more tablets; I ran out last night. Janet said as she rubbed the sore area on her back.

"I meant to get some to you. I thought you would be getting low; why did you not ring me? You could have done that instead of coming down here; you are doing too much, and you have a serious injury" with that, he invited her to his room which was set up like real surgery; Janet thought it was odd the fact she thought it would be different. He walked over to a locked wall cupboard, branded a key, and then swiftly unlocked it. He took out a small bottle of tablets, checked the label to make sure he was giving her the right prescription then handed it to Janet. Janet thanked him and then put the medication in her pocket.

The doctor asked Janet if she wanted to take some now, which Janet thought would be a good idea. He went to his sink to get some water in a glass which he handed to her. Janet unscrewed the bottle tipping out two tablets. The doctor suggested that she takes three, which she did. After she had taken the drug, the Doctor asked if he could examine her, which she agreed to. He gently checked her spine and lower back. "Yes, it is in spasm, and it looks like you have an area of inflammation at the base of your spine. I would like to give you an injection of cortisone to deal with that; then, I will ask our technician to take you to your dorm in a wheelchair; how does that sound?" Janet nodded her approval.

"Have you looked at that book yet?" She enquired.

"Yes, though this is not a speciality to me. It is very complex; it seems to me that the drug damages specific DNA, causing toxicity and resulting in the form of Progeria, a condition that causes premature ageing. I am not sure how these fit in with Graduation, though. Now enough of this; let me draw up this injection."

The injection was painful, and the needle seemed very long, but Janet endured it, knowing that it would help her. Once done, she re assembled her clothes and went with the receptionist down to the basement, where Janet was introduced to the technician who managed the equipment stored there. The technician selected a power wheelchair that was charged, bringing it to Janet to show her how to operate it. Janet sat in it gingerly and then looked over towards the exit. It was then that Janet spotted a chair that looked like the one Debbie used. She had personalized it with stickers and ribbons. On closer inspection, Janet was convinced of the fact.

"Where did this come from? It's Debbie's." She slumped in the chair with tears cascading down her face. She sobbed until she ran out of energy. The technician was at a loss of what to do; she found some tissues, which she offered to Janet, who took them gratefully. Her body hurt, and she felt drained with the knowledge that Debbie was dead again. The technician relieved that the tears had stopped, hurriedly asked Janet to sign a form releasing the chair into her care.

"I'm so sorry, but she was my friend," gulped Janet, dabbing her nose with a paper tissue. She then pressed the start button on the control unit on the chair and set off through the open door, and headed back to her suite of rooms. The technician did not attempt to go with her, she felt very awkward, and it seemed to her she had good control of the chair. Sighing, she closed the door and then went about her business doing an audit of the stored equipment. Janet felt like she needed some air, so she went over to the park and rode the powerchair around the lake. There were quite a lot of people out; it was lunch time which probably accounts for that. Janet left the park to go to the waterfall. Once there, she looked at the tumbling water imagining the power generated by them. She could not go to the spot she normally sat because there was a young couple sitting there.

Janet watched them, and they were clearly in love, and they kept touching each other and kissing. Janet thought that was lovely to see; it made her feel warm inside; it was either the couple or the morphine; it was hard to tell. Once she had had enough, she turned around and headed back to her wing. Joe would be serving food now; she didn't want to be late. She got back in time for food which she ate slowly, savouring every mouthful.

Joe had made a lovely veg crumble, and the pudding, sticky toffee pudding with custard, was light as a feather. After food, she went to her room; she felt drained. She rested for a while to regain her strength, and she needed to be in good form for that evening. She slept through to mid-afternoon and then made a brew. After drinking the tea, she checked the time and then decided to make an appearance to get something to eat. Joe was in the kitchen; he hurriedly moved some chairs around to accommodate her wheelchair. He got her a slice of cake with a mug of tea and joined her in consuming the food. She had a few hours until dinner, so she killed some time sitting in the day room reading a crappy romantic novel.

Why do they write trash like that, she thought. The heroine was always beautiful, and the hero was always not a nice person. Anyway, she thought, they must have people who like these escapisms, or they wouldn't publish it. One of her wingmates came over to chat. He had finished his shift and was like her, killing time before dinner. He asked Janet if her back was any better, which was kind of him, she thought.

She assured him that things were improving and then moved the subject on to his work. It sounds as if he had a bit of a day from what he was saying. With time killed and lovely smells coming out of the kitchen, Joe let them know that food was ready. He served her soup with freshly baked bread, followed by a jelly trifle. Janet left the dorm after eating; she was keen to track down her friends. She didn't bother changing her clothes into her Brownie ones; she was really passed caring. Once out of the Nerve Centre, she headed towards the nursery to see if Gary was working there that day. She took her time manoeuvring the clumpy power wheelchair. Any bumps in the path sent electric jolts up her back which felt very fragile. The sun on her face revitalized her making her feel less tense; the outside always had a positive impact on her; she waved to a few people she knew on the way until she arrived at the nursery. To her delight, she spotted a head with an axe in it; she called out his name, and he turned round, waving to her when he saw her. He wove through the raised beds until he reached her; he leant down to place a kiss on her cheek. "You don't look too hot. Are you OK?" he asked, cupping her chin in his big man's hands.

"I've been in a lot of pain; also, my friend Debbie was killed yesterday," Janet replied.

"Yes, I heard; it's caused a lot of upset. She was neither old nor too disabled to work, and there was no reason to Graduate her," he said with a touch of anger in the tone of his voice.

"She was a member of the Resistance; I think she was killed to make a point," Janet replied.

"Well, quite a few people are looking to join the Resistance on the back of this. The Inner Circle probably didn't see this would happen when they decided to take her," Gary pointed over to the beverage table, inviting her to join him in having a mug of tea or coffee. Janet nodded, asking for coffee; as he made the drinks, Janet asked him how things were going with Mel. His face was alight when he talked about her; it was clear he was smitten.

"Do you think you will marry her?" Asked Janet, at this Gary smiled, took a sip of his coffee

"Maybe," he answered her in a furtive manner.

"Oh, come on, Gary, you can tell me."

"Maybe" he repeated, Janet considered he was not likely to budge on this subject so switched the conversation to the evening ahead checking to see if Gary and Mel were going to the social club. Gary confirmed they were going and asked her if the Resistance were meeting that evening as usual. Janet said she was not sure but felt it would be important to as they were making good progress in finding out what Graduation was. Gary did not press her to shift the dirt, he knew as much as he knew to keep him safe from the security guards. He had a feeling he was being watched at times but could not prove it. Life was going well for him on Second Chance he really did not want to mess it up.

Gary and Janet arranged to meet at the social club later that evening to join in the monthly general knowledge quiz. The dream team had failed to get placed from their previous attempts they usually ended up writing down silly answers to the questions, giggling like naughty school kids. Janet left Gary to tend the young plants and started off to return to the wing for a rest which she felt ready for. On arrival at the Nerve Centre building, she got out her fob key to gain access but for some reason it failed to unlock the main door. She tried it again and again. Janet pressed the button for assistance on the intercom which burst into life very quickly. She spoke to the voice at the other end when asked her name and purpose, eventually the door buzzed releasing the lock giving her access.

She entered the foyer through the whoosh door straight in the path of two blue clad security guards. In dread Janet looked up at the men who blocked her passage. One of them handed Janet a buff-coloured envelope then they both side stepped allowing her access. Janet put the envelope on her lap and set off towards her dorm as quickly as she could. Her anxiety levels quadrupled at the sight of the envelope. She dared not to guess what it could be, instead she focused on getting in her room and closing and locking the door. She slowly tore the seal on the envelope and extracted the single sheet of paper it contained. She opened the paper to its A4 size and scrutinized the words written on it. Upon reading it several times, she sighed, sat down on her sofa and sighed again. She had been given a second warning for entering a forbidden area, the library. Despite her efforts to conceal her identity by blocking the security camera the Inner Circle had sussed it out. Now Janet was scared. She felt fear creep over her body top to tail feeling exposed and vulnerable.

It felt awful knowing you are under surveillance, she really was not a dangerous person, just an inquisitive middle-aged woman who had a riddle to solve. She was debating if to go to the social club that evening wondering if to separate herself from any contact with the Resistance even though they were desperately close to finding the truth behind Graduation, surely Debbie had not died in vain, that thought alone plus the need to be with her community hardened her opinion that yes, she should carry on, after all, she was already dead she could not be killed though that seemed doubtable now. Janet, having made her decision swallowed a couple of pain killers with some water then sat in her armchair dozing. She woke up just after seven, had a cup of coffee then readied herself for the evening ahead.

Once out onto the main corridor Janet looked around her thinking that she may be being followed. She couldn't see anyone so carried on her way. At every turn, she stopped to look feeling utterly paranoid. But she left the Nerve Centre in her wheelchair defiantly, determined not to let them get to her. She arrived at the social club quickly. The power chair could get quite a speed up even though it was a rough ride. At the club, she saw Mel waving to her. She came running up to her and they embraced. Gary followed Mel carrying two glasses of beer, offered one to Janet. Despite being on strong pain killers she took the plunge slugging a generous mouthful of the brown liquid. She spotted Martin, Kim's friend and member of the Resistance come towards her, he hugged her and whispered a warning of guards in civvies at the bar, Janet nodded her understanding then tucked into her beer. The mood was buoyant and defiant. Word of Debbie's Graduation had spread around and was at the forefront of conversation between groups of people at the bar. Kim and Lisa were holding a table at the back of the hall for everyone. Janet and Mel went over and put their drinks on the table. Kim and Lisa got up to hug Janet and asked her how she was.

"I'm still in a lot of pain but it is tones better than it was." She said setting down her pint on the table. Janet could feel the tension in the room, several people she vaguely knew came up to ask her if she was OK which was very nice of them. Janet assured people that she was fine then got into conversation with Lisa who was asking her what she knew about Graduation. Lisa had particular interest because her young daughter had been taken away from her to go 'somewhere more suitable for her needs'. Janet told her they were getting really close to the truth then the Inner Circle would have some questions to answer. Gary came over after talking with Martin and asked Janet if she was OK. She was feeling a bit giddy from the mix of drugs and alcohol but managed a nod and a thumbs up. She realized it had been stupid of her to mix her drugs. Martin came over to the table and asked if he could have a chat with Janet. Janet moved the wheelchair away from the table and outside in the night air. Janet showed Martin her letter from earlier which he quickly read. "You must keep a low profile; we cannot lose you as well" he said earnestly. "The Doctor told me that you had given him a book on genetics, he thinks it holds the answer. The potion causes degeneration of the DNA leading to toxicity and decay. It sounds horrific, in effect from what the doctor said is it brings about premature ageing." Janet stared at Martin trying to be logical in her thinking but failing because she was ever so lightly pickled.

"It makes people old?" She semi asked semi surmised.

"Yes. Graduated people die from old age." He said dramatically. He moved away to join some people at the bar leaving Janet feeling stunned. It made people old, but why? She couldn't join the dots her thinking process was temporarily indisposed due to being drunk. She went back in just as the music started. Some people got up to dance but most of them stood around drinking and talking. Debbies disappearance was high on the list of conversations around the hall. Janet watched the undercover security guards edging ever so slightly to where pockets of people stood talking seeing, she assumed, if they could pick up on what they might be saying about Graduation. Janet spotted the doctor at the door of the club who went up to the bar to place an order. It looked from Janets perspective that he had ordered orange juice but almost as soon as he had been served Janet saw Martin go up to him. They were discussing something and looking at the body language Janet thought they were discussing her. Janet felt like she had a 'dead man walking' sign above her head seeing that she was on her last life. She felt concerned about that thought because she only needed to take one wrong step then she would disappear like Debbie and the others. It felt like a private club where only a few are allowed to attend. One that you had no say about the membership. Janet stopped watching Martin and Gary and paid attention to the girls who were talking about getting up to dance. They all decided to get up and asked Janet if she was going with them. Despite everything saying no, it would not be right she moved over to the dance floor to see if she could make some moves just using her arms and torso. She became one with the beat of the music and started to move with rhythm. She gave into it and let herself go. After a few dances she felt satisfied and tired. She decided that she should go home before the pain started to come through. She hadn't taken her tablets with her so said her goodbyes to the girls and the boys at the bar. She promised to come back the next day then left leaving the pulsating sound of the music gradually getting softer as she moved away. She felt a bit sick and really wanted to get back where she could vomit in privacy. Even that thought made her feel sick so she trained her mind onto something else as she completed the journey as far as the garage. She stopped there for a moment or two noticing that they had got some more bikes. Cycling had really taken off on Second Chance with many people preferring to cycle than use the buggies. Janet went through the side door using her fob key then went to her wing which was a short journey away. She let herself into the wing then went to her room. She made herself coffee in the kitchen then drove the chair with the mug of hot coffee into her garden. She put the mug on the table then just sat in the cooling air taking stock of what had happened at the club. They were inches away from the truth, Janet felt sure that when her brain was less pickled that she would work it out. The missing bit can't be that far away, she thought but didn't try to make all the connections because she needed to be fully alert. She was annoyed that she had drunk the beer, it was a silly thing to do and it could have jeopardize her safety. She could very easily have said the wrong thing to the wrong person and made things worse for herself. Janet drank the rest of her coffee then went in to take her meds. Once she had done that, she got ready for bed then got into her bed to find sleep. Sleep didn't want to be found. She tossed and turned so much she got herself knotted in the bed covers. Janet got out of bed several times to see if that would break the cycle of thoughts, but it didn't work. In the end she gave up on the idea of sleep and went into her lounge and sat on her armchair with her book. Then she remembered that her glasses were in the bedroom so get up to go and get them. Finally, she was settled to read her trashy novel but she could not engage with the words. She gave up on that idea and reached to the sofa where her diary was hidden behind a cushion. She got hold of it and found a pen then started to write. In no time at all, she was scribbling nearly as fast as her thoughts hoping that getting it out would mean she could sleep. She wrote three pages worth of words then put down the diary on the coffee table. Janet got up to make herself another drink and looked in her fridge to see if there was anything to eat. She saw immediately that there was a large slice of carrot cake which Joe had made earlier that day. He must have put it in there for her. She took it out and cut it in half with a knife then placed one of the halves back in the fridge taken the other one to eat in the lounge. Everything feels better with cake, Janet thought enjoying the spices and creamy filling. She drank her tea after consuming the cake then went back into the fridge for the other slice. She ate it quickly and justified it to herself by stating that she might not be here tomorrow, and it would be such a waste. It seemed to her that one of the good things about Second Chance was that you could eat what you want and not gain weight. They could do with having that on earth. She felt quite sad when she thought of earth. She missed it terribly; she would have loved to have been at her funeral if she had one. Maybe there is no body to bury or burn because it had gone to Second Chance? Janet was not sure of that one. Maybe it's not a real body in the casket, a dummy one or someone who had no family to mourn over them. Janet thought that it was so easy to get caught up with this kind of thought. It sounded more like a story line in a book than reality. But the reality was that she had died and ended up here. So, if she dies again, where will she be, third chance? No chance? Janet stopped her thinking and went to bed where she fell quickly and easily to sleep. It was already five in the morning, soon the birds would start their morning song heralding the start of the day.

Back at the social club things were winding down. Martin was one of the last to leave having spent the evening talking to the many people who were upset about Debbie's disappearance. Things were coming to a head, they were inches away from the truth, thanks to the hard work of Janet who now was treading on dodgy ground. Martin picked up his glass half full with beer and thought about what he needed to do to lead the revolt.

Martin had experience of leading movements; he was a trade unionist in his past life. He worked at Vauxhalls for many years and got into the role of unionist when the management would not or could not pay the workers any more money to match the rising cost of living. He turned out to be a good speaker and a good negotiator which worked to his credit dealing with the management. One day, he was working on the production line constructing work vans when he was approached by one of the workers who was going through some workplace issues. He had been accused of bullying and was up in front of the board about it. He wanted Martin to go with him and help him fight his corner, which Martin was happy to do. He arranged to meet with the man later in the day to discuss strategy. That meeting didn't happen, Martin died a few hours later when there was a tragic accident on the production line killing two people and injuring many more. Martin was a hard worker he enjoyed his status at work and always was willing to support his fellow workers. No doubt, if he had not been killed, he would have been supporting the injured parties to get a good settlement. Martins' death was slow as his life's blood left his body. His right arm was mangled in the machinery causing him severe and agonizing pain. They had to dismantle the machine to release his arm but by the time they had done that, he was close to death. They laid him gently on the floor as the ambulance staff tried to stop the flow of blood. They knew he was not going to make it, but they went through the procedures. He did not gain consciousness throughout the ordeal, but he could hear. He felt soothed by the reassuring words of his comrades and the ambulance crew but as he neared death, his hearing muffled then failed.

Martins wife and children were helped to manage their grief with a large settlement. His wife, Sandra appeared on the local news when they covered the accident at the plant. She looked shocked, like a rabbit caught in the taillights of a car. The chief executive of the Vauxhall plant spoke about Martin in glowing terms, as he did with the other dead men and those who had been injured. It was just as well they had good liability insurance as the pay-out went into the millions. Martin was a good worker and a good unionist. He died doing the job he loved and now, on Second Chance he was putting his skills to good use by challenging the whole process around Graduation. He was so near the truth.

Chapter 16
Happy Birthday

The next day Janet woke up with a hangover. Her mouth felt like a sand box, her skin was blotchy even her eyeballs hurt. However, her spine was feeling OK, and she felt hungry. She got washed and dressed then splashed cold water on her face to make her more alert. She found the sensation of water on skin rather lovely so repeated it a few times. She studied her face in the mirror, thinking that she was looking old. Her hair had bits of grey in it and her skin was showing signs of wrinkles. Well, today was her birthday not that anyone else knew. She was determined to mark it somehow. Afterall, you are only sixty once. She remembered back to life on Earth and the holidays she went on on some key birthdays. Off to explore Rome on her fortieth, enjoying a Caribbean cruise on the fiftieth. She tried to come up with things she could do to make this one special. For her, the best she could think off was to spend time with her friends. With a decision made Janet walked down to the dining room where Joe was wiping down a table. "You look rough, too much to drink?" He said looking up from his task.

"Yes, last time I did that, at least for a while", she remarked, sitting down at her usual table.

"What do you fancy? Something on toast? Fry up?"

"Fry up, yes, definitely a fry up, thank you," Janet said, smiling up at him. He went into the kitchen whistling as he worked. He bought her a mug of tea as lovely smells wafted out of the kitchen. In no time at all, Janet had a plate full of cholesterol and calories, which tasted fabulous. She tucked in with relish enjoying every mouth full. Joe sat down with her with mugs of tea. He pushed one of them over to Janet, who muttered thanks with a mouthful of egg. She could not help herself but say,

"Joe, did you know, I'm a year older today. It's my birthday."

"Is it? Happy birthday Janet, are you going to celebrate?" Joe asked her. She stopped to think for a moment, remembering she was going down the social club in the evening. Maybe she could drop lots of hints, so they arrange a surprise party for her. No, she thought, Debbie had not long died, everyone will be focused on that. She would have to celebrate by herself.

"You know what? I am going to swim in the lake this morning then look after my garden then tonight I am out, that will do for now" Janet said smiling at Joe. He headed off back to the kitchen to start the washing up. Once she had finished her breakfast, she went back to her suite to take her painkillers. The cortisone injection really had helped, she felt a lot more comfortable. She changed into her swimming costume putting it on under her uniform. She grabbed a towel them checked her hair for tangles then smiled at herself in the mirror. What is another year? It is pretty meaningless here on Second Chance. Janet left her room leaving the wheelchair behind, she was determined to walk to the lake. It took her a bit of time but when she arrived, she sat down on her usual bench for a while. She knew she had time to kill before the evening so wanted to stretch this out as long as she could. Like every day, it was a lovely day. The temperature just right with the artificial sun in the blue sky with the same usual clouds gently rotating. The people who designed Second Chance had really put a lot of thought into it.

Janet stopped her daydreaming, took off her clothes revealing her swimming costume, then gently submerged herself in the water of the lake. The water was lovely. She was able to do more than she could last time she was here when she had not long injured her back. She swam around the island in the lake twice before stopping to get her breath. She floated on her back for a while letting the water take her weight. Just then she thought she had heard someone call out her name. She was not certain so turned over onto her front to do breaststroke around the lake for the third time. Then she heard it again. This time she stopped, turned round and had a look as to who was calling her. She saw Lisa on the bank waving to her. Janet waved back then swam back to the shore of the lake. Janet got out of the water and grabbed her towel to put around her. Lisa came over to her and they both sat down on the bench.

"How are you Lisa?" Janet said.

"Me, I'm doing OK, I've been hearing things about you from the others. Are you OK?' Lisa said wiping a stray lock of her hair from her face.

"Me, yes, well, I cannot really tell you I'm afraid. I don't want to get you into trouble. I am being watched, enough said." Janet replied looking around her to see if anyone might be listening.

"OK, what are you doing for the rest of the day, I guess you are not ready to work."

"No, the doctor hasn't cleared me yet. I can't wait to get back though. I might pop in later. Are you going to the social club later?" Janet asked.

"Maybe, I don't go there as much as I used to. I have met someone; I like to spend time with her."

"Her?" said Janet immediately regretting it. Janet did not know she was homosexual.

"Yes, Christine. She is so nice and kind. She is very quiet, a bit like me."

"Where did you meet her?" Janet said using the towel to dry her hair.

"At work. We work together. She has not long come out of the Mind Complex." Said Lisa.

"That's great Lisa, well done."

"You found anyone?" Lisa asked.

"Well, no not really, you know I had that thing with Gary, that was the last time" she said sadly. Janet was pleased for Mel and Gary, but she had hoped that Gary and she would be an item. Still, she had a good relationship with him which was nice. Lisa stood up to take her leave, Janet stood up as well to say goodbye. "I'm pleased you have found someone, you take care."

"I will, see you soon" Lisa said as she went on her way to work. Janet sat on the bench letting herself dry in the sun watching the comings and goings in the park. She had a lovely restful time, immersed in her surroundings. She was not far from the nurseries; in fact, it was next door to the park. She wondered if to go over to see if they had a rose bush she could have for her garden. She mused over her experiences as a gardener which she did with fondness, before things got complicated. Just then she spotted Gary, or more to the point, the axe in his head, instructing some new Brownies in the art of potting up. Janet waived to him in the hope he could see her. Eventually he spotted her and waived back then came over in his long-legged gangly manner. He sat on the grass near her feet mindlessly teasing out weeds in the flower beds. They chatted about this and that both avoiding taking the discussion to deeper darker levels. He really was a lovely man; Mel was really lucky. Janet wandered if she ever had a chance of romance with him but knew somehow that Mel and Gary made a fantastic couple. Janet asked him about setting the date to marry, his face lit up with the prospect of formalizing his relationship with Mel. Janet felt so good to be dead alive and not dead dead at that moment in time. He invited Janet to help in the nursery teaching his new staff. She was glad to, she pulled on her clothes over her now dry costume then they walked together into the covered area where Janet was introduced to Sally and Linda, his fresh faced Brownies. The girls were suitably impressed when they learnt she worked at the Nerve Centre they questioned her intently about the place filled with awe. Janet enjoyed her spot of work but after an hour became aware of pain in her lower spine that stretching failed to ease. She made her excuses to Sally and Linda found Gary to say goodbye then walked carefully back to the wing in the Nerve Centre. Back in her lounge she took some medication, thought about having some lunch then a sleep. Joes cooking was enticing, the smells from the kitchen ebbed and flowed down the corridor hitting Janet's nose making her salivate. She followed the scents to the dining room, sat down, then silently hurried Joe along to plate up and deliver the food. It did taste good, after her lovely morning she felt like her day had been worthwhile. She decided to catch up with some entries in her diary that afternoon a lot had happened over the last few days she felt it necessary to record it carefully in case it is read by another person further down the line. Maybe, she thought, she could put it in the library next to the other diaries before she died. She felt sad when she said that. But, she was on her final warning, one more thing then she would face Graduation.

Writing her diary helped her to think more clearly. She tried to focus on facts, but emotions and feelings interrupted her flow. Seeing the recent events in writing really helped to soothe her mind. She reminisced about the journey she had taken so far. From waking up in the Physical Complex and her time with Mark to life as a Greenie and a Brownie. As she thought she remembered her first sights of Second Chance, going to that strange induction meeting which really was not that informative. She remembered that they told them briefly about Graduation, a term, back then she really thought did not apply to her because she was going to make sure she did not reach old age. Then it hit her like a thunderbolt making her sit up from her writing in order to hold on tightly to what she had just recalled. Old age, old age, they were informed that they stay on Second Chance until they die of old age. Suddenly things made sense. Now she could see that Graduation was the process of causing death by using this drug to bring on premature old age. The knowledge gave her a cold shiver over her body. It was now obvious that Graduation was painted to be a good thing by the Inner Circle. Naughty people were dispatched to somewhere more suitable for their needs, the very infirm the same, the newly retired had earned Graduation, they were all not contributing to society. Eugenics and euthanasia.

Knowing now and understanding the controlling nature of the people in the Inner Circle was one thing but what to do with this knowledge? That question rolled around and around in her mind. She jotted down ideas then crossed them out. She needed the support of other members of the Resistance but at what risk? Janet was on her final strike. She was of high risk of Graduation. It seemed clear that dispatching Debbie was a message to the Resistance to stop their actions. She paid the price, but could Janet do the same? She always thought her life as meaningless but now it comes to the quick, could she face it? With so many thoughts tumbling around Janet wrote down as much as she could. Her journal rapidly filling up with the work from her brain. She stopped writing for a minute to read what she had just written. She wanted this to be able to be seen by others should she not make it. Next, she needed to speak to Martin to get a message to the Resistance members. She needed to find a way to get to him, but she was not too sure where he worked. She knew he hangs out at the Social Club, but it felt too open to accost him there. She wondered if she met up with Kim to get to Martin through her. It might work. Kim was now working in one of the offices managing supplies. It was easy to get to and not too far away. Janet decided she needed to act now so she wrote a note to Martin then set off in the wheelchair to see Kim. She set off down the corridors to the main entrance way of the Nerve Centre. She spotted Stuart working on one of the cars, he waved to her and came over to speak.

"Janet, are you coming over to clear up the office" he joked.

"Sorry Stuart, I can't stop. I need to be somewhere." Janet said hurrying away from him.

"Where are you going?" he asked.

"I'm meeting a friend, and I'm late," Janet said, trying to get past him in the wheelchair.

"Whoa, hold on, why in such a hurry. Who is it, a mystery man?" Stuart asked, "I hope you are not up to anything dodgy, you are on your last life." With that he got on tuning up the engine of the buggy dismissing her.

"No, just Kim. I told her it was my birthday. She is holding a party for me," Janet said, grabbing for anything to say to give a legitimate reason for her rush. It was pretty feeble she thought to herself. She carried on entering the building through the whoosh door then up another corridor, round the bend to the place where she saw Sally, the work advisor all those months age. Kim was working in a back office where she was sitting behind a pile of papers on a desk. She saw Janet then immediately called a tea break, reaching for the kettle and loose-leaf tea.

Once the brew had brewed, they enjoyed the beverage with some biscuits Kim hid in the drawer of her desk. Janet quickly came to the point of her purpose. She asked Kim to ask Martin to call a meeting of the Resistance as an emergency as decisions had to be made. She handed Kim the note she had written for Martin. Kim was concerned about the level of surveillance Janet and other key members of the Resistance were under. Janet responded that they needed to bite the bullet and have the meeting in the open. With that, their chatter turned to the subject of love and friends which felt cozy and false in the circumstances but a great cover. Janet left Kim to manage her growing pile of filing and set off to see Stuart on the forecourt.

Something he had said earlier in the day was sitting on her mind. He was out and about in one of the buggies on a job when she arrived. She stayed for about half a hour then as she was leaving he returned. He dropped off the passengers in the buggy then came over to where Janet was sat. He smiled at her then asked her when she was planning to get back to work. Janet smiled back shrugging her shoulders, then nodded her head towards the tea table. She went over to it and started to make Stuart a brew. Janet was all tea'd out by now but munched on a biscuit. Stuart supped his drink, periodically dunking his biscuit in his tea for two seconds at a time. Janet was well used to this routine from working with him. They spent an hour in more silence than banter. Stuart was a man of few words which put Janet under pressure to fill the gaps in conversation. She did this pretty well until the defined end of the break. Janet knew that she had to say what was on her mind to Stuart.

"Stuart, how did you know I had another strike?" Janet asked.

"You told me." He replied.

"No, I didn't tell you. How did you know?." Janet asked dropping her head to one side of her body and looking at Stuart straight in the eyes. Stuart could not hold her gaze. He got up walking away leaving Janet alone with her thoughts. Janet was now sure that Stuart was the one feeding back things to the Inner Circle. He was a spy. That sounded outlandish to Janet, but that was the only conclusion she could think of. Janet left the forecourt after washing up Stuart's mug.

Feeling tired now, she made her way up and down and along numerous corridors to her wing and rooms. She took herself to bed for a rest, feeling she had filled her day well but needed a recharge before facing the Resistance with the truth. Janet knew she was in danger; she was scared but realized she was in too deep now. She did manage to sleep, she felt exhausted and stressed but resting her body gave her mind chance to also rest. When she woke up, she got out of bed and checked the time. It was only three o'clock. She went to her kitchen and put some water in the kettle to make tea. When the kettle had boiled, she poured water into her mug only remembering that she had not put in a tea bag. She rectified that then stirred the tea until it reached the right colour. Janet added the milk to the brew then picked up the mug carrying it out through the lounge then outside into her garden. She sat down on the chair then slowly sipped her tea looking at the activity in the park. She could just about make out some people walking hand in hand heading down the path to the lake. She looked at the people sitting on the ground; some of them reading, others making daisy chains and others just sitting and watching just like her. She wanted to capture the images in her brain and the sounds. The gentle ebbs and flows of conversation, the breeze tickling the plants in her garden. And the smells, her rose was sweet with the magnificent heads bobbing with the breeze. She wanted to capture all of it, all of it; it was important to her. She didn't know if she would get another chance. She finished off her cooling tea and then got up to go into the bedroom to grab her book. She read for about an hour; the book was all about love and desire for buxom Abigail and muscle-bound cad Grant. He treated her badly; she lusted after him. The story was a typical light romantic novel much loved by some people on earth. It was not the normal type of book she goes for, but there was not very much choice here on Second Chance. But it was a bit of escapism.

Later that day, she decided to go to see what Joe could muster up for her evening meal. She didn't really feel hungry, she was too nervous for that, but she needed food to energize her to do what she needed to do. She walked down to the kitchen and poked her head around the door to see if she could see Joe. He wasn't there, but she did see a cake, iced with the words Janet piped on the top. Janet started to cry. She was so overwhelmed by Joe's kindness. She went into the dining room and sat down, waiting for him to return. Joe came back a few minutes later; he came into the dining room and went up to where Janet was sitting.

"Janet, it's not much but I wanted to get you something for your birthday." With that he presented her with an envelope. Janet opened it up and took out a card from the inside. On the card was a hand drawn picture of a bird. It was lovely. Janet's tears cascaded down her face. Joe, concerned, asked her if she liked it.

"Its perfect Joe, thank you so much. Did you draw this?" Janet asked.

"Yes, it's just a hobby, I've been trying to get hold of oil paints but they don't have that here so pencils have to do." With that he returned to the kitchen and brought out the cake.

"Sorry, I don't have any candles. Happy birthday Janet." Joe put the cake down on the table then went into the kitchen to get a knife and some plates. Janet could only gaze at the card and at the cake over and over again. The tears had stopped, she had no more tears to cry, she just looked at Joes kindness. The cake was delicious and enjoyed by her dorm mates who all wished her a happy birthday. Janet thought the day could not get any better, maybe this evening will be OK.

Janet popped into her suite after dinner and cake and went to sit in her garden for a few minutes. She watered the rose which was looking thirsty. Then she stood up in order to go and take her medication. She checked herself in a mirror then climbed into the power wheelchair then made her way out of the Nerve Centre to the social club. She hoped that Martin and the others were already there, she was running a bit late. She felt nervous about going but knew this had to come to a head, they needed to decide what to do with all the information they had about Graduation. Janet was astute enough to know that she and she alone had found out about Graduation, the resistance did not have anything as evidence only a theory. Still,

Janet was pleased that there were some people in Second Chance who had the same thought as she.

Janet kept checking the area around her looking out for security guards but there were none obviously around. Along with feeling nervous she felt excited and rehearsed again and again to herself what she needed to say. She knew that others needed to know about Graduation but was still unclear how, hopefully they can look at that during the meeting. She arrived at the social club just as Martin arrived from the opposite direction. He hailed her and urged her to go around the corner of the building. He looked worried, pretty similar as to how Janet felt.

"We have got to do this now when we go in. We need to tell them what happens during Graduation," he said

"I'm on my second strike" Janet stated, "Maybe if it's out in the open the Inner Circle will leave us alone."

"Maybe you should not come, you have to look after yourself."

"No, I'm in it for the long run" said Janet determinedly.

"Come on let's do it, I will tell them, you chip in as you feel fit" with that Martin held her hand as they entered the crowded hall. The room was packed which increased Janets fear level but the mood in the room was strong and positive. Martin went to the mike on the small performance stage at the head of the room, Janet moved to be near him on the floor. Martin got hold of the microphone and spoke to the crowd.

"As you all know, Debbie was Graduated the other day for no apparent reason. We have been investigating Graduation and have found out some horrific facts." Martin stopped to draw breath, "People who are graduated are taken to a unit at the far edge of Second Chance. Once there they are taken into a room on their own and they are drugged. They are given a drug that causes them to become old very quickly then they die of old age. Then their bodies are burnt in the furnace at the back of the unit." He looked intently at the crowd; Janet decided to add her two pennies worth.

"The drug damages the DNA causing rapid premature ageing. Debbie was killed to give us a warning. I am now on two strikes from finding out what goes on, but we felt you had to know that unless these poor people's souls go to a place more suitable for them because their bodies are unceremoniously dumped and burnt. The Inner Circle use Graduation to control you. If you don't fit in or can't participate you are deemed unsuitable and killed" Janet felt a mix of relief and fear knowing she had probably signed her own death warrant. Some people called out some questions which Martin was able to answer, there was a lot of chatter between the audience as they digested the news. The noise in the room reached fever pitch and the mood of the room changed to one of anger. Janet felt a bit worried about how they could contain it if it got out of control.

"Well, what happens now," asked a woman near the front.

"We need to get answers from the Inner Circle. They need to stop Graduation and allow residents of Second Chance to live out their years naturally" responded Martin. With that Martin got off the stage and went over to Janet checking that she was OK. Several people went over to Janet to ask her some questions. Janet did her best to answer them. One of them warned her that there were guards in the room under cover and to be careful. Janet thanked her for her concern. Janet felt she needed a drink, made her way through the crowd to the bar. It was slow progress as people stopped her with a mix of questions and praise. Finally at the bar she ordered two beers, carefully balancing one on the knees she maneuvered her power chair back towards Martin to give him a drink. He gratefully took the drink from her then Martin continued to answer questions and concrs, as did Janet. Janet spoke to two people who were getting to retirement age who were concerned about what would happen to them. Janet could sense their fear and did her best to try to reassure them when there was no reassurance to give. Janet knew that Martin and the others needed to confront the Inner Circle and had assumed that the undercover guards would be the ones to convey that message to them. She looked to see if she could see them from where they were earlier that afternoon but there was no sign of them. Maybe, Janet thought, they had gone to report back. She took sips of her beer while talking to others then when she had the chance she went to the girls who were around the table at the back where they usually go.

"Is all that true Janet?" Asked Lisa, "was my baby killed that way." Lisa started to cry imagining just how frightened her baby Linda must have been in the hands of strangers then being drugged and set alight.

"Oh, Lisa, I wish it wasn't true, but it is, baby Linda had to go through all of that, bless her. We need to stop it happening to anyone else." Janet put her arms around Lisa and let her cry on her shoulder. Eventually her tears stopped, and anger took its place.

"I'll fucking kill them," Lisa said with venom in her words. "How dare they think they can get away with murdering babies." Janet moved a bit away from her, feeling her pain. Mel put her hand on Lisas, which was on the table clutching her wine glass. She was holding it so tightly Mel was concerned she would break it, so she peeled her fingers away from the glass while looking with sad eyes at Lisa. Janet felt like she was waiting for something to happen, something to kick off and kept scowling around the room to see if she could see anything happening.

At that point, Martin came over with a dink for Kim, who took it from him and stood up to kiss him on the cheek. Martin was hoping they could contain the anger and use it to good effect once word had got to the Inner Circle and someone made an appearance. Janet heard a commotion near the main door to the club. She then saw about ten guards come in and split up, so some went to the front of the room, some to the back and others stayed by the door. It gave the illusion that something was about to happen. She put down her drink and looked towards the stage where one of the guards had hold of the microphone. The occupants of the room hushed to allow the guard chance to speak. He checked that the mike was on by testing it by tapping on the head. Satisfied that the microphone was working, he spoke,

"Right, your attention. The club is now closed; please leave quietly through the main door. Anyone who is left and refusing to leave will get a strike." He said, gesturing to the door where two guards stood on either side. The noise in the room reached a fever pitch, and someone called out

"So, you tell us, who excactly will give us a strike."

"We have the authority to; it is in your own best interest if you leave and leave now, nothing will happen to you." A few people moved towards the door and left the club room. The majority of people stayed put despite the guards going around to 'persuade' them to leave. Two people reacted badly to being pushed by one of the guards and swung a punch, hitting him squarely in the face. The guard moved backwards from the hit and then put his weight back on the front of his feet. He got hold of the man and dragged him out of the room. At this, the noise in the room escalated, and more and more areas of violence started up. Janet was worried that the fighting would mean people would get strikes and spoke to Martin, encouraging him to go up on stage to see if he could settle things down. Martin made his way to the stage, and Janet went to the front of the room near the bar to give him moral support. The noise in the room abated when Second Chances saw Marin, and he started to ask for people to calm down so there would be no reason for the guards to arrest people. It seemed to do the trick, and then Martin put down the mike and went over to the DJ, encouraging him to play some music. It might sound like an odd thing to do, but he was in an odd kind of mood on an odd evening.

The DJ started playing some well-known anthems to bring a sense of unity to the residents. Janet and Martin made their way back to the back of the hall to their table. They had a good view there of the room and the doors. Janet kept looking towards the door for someone dressed in silver to appear, but no one came. Janet and Martin considered what they should do now. Janet suggested a silent protest outside using candles. Martin thought that that would be a good idea and also to draw up a list of demands. Janet went to the bar to get paper and a pen but decided to visit the little girl's room while she was in the area. She opened the door to the ladies and went into the foyer. She went to the toilet to do what she needed to do, then went to wash her hands and check her hair. Just then, someone grabbed hold of the joist stick, steering her away out of the ladies towards a fire escape door. Janet called out, but no one came to her aid. They probably couldn't hear her over the loud music.

She thought panicking. She could not clearly see her assailant. He or she was wearing blue with a black balaclava. Once through the door, Janet shouted for help again, but this time her voice, due to fear, was croaky and strained. She tried to get out of the chair but was pushed back in by the guard. Janet tried to pull the hand of the joystick and tried to turn the chair off so she could try to run to get away, but the guard wouldn't let that happen. He/she held the joystick tightly. Janet swore at the person and threatened them with whatever she could think of to say. Just then, the person stopped the chair, walked to the front of the chair and said,

"Third strike. Time for Graduation." So, she was able now to determine that her assailant was a female, Janet tried to engage with her on a human level. Inside her fear had tripled, quadrupled as they moved her away from the social club towards the Nerve Centre. At some point on the way she saw two guards come over in front of her. One of them was pushing a manual wheelchair. When they got up close, one of the new guards, a man, lifted her up from the power chair into the manual chair in one movement. Then one of them pushed her leaving the powerchair where it had stopped. Janet kept trying to scream and to get out of the chair, but she was forced back. They took her past the garage forecourt and around the Nerve Centre to a door she had passed before but didn't know where it went to. The guard used a fob key to open the whoosh door and she was wheeled down a few corridors with various doors coming off it. One of the doors was open, it was a small kitchen and there was a toilet opposite. There was a wide door ahead with a keypad near the door handle. One of the guards keyed in a six-digit number then opened the door with a click. Janet was quiet now; she was watching intensely to see if she could see the door code to use if and when she was able to escape. She had memorised the way to this point, she was sure she could find her way out.

The door opened out into a large room with four rooms coming off it with half glass doors. It was the same place that Debbie had been taken to, not that Janet knew that. She was seeing it with the same fear Debbie felt two days earlier. Janet was wheeled into the same cell Debbie had been placed in and the door closed and locked with a heavy key. The guards left the room leaving a large woman dressed in blue. She sat down in the centre of the room where she had a good view of all the cells. Janet heard movement from one of the other cells. She stood up to see if she could see anyone in one of the other cells. She couldn't see anyone so called out saying her name. Then she heard a voice from the one two down from her. He told her his name, Gareth, then they tried to get into a conversation both fully aware of the guard. She didn't stop them from talking she seemed OK about it.

"Why are you here Gareth?" asked Janet.

"I got arrested at the social club for hitting a guard" he replied.

"Oh, that was you? What did they bring you here for?" she said.

"I am here to apparently cool off. I have been given a strike. Are you still on your second?" he asked Janet.

"No, third, I'm going to be Graduated" she replied.

"Oh boy, you feel OK?" he said

"Yes, I'm OK, I have been expecting it" said Janet speaking the truth. She did feel OK about it. In some ways it had come as a relief as it was very stressful being followed and spied upon. At least now there was certainty.

"When I get out, I will get you help" he said with bravado.

"Do you know how long they are keeping you here?" Janet asked him.

"No, hopefully not much later. I have said I'm sorry to the guard I slugged.

"Yes, I saw you are doing it; you must have given him a black eye," Janet said.

They both stayed silent for a while, each to the privacy of their own thoughts. Janet was thinking about dying. Death did not fear her, after all she was already officially dead. The whole of Second Chance was a fabricated island, even the sun. The air was filtered and pumped around; stars were illuminated from a backdrop. There was nothing real, nothing. No, that's a lie, what was real was friendships, laughter, warmth. That, she thought, she would miss. Janet thought about her friends and what they would be doing now. She wondered if they had realized she had gone, maybe they thought she was tired and gone back to her flat. Perhaps they knew where she was and was organizing to overthrow the guards and release her from this place.

The guard stood up and went over to the door of Janet's cell. She pulled down a flap in the glass and asked her if she wanted a drink. Janet asked for a tea then the guard went to Gareths door and asked him the same. With drink orders ready, she left the holding area to go into the kitchen next door to make both her charges drinks. Janet took advantage of having no guard and asked Gareth some more questions about what he thought about Graduation. He said that he had no knowledge of anyone who had been killed that way though several of his friends had had strikes. He didn't seem to be particularly worried about being given a strike, maybe if it was his third, he would be more concerned. The guard came in with the drinks and handed her guests drinks through the hatch. Janet sat down on the bed to drink her tea. It was nice and strong though the guard had put sugar in, she didn't usually drink it with sugar. She decided not to ask her to make one without sugar but thought she would be pushing it and let it ride. Janet sat quietly with her thoughts she felt surprisingly calm and had a clear mind. She began to try to imagine what was happening outside.

She listened out to see if she could hear any noise from a gathering but there was no noise except for the breathing and the sound of the guard flicking through a book. At one point the guard looked at the clock then looked at the main door looking as if she was expecting someone to come in. A few minutes later a male guard opened the door and the female one got up and went over to him. There was a bit of a hushed dialogue then the woman left the room, and the male came to sit in the chair she had vacated. Janet assumed it was a change of shift and watched the guard trying to size him up. Just then Gareth asked the guard if he could go to the loo. The guard got up and went over to the cell he was in and unlocked the door. Gareth walked with the guard out of the main door and to the toilet opposite the kitchen. Janet watched this wondering if it might be possible to escape from the guard at that point. She considered the risks and decided it might be worth a go, after all she had nothing to lose. After a few minutes both men came back in and Gareth was locked in his cell. Janet called out to Gareth to see if he was OK.

This time the guard wouldn't let them talk by shouting at them to shut up. Janet stopped talking immediately, she didn't want to get on the wrong side of the guard. The guard made them both another cup of tea a few hours later and offered them a sandwich to eat. Janet took him up on his offer as she was feeling peckish. He went out then came back in a few minutes later with two teas on a tray and two plates piled up with cheese sandwiches. Janet thanked him when he handed her her food and drink then she went to sit down on the moulded bed. She ate the sandwiches slowly, relishing every mouth full. She was surprised at just how hungry she was. The food tasted good, the bread and cheese tasted fresh and the tea was the perfect colour. When she had finished the guard dropped down the hatch on the door and took away the empty plate and mug then closed the flap back down. Janet was beginning to feel in pain, her pain relief was wearing off and she didn't have any on her. She debated whether to see if the guard could get her some pain medication or if she should just try and bare it. She decided the latter knowing that she could change her mind at any point. She lay down on the bed and tried to get into a comfortable position. The pain was not too bad, she was sure she could manage OK without pain killers. Janet had no idea what the time was. She assumed it was nighttime though could not be sure of that.

At one point, the guard looked up at the clock then looked towards the door. He did this a few times Janet thought he must be waiting for someone. A few moments later, the door opened and two people came in and went up to the guard. The new people were guards, they were wearing the navy-blue top and trousers. There was a bit of quiet discussion and now and then one of them would look over to where Gareth was in the cell. Eventually, the guard went to Gareth's cell and opened the door. He gestured for Gareth to come out then the two new guards went one of either side of him walked him across the middle part of the room and towards the exit.

"Where are you taking me, what's happening?" Janet heard Gareth saying.

"You are being escorted to your flat, then that's it for you, you have your strike, now you can go." Said one of the guards walking beside him on the left. Janet watched as Gareth left through the door. Hopefully the guards were telling the truth and were releasing him. She wished it was her but didn't let on. The remaining guard sat back down on his chair then picked up a book and started to read while Janet watched him. He must be used to being stared at as he didn't flinch. She was giving him the evil eye hoping it would make him let her go, but that was just her fantacy.

Maybe Gareth would be able to get word to Martin and the others so they could come to rescue her. She pulled the blanket that lay on the bed over her then settled down to sleep. To her surprise she felt herself falling to sleep quickly, she was exhausted. She was sure that nothing would be happening until the morning, so she rested.

Chapter 17
Graduation Day

In the early hours of the morning, Janet woke up. It took her a moment or two to get her bearings, then when she realized this was for real, she looked over at the guard who was snoozing, then looked around the area outside of her cell to see if there was anything useful she could use to escape. Janet sat quietly in her cell, desperately trying to keep calm and plan. She moved off the bed and went to sit in the wheelchair next to it. She was surprisingly coping with this kidnapping, she thought. Janet got up now and then to move around. She was getting desperate for a pee but felt embarrassed to ask the guard who sat in the centre of the room asleep. Janet tried not to think about weeing in the hope her bladder would get the message, but it only seemed to make her want to get worse. In the end, she called over the guard,

"Excuse me, sorry to bother you but I really need to wee," she asked. The guard grunted a bit but looked like he was heading back to sleep land so she repeated what she said louder. This time, he shot up and looked over at her.

"What, oh dear, let me see if I can find a female guard to escort you." The guard said as he stood up. He went to one of the doors, opened it, and looked out. Janet was not entirely sure what he was doing but watched him hoping he would find someone quickly.

"There is no one around at the moment. Can you wait?" He asked.

I can try" she said lying, the fact was that if she didn't get to the toilet very soon, she would soil herself. Sometimes British people are too dam polite she thought. She sat back down wondering what she should do, she really did not want to wet herself. She stood up again and went to the door. This time she would get the message through she thought.

"Sorry, I need to go now," she said clutching at her pubic area. This time the guard got up and went to the same door he went to before. He looked down the corridor but still could not find a female guard to escort Janet to the toilet. He scratched the balding part of his head then came back in then went back out again into the kitchen. He came out with a washing up bowl and came over to the door where Janet was.

"Can you go in this; I will turn my back?" he said, opening the door and passing through the receptacle. He then locked the door and turned around while Janet dropped her lower clothes down so she could wee. She tried to go quietly, but her bladder had better ideas. She felt embarrassed by the noise she was making when urinating. She felt herself cringe. When the flow stopped, she pulled back up her garments and let the guard know she was done. He opened the cell door, took the washing-up bowl then relocked the door. He went out of the first door to the toilet, where he disposed of the urine. A short while later, he came back in and asked her if she wanted anything. Janet feeling a lot more comfortable said that she would love a cup of tea. Then as he left to make it, she sat back down on the chair, wondering how much longer she would be held there. She tried to pass the time by naming animals the letters of the alphabet, another technique for distraction and control she had picked up in the Mind Complex. She was pleased that she had been able to make good use of her time there. It certainly helped her to deal with lots of difficult situations. The guard came back with her tea and looked at her; he said

"Can you hear them, there's a vigil outside going on for you, here, listen" Janet heard something that sounded like people shouting. She could not be sure if it was for her benefit but took the guards word on it. She wondered if Gareth had got word to Martin where she was being held. Maybe Martin could persuade the Inner Circle to let her go. May be this, maybe that maybe just maybe it was all too late. Janet got stuck finding an animal beginning with X so gave that actvity up. She started to ruminate on what she knew about the process of Graduation from being a driver taking someone to their destiny. She knew it was a distance from these cells and the place of execution, maybe she could get away then, it might be a possibility if she was not nursing an injury. What else, what else? Janet felt her heart quicken; it sounded as if it was trying to get out of her chest. She calmed herself down by repeating a mantra, she needed to keep a cool head. The guard got up and came over to Janet. He asked her if she wanted anything. She had just had tea but thought she might like something to eat. The guard said that he would have a look in the kitchen to see what they had. He was gone just for a few minutes then came out with something on a plate. He came to the hatch which he lowered to pass her through a plate with a generous slice of Victoria sponge cake on it.

Janet accepted it and then asked the guard if he could tell her the time. He looked up at the clock and then told her it was six thirty in the morning. With that, he went to sit down on his chair in the middle of the room. On receiving the cake, she set it down on the chair she had just vacated, then went to sit down on the bed. She was feeling stiff, and in pain, so she did a few small stretches to see if that would help. She did wonder if she could ask the guard for her painkillers but thought that that might be a step too far. The pain in her lower back was annoying her; she wanted to have a good body that would fight and run. Just then, the guard came back over to the door; he looked around him, beckoning Janet to the bars. She went over, asking him what he wanted.

"You are causing quite a stir; lots of people are rioting, wanting you to be released. Security is overwhelmed."

"What, what is going to happen to me?" She asked him, feeling a sense of nervous excitement in her stomach.

"I don't know, the Inner Circle are discussing it at the moment; the last thing I heard was that you are being Graduated in the next hour, just to let you know," with that, he backed away and sat down at his station. He took out a sandwich from a bag on the table next to him which he took over to Janet.

"You want one to go with your cake? They always pack me too many" he then handed Janet a jam sandwich through the hatch when she nodded a yes. Janet was grateful for his thoughtfulness and for the information. She did not know what to make of the civil unrest, but it could give her her freedom, or the Inner Circle would use her death to exert control like Debbie's. Janet picked up the mug on the chair and sat down. She peered at the sandwich and then took a big bite enjoying the sugar hit of the jam. It gave her a bit of a whizzy head for a moment or two; then, she quickly scoffed it down before tackling the cake. She ate the cake slowly, focusing on the mechanics of eating and the taste of the food. She ate it mindfully, afraid that this was the last meal she would have. When she had finished her meal, she went over to the hard bed along the back wall and gingerly laid down.

She reflected on the past few days which had unfolded to this, whatever this was. Janet heard the tell tale sound of a key fob being swiped and a door opening. She then heard the footsteps of two people. The guard on duty stood up, his chair legs scraping the floor; he brushed the crumbs off the front of his blue tunic as the duo came over to him. Janet stood up slowly and then stood where she could see the officers. She heard voices talking in hushed tones, too hushed for Janet to make sense of the words. Then, one of the two came over to the grill in the door of Janet's cell, calling her over. The woman wore the colours of someone from the Inner Circle, a silver tunic and trousers. Janet walked the short distance to the door facing the woman. She made eye contact holding her stare constantly. Janet hoped it would intimidate her, but the woman did the same.

Eventually, Janet dropped her gaze once she saw that it had not worked. The woman smirked when Janet caved in, which made Janet laugh, it was oh-so childish. Janet waited for the woman to speak, but she just stood there. Say something, anything, said Janet in her mind. She was wondering what mind games she was playing; maybe this was another way to let her know they were in charge. As the silence grew, Janet felt herself get angry but got it in check as she just had to keep calm. "Yes, what do you want," Janet asked eventually.

"Who are the ring leaders of this not-so-hidden Resistance? Tell me; then you can go," she barked. Now Janet knew the plan. She knew she had a chance to get some control. "I will not tell you that, do what you want with me", Janet replied, feeling that calm she had strived for. Now she knew they did not know the key members of the Resistance; they were safe, and she felt relieved about that.

"OK, I will give you ten minutes to change your mind after that we are going on a little journey" said the silver clad woman who turned away from the hatch and left the room with the person she had come in with. Janet sat down she noticed a tremor in her hands, adrenaline was pumping around her body. She did not feel frightened despite the imminent threat to her life.

A few hours earlier, the social club was alive with chat. Martin was going around the space, answering questions from people who were angry and scared. Some of them wanted to relay their experiences of people they had got to know just disappearing for no reason. Each story strengthened Martin's resolve to stop Graduation no matter what happened. The undercover guards seemed to have dissolved in the mass of people, making it impossible for members of the Resistance to keep an eye on them. At one point in the evening, Martin asked where Janet had gotten to. He assumed she had left the meeting as her job was done, but he had hoped she would help her with this part. He found Mel with Gary and asked them if they had seen Janet.

"Last thing I heard was that she was off to the loo. I haven't seen her for a while. Do you want me to go and see if she is in her room? Those painkillers make her drowsy; chances are she has the head off for a rest," Mel said, getting ready to set off.

"I hope she is OK. Are you sure you saw her at the ladies? How long ago was that?" asked Gary.

"That must have been about a quarter of an hour ago. I'll go off to her room and see if she is there," Mel said, knowing she could ask the concierge to let her in to go check on Janet. She weaved her way around the groups of people preoccupied with talking loudly about what had been said that evening. Eventually, she went through the doors and outside into the evening air.

It felt good. The temperature in the social club was high in all respects. She started to walk to the Nerve Centre when she spotted something ahead of her. Curious, she went over to see what it was, but it did not take long to identify it as a wheelchair. Mel immediately knew to whom it belonged. It had some stickers on, just like the chair that Janet had been using that evening. Fearfully, Mel looked around her and then headed back to the social club at a run. Once back, she tried to spot either Gary or Martin to tell them what she had found; they would know what to do. Why would Janet abandon her wheelchair on the way home? She thought.

She found Martin drinking a pint at the bar. He had a couple of comrades with him, probably trying to think of their next actions. Mel told him about the discarded chair, and he asked her if she was sure. Martin quickly came to the conclusion that Janet had been taken by the guards. Just to be sure, he mounted the small stage and grabbed the microphone. He checked it was working by tapping the head and saying testing, which got the attention of the crowd. 'Has anyone seen Janet recently?" he shouted out. The crowd fell silent as they digested his words and implication. "I have reason to believe that she has just been taken by the guards under the order of the Inner Circle."

Martin said, then stopped to gauge the mood of the room. "We have to save her. Let's go and protest by the Nerve Centre where she may have been taken. Who is with us?" he shouted. "Who is with us?" he repeated as a multitude of voices shouted out 'yes'. With that, he put the microphone back on its holder, then jumped off the stage, heading towards the door.

Martin led the enraged crowd to a spot near the main entrance to the Nerve Centre, holding up his hands to stop them when they reached a suitable space. In no time at all, the Brownies in the crowd were all calling out for the end of Graduation and liberty of Janet. Mel and Gary stood with Kim near the front keeping the slogans being shouted again and again. Here and there, amid the sea of brown, grey uniforms of workers in the Nerve Centre, joined in. Then they were joined by the dark blue and dark grey uniform of the work detail. Some banners had been made from sheets and painted, mimicking the slogans.

Martin kept stirring up the crowd by telling them about the plight of the Doctor due to retire shortly. He reminded them of the recent Graduation from Debbie. The crowd were noisy, and the shout went out demanding a member of the Inner Circle come and answer their concerns. They all got behind that, shouting out, creating a united front. About half a dozen blue security guards stood silently at the back and sides of the crowd. It was hard to determine what side they were on, but they made no effort to disperse the gathering. Just then, someone who worked in the Nerve Centre came out of the building and signalled for Martin to join him. He spoke in a hushed tone, not wanting everyone to hear what he was saying. Martin, relishing in his role, immediately relayed what the man was saying to him out to the crowd.

The Inner Circle want to talk to the ring leaders inside the building. What do you think?" he yelled out. There were a few far-from-polite answers shouted out, but the general gist was that they put two fingers up to that idea. Martin responded that what needed to be said should happen here so everyone could hear. On hearing this, the man bustled away into the building to pass on the message. A few minutes later, he reappeared, making his way back to Martin. Martin looked at him feeling sorry for the fella; he was being put in such a dangerous position.

"If the ring leaders come, they will let Janet go; they want you to go inside to the meeting room," he said out loud, then averted his gaze to the ground while he waited for an answer.

"I hope the room is big enough for us all to fit in", Martin replied, motioning to include all the people standing there, "I suggest they come out here" with that, he walked away from the man who scuttled back to the door. Someone started singing, 'we shall not be moved', which grew in intensity like a wave above the heads of the crowd. A couple of the guards let their guard down by joining in, which did not go unnoticed by Martin. The messenger came back out quite quickly. He was joined by a good number of grey-clad Nerve Centre members who had been ousted from their sleep by the noise. They came out to join the crowd. Most of them asked what was going on, and they were quickly filled in. There was a good turnout, probably about a hundred people, maybe more, Martin thought, looking at the people fighting this cause. The messenger turned around without speaking and walked first slowly, then quickly as jeers started to rally him to the entrance way. It was a good ten minutes before he returned, looking exasperated. He approached Martin handing him a notebook and pen. "They want you to write down your demands and the names of the ring leaders.

Do that, and they will let her go," he waited for a reply, took a step away, and then breathed. Martin waived the book in the air. He stood up tall and then addressed the crowd.

"So, our demands, stop Graduation and release Janet, yes?" In agreement with the crowd, Martin wrote this in the book; then, he passed the book to a Brownie in front of him, asking him to sign it and pass it on. One by one the majority of people wrote down fictious names and passed them around until all those that wanted to have them signed them. Martin noticed that the guards did not join in with this, which was understandable. once the book had been passed around, it was delivered, hand over hand, back to Martin, who ceremonially presented it to the messenger, saying, "When the Inner Circle are ready to talk, we are here." With that, the messenger turned on his heel back to the Nerve Centre. Martin took himself off to the side to talk to a couple of members of the Resistance, asking one of them to get him a drink. With that, the woman turned around to go to the social club to get him a beer. She had an idea that it was going to be a long night.

Janet could just about make out the sounds of the crowd. She wondered what was going on and tried to find out, and she called over to the guard. He came over, but when asked, he had no more news to give her. "Just tell them what they want to know; they will Graduate you; you do know that don't you? You haven't got long. They are getting ready to remove you."

"If I do that, how can I be sure the members of the Resistance will not be Graduated? It's too risky" she knew she was doing the right thing; she was no heroine. Ten minutes passed slowly; Janet used the time to meditate. She felt calm and in control. In time, the two people returned. Another stilted conversation occurred before the woman from the Inner Circle came over to the cell. She looked straight at Janet with a wry smile on her face.

"Right, are you going to give me your answer? Who are the ring leaders?" She put a lot of emphasis on the word 'who', which struck Janet as weird. Then Janet thought that she must be weird thinking the woman weird; it odd how the thoughts go when up against it.

"No, do what you want with me. I don't care." Said Janet smiling a false smile. The woman gave her a stare before stomping out of the room, barking an order to the guard and the other person in the room. This person came to Janet's focal point, and it was another member of the Inner Circle, a round middle-aged gentleman. He told the guard to cuff her wrists and take her to the car. The guard picked up his fob key to unlock the cell door, then took care of putting the hand cuffs around both of Janet's wrists. He apologized to her for what he had to do and asked her if the hand cuffs were not too tight. He then steered her by the elbow, taking care to the door and down the corridors and ramps to the forecourt with the Inner Circle guy. Janet was in pain; walking was only aggravating her injury, but she did not let on. She had to look as if she was OK.

Janet noted everything on the journey. The doors, windows, and corridors all seemed relevant at that point in her life. She was walking the green mile, she thought to herself, then giggled. She wondered if she was losing it, but at the end of the day, what did it matter?

At the end of the corridor they were walking along, they came to a whoosh door. The person from the Inner Circle zapped the door open and then stood aside so everyone could get out. Janet looked around her and saw the posh car waiting, she presumed, for her. It was nice, she thought; they had made an effort to get the best car. With her thoughts running riot, she tried to ground herself. It was failing miserably.

She stopped walking for a moment to look at the car, and she was wondering who would be driving it this early in the morning, to her point of execution. Janet laughed out loud at that; who cares, she thought to herself. She could say and do whatever she wanted. It was all going to end the same way. She might as well get out of it as much as she could. Janet was 'helped' into the car by the guard, followed by the two members of the inner circle.

The guard looked around for the person who was meant to drive the car to the place of Graduation. He was nowhere to be found; the truth was that he was attending the rally as a deliberate act of defiance. The woman Inner Circle member ordered the guard to drive the car, but he refused as he didn't know how to drive, and neither could her counterpart. It seemed that none of them could drive except Janet. Janet thought that that was amusing. She told them that she could drive, wondering if she could take them anywhere but the Graduation building. They didn't take her seriously and discussed the options between themselves. The male person from the Inner Circle left them at the car and walked back into the building to see if he could find someone to drive the car.

He double-checked the person on call from the garage team but had no joy getting hold of him. He then rang a couple of numbers of the Inner Circle team to see if he could rouse one of those to drive the car. He was coming up blank with that. So, he came back out and explained the situation to the others. Outside they could hear the sound of the enraged mob. Who could find out where they were very quickly? It was just around the building from where they gathered. The people from the Inner Circle debated whether to take Janet back to the cell until they had found someone to drive the vehicle because of their concern about being confronted by the mob. They discussed this coming to no decision; they had been given orders to Graduate Janet as soon as possible. One of them went over to Janet and asked her if she would drive.

"You have got to be joking. Why would I drive myself to my own place of murder? Fuck off." She laughed at the absurdness of the situation. The female Inner Circle member went over to her saying, "We now know who the ringleaders are. We will not give them a strike if you drive the car. You have my word on that."

"How can I be sure of that?" Janet asked.

"You have my word," she repeated.

"I don't believe you. But I will drive the car." Janet said, just wanting all of this to come to an end. She knew that whatever she said or did was not going to make any difference to what was about to happen to her. The woman asked the guard to take off the handcuffs, which he did. Janet rubbed the sore area around her wrists. The guard apologized to Janet for hurting her, which Janet acknowledged with a smile. He was only doing his job, she thought. Janet, with her odd sense of humour, found something funny in the fact she had to drive herself to her own death and that the three passengers would have a long walk back afterwards. The guard walked with her around to the driver's side of the car, and he opened the door motioning for Janet to get in. He got in beside her in the passenger seat; then, her other two passengers got into the back of the car. Janet made sure everyone was in, seat belts on, and the doors closed before turning the ignition to spark the car into life. As the car was electric and had an automatic gearbox driving, it could not get any simpler. It was just the case of steering, no clutch pedal to depress, no gears to select. She adjusted the speed of the vehicle as they made their way to the Graduation Centre. Janet deliberately took the path that went where the demonstrators were, but the guard intervened, telling her to go the other way.

She did as she was told and turned the car around in a three-point turn. She debated with herself about crashing the car deliberately in the hope she could escape but could not think of any possible hazards she could use to make the crash seem accidental in case it came up at a later date. However, Janet could not fail to notice the angry faces of Brownies they passed en route. Some hurled abuse at them, and others chucked rotten fruit in the vague direction of the passing vehicle. Janet assumed it was done with the intention of showing their support and found it comforting. She just wished that someone would help her escape. Why doesn't someone jump in front of the car so she would have to stop? Then the Inner Circle people could be overwhelmed, so she could run off, she thought. Or maybe they could set alight on the Graduation Centre and raise it to the ground getting it out of action now and in the future.

So many things that could have been done to save her. Janet's head was spinning with her thoughts. She felt rather vulnerable and insecure, and she felt so helpless. She drove carefully past the buildings and farming equipment she recalled from her last trip there. She drove slowly and with care, just hoping there would be some sort of intervention. Brownies feared the Inner Circle. They were in positions of power and had to be respected, or at least that is the line that they lived by. On arrival, she noticed about twenty people standing in front of the Graduation Centre door.

Janet was instructed to drive towards them so she could stop the car at the entrance. Janet was not happy about doing that; she would be driving right at the protesters. She chose instead to just stop the car where it was. She pulled the handbrake on and then turned off the engine. She ignored the curses from her backseat passengers. They were still telling her to start the car and disperse the crowd with the car. Janet refused; after all, what could they do to her? The guard lent over to her side of the car,

"You better do what they want; you don't want to make it worse for yourself," he said quietly.

"Things can't get any worse. They are going to kill me tonight," Janet retorted. Her passengers concluded that Janet was not going to move the car, so they alighted. Then the guard came round to Janet's door, opened it, then helped Janet to get out. Once she was out, he put the handcuffs back on her and then gently pushed her to start walking. The two Inner Circle members asked the crowd to move aside, or they would all receive strikes. They took no notice. The silver-clad woman asked the guard to disperse them. He refused at first until he was threatened with the same punishment. She then asked for the name of the person behind this. One person spoke up, saying, "Peter Pan," "no," said another, "Bill and Ben," 'No, it's Terry Wogan," said a third. All the other people came up with names; it was clear they were united in their views. The Inner Circle workers continued to walk with the guard and Janet reaching the edge of where the protesters were standing. Janet wondered what they would do next; they were seriously outnumbered, and maybe this was going to be her rescue story.

The crowd remained in place, with some of them jostling the silver-clad persons as they tried to walk through. One of them asked for Janet's release as the woman instructed the guard to put that person in cuffs as he was under arrest. The guard let go of Janet and headed towards the man who stood tall with defiance. The guard tugged the man away from his comrades and then slapped him on some cuffs.

He then pulled the man over to where the members of the Inner Circle stood and waited for more instructions. The round male Inner Circle member said to the rest of the people gathered there,

"Let us pass, or he will join Janet to be Graduated" the silence from the crowd was like clouds, and then they began to talk, weighing up the pros and cons.

"Do as they say; let us pass. We don't want to make it any worse for anyone," called out Janet. The crowd, as one realized that they were serious in the threats, the crowd opted to allow safe passage for the two silver-dressed pair and Janet. The guard stayed with the arrested man to wait for further orders. Janet watched all that went on with dread, "You can't let this happen; please, stop them", someone called out from the crowd. A few of them could be heard calling out about releasing her, but Janet could not stop the thought that it was all over. The woman led her into the building, followed by the man. Janet walked past the reception desk and then was taken to a room near the toilet. The room was small, with only a chair and a bed in there. There were no windows or decorations; it really was more of a cell than a room.

The door had no window in it and no door handle. Janet noticed a large bolt on the door on the other side so there was no way out. Janet sat down on the chair them the woman removed her hand cuffs. Janet rubbed her wrists looking up at the woman with pleading eyes. The woman would not make eye contact, instead she turned round to leave the room. Janet felt like a saggy balloon, one where all the air had blown out. She had lost her fight. She knew for a fact that she had tried so hard to be part of Second Chance. Her fear left her as quickly as it had come and in its place she felt relaxed and calm. Janet did not know what to expect she just hoped it would not be painful.

The male member of the Inner Circle went to the door outside the building with a bottle. He took the lid off then inverted it into a receptacle. Satisfied that all was as it should be, he stepped out of the annex and closed the door. His part was done. He realized too late that someone had been watching him administer the drug he stood still for a moment then went through the main door using a fob key to gain entrance. The person who had watched him went up to the annex to see if he could remove the bottle which he located easily. He moved to take hold of it to pull it out when the guard pulled him away and onto the ground. The guard pulled him upright, shook him a couple of times then released him.

The man scuttled off back where the others were, and the guard stopped by the annex in case he decided to come back. As little as he liked this aspect of his job, he didn't want to end up the way Janet has. Janet sat still on the chair staring at the door. She couldn't hear anything then she noticed that the light in the room dimmed a bit making things less glared. Janet began to sing. She sang a mix of songs mainly taken from her youth. She moved her body side to side in time as if there was a drumbeat, she moved her head side to side, back to front, really getting into her stride. She ignored the odor she could smell coming through the walls belting out Simply Reds hit 'Stars" followed by Bon Jovis 'Living on a prayer' the irony of both songs made her lift her voice more, louder and louder. She felt something in her hands, they looked different, several fingers were warping, the skin looked thinner her fingernails looked brittle. It was starting, she was ageing.

Gareth left the building after being released a couple of hours back and headed home... He had had enough of that day and only wanted to sleep in his own bed. He heard the sound of the protest; it was hard not to miss it. He went to a window in the corridor to his room, looked out and saw the mass of people with handmade banners. He stopped to watch them, and then out of curiosity, and he decided to go out and join them. He knew he could get in trouble being there, he had already been given one strike that night, but Janet's plight had hit his heart. Once he reached the outer space of the protesters, he looked to see if he could identify the person responsible for setting this up. He asked one lady if she knew who was in charge and pointed out Martin, who was facing the crowd urging them in their chants. There was a tall man with an axe in his head next to him and three rather good-looking young women. He gently pushed people out of his path as he made his way to the head of the crowd. Once there, Gareth went over to the five of them and introduced himself. He told them that he had been held in a cell where Janet was and that she was due to be Graduated that day. Mel asked him if she was OK.

"She seems to be coping OK; well, she wasn't freaking out; she seemed pretty calm," Gareth said.

"Could you take us where she is being held?" asked Gary.

"Probably though you must go through pass only doors. You need someone with the right fob key" replied Gareth.

"What about the doctor, doesn't he have all an access pass?" Martin piped up looking around at the crowd to see if he was there.

"Do you want me to go and get him. He has rooms next to the medical centre, what do you think?" said Kim who works now and then there.

"Yes, Go, Kim, let me go with you" said Martin then they set off for the medical centre at a fast walk. It didn't take them long to get there. They knocked on the door of his flat rapidly until finally the doctor opened the door to see what was going on. Martin quickly filled him in with what he knew and answered the doctors' questions. Then the doctor went into his flat to get dressed and to get his all-access fob key. The three of them left and headed back to where the others were waiting.

Gareth stepped forward when he saw the three of them coming then got set to show them the way to the holding cells. Martin, the doctor, Gary and Gareth negotiated the route opening up the doors as they went until they got to the room which held the cells. The doctor used his key to open the door and all four of them piled into the room. The room was in darkness and empty.

Despairing Martin hit his fist onto the table in the middle wondering what to do now. Janet had gone to the Graduation Centre; she may already be dead dead. None of them knew the way there, but Gary knew a person who could take them there, Stuart. They left the room with the cells and retraced their steps out and went to the garage. They didn't expect to see Stuart there but in the office there was a list of on call staff and room numbers. Stuart was on call that night, he may already be driving them to the centre, but Martin thought it would be worth a try to see if he was in his room. The doctor asked if they had a bleeper or phone when they are on call which would be quicker than going to find his suite. They looked at the list again and at the bottom of the page was a phone number.

Without haste, Gary picked up the receiver of the phone in the garage office and rang the number. It took about a dozen rings before Stuart picked up. He sounded sleepy which was not surprising as it was the early hours of the morning. Gary told him that they needed to go down to the Graduation Centre to save Janet. It all sounded very dramatic and Stuart replied to the demands saying it all might be too late. He told Gary that he had been summoned to drive the car to the Graduation Centre earlier that evening but he decided not to go. He had left the car by the Nerve Centre where he normally picked up passengers going to the Graduation Centre, then returned to his rooms. He knew it was for Janet and wanted nothing to do with her death, hence why he deserted his post. However, he offered to take them to the centre in one of the buggies but just needed to dress first.

Five minutes later he came out of his room and joined the men on a mission. They charged down to the garage then Stuart went into the office to grab the open-air buggy keys. Martin went to illicit help from people in the crowd to go with them to save Janet. Three men and two women offered to go with them then they all headed to the garage where Gary had got the vehicle out for everyone. Once all of them were on board, Stuart set off for the Graduation Centre. He drove the vehicle quickly knowing as he did the journey and the short cuts. En route they discussed tactics expecting to find a whole load of security guards there. They assigned roles, with Martin and Gary opting to go into the centre when they get there to release Janet. The others would deal with the security guards and the people from the Inner Circle. Stuart let them know when they were five minutes away so they could start to look out for the posh car. They saw it at the entrance to the Graduation Centre surrounded by twenty or so people. Gary and the others got off the vehicle and Martin asked them if Janet was in there.

'What the young lady? Yes, she is in there but there has not been any smoke from the furnace so she still might be alive." Said one of the men.

"Can I help?" asked one of the men in the crowd.

"Martin thanked him and asked him to watch the cars and alert them all if anyone comes out of the main door. There was no sign of the security guard who had been with Janet on her final journey, but there was one person wearing handcuffs sitting on the ground near the annex. Martin had asked the doctor if he could use his all-access pass while Stuart was getting the bus. The doctor handed it over which broke the rules but he thought he would just have to deal with what may happen to him later. Martin and Gary went to the entrance of the Graduation Centre and used the pass to gain entry into the building. They looked around them trying to suss out the best route to go. Just then, one person dressed in the silver outfit of the inner Circle came out of one of the doors down a short corridor.

Martin and Gary went over to the lady who immediately called out for the security guard. He didn't turn up, truth was that he had had enough and didn't want to be part of this, so he decided to start to walk home leaving the man in cuffs for the Inner Circle to deal with. The lady yelled out again "Security, now" but quickly realized that help wasn't coming. She went back into the room she had come out of and Gary and Martin both heard the sound of a door locking. They looked at each other then went down the corridor and tried the door to put the frighteners on her. They couldn't hear any noise coming out of the room so carried on down the corridor. They came to another locked door bolted from the outside. They looked at each other then pulled the lock back.

A little earlier Janet sang and sang as she changed from a middle-aged woman to an old one, her hair turned grey and thinned, her ear lobes and nose grew and altered in shape, but still she sang. She shrank as her spine curved as her skin thinned, but the words of Sir Elton John, 'Tiny Dancer' stayed strong, her heart behind every word. Her eyesight darkened as she developed bi lateral cataracts making the room, her surroundings blurred and hard to make out. So she closed her eyes and gave a new dimension to the power ballads she was belting out. She felt liberated, defiant, powerful, she noted each change in her body then moved on, not dwelling on anything but re focusing on the songs, as she sang 'The Power of Love' she felt her heart flutter, but she sang louder. When her hearing diminished, she sang, as wrinkles formed and skin sagged, she sang. Her breasts headed downwards as the elasticity softened, Janet noted it then quickly refocused on her singing. Her voice changed, she tried a different key, bunions grew on both large toes, she kicked off her footwear. Throughout all the accelerated ageing process she felt no fear, in her mind she was surprised she lived into old age, she felt sure, with her track record, she would die young from her own hand, which in reality is what happened. This time she felt sure there was no coming back, her body was finally going to die and decay. Janet began to feel really tired; she realized the end was near so changed her song to 'Amazing Grace' gospel edition. She felt uplifted and oh so ready for this. She felt the loose skin on her arms and her bony hands, she tried to see through the milky cataracts. She stood up on strange legs moving to the bed to lie down. She carefully felt her way there then with a sigh rested on the hard bed, her head indented the pillow. She felt the need to wee so allowed herself to wee, the urine saturating the sheet. She continued singing but was aware of her voice losing its power as she felt so so tired. She closed her eyes singing gently anything that came to her mind, she was fading, slowly, slowly going down. It felt as if the bed was consuming her body as her stature continued to shrink. She was ready for this; she crossed her hands across her chest and just gave in. She slept, her breathing altered, became intermittent then stopped. Her old heart stopped beating shortly after. Janet died an old woman within fifteen minutes of entering the room.

The two people from the Inner Circle, overviewing the execution, entered the room. They checked Janet for signs of life. Satisfied that she was not breathing, did not react to painful stimuli, and had no pulse, they covered her body with a sheet. They then pushed the bed out of the door in the room towards the back of the building. A couple of the work detail took over manoeuvring the bed towards the hearth of the furnace. Her body was grabbed at the ankles and shoulders, lifted off the bed and unceremoniously dumped in the furnace. The furnace was not lit at this point. That would be done a bit later when the crowds have moved on. They felt that they could run riot if they saw the smoke and saw it was all over for Janet and that she had gone.

Gary pushed the door open expecting to see Janet. He saw instead an empty room, or at least empty from people. There was a bed and a chair in there and what looked like water on the floor near the bed. They looked at each other then left the room and carried on down the corridor. They checked each room in turn with no joy, the door at the bottom of the corridor was locked and did not open with the fob key. Gary tried to push it open, but it was not going anywhere. Martin suggested they force the door open which Gary nodded his agreement. Gary tried to shoulder open the door with no joy then tried it with a bit of a run up. The door refused to budge. Martin and Gary went and tried to force it together; on the first run up they heard a bit of a scratching sound as if the door was beginning to give. They felt reenergized from the noise then tried again and again and each time they tried the door gave a bit here and there. Gary then tried a different tactic and kicked the door near the hinges. The door splintered even more so Gary did it again and again. Finally, the door literally fell off its hinges, Gary and Martin moved the door out of the way to see what there was behind it. Behind it was another door. This one actually had a key in the lock which made access ridiculously simple. Martin used the key to unlock the door then they went through the gap left by the door. It opened into a short corridor type room with a large opening opposite the door. Martin identified the opening as belonging to the furnace which was unlit at this point. On the floor of the furnace was a white sheet concealing Janet. The men approached her body then gently pulled away the sheet covering her face. Gary and Martin both took an in breath when they saw her old face then scanned the rest of her body. It was clear she was dead, her withered features still showed much of who Janet was, even in death. Gary stood up and scratched his head.

"I can't let her be burned like this. What should we do, what do you think?" he asked Martin.

"I don't know, she had just been dumped here, we can't leave her. They could be back anytime to fire up the furnace." Martin replied.

"Why don't we take her now and give her a proper send off. Maybe we could bury her somewhere on Second Chance, somewhere where she liked to go maybe." Gary said. "She used to like to swim, maybe bury her somewhere near the lake?"

"That's a good idea. She used to swim there didn't she?" asked Martin. Gary bent down onto his haunches and scratched his head again. Martin mimicked his posture while Gary quietly thought.

"What about burying her near the waterfall? She used to go there a lot."

"Good idea, let's do that. We could carry Janet to the car and take her there. I expect we could borrow some spades from the workmen outside. What do you reckon?" Gary said, looking up at Martin. Martin nodded his agreement, and then Gary gently scooped Janet's body up off the floor of the furnace and walked with her back through the two doors and the short walk to the reception desk. The member of the Inner Circle who had decided to hide in the room was standing in the doorway leading outside. There was still a good number of people standing around out there, and the mood was ugly. Gary carried Janet through the doorway as Martin shoved the Inner Circle worker out of the way.

"Is that her?" asked one of the women standing in the crowd.

"Bless her, what have they done to her, is she dead?" asked another.

"Yes, she is dead. They have killed her." Responded Martin. The crowd parted so Gary could make his way to the posh car. He gently placed Janet on the back seat of the vehicle then he sat in the drivers seat. While he was doing that, Martin asked the workers for shovels which they produced without a word. Martin took the shovels and put them in the boot of the car. He got in the passenger side then Gary drove carefully back towards the Nerve Centre. He stopped the car near the waterfall and the men alighted. They had a look around for a good spot to dig settling on a spot near a fallen tree trunk.

The soil was easy to dig and in no time they had dug a long deep grave to lay Janet in. Once they were satisfied with it, they put down the shovels and went back to the car to get Janet. Gary lifted her up and carried her to her last resting place. Between them they lowered her into the grave, her body covered in the sheet. Gary said a few poignant words before they started to infill the grave with the soil. When they had finished Gary found some twigs to make a crude cross, he would make something permanent at a later date. They both stopped and looked at the grave in silence then turned around making their way back to the car. Gary drove the short distance back to the garage where he alighted to open the gate into the forecourt.

He drew the vehicle to a stop then they both got out of it feeling at a bit of a loss; for what to do now? They could still hear people chanting over by the social club, and Martin started to walk over to where the people gathered. He rehearsed what he needed to say to the protesters as he walked, trying hard to think what a fitting epitaph would be.

As he approached the group, the people fell quiet as they saw him. Martin walked through them and then spotted Mel and Kim at the front of the crowd. He saw them looking at him, then slowly shook his head 'no'. Mel started to sob, and Kim saw her distress and put her arm around her shoulder, pulling her in for a full embrace. Martin stood looking at the crowd, then realised that he had their full attention, stuttering over a few words until he was finally able to tell the people what had happened. He told them what had happened to her and where they had laid her to rest. All throughout his monologue, the crowd stayed silent. A few of them patted him on his back when he made his way back through the crowd to where Mel stood. Gary, at this point, was standing next to Mel and had his left hand draped around her shoulder. She turned towards him needing to be held, then asked Gary and Martin,

"What happens now. Martin, you will be in serious shit. They are saying everyone here is going to be in deep trouble. We can't let them get away with this. But what can we do? We have no power." Mel's words probably were echoed in everyone's thoughts. There were no answers to that, certainly not at that point. They needed to sleep. See what happens in the morning. Mel and Gary stood where they were until the last of the group of people had left. Kim went over to Martin to check he was OK then they left. It had been a long evening; dawn was just around the corner and tomorrow was another working day. Mel and Gary went to the social club and went around the business side of the bar helping themselves to a glass of wine. They took their drinks and sat down at their table at the back of the room. They talked and talked about the important things in their lives. They shared experiences and memories of their lives on Earth. The chatted through the early hours then left the social club to walk in the park. Gary was going to take Mel to Janets grave, Mel needed to say her own goodbye. They walked towards the lake and sat down on the bench that Janet used to use. Mel then looked around her to see if anyone was about. With that she stood up from the bench, Janet's bench, and started to remove her top.

"What are you doing Mel" Gary asked her.

"I'm going for a swim, you coming?" she replied removing her shoes and trousers.

"What now?" he said.

"Yes now, come on" she said removing her underwear. Gary stood up and undressed himself. Once they were both naked, they walked down the sandy part until they were in the water. The water felt like silk as it maneuvered around them. Gary was the first one to fully immerse himself in the water, Mel quickly joined him. They swam together around the island in the lake a few times then climbed out of the water resting on the grass.

"That was for Janet," said Mel.

"Amen to that" replied Gary.

Chapter 18
De Ja Vu

In a quiet room, somewhere and no where a person laid on a gurney covered in a sheet. The room was airy with the light hum of air conditioning to be heard. The room was brightly lit by a fluorescent light which flickered now and then. The air felt clean and cool thanks to the ventilation, but it was the silence that engulfed the air the patient on the gurney first experienced. The woman lay still, dead still, except for the almost indetectable rise and fall of her chest which indicated that she was alive. The woman lay sleeping, deep in her slumbers. She was not aware of the cool of the metal gurney or the lack of warmth the cotton sheet covered her offered. She just lay there with no dreams and no hope. She had been in the room for about an hour or so, it was hard to be more accurate, there was no clock in the room.

In fact, the walls were bare except for a dial on the wall to control the air conditioning unit. The woman on the gurney began to come around. She first heard the silence then felt the cloth on her body about the same time she felt the hardness of her bed. Her thoughts were slow to come, she was just feeling the physical things at this point. It took an hour or so before she was ready to think. She opened her eyes taking time for them to adjust to the light. Her gaze was unfocused at first, gradually her sight returned to normal. She lay still trying to use her senses to work out where she was but there was so little to go on, she knew the next thing she had to do was to move. Her right hand moved first, quickly followed by the left, then she moved her head from side to side, so far OK, no pain. Her legs responded to her muscular request to move, that all was unproblematic. The woman stopped to rest; she was feeling tired again. She did not try to fight the fatigue but just went with it back to sleep.

After about two hours she woke up. This time she felt alert and ready to move. She sat up and tried to swing her legs over the side of the gurney but realized she was naked under the sheet. She pulled it up to wear as a sarong as she got down off the bed. She looked around her, taking in the pale cream walls and vinyl flooring which was quite bright and attractive. Everything looked so clean, including the sink in the corner. The porcelain bowl sparkled in the light. The woman noted it all with her fresh eyes. Trying to find a connection, a reason as to why she had woken up there. She noticed a small mirror on the wall above the sink, she decided, out of curiosity, to check it out. She took a moment to see if her body was intact, she mentally checked herself over from top to bottom, finally satisfied her body was fine. She felt no weakness or dizziness as she stood there then made her way carefully to the sink and mirror. The woman looked at herself in the mirror, first a quick glance, then a longer one until she properly stared at herself. It was not clear in her mind what she expected to see, certainly the mirror gave her no answers to her no questions. What her reflection told her was that she was a young woman, probably in her early twenties.

Her hair needed a brush, and her mouth and teeth needed a clean. She put her hand down to the cold water tap on the sink and turned it on. She used both of her hands to splash her face with water then, feeling thirsty, she brought handfuls of water to her mouth to drink. Her thirst sated she looked around the room, seeing if anything could give her a clue as to where she was. There was a door set in one of the walls which she made her way to, noticing immediately that it had no door handle. Panic spasmed her body as she realized she was trapped. She tried to push it to see if it would open to no avail.

She concluded that she was not going anywhere so sat back down on the gurney. Within a few minutes she was lost in her thoughts when she heard a sound behind the door. She quickly pulled up the sheet to conceal her naked body as the door moved open with a whoosh. Daring to look, the woman glanced over at the doorway which revealed a young lady dressed in white. The lady smiled at her with a glorious display of white clean teeth and red lip sticked lips. The woman felt her nervousness ease as the lady came in. She had a badge on her by her right lapel, which was just too far away, at that point, for her to read. She was carrying a bag which she put on the gurney then held out her right hand to the woman.

"Hi, my name is Iris; I am your Fetcher. I am here to help you adjust to life here. I have these toiletries and clothes for you; I think they will fit you. I will leave you to dress. I will be back soon," said the lady, Iris. With that, Iris turned around and pressed a button on the fob key, which hung around her neck, and activated the door. It closed behind her as Iris headed off down a corridor. The woman reached over to grab hold of the bag and then looked inside it. She pulled out a plastic bag that held soap, flannels, toothpaste and a toothbrush, deodorant and a comb. The woman got up and went over to the sink to wash. She dried her underarms with one of the flannels before applying deodorant. She was already feeling better about her situation; maybe it wouldn't be too bad. Once she had attended to her toilette, she went back to the gurney to check out the clothes. She then, one by one, picked up the garments before dressing hurriedly in case Iris came back mid-dressed, which would be embarrassing. The clothes were pretty good, good quality, fit well, and very similar to what she would buy. Now she was washed and dressed. She wondered what would be next; one thing she did need was to take a wee. She hoped Iris would come back sooner rather than later. This she did just a few minutes later. Once in her room, she asked Iris

"Where am I? What am I doing here?"

"You will find out very soon in the induction meeting which will happen in ten minutes time, shall we go?"

"Before we go," said the woman, "you couldn't tell me where the ladies are; I'm bursting." Iris laughed and then said. "Of course, it's just around the corner, and we pass it on the way to the meeting room. With that, the young woman got up and walked out of the room through the whoosh door led by Iris. The woman had so many questions for Iris, who replied to them that all would be made clear at the meeting. They walked down an artificially lighted corridor, which was fresh and clear. Coolish air wafted down from vents in the ceiling, making a pleasant temperature. There were no works of art adorning the walls, just doors here and there. The doors had numbers on them; what they contained, who knows.

At the end of the corridor was a double door, this Iris opened with a push, the door opened into a large room with many doors leading off it. There were about twenty people in there, their Fetchers stood together at the back of the room. On a small raised platform a brown suited man stood there with his shirt opened a button showing a hint of body hair. He waited until the noise in the room abated then addressed his audience.

"Hello, my name is Ron; I hope I can answer your questions and tell you about this place. Now, most of you arrived here last night; I do apologise for keeping you in the dark for so long; something went wrong somewhere. Anyway, to be clear, your Fetcher is here to assist with your transformation; they are skilled in what they do. Please treat them with respect. We have a few rules here that people are expected to follow; this is all written down in your manuals which your Fetcher will give you after this session. Basically, you all must respect one another, no violence, no fighting and that kind of thing. There is a no violence policy here, and any violence towards the staff and others will not be tolerated."

"But where are we? What is this place?" Demanded one of the men in the group. Others nodded at this,

"Yes, of course. This is a place where you will adjust readily for your Graduation. You will learn how to act, react and fit in with the way we do things around here." Ron said. The young woman felt as if nothing really had been said, there was so much to ask, but she felt too shy to speak. Instead, she kept quiet, hoping that someone else would ask the questions.

"Many of you will pass through here relatively quickly, a few will struggle, but we are all here to help" Ron spoke with confidence.

"You have told us nothing, why are we here" shouted out a woman wearing a rather nice yellow top.

"You are all here to prepare you for life when you will graduate" Ron replied, really not helping at all. With that, he stood down off the platform making a hasty retreat through one of the doors. Iris went up to the young woman leading her away back down a corridor. She led her to a rather nice room with a large window overlooking parkland. The room was painted a pink rose colour with corresponding pictures. There was a bed, seating area, shower and desk come dressing table. It all looked very comfortable. She checked the wardrobe only to see several outfits hanging up, they were all things she would buy herself.

"Iris, how do you know what I like to wear?" She asked

"We get a prior notice about our new arrivals, so I could get them for you; I am pleased you like them," Iris said as she smoothed wrinkles out of the bedspread.

"What is this place, what is Graduation?" Asked the woman.

"Janet, this is Earth, people who have been through Second Chance stations come here to prepare them for re-joining Earth life, that's Graduation."

"But, I thought, I thought I was back there again. It is all so familiar. Am I really back on Earth?" Janet said, struggling to take everything in. Janet looked in the mirror, seeing a young woman, probably in her early twenties.

"How come am I so young?" Asked Janet.

"You came here at a crucial part of your life to take you down an alternative path. You have a chance to change your personal history," Janet stared at Iris and then at her reflection; *wow*, she thought.

"I don't think you will be here long; I am sure you can take everything you have learnt and experienced in Second Chance to good use. You can do something about your depression and your other destructive behaviours. I have the privilege of helping you to do that until you are ready to jump back into your life; now, are you hungry?" She said, turning towards the door, "What do you fancy to eat? Will Macaroni Cheese do? They make it pretty good here. It's what I'm going to have on my lunch break" she walked through the whoosh door and then turned around. "Oh, by the way, there is someone here whom you know, Debbie?"

"Debbie, here, when can I see her, how is she, is she well?" Janet nearly jumped up and down at the prospect of seeing her friend.

"First food," insisted Iris, "then I will take you to see her; she came yesterday. She's doing well. Anyway, I'll get your food," Janet nodded to her and then thanked her for her kindness. Iris finally left the room, leaving Janet alone with her thoughts. She stood up and looked in the mirror again, and she barcly recognised the young Janet. She had forgotten just how pretty she was. Her figure was trim, and her complexion clear. Her hair had no sign of grey in it; yes, she thought that she looked good. She felt quite excited about the thought of going to earth at this age.

All her wisdom to make better decisions, good choices. It was down to her to make the most of this opportunity. She went over to the wardrobe to check out her clothes. They were the very nineteen eighties, she thought. When new jeans were shrunk to your size in the bath, pulling them up in the water, so they were skin tight, she remembered that. What about the shoulder pads in tops and jackets? She checked to see if any of the tops in the wardrobe had them. She fingered the material; polyester was the material of the decade. It held the bright colours well and was cheap to make.

Janet went over to the mirror and got hold of the comb she had left there. She set about trying to style her hair in an era when hair spray was used to set hair, too soon for the likes of mousse and hair gel. She gave up on that, her hair had always been reluctant to do anything she wanted. She sat down on the bed then stood up to look out of the window. The park was not as large as the one of Second Chance and did not have a lake in it but the flower beds looked lovely and well cared for. Maybe she could go out for a while, maybe after lunch, she thought.

Janet heard a noise outside her door then the whoosh as it opened revealing Iris with two plates of food on a tray. She set it down on the desk then invited Janet to eat. Janet took off the lid on one of the plates and instantly got the scent of melted cheese. She felt a rush of saliva fill her mouth as she picked up the plate and a fork then sat down on her bed to eat. Iris joined her and after a couple of mouth falls both agreed that the food was good. Iris told her that from now on she will be having her meals in the dining room with the others starting from that night. She said she would give Janet the grand tour after they had finished eating. Once she had consumed her food, she pushed the plate away from her. It was not, by far, the best Macaroni Cheese she had eaten, but it was up there with the best. She had not realised how hungry she was. She drank her tea with relish then once downed, she put the cup down on the tray. What now? She thought. Within a few minutes of consuming her meal Iris finished hers and put her plate on the tray.

"Oh, before I forget, I have this for you," she handed Janet a fob key to wear around her neck, which would give her access to what she would need during her stay there.

"Now, do you need a rest, or shall I show you around," Iris said as she picked up the tray.

"The journey here can take its toll on you; it will take you a day or two to adjust."

"How did I get here?" Janet asked.

"Well, the best I can tell you is that we were told you were due to arrive, so the porters got the gurney ready at the arrival door. Beyond that, I really don't know." She said leaving Janet not really any further forward. She did feel a bit tired so lay down on her bed. Iris took the tray away and left Janet to rest. She was asleep within minutes. When she woke it looked like it was getting dark. The window of her room showed that dusk had fallen and that it looked like it was raining. She sat up then swung her legs over so her feet were on the floor.

She pressed the call button on her fob key to call for Iris then stood up to walk over to the window. As she looked out at the pouring rain she felt as if she was being hypnotised. She was focused on tracing rain droplets as they hit the window then left a wet trail as they fell. She did not hear Iris entering her room and made her jump when she said hello to her.

"Iris, you made me jump. Is that clock right? Is it really two in the morning? Oh my gosh, I am so sorry for having called you. You must have been asleep." Janet said feeling guilty at having summoned her.

"Yes, well I am a light sleeper and know I have to be alert to be there for you for the first twenty-four hours. Please don't worry about it. Now, what can I do for you."

"I would love a cup of tea. Would I be allowed to have a shower?" she asked.

"Yes, of course, I will get you some towels. The shower is a bit temperamental; it may take a little while for the temperature to get up." Iris turned around and left the room. She was back within minutes with a mug of hot steaming tea and two fluffy towels. There are shower gel and hair shampoo, and conditioner in the shower unit. Do you need a hand with anything? Iris asked, handing Janet her tea and putting the towels down on the bed,

"I will get you some night clothes and leave them on your bed if you like."

"Thank you," Janet said, then waited until Iris had left her room to get undressed. The shower room was pretty standard, with white tiled walls and an anti-slip dark-coloured floor. There was a fold-up seat that Janet left in position, and then she turned on the water to start her shower. The water felt lovely on her body. She relished it for a short while, then began to wash her hair and then her body. She wanted to spend longer under the waterfall, but she thought that Iris might be waiting for her.

Janet was still very aware that she was in a strange new place, she was not yet sure of the rules. She didn't want to do anything to upset anyone, a bit like finding your way on the first day of school. Once she had finished her shower, she grabbed a towel to dry herself then wrapped it round her body to go to her bedroom. Iris had left a nightdress on the bed as promised along with a book. Intrigued, Janet took hold of the book and checked out the title. It was a manual detailing what to expect in this place.

Janet didn't know what it was called, she vowed to ask Iris next time she saw her. Janet pulled on the nighty then gave her hair another dry with the towel. She ran a comb through her now clean hair then sat down on the bed to study the book in more detail. It said in there that this place, thought Janet, is actually called the Time Complex. Now she knew that she started reading the manual. It told her what to expect from the various members of staff, what would be happening during her stay and the expectations they have of the residents. It all looked pretty straightforward to Janet. It looks as if residents are only there for a week, often shorter than that, just enough time for them to adjust back to Earth and their new selves.

For Janet, she was a sixty year old woman in a twenty year old body. She had changed to the time she first started to have problems with her mental health. Janet was thrilled that she now had the opportunity to do things differently. To, as Iris had said earlier, to re write her own personal history. Janet tried to settle down to sleep but found it hard. In the end, she got out of bed to make herself a drink. While the kettle was boiling, she looked outside at the parkland through the window. She wondered if she could go out now to walk in the park. Her interest piqued, she pulled on her clothes on top of her nightdress, turned off the kettle then grabbed her fob key. She opened the door to her room and looked up the corridor to see if anyone was there. Seeing nobody she set off heading towards the exit that led to the park. She found it with no problem, helped by some excellent signage.

Once she stepped outside, she was aware of how cold it was. She had been so used to the warmth of Second Chance air that she realised she would need to climatise to it. She found a path that went into the park, she followed it as far as she dared in the semi dark. It was getting darker by the minute; Janet was not sure she would feel safe continuing on her adventure so turned around heading back to the building. She would explore more tomorrow, she thought. Once back in her room, she proceeded to make herself a mug of tea then took off her day clothes. She drank the tea while sitting up in her bed, when she had finished, she lay down on the bed and tried a meditation technique she had learned in the Mind Complex. It helped her to unwind enough to feel sleepy. Janet turned off the bed side lamp and fell into a deep refreshing sleep.

The next day, Janet woke up feeling good. She got out of bed without the aching joints she was used to and was surprised at her energy levels. It took her just a few minutes to remind herself that she was now twenty. She had all the body of a young person, not the sixty-year-old she was. She looked at herself again and again in the mirror, admiring her youthful self. She washed and dressed, then wondered what the day would bring. Iris knocked on her door and then entered.

"Are you decent?" Iris asked, pocking her head around the door.

"Yes, you can come in," replied Janet.

"Did you sleep well" Iris said as she came in the room closing the door behind her.

"Yes, thanks, I did. I can't get over the fact that I am so young. I look so different and feel different." Janet said standing up. "How long is it likely to last until I am sixty again?"

"Forty years, Janet, this is you," Iris replied.

"Oh wow, really. What am I doing today?" Janet asked then grabbed the comb to try to brush her hair which had tangled during her sleep.

"Today? Well, first I will take you to the canteen for breakfast, then how do you feel about meeting up with Debbie?" Iris said.

"Yes, that sounds good, thank you," Janet said as she finally won the battle with her hair. With that, Iris and Janet left the room and headed off straight down the corridor. They took a left, then a right and the dining hall and canteen were right ahead of them. Janet heard the noise before she saw the place. It was not as big as the ones she was used to, but it was still a bustling noisy place. There were a couple of other people in there eating their breakfast. Janet looked at them to see if she recognised them from Second Chance, but they did not look like anyone she knew.

According to Iris, The Time Complex took people who had Graduated from many Second Chance places so what with the fast turnaround, the chances of her coming across anyone was small. Janet opted to have porridge and tea then took her tray to one of the free tables. Iris had selected cereal came to sit with her. They ate in silence; Janet was too lost in her thoughts about possibilities for her new future which delighted her. She felt excited about what she could do in her young body. The world was open to her, as long as she got on top of the bipolar disorder, she had first experienced at twenty. What could she do differently, she thought to herself?

"Penny for them," said Iris.

"Oh, sorry, I was just thinking. How much of my future do I have control over. I mean, can I stop myself getting ill?" Janet asked.

"No, you can't change that because you inherited it, what you can do is change how you behave with it. Get to the point that you manage it better a lot earlier than you did in your past." Iris said.

"Yes, I see. So if I get help before it gets too bad, then I might not suffer as much as I had. That would work" Janet said as she put down her empty mug.

"Yes," said Iris. "That's right, then you probably wouldn't get as ill as you did because you know better how to manage it from your sixty year old self. What's more, you would not be in the position to jump off the bridge breaking your back and legs which killed you. Do you get it?"

"Yes, I do. I can see better where I could change things. I feel really excited about this. When will I return to my life on Earth?"

"Well, hopefully by the end of the week. It is Wednesday today." Said Iris. "Are you done?" she asked gesturing towards Janet's empty bowl and mug. Janet nodded then they both stood up. Janet started to head back to her room when Iris held the lose part of the sleeve of her jumper.

"Let me take you to the day room." With that she led her down a short corridor from the canteen into a room with a number of armchairs, low tables and a television set. Janet looked around her at the room and at the tv.

"Does that work?" she asked Iris pointing to the tv.

"Yes, we put things on like recordings of the news and other lifestyle programmes, so residents have an idea of what is happening on Earth at the time of their death."

"OK" Janet said as she sat in one of the comfy chairs. She then stood up and went over to cabinet that had three shelves of books. She picked up one checking the title on the cover.

"Janet is that you?" she heard someone say. Janet turned round seeing a woman who had just come into the room. She stared at her for a moment until it finally clicked.

"Debbie, Debbie wow you look amazing" Janet said going over to embrace her.

"I've got my legs back. You look fantastic, young," Debbie said. They both sat down to chat while their fetchers left them to it. Debbie excitedly told Janet about her experience at the Time Complex filling her in about the regime. They talked for hours about their time on Second Chance and their experience of Graduation. Debbie was astounded about how her re death had touched so many of the residents and stirred them into action. She recalled the ageing process seeing what she would be like as an old woman. Janet asked her if she knew when she was going back to her life on Earth. Debbie said, "I'm going back tomorrow. Because my history is quite recent, they don't think I need much reintroducing."

"Now I'm young again, and I think it's going to take a bit of time for me. I've, in effect, lost forty years." Janet said, looking a bit concerned. "We won't know each other; we will be at different times," Debbie said, leaning over to take one of Janet's hands. Janet fell silent at this. They would have to make the most of the time they had together, she thought. At least there will be the memory.

Debbie went over to a small kitchen just outside of the day room to make them both a coffee while Janet mused over everything she was learning. She was keen to pick Debbie's brain more and more but the thought of losing her again was playing on her mind. When they had finished their coffees, they sat and talked some more until Debbie looked up at the clock on the wall.

"I've got to be somewhere, I have a counselling session, will you be alright by yourself?" Debbie asked as she got to her feet.

"Yes, of course, will you be free later on?" questioned Janet looking up at her.

"How about lunch, they start serving at twelve thirty. See you in the canteen?" Debbie replied.

"Yes, that would be great. I hope your session goes OK" said Janet then watched as Debbie left the day room then headed off to the left. Janet decided to explore the park so found her way to the door she had used the night before. She stepped outside then realised that it was raining and cold. This was something she would have to get used to she thought then she wondered where she could get wet weather gear from.

"Do you need a coat" someone asked her, she turned around only to see Iris standing there holding an anorak.

"How did you know that?" Janet asked her taking the coat from Iris's grasp.

"It's my job to know. Iris said, "You have a session with the counsellor at two after lunch. I will take you there if you like."

"Thank you, shall I meet you at the day room, will that be OK" asked Janet.

"Yes, that will do fine. It's only a very short walk from there." With that Iris turned around heading back through the door to the corridor beyond. Janet put on the coat then started to walk down the path into the park. She admired the autumn colours and the growth of fungi at the base of a tree. Everything seemed so alive she thought to herself. Second Chance only had one season, late spring. It felt great to see such a lovely November day. It was then she noticed some ants running along a set path on the concrete, one by one they head off in the same direction. Janet sat down on her haunches to watch them for a while. Then she heard a scurrying noise, looking up she spotted a grey squirrel frolicking around in a pile of fallen leaves. Janet watched it as it stuffed some acorns into its mouth then ran to a tree and effortlessly climbed up it then disappeared down a hole at the top of the trunk. Janet had a look around her for a moment or two then continued down the path enjoying the sensation of the light rain on her face. She came to a couple of benches on top of a small hill that offered some lovely views of the park. She pulled down the back of the anorak to cover her bum to sit down on the first bench. It was not a day for skinny dipping she thought realising to her embarrassment she had actually said it out loud. But there was no one around to hear her, the place was empty apart from the squirrel and the ants. Janet sat there until she felt the cold of the day then got up and started to retrace her steps back to the building. She unlocked the door with her fob key then found her way back to her room. She wanted to change; her trousers were damp from the drizzle. She took off the anorak and her trousers then went to the wardrobe to grab another pair. She took out an outfit, a jacket, it had shoulder pads in it. The blouses all had grandfather collars. The jeans were high fitting. Janet then surmised that these were the clothes she would have worn in the nineteen eighties. Maybe, she thought, that that was part of her acclimatising to the era she was returning to. Excited at the thought of how she would look she took off her top then once down to her underwear she tried on some of the clothes then looked at herself in the mirror turning from side to side to admire her reflection. She settled on wearing a pair of jeans with a light-coloured blouse with a tailored jacket. She felt surprisingly comfortable wearing the clothes. She checked the time to see if it was nearly time for lunch, seeing that it was nearly half past twelve she left her room to show of her new clothes to Debbie.

Debbie thought it was funny seeing the fashion of the day. Janet did a twirl in front of her then showed her the shoulder pads giving her the 'V' shape. Then they selected their meals, sat down and chatted. Debbie had had a good session with the counsellor. He was happy with her progress and if the physio department were sure she had the lower body strength she needed then she was going to be going home the next day. She was thrilled with the thought of stepping back into her sons lives and she knew what she needed to do to prevent the action that lead to her entering Second Chance.

"I will miss you," Janet said.

"You will soon be back in your life, do you know what you need to do differently this time?" Debbie asked.

"Yes, I get help quicker and make sure I am in charge of my mental health. That way I can lead the professionals to manage my care. Or at least that is what I think I need to do. Its not straight forward is it?" said Janet emotionally.

"No it isn't, I think you will find that the counsellor will be helpful. He helped me to priorities things. I'm sure he will help you find the way." Debbie said. After their meal they went back into the day room. Iris came along a few minutes later and sat down with the girls. Do you fancy a laugh? Iris said, reaching for the remote control to the television set. "Watch this, its top of the pops from the eighties, Janets era." With that she put the tv on then sat back to enjoy the show. The music was so familiar to Janet, and the colourful clothes were a delight to see. Everything was big, from hairstyles to shoulders. The mullet haircut was evident on many people performing and in the dancing audience. It felt like a trip down memory lane for Janet, but Debbie watched with delight. She had heard some of the music, but the range of fashions were new to her.

"Perhaps I could lead a revival of eighties fashions," said Debbie.

"Good idea," said Janet singing along to one of the tunes. It took her back in time to what she was doing at that point in her life. She was training to be a nurse. She had to give it up when she became unwell but maybe, Janet thought, she could change that. She had loved nursing but had felt pushed out due to the state of her mental health. She figured that if she showed she had got control of things, she could have stayed in the job that she cared for. There was just a little bit to sort out and that was taking control. Her illness was marked with psychosis, something she could not manage as she would not be aware that she was ill. With all of these thoughts invading her mind, she tried to home in just focusing on the tv. It was fun looking at how things were in her history but the thought of re-entering her life as a twenty-year-old was quite daunting. She would be able to predict what was going to happen, not only to her but to the wider society. Changing her history would impact on the rest of society one way or another. That was a lot of responsibility. What if she mucked it up, made things worse? She assumed she couldn't go through this process again! Janet spoke her fears to Iris and Debbie as they watched their programme. Janet got to think that in some way she might actually influence Debbie in her life. Janet felt fearful of her new destiny, maybe she was looking at it on the bigger picture, thinking that she alone had all the power and influence. She focused back into her own life. Yes, her decisions and actions will most likely affect those around her but would be so diluted in the wider society to barely alter the status quo. At the end of the programme, Iris tuned the tv into a news programme on the BBC from 1983. Janet would be twenty then though at that age had no real interest in politics, that came along a lot later in her life. Top of the news that day on the telly was that Margaret Thatcher was on the campaign trail and the cold war was raging on. Also, the fear of nuclear attack was in the news. Janet could recall these events. The world was quite the place in turmoil with threatened strikes and the rise of the trade unions. Yes, she could get herself well immersed with the politics of the day. At the end of the programme, Iris showed Janet how to access the programmes they had for the decades. They had quite a library of programmes that Janet would be happy to explore. But now, Iris told her that they had to go as she had her appointment. They turned off the telly and Iris showed Janet the way to the therapist.

At exactly two o'clock, Janet knocked on the door of the room where the counsellor worked. He opened the door and invited her in. She selected to sit on a chair with arms while he sat in one in front of his desk. He introduced himself as Simon and welcomed her to the Time Complex.

The session lasted for an hour. During her time there, Janet was asked to list the early warning signs and triggers that she experienced before getting unwell. Janet was able to list them easily but stumbled a bit when he asked her what she does to minimise the impact of her mania or depression. She found it hard but with a bit more exploring, Simon was able to tease the information out of her.

She had a lightbulb moment when she acknowledged to herself that she doesn't have to do it all on her own, that she was under a team of professionals who would be more than happy to work with her. Also, the value of taking medication to control her psychosis for either a short or long term. Janet had always struggled with the idea of taking medication regularly even when she was not ill. She had hated the side effects one of which that caused her weight gain. She realised that if it kept her well, then it was a small price to pay then to spend many many months in hospital. At the end of the session, Janet felt tired but pleased with what she had achieved. She could see how her life experiences could now to used to educate her in her new old life. Satisfied with her progress she left Simons office and walked to the day room. No one was in there, so she decided to have an explore. According to the manual there was a fully equipped gym on site, she wanted to find that then she would get changed in some gear to have a workout. She assumed it was along the same corridor as they day room so wandered along it looking for any signage on the walls or doors. Near the end of the corridor, she found a door which looked like it was what she was looking for. She opened it and peered in. There were a good number of resistance machines and some free weights. She closed the door then retraced her steps back to the day room. She made herself a coffee then turned on the tv. When the screen came to life there were a list of decades on a page. She scrolled down to the nineteen eighties which opened up on another page. There was list of genres from music, films and news channels. She selected the news then the tv burst into life with the nine o'clock news on BBC1. She settled down in one of the armchairs to digest the news. Headlining was the IRA bombing outside of Harrods and the birth of the internet. Janet tried to memorise as much as she could, so she was familiar with the main points. She was sure it would all help for when she returned to Earth. She was so engrossed in watching the telly that she did not notice Iris coming in.

"Are you OK, Janet?" she said, making Janet jump out of her skin. "What's that you're looking at?"

"Just the news from the nineteen eighties. Thought I would do some homework," Janet said, shifting her seating position.

"How did your session go?" Iris asked.

"Yes, it went well; I found it very helpful. I feel really optimistic about going back. Though I will miss Debbie," Janet said.

"Well, you never know; your paths may cross in the future. Have you thought about how you could make that happen?" asked Iris.

"No, I hadn't. Is that possible?" enquired Janet.

"Well, yes, if you make a pact to meet up at a certain location and time. You will be back at the age of sixty then, what do you think?" said Iris.

"Yes, I guess that is possible. Do you think that is something Debbie would want to do? She may want a fresh start," asked Janet.

"Yes, she might. I guess you will have to ask her." With that, she left the room, leaving Janet to her thoughts. She watched until the end of the news programme and then turned off the tv. She went to her room to see if there was anything in her wardrobe for her to wear at the gym. There was a brightly coloured jogging bottom with a t-shirt she selected to wear. Iris had given her some trainers, which she pulled on and then set off to the gym. Janet had a good workout, though, of course, the last time she exercised, she was forty years older. Another promise she made to herself was to exercise regularly, and she had learnt too late in life that it was pretty therapeutic.

She left the gym, then went home to shower and change into brightly coloured clothes. Debbie knocked on her door on her way to dinner. Janet opened the door and invited her in. She spoke to her about making a meeting pact which excited Debbie. They decided to write each other a letter with the date, time and place they would meet when their time paths would collide. Janet joked that Debbie would not want to meet up with an old fogie like her. Debbie laughed at that "you are so special; I would love you if you were old and decrepit."

"No, you wouldn't. I went through that when I Graduated, and it was not a pretty sight," Janet said as she reflected back on her ageing process. They had been through so much together; their shared history would always be their bond. They set off for the dining room, saying Hi to some of the other residents. It was Debbie's last but one meal on the Time Complex, and she was returning to her life on Earth the next day. Janet selected roast pork with all the trimmings, while Debbie went for a vegetable curry with rice. They sat down to eat their food when movement at the hatch got their attention.

Looking up, they spotted someone whom they had not seen there before who looked familiar. It took a short while, then both of them realised it was Martin from Second Chance, leader of the Resistance. They waved to him; it took a moment or two to recognise them in their new identities. He didn't look much different, possibly a year or two younger. His Fetcher stood back while he joined the girls at their table.

"Oh my god, it's so good to see you two," Martin said as he picked up his knife and fork.

"What happened, Martin? They got you?" asked Debbie.

"The following day, after you, Janet, they arrested me. They didn't give me any chances. They just took me to the holding cell and then to the Graduation Centre. What a turn-up for the books, this being the route back to Earth," he said excitedly. Janet wanted to say something about how he had gotten it so wrong but decided to stay mum. They ate their food, with Martin especially interested in Janet's shedding off the years and her new clothes. He told them that he sustained his injury, like Debbie, quite soon before he died for the first time. They took Martin to look at the day room, where there were a couple of residents looking at programmes from the nineteen nineties on the telly. Once they had finished and wandered off, Janet asked the others if they could look at some more stuff from her era. With their agreement, they selected from a list to watch the film 'Saturday Night Fever'.

Again, the music of the time and the fashions were enough to make them giggle. At the end of the film, they stopped to chatter then Martins Fetcher came to show him back to his room. He was flagging having made the journey to the Time Complex not long ago. Once he had gone, Janet and Debbie looked at each other, each one daring for the other one to say what needed to be said. Debbie caved in first,

"So, the work of the Resistance, it was all for nothing," she said.

"Yes, it's a bit ironic. Isn't it for the leader to be here after all of that?" Janet replied. With enough said, Debbie left to go to her room; she had been told to get to bed in good time because she had a busy day the next day when she was due to be Graduated. They said goodnight to each other, Janet following suit, then back to her own room to start the winding down process before sleep.

The next day, Janet woke up feeling great. She remembered that Debbie was going that day and she needed to sit down somewhere quiet to write her a letter.

They had agreed on a place, date and time to meet in the future so their two worlds could collide. It didn't take long to get in her stride with the letter, and she poured her heart out into it, mainly with memories of their time on Second Chance. When she had finished, she got washed and dressed, then made her way to the canteen for breakfast. She chose to have a cooked breakfast, vowing to use up all of the calories down the gym later in the day. Debbie wasn't there at breakfast, but Martin came along and sat down with her to eat.

"What was it like for you, Graduating?" he asked Janet quietly, almost as if the word could not be said.

"It was far from pleasant, seeing your body age so quickly. I just gave in to it," she explained, finding it quite hard to verbalise. "What about you," she asked Martin.

'Terrifying now I know what I will look like when I am old; it makes me want to treat my body better," he replied.

"Yes, I know what you mean. Now I have a nice new body. I am going to really look after it." Janet responded.

"Has Debbie gone?" He asked.

"I don't know; I hoped she could have said goodbye beforehand," Janet said, hoping that she would see her give her her letter. At that point, Iris came over to where Janet sat and called her aside. She told Janet that Debbie had gone back to Earth and that she had a letter for her. Janet exclaimed that she had not been able to get the letter she had written to Debbie.

Nevertheless, she accepted the letter when Iris handed it to her. Hopefully, Debbie would remember the details they shared. It was not too far into her future compared to the many years in Janets. Janet said a quiet prayer for Debbie to help her on her way, then, deciding she was no longer hungry, left the canteen to go into the day room to have a look at the politics of her younger day. She planned to go out for a walk a bit later on and then have a session down at the gym. She half hoped that Martin would not want to hang around with her. Mealtimes were fine, and she could put up with that though she confessed she did find him annoying.

Janet had another counselling session later that same day, and she felt like she was really benefitting from it; she wondered if she could seek it on the outside. She went to the gym afterwards, enjoying just how much more she could use her body in her younger self. She had come to realise that she had not done much of this when she was twenty; she was too busy lashing out at the systems that were supporting her. Her maturity was certainly coming out, she thought. Next time round, it would be very different. She couldn't do much to stop the manic and depressive episodes, but she knew better now what to do to look after herself and minimise the time she would spend in the hospital. Iris caught up with her at dinner time, where they both sat down to eat while Janet disclosed her insights. Iris listened and piped in when she thought it appropriate.

"I think you are ready; let's see if we can get you graduated tomorrow," Iris said.

"Just one thing, will I go through the rebirth the same as before, am I going to be old" Janet asked feeling a bit concerned about the process.

"No, you go through a door right back to a place you know. It could be your bedroom or outside. Either way, it will be familiar to you. I will have a word with my boss and tell him my recommendations; how does that sound?" Iris asked between mouthfuls of fish pie.

"It sounds good. Will it hurt, you know, going back?" Janet asked, still feeling worried about the process.

"No, I don't think so; it will be the old cliché of one door closing and another one opening. It's the best part of my job, seeing people move on." Iris answered.

Janet needed a bit of thinking time, so she went out into the park back to the bench she had sat on before. It was not raining that day; in fact, it was quite a pleasant autumn day. She had her cardigan on to keep warm. She let her mind drift and then pulled herself up to focus on what she was going to do when she went back. The nineteen eighties were a long time ago; how would she cope with a place in her distant memory?

Not only were the clothes different, but so was the language; she felt ill-prepared to go, she thought. Panic began to come, and she got up and walked fast along the path heading down the hill to the other side. She began to shout out loud, no, no, no, louder and louder, until her throat hurt. Then Janet sat right down on a mound to try to calm herself down. She looked down at the mound and then realised she was sitting on rabbit poo. She stood up, brushing any debris off her bottom. She then stopped thinking about what she was doing.

There were rabbits here; after the no-creature world of Second Chance, she focused on what she could see or hear around her. In a short while, she felt grounded; she was pleased with that. Another skill she could add to her toolbox, she thought. She started to head back to her room, feeling a lot calmer. She had a busy day tomorrow, she thought. She went back to her room to change for the gym and, once dressed, walked the short distance to the gymnasium. There was a man already there exercising.

She hadn't seen him before, so she assumed he was new. Janet introduced herself to him and then waited until he replied with his name. He didn't say anything, didn't even react to her presence, so Janet just got on exercising. She actually managed to run on the treadmill, something she hadn't been able to do on Second Chance. She increased the speed of the belt and then fell into a steady jog for ten minutes until she felt winded. Back in the eighties, she didn't really exercise; that was something she could do something about, she thought. She moved off the treadmill and onto the rowing machine setting off at a fast pace which she held steady for ten minutes. Feeling warmed up, she went on target muscle groups with the resistance machines. She was pretty sure they didn't have them back in the day, but she couldn't be sure. The quiet man finished what he was doing and then looked like he was getting ready to go. He turned to look at Janet, then,

"Can you believe all of this crap?" he said. "Some fucking time machine, give me a break," he slammed his fist down onto a table in the centre of the room. "They mess you around then tell you your going fucking home, my fucking home was crap. What if I don't want to go there. I had a good life on Second Chance. Best place I've been to. Why can't they send me there?" He looked at Janet as if she had an answer.

Janet shrugged her shoulders; he had a point. Not everyone had what she had back home. She knew that her friend Mel thought her life on Second Chance was best, better than her life on earth with a bullying husband. The man left the room leaving Janet feeling a bit deflated. She had wrongly assumed that it was a positive thing for everyone. Maybe they could put the man in a place less bad for him, before his troubles started. Janet went back to her exercise still reeling from the comments but soon got her head back onto her work at hand. She had a go on all of the equipment until she felt she had no more to give.

Then she walked to her room to shower and change. She couldn't wait to try on another outfit then she had to go to her appointment with the therapist. She set off to walk to see the therapist going over things she wanted to say to him. This would be her last appointment with him if she was leaving the next day. The session went well. He was satisfied with her progress he just urged her to watch more tv of the decade so she could be clear what she would be going back to. This she did once she had finished. She made herself a hot drink then settled down to watch more programmes.

It was funny watching Coronation Street, with all the old characters. Some of which were still there in the programme. She then watched more of the news thinking that was important especially day to day life in a traumatic time in history. At least she knew the outcome of some of the troubles, though was not too sure if she could keep it to herself. She could make her fortune as a fortune teller, she thought. But, this was serious. What if she did let things slip. Suddenly the thought of going back tomorrow was daunting. Was she ready?

Chapter 19
Back Home

In the morning, Janet stretched her body then got up glancing at the clock on the wall. She got out of bed then washed her body and dressed herself in her eighties gear. She tried to style her hair big, but it simply would not go, it was unhappy with the back coming just ending up in tangles. She gave up on that, checked the time again then made her way to the canteen for breakfast. This could be my last meal thought Janet as she walked along the corridor. Martin was already in there eating his fried breakfast. The bacon smelled gorgeous, Janet thought quickly settling on her choice of breakfast. She placed an order for a full English breakfast and a mug of tea then waited in the queue until it was served. As Martin had seen her, she didn't really want to appear rude by sitting somewhere else, so she chose a seat at his table.

"Hi Martin, how are you doing" she said amiably.

"Me, I'm fine. Are you going today?" Martin asked.

"Yes, sometime soon" Janet said as she sliced her bacon. Her mouth was salivating from the smell of the food, she really wanted to savour it than talk to him.

"I've heard it's pretty horrible" he said to Janet.

"Have you, where did you get that from" Janet asked Martin.

"Someone told me last night in the day room" he said, "How's your food" Martin rapidly changed the subject.

"No one can tell you what it's like, nobody comes back. There is no third chance. It may be horrific, but if it gives me my life back, its worth it" Janet said closing the conversation. She ate her meal making small talk then excused herself at the earliest possible time to not cause offence. After breakfast she went into the day room which was empty. She turned on the tv then scrolled through the eighties programmes until she found one she liked. It was a news programme with the interviewer questioning a sports man who played for Chelsea football club. Janet just sat watching tv, hoping that Iris would come soon to let her know what was happening. Iris turned up during Nationwide and sat down in an armchair next to Janet.

"Well, today is the day, how do you feel" Iris asked Janet.

"Nervous but ready. Are you sure it won't hurt?" Janet said to her.

"I can't say for sure, but I've never heard any shouts when the door closes. I expect you may feel a bit muddled headed for a while, but the door opens in a safe environment for you." Iris replied.

"When am I going" asked Janet.

"After you last counselling session with Simon. So you have the morning to fill, what are you going to do?" Iris asked.

"I'm going to the gym; do I need to pack anything?" Janet asked.

"Only the letter from Debbie, have you read it yet?" Iris said.

"No, I thought I would read it when I get back home, then I can put it somewhere safe, do you fancy a coffee?" Janet said getting to her feet. Iris nodded yes so Janet went to the little kitchen to put the kettle on. Janet asked Iris some questions about her and how come she worked for the Time Complex. Iris told her she was head hunted while she was at university studying behavioural psychology. She works two weeks on at the Complex then one week back at home.

"So, when you go home, do you go through that door" asked Janet intrigued.

"No, we have our own door, which is at the same time as Earth. I don't know how it all works; all I know is that I love my job, and I get to meet some lovely people." Iris said, smiling at Janet,

"Thank you, I think your amazing. You just seem to know when I need help" Janet said then finished her coffee.

"Right, I'm going to get ready for the gym. See you later?" said Janet getting to her feet.

"Yes, how about lunch together before your session with Simon?" said Iris then she got to her feet without waiting to hear the answer. There was a pile of paperwork to be done to make sure everything was ready before Janet went back to Earth.

The gym helped, Janet, thought on her way back to her room to shower and change. She had worked very hard and felt very sweaty, but it all felt good. After her shower, she made her way to the canteen. Opting for a cheese salad and trifle, she sat down at an empty table. There were only a few people in the room and no sign of Iris yet, or Martin. She picked up her knife and fork to eat her food, glancing up to the door now and then to see who was coming in. Iris came in just as Janet was starting to eat her trifle. She smiled as she came over with her tray of food.

"Not long now" Iris said as she sat down. At that moment Martin came in waving to Janet as he went to the counter. He joined the ladies setting down his tray of shepherd's pie and vegetables.

"I'm going tomorrow," he said, "I'm really excited about going back home. I will get to see my wife and daughters."

"I didn't know you had family on Earth" Janet said then took a mouthful of jelly.

"Yes, Claire, is my wife, and Emily and Rose are my daughters. They are fifteen and Rose is twelve."

"Hopefully they have not missed you. You had an accident at work, didn't you?" Iris questioned.

"Yes, there one day then gone the next" Martin replied.

"So, you will be going back a few minutes before the accident so you can take evasive action, how does that sound to you?"

"I look forward to it. One thing I am going to do is resign from heading up the trade union." Martin said then started to eat his meal. They ate in silence for a while then started some chit chat to pass the time it took to finish their meals. Janet thought that she should have expected him to be part of a trade union as he was an activist. She thought that maybe she should look to work for a trade union at the hospital where she was doing her nurse training. Maybe she could change the practice of encouraging people with mental health problems to leave the profession. She remembered that the director of nursing came to see her when she had her first breakdown to inform her that it would be best, she should leave. Janet could see that the practice did change over time, but maybe she could make it happen sooner. She was getting excited about the things she could do when she got back, it all sounded very positive, not much longer, she thought.

The session with Simon was spent with Janet going through the changes she was going to make once back on earth and how she could avoid getting to the point of trying to take her life. Having died once, she couldn't get to the point where she would contemplate taking her own life. She felt privileged to have been given a second chance, she was not going to muck it up, but on the other side, she knew just how ill she used to get; she would need all her coping mechanisms to get her safely through. At the end of the counselling session, Simon offered her his hand to shake, and he wished her the best of luck. Janet left the session feeling a little less buoyant than when she went in; she was feeling rather nervous now, worried about what was to come with her Graduation.

She popped into the day room to see if anyone was around. The room was empty, so she headed to her room to get herself ready for her next step. She had decided what clothes she was going to wear, selecting a pair of high waist loose-fitting jeans with turn ups and a grandad shirt. Because she was unsure of the time of year she would be returning to Earth, she took a brightly coloured cardigan to wear. Once dressed, she wondered what to do with herself. She knew her time was limited and that Iris needed to find her, so she went back to the day room. She spotted Martin there reading a magazine.

"Your still here, I thought you were going today?" he asked her.

"Yes, I am; any time now, I'm waiting for Iris to get me," Janet replied.

"How are you feeling?" Said Martin.

"Nervous, there is so much going on in my head; I'm worried I will forget everything I've learnt," Janet said, sitting down on a comfy chair. She sat in silence for a while then she picked up a magazine. She looked at the cover, and it was dated nineteen eighty-three; she flicked through it, reading up on the celebrities of the day and all the gossip. It was certainly something she would buy to read back when she was twenty. That was quite a thought, she thought. She is now twenty, twenty!

How does a twenty-year-old behave in the eighties? She began to feel edgy, worried about heading towards a panic attack she left the day room heading out to the park. She felt claustrophobic indoors, outside it felt less busy, she could get control of her breathing and pulse rate gradually, gradually the panic subsided.

She stood on the grass near the bench just staring out at the view. It was a lovely autumn day; the sun was shining, and the colours of the leaves were fantastic.

One tree in particular, still had most of its leaves on the branches. The gold and reds and oranges were striking. She just looked at it, focusing on as many details as she could. It's alright, I'm in control now she said to herself when she let go of her gaze. Feeling less stressed, she sat down on the bench just looking around her. She spotted a squirrel scurrying around in a pile of leaves its grey body disappearing at times.

Janet watched its antics until it realised she was there and hopped off up one of the nearby trees. She could hear the call of birds in the distance, she looked up to see if she could see them. There were dots in the sky, but Janet could not tell if they were the birds that called out. Janet was unaware of time while she sat there, so much was she engrossed in being with nature. She laughed as the squirrel reappeared with another one. They ran chasing each other around the trunk of the tree.

Jumping from branch to branch in an elaborate dance. Then they both disappeared from her view but she could still here the scurrying noise they made. Janet decided that she needed to be getting back. She didn't want to keep Iris waiting as she was now in a state of mind to leave. She felt ready for Graduation, today, she was going home. Home, at that point in her life would be her room in the nurse accommodation. She could be working tomorrow she thought, boy, could she remember what to do? Not wanting to panic again she moved her mind off that and set off for her room. She had just gone through the door when she spotted Iris coming up the corridor.

"There you are, I've been looking for you, are you ready?" Iris said as they approached each other.

"What now? Well, yes, I'm ready." Janet replied her heart fluttering.

"Lets go then, follow me. Have you got that letter?" Iris asked.

"No, let me quickly get it" Janet said then went off to her room to pick it up.

"I'll meet you in the day room" Iris shouted at Janets disappearing form. Janet took no time picking up the letter then hot footed to the day room to see Iris talking with Martin.

"This is it then; you are going back to Earth," said Martin coming over to give her a hug. "I hope all goes well, and thank you so much for supporting me back on Second Chance."

"Good luck for tomorrow when you go back Martin" Janet said returning the hug. Breaking apart Janet looked at Iris indicating her readiness. Iris started walking towards the door expecting Janet to follow her.

"Can't I stay here?" asked Janet looking at Iris.

"No, there is a place for you on Earth ready for you to carve out of it the best you can. It's time to live your best life, and you will do well." Iris said, putting her arm around Janet.

"Now, come on, let's go." Janet walked alongside Iris down a corridor that she had not been before. Iris used her fob key to enter through a door into a room. The room was covered nearly entirely by computers, screens, dials and buttons with a bare space where there was a door.

"Is that the door?" asked Janet pointing to it.

"Yes, it's not very impressive is it."

"It's a time machine," said Janet.

"Yes" replied Iris. Iris went over to one of the computers pressing a sequence of buttons. "I'm just setting it up, it's all been programmed but I have to put in a code." She continued pressing buttons until it bleeped. "All ready. Right, when you step through the door, it's a very short passageway to another door. Once the door from here has closed, you need to go to the other door and push it. It's going to open out into your room at the nurses home. Then, the rest is up to you. Is all that clear?" Janet nodded and on Iris's command went over to the door. She got ready to open it but turned around to face Iris.

"Thank you so much Iris, you have been brilliant. You never know we may meet again." With that she turned the handle on the door, swung open the door then stepped through. She stopped for a second before closing the door. She heard some weird noises during the three steps to the second door. Taking a deep breath, she put her hands on the door then gently pushed. The door moved easily to her surprise. She stepped out through the door and looked around her. The door closed behind her with a clang.

She turned around just in time to see the door disintegrate into millions of pieces. The pieces shimmered like metal confetti as they fell to the floor then continued to break down until it was just dust. Janet looked back out ahead seeing her things in a room. The room was the one she lived in as a trainee nurse. She recognised it easily. She took in a deep breath looked around her then went to sit on her bed. She was back, and this time, it was going to be different, better.

Chapter 20
Home

Janet stayed sitting on her bed for a good few minutes. She looked around at her things everything looked somewhat familiar but strange. It looked like she had just got up and left, which, Janet thought to herself, is exactly what she did. She got up and went over to her desk where a few pieces of paper were settled on it. She picked up one of them seeing it was a work schedule. She checked to see if there was anything on it that could help her see what she needed to do. The calendar on the desk indicated the day, month and year meaning that she could cross reference it with the schedule. It was a document listing her shifts working on the wards as a student nurse. She was not due to start work for two days which, she hoped, would give her chance to acclimatise.

Also on the desk was a personal diary. She picked it up then put it down again without looking inside, Janet had decided to save that for another time. She looked in the wardrobe where her uniforms were hanging touching the material gently. She saw her hospital cape and her work shoes and the funny white striped head piece she had to wear. Alongside the uniforms were her own clothes. There were some outfits suitable to go out in at night time, she remembered the club herself and other nurses went to to unwind. That would be nice thing to do she thought.

She wondered if she had anything in her diary about any social gatherings coming up. She would look later once she had had a good look round. She moved to the chest of drawers, picking up some of her underwear, cardigans, jumpers and jeans. Then putting them back thinking she could wear her donated clothes a bit longer. Seeing a kettle and a small fridge she thought about making herself a cup of tea. A quick check in the fridge confirmed that she had milk so used the washbasin tap to half fill the small kettle. It took ages to boil but when it finally did, she made her brew. She sat down on the swivel chair by the desk with her mug then flicked through the diary while she drunk it. She focused on the more recent entries hoping it would tell her her state of mind. Afterall this time was just before she had her first mental episode. Though she did not feel too bad at that moment something had had to happen to make her ill. The diary entries did show a gradual decline, the writing looked laboured, and the language used gave Janet the real feeling that things were not right. Janet realised immediately that there was a problem. How could she have a breakdown the next day when she was feeling so good? Maybe, she thought, just maybe she would not break down!

Perhaps she could avoid it happening by learning what was going on for Janet in recent weeks and putting what she could right. Janet settled in the chair then turned back the page a day sheets of her diary back to a month before then started to read. She not only read the words she tried to imagine the emotions behind them. Despite the fact the diary was forty years old, no, Janet thought, it was less than a year old. She was just reading it with forty years of experiences. It appeared that her young self had had a few things go wrong at work. She had made some errors and had been told off by the ward sister. It seems she did not attend to someone's catheter bag twice in a row despite having asked a junior member of staff to do it. She also was not paying attention during a drug round where she was assisting the qualified nurse nearly giving someone the wrong medication. So, she was not paying enough attention Janet thought. To understand why she was distracted, Janet delved further back in the diary for clues as to what was going on. Three months earlier, Janet found out, that there was a knock on her door one day. She opened it to a young man who was the boyfriend of one of the other nurses on her corridor of the nurses home. He asked if he could come in to wait for her to get off duty. Janet agreed and let him in asking him if he would like some tea. She had put the kettle on then while it heated up to boiling point, he made a move on her. She pushed him away suggesting strongly that he should go. With that said, he went over to her and pushed her onto the bed and raped her. Janet was frozen in fear, she couldn't move her body and voice. She tried desperately to scream out, but nothing came out. When he was done, he straightened his clothes then left the room leaving Janet half undressed on the bed. She lay there for a few minutes her mind blank. When she felt she could, she got up and went to the door to lock it. Janet re read the horrific experience she had gone through. She had not remembered the attack but now that she had read it, it felt familiar. She put down the diary and went over to the door to see if it was locked or open. It was locked. Janet's diary never mentioned the assault again, it was as if it had never happened, though clearly, thought Janet, it was a catalyst for her breakdown. Janet tried to imagine what she must have been feeling during the rape. It was too far behind her to evoke any emotions now, perhaps she was healed enough for it to stave off the start of her Bipolar. She tried to think about what she should do. Should she go to the police, maybe talk to the man's girlfriend. Or maybe just to keep it to herself and work extra hard to be nice to herself. To Janet, that seemed the best option. The attack was, in the diary, three months ago, it was a bit too long ago to go to the police. What she could do, she thought, was to get counselling to help her deal with it but again, Janet was not really convinced that that was the answer. She moved from the chair to the bed then saw her telly. She looked around for the remote control but couldn't find it anywhere. She went over to the tv then saw some buttons on the top part of it. She pressed one of them switching on the telly. She assumed the buttons with up and down arrows would change the channel. The tv took time to fully load up, then showed some childrens tv. Janet checked the time on the clock on her wall, it was ten past five, late afternoon. She watched Blue Peter marvelling at the fact that it was still going on now. She made herself another tea to settle down to focus on the programme. The news should be coming up soon, she thought. So far, so good, despite uncovering something as horrific as rape. The rest of the day passed quickly. Janet left her room a few times to go to the bathroom at the end of the corridor. She spotted some shower cubicles deciding to have a wash the next day. She had planned what she was going to do tomorrow she needed to buy some food and to read up some of the things she needed to know when she went to work on the ward. Janet thought it would be interesting to see the price of food and clothes. She had found a purse in a handbag with some notes and coins in it. She sat down to make a shopping list then tried to see if she could remember where the nearest supermarket was.

At around eight, she heard the sound of voices and other sounds coming from the corridor, Janet froze then tried to be as quiet as she could so they would not hear her and maybe come over to see her. She assumed that they had just gone off duty from the afternoon shift. Quite quickly the noise dissipated with the sound of doors opening and closing. Janet went to look out of her window. It looked like she was on a second floor going by the drop from where she was to the ground. Her room faced the hospital entrance with the Accident and Emergency at the end of the façade. She watched an ambulance spewing out a casualty and two paramedics who was wheeled the gurney into the wing. A couple of people parked their car near the entrance then hurried into the building. Janet assumed they were relatives of the patient just gone in. She wished them well in her mind then went back to the chair. She felt that she should be doing something, so decided to get ready for bed donning her floor length nightdress and dressing gown. She picked up a textbook then looked at pages where young Janet had written notes. All of it made sense to her, she recalled what she could and promised to herself that she would not forget to empty a catheter bag again. At ten o'clock she turned off the telly and brushed her teeth ready for bed. She pulled up the sheet and blankets then turned off the light using the switch by the door then did her best to create a good sleep environment, another technique she had learnt in the Mind Complex in Second Chance.

Janet slept well, she woke feeling nicely refreshed and raring to go. There was definitely something different between the sleep of the young and the sleep of the old she thought.

It was quiet along the corridor, the morning shift on the wards having already gone. She took her towel and toiletries to go to the toilet then the showers. She did not dare spend too long washing in case anyone came in. She did not yet feel ready to meet anyone she knew in case they sussed her out. When she had entered the Time Complex, she had to sign a document that prevented her from sharing anything to do with Second Chance with anyone except those people who had visited Second Chance. Janet understood why she had to sign the paper but could not imagine how the Time Complex would know if she had told anyone. It made her wonder if they keep an eye on their students when they Graduate. Maybe they do, she considered, the thought of it made her feel less alone. Being alone or being lonely is something Janet had experienced throughout her life. She was naturally shy and found it easy to make friends but difficult to keep them. She knew that now; she had a chance to change that. Maybe she could find love, maybe if she was less guarded she would find her soul mate. Janet thought of all the possibilities and came to the conclusion that she should aim to go out of her room every day. It would be easy when she was on shift, but she would need to find something to do on her days off. She tried to remember what facilities were around the hospital area. She then remembered there was a gym about ten minutes' walk away. Thinking that she should check it out that day along with grocery shopping would do for that day. Then, she really had to focus on returning to work to the standard or above she used to work as a third-year student. Once dressed she poured some cornflakes into a bowl then added some milk and a teaspoon of sugar. Janet stopped at that point, she did not put sugar on her cereal, not in her old self. She had weaned herself off sugar when there were so many reports saying how unhealthy sugar was. The action of putting sugar on her cereal was automatic. She was adjusting to her new old life, Janet concluded. She ate her breakfast while listening to the morning news programme. The top story was the IRA bombing London and using letterbox bombs to target certain government buildings. It was worrying times thought Janet though history would put things right. It made Janet think about how she could change not only her own personal history but for others, her country, the world. She could use what she knows from the twenties decade to influence change. That kind of thought scared her; it made her feel powerful but knew it could easily turn round to bite her on her bum. She could be outed as a witch or psychic neither of which was something she would not like to be known as. Janet finished her breakfast then pulled on her trainers to go out to find the food shop. She grabbed her handbag which had her purse in with the money. She looked out of the window to gauge the weather. It looked like a lovely spring day. It was odd, she thought, she expected it to be Autumn like in the Time Complex. Having decided she did not need a coat she left her room and headed down the stairs of the nurses home. She passed someone on her way who she recognised but for the life of her could not remember her name. The woman said Hi to her as they passed. Janet returned the greeting feeling pleased that she did not want to stop to chat. Janet did not yet feel ready for that. Fine Fair supermarket was just on the corner of the road from the hospital. Janet went in and was immediately aware of the change of supermarkets over time. The area was dark, with a lot of the packets in boxes instead of being displayed on shelves. The cold food was not in cooled refrigerated shelves but in fridges with doors. Janet managed to find everything on her list but had to use her imagination for some of the items which were not stored where she thought they should be. The biggest change Janet found was that all the groceries were lose for someone to select the produce they wanted, not prepacked. She took a bit of time selecting some fruit realising that she naturally gravitated to the perfect specimen as opposed to the 'wonky' fruit. It was great to see that they were not so rigid about the weight, size or shape of an apple. Everything was on offer to select. She deliberately, to challenge herself opted to get odd shaped potatoes. By the time she had everything on her list it was time to pay. She was pleasantly surprised at how much she got for her money, it seemed that everything was reasonably priced. She left the shop feeling content. She carried her shopping in her bag with lose fruit and vegetables in paper bags. How did grocery shopping drift into what it was like in twenty twenty two? She thought. Shopping done; next thing was to go to find the gym. She didn't know what to expect there, she was not sure what was available in this era, nevertheless she went in. Immediately she regretted going. Everyone there was male, the only female was the lady on the reception desk. Nevertheless, Janet walked over to her,

"Can you tell me what you have going on here?" Janet asked her. She saw her name was Claire from her name badge pinned to her blouse.

"Well, we have a boxing ring, weights and run some dance classes for the girls. Are you interested in joining?" Claire said pushing a brochure to Janet.

"What kind of dance?" asked Janet.

"Jazz dance, ballet and tap" she replied. Janet remembered trying out jazz dance before she became a nurse. It was very energetic; she was not too sure that is what she wanted to do. She took ballet classes as a young girl she was never any good at it so that was a no no. She asked Claire about the boxing she was quite interested in doing that to keep fit but Claire let her know that it was for the men. Janet asked Claire if she could join in.

"Well, there is nothing to say that you can't but I'm not sure what the blokes will make of that."

"How much does it cost?

"We charge two pounds a session, each session lasts an hour and a half. These are the times of the sessions; you don't have to book." Claire said turning the pages of the brochure to show Janet.

"Thank you, you've been very helpful." Said Janet as she put the papers in her bag with the shopping. She wondered what people wore in the gym but came to the conclusion jogging bottoms and a t shirt would be OK. She walked out of the gym mentally planning to attend the next day. With her tasks done, she walked back to the nurses home then put away her groceries. After making herself a hot drink with some pretty awful instant coffee, she sat at her desk with the diary in front of her. She read some entries to try to get a feel of what Janet was about in her youth. It was clear that she was dedicated to her work, she often mentioned her sadness when losing a patient or if one was especially ill. She was also a bit of a party animal enjoying being let loose on the dance floor. She was a twenty-year-old woman living a full and interesting life. It was so hard to imagine all of this going when her illness took hold. What a terrible waste. Janet vowed to make it different, so she did not end up spending years in the mental health system. She knew she battled against the system so strongly which only resulted in her being in hospital longer. Well, she thought, that is something she could change. She would be compliant and try to work in a true partnership with the services. Janet felt happy with that decision then re-read the last few entries in her diary. Her breakdown happened that day forty years ago. She had attempted to take her life struggling to deal with depression and the impact of the rape. Janet stopped reading for a moment, there was absolutely no way that that would happen this time. She was going to go on duty the next day with energy and openness. She would make sure she did not repeat the things that showed she was not coping because this time, she was on top of things. She was changing her future. She spent the rest of her day swatting up on information from the textbooks, in particular medical nursing as the ward she was working on was a medical ward. She wanted to be armed with as much information as she could. No one could know about her past. She was starting work at seven fifteen in the morning so took herself off to bed at ten. She felt ready, having got out her uniform and practicing putting on the cap with a few hair grips.

Janet woke with excitement. Today, she was going to work in the profession she loved. She had not broken down; she was in control. She washed and then changed into her uniform. It felt really early to be having breakfast, but she ate anyway; she was not sure when she would get a break; from her memory, often, if it was very busy, breaks went out of the window. Cereal eaten and tea drunk, she cleaned her teeth and then got ready to leave. She was working just over from the nurse's home, so she would not need to wear her cape. She put the cap on her head and then had a look at her reflection in the mirror. With no mobile phones with fancy cameras invented yet, she could only record this moment by holding it in her mind's eye. She left her room at seven o five to walk to the ward. She passed a couple of other nurses on their way to work, and they called hello to her, which she responded to. At the entrance of the ward, she stopped for a couple of seconds and then took a deep breath.

Then she moved forward to go to the sister's office for handover. The room was crowded with nurses with no space to sit. Janet got out her notebook to write down anything she particularly needed to know about in the handover then the nurse in charge, Rita, allocated nurses to patients. Janet had five people to care for on her shift, so she took care to make sure she had all the information she could have about them so she could do a good and thorough job. Once the handover had finished and the night shift had left, Janet went over to her patients to introduce herself and to see if they were OK. She was back, she thought.

She was back better than ever, with forty years of life experience to guide her. She was a good nurse, and now she would surpass that and be a brilliant nurse. The shift passed quickly. She was kept busy but managed to get a lunch break which she took in the canteen. She was pleasantly surprised by just how much she remembered but wrote what she was less sure about to look up when she got back to her home. At the end of her shift, Rita, the ward sister, came up to her. She said that she was glad to have her back working at the level she expected. Janet replied, "I had some things to work out; I was not in a good place. You see, someone took advantage of me a short while ago, it affected me more than I thought it would, but I'm OK now. I have dealt with it."

"I'm glad to hear it, was it something that happened to you at work?" asked Rita looking concerned.

"No, in the nurses' home, a man came into my room with my consent then he sexually assaulted me," Janet said surprised at what she was saying to the top nurse.

"Did you go to the police?" Rita asked.

"No, I just want to forget it and move on; it's been helpful telling you, though, I had kept it to myself," Janet said, gently smiling at the older woman. Rita dismissed her then Janet went back to her room to unwind. It was four thirty in the afternoon; she had a bit of time before she needed to eat, so she decided to go to the gym. She changed into some suitable clothes and then headed out to the gym she had visited the day before. On arriving there and booking in, the receptionist called a very fit man over to give Janet a tour of the place. As he showed her the facilities, he asked her what she thought she would like to do.

She took particular interest in the room with weights, kettlebells and dumbbells. She looked at them then made her decision to work out there. The man left her alone after checking to see if she knew what she was doing. She assured him that she had experience working out in gyms and proceeded to warm up using a skipping rope. The cardio work out got her body working ready to start to use the weights. She knew what weight she could manage before but found them too easy so upped the pounds. Janet was seriously impressed with the weights she could manage; youth had some advantages she thought to herself. After her work out and a shower she went back to her home. She passed a couple of girls on the way up the stairs who looked familiar.

"Hi Janet, are you coming out tonight, we are off to Charlies. Meet us at eight?" one of them said.

"Yes, great" Janet replied trying to find the filing drawer in her brain for their names. Eureka, it was Debbie and the other one was Dawn, her next-door neighbour. They parted company with Janet going into her room and closing the door. She felt brilliant, her first day back at work went well and now she was off to a nightclub with some friends. There was absolutely no sign of a breakdown, it looks as if it was not going to come. She sat down at her desk getting out her notebook at the entries she had made. She went through them one by one, seeking clarity from the textbooks in front of her.

There were a couple that she could not find so she made a vow to check them out tomorrow when she was back on the ward in the afternoon. Janet got out her diary from nineteen eighties to the page for that day. She wrote about her activities and her feelings about how her day had passed. She was going to make sure she wrote something down every day and what's more she was going to make every day count. She had been given her life back she knew she would not get another chance. Her future looked clear and bright. She was going to succeed as a nurse, she will meet her soul mate and settle down with children. With that, she closed the diary then got up to see what she could wear for her night out with the girls. She was back.

Chapter 21
Reunion

It was twenty-twenty-two on a cold and rainy November day. The weather was not the only thing that was abysmal; the state of the country was just as wet and miserable. Janet sat in her car stuck in a traffic jam on the motorway. Politicians in the past had said how motorways would change the lives of many by getting people to where they want to go faster. Just one of the mistruths, along with many more in the language of change. Janet checked the time on the clock in the car; she had forty minutes before the time of her meeting; if the traffic got moving now, she should just make it. Janet had left her husband in charge of the animals and the grandchildren, her daughters having dumped them at her home while they went about doing something or other. They were in good hands, she thought to herself.

Now, if only this jam would go so, she could get to the hotel in good time. She checked her rear-view mirror to see what was happening behind her. Some impatient people were tooting their car horns expecting, she assumed, that that would clear the accident ahead, causing the backlog. She hoped no one was hurt, and a police car had wormed its way through the traffic to go to the scene, but no sign of an ambulance. Then she heard the sound of a siren, maybe that was more police or an ambulance. She looked in her mirrors to see if she could see where the noise was coming from. It would be a bloody miracle if they could get through this jam. Especially as some idiots had stopped on the hard shoulder, probably thinking they could bypass the jam.

Janet put on her radio and listened to that for a while, then looked in her mirror to see if her hair was behaving itself. The grey was coming through, she thought; time to dye it again. She was not yet ready to embrace her age and just let it all go grey. She looked at her face smiling at herself in the mirror. She felt nervous about what she was about to do, what if she didn't recognise Debbie. What if she didn't turn up? Janet knew that Debbie should remember what she looked like. After all, it was only, for her, a couple of years since they first met. For Janet, it had been forty years. She wondered if her own appearance was as Debbie remembered. She thought she looked younger than she did back on Second Chance.

It still felt odd going to meet with Debbie. Her life was so different to the first time around. She had graduated as a nurse and worked as a staff nurse and then as a sister in a stroke ward. She enjoyed the work; it was great to see people recover the best they were able to after a stroke. It was not the glamorous side of nursing; a lot of it was very physical, with no help from hoists in the eighties. She had decided on a change of job by going on to train to be a psychiatric nurse thinking that it would give her a fresh challenge. She did well working with the mentally ill.

Again, it was a very challenging job, but a lot of what she did she could relate to with her own personal history. She met her husband, Tim, at the local pub where she and a work colleague went to hang out for an evening. Tim asked her if he could buy her a drink which Janet agreed to, and then the romance all started from there. Janet's workmate tactically withdrew, leaving Janet and Tim to get to know each other. He was a quiet, thoughtful man who had worked in IT since the nineties. He lived and worked locally and seemed to be quite big in his field.

He earnt a good wage, a lot more than Janet would ever get working for the NHS. They dated for a year and a half before he popped the question after asking Janet's father if he could marry her. The proposal was romantic; he took her to the seaside for the day, they paddled in the sea, then had a late meal at a local hotel. After dining, they went for a walk on the beach as the sun was setting. It was at that point he went down on one knee to propose to her. Janet had burst into tears. It was just so perfect; through her tears, she said yes, please, and then he put a beautiful diamond ring on her finger.

They planned for a white wedding in two years' time. Not that they really needed to save for it, as Tim's wage would more than cover it. But it was the done thing back then, so Janet was happy to wait and plan. Their wedding day was beautiful, and everything went to plan. Janet wore a long off-white dress with a long train and a high neck. They had deliberately chosen to marry in the winter so there would be no worries about the weather spoiling an outside party; it would take that problem away by holding an inside party. They had planned to honeymoon in Jamaica on a yacht which Janet was really looking forward to. She had romantic visions of nights sipping wine on the deck, watching the sun slip down the horizon. The truth was, she got her vision and more.

Tim and Janet settled down into married life. Janet gave up her job to be a housewife but joined a few committees here and there to keep herself busy. She missed her work, so they discussed it with both agreeing that she should return part-time. That seemed the perfect compromise. She found work running a project for a mental health trust and excelled in her post. She felt like she was really making a difference in the lives of people with mental health problems.

She worked three days a week which sometimes became four with the demands of the role. She made sure everything came to budget, and goals were achieved by planning ahead. She was setting up a peer support scheme, where people with mental health problems supported their peers in the community. Employing people who have mental illness came with its own bucket load of issues. Many had never worked before so had little in the way of work ethics. She wondered if, in her past life, she would have opted to become a peer worker. She expected that she would. She tried to use her past experience in developing the project. As for her own mental health problem?

Well yes, her bipolar disorder did raise its ugly head, and she was admitted to the hospital a few times when it was at its worse. She had been stabilised with a cocktail of medications which she took religiously. Subsequent attacks were relatively mild because she sought help quickly. She drew on all of her toolbox skills to manage things went they went tits up and added to her arsenal as she went along. She had not acted on attempts on her life when depressed because she remembered oh too well where that took her before. She didn't think they allowed people to go back to Second Chance when their lives were cut short. She found her husband and her girls were enough to keep her on track, and she was proud of how well she coped. She had considered not going to meet Debbie again. She was not too sure if meeting her would be of benefit to her. Maybe it would set her off again, but on the other hand, it would be so good to see someone from her past. It was hard to get around the time difference thing.

For Debbie, it was only a year and a half that she had been back on Earth from Second Chance, whereas for Janet, it was over forty years. Janet sat in the traffic queue in her car, tapping the steering wheel with one of her index fingers. She reached over to turn on the car radio tuning it into a music channel. She had to move the car now and then. As the queue moved, Janet dreaded to think how much pollution was being discarded from all these cars. Someone on a motorbike weaved his way around the traffic.

Janet watched that, thinking that she wished she still had her bike. It had always been a dream of hers to own and drive a motorbike. She used some of her savings to buy one as a treat when she graduated from nurse training. She had a few lessons to get her going on her Suzuki 125cc, and then she went everywhere on it, enjoying the freedom. It was cheaper to run a bike than a car, and the insurance was more reasonable. She kept her bike up to the time when she got engaged to Tim when she swapped it for a little car.

She passed her driving test the first time, which surprised her. She had been so nervous during the test she was sure she had mucked it up. Anyway, Janet and her Fiat made a good couple, and in time, she moved on emotionally from her motorbike. Tim had always expressed his concern when she rode her bike. He was worried about how vulnerable she was with some of the idiots on the road. Janet listened to his concerns and then asked him to go with her to look at some cars while she found a good trainer. Now Janet drove a Toyota Yaris, which had a dashboard like the one you would expect to find on an aeroplane.

She liked the comfort it offered, and she had good visibility, things that were important to her in a car. She edged the car forward a little way, wondering if the accident on the motorway would make it in the radio update on the state of the roads. She thought about reaching for her bottle of water in the pocket on the door but decided against it as, at that moment, the traffic started moving. Janet gathered up speed, and in time, she saw two damaged cars on the hard shoulder where the fire brigade and police had moved them. They had also swept the debris from the cars from the road. Janet tried hard not to look at the wreckage but could not help herself. She just hoped that no one had been badly injured. More to the point, if one or more of them had died, if they would wake up on Second Chance.

She shrugged those thoughts off her mind and focused her eyes on the road ahead. She again checked the time, trying to work out if she could still get to her destination in time. She had allowed a lot of time to drive the twenty-odd miles to the hotel. Janet had booked them a table for lunch at a hotel she had visited a few times in the past. They had a good French chef and good polite service, and she only hoped that Debbie liked French food. When they had agreed on a date and a venue, the restaurant used to be one that sold good old English grub; you know the type?

Your full roast and steak with chips, along with fish and chips and house wine. Janet chose it because it was easy to get to on the motorway. It was just off the M1 near Luton. There is another building next to it where they have exotic dancers as entertainment. Janet hoped that Debbie did not go into the wrong building. Now, that would be a story to tell her children. Thinking of which her eldest, Katie, who had a promotion meeting that day, Janet reminded herself to ring her when she got back from meeting Debbie. She had worked hard for it, but it would give her more money each month. Her wife Kim worked as a schoolteacher in a primary school. She loved working with the little ones especially watching them grow and develop their personalities. Kim and Katie had adopted two little boys who were now teenagers. Both boys were on the autism spectrum and had challenging behaviour, but they were loving and kind.

Janet loved them to pieces as she did her other daughters' kids. She had recently divorced her husband and had moved out of the family home. The children were living with their father, so they could stay at the same school. Evie, Janet's daughter, had moved in with her and Tim for a while until she found herself a flat. This she did within a couple of months and had a spare room for the girls. Janet had a tight nit family who understood that Debbie was an old friend from her student nurse days. She had, when they were small, told them stories about Second Chance, but now her girls were adults; she sensed that it was not a good idea to tell as they would probably think that she was mentally ill. So that was it, her history told in a couple of pages.

Janet was nearing the hotel now, having taken the turning off the motorway and going up the slip road. She located the parking area and found a space where she parked her car. She looked around the car park to see if she could possibly see which vehicle may be Debbie's. It could be any one of them, she thought, then patted down her skirt, took hold of her handbag then started to walk to the entrance of the hotel. It had one of those revolving doors, which Janet detested. She always felt that she would get caught in it and end up going around again and again until she felt sick. She saw that next door to the revolving one was a door with a disabled person pushing a button to open it.

She opted to use that one and pressed the pad. The door opened with a whoosh, which took Janet back immediately to Second Chance, where most of the doors were whoosh doors. She stepped into the reception area of the hotel and looked around for the door to the restaurant. She spotted it and then started to head towards it. Just then,

"Janet, is that you? Yes, it is, Janet," she heard someone say. Janet looked around and then saw Debbie. She hadn't changed at all from when she saw her on the Time Complex all those years ago. Janet went over to her then they hugged. Debbie was crying, which surprised Janet.

"Are you OK? Yes, it's me. Debbie, it is so good to see you; please don't cry," Janet said, hugging her tightly.

"I didn't think you would remember. It has been so long for you." Debbie said.

"I've been counting the years," Janet said, linking her arm with hers. They walked together into the restaurant, where the maître de showed them to their seats. The table overlooked the car park just where Janet's car was parked. They sat down opposite each other, still holding hands.

"How have you been? How is the family?" Janet asked Debbie.

"My two, getting bigger by the day. I arrived back on earth in enough time to avoid what brought me to Second Chance, did you?" Debbie asked.

"Yes, I was able to head it off. I sought help and actually accepted help. I have been really well really, I still get mood swings but they are not as bad as they were." The waiter came over to give them the menus and told them about the specials that day. When he left they both looked at the menu and discussed what they wanted to eat. Janet selected Duck in plum sauce with seasonal vegetables while Debbie selected nut roast.

"You are still eating veggie meals?" Janet asked Debbie.

"Yes, that's something I kept on doing after I left" she replied. They fell into gentle chatter only stopping when the waiter returned to take their orders. Debbie looked great, she looked healthy and happy and young. Janet felt old in comparison even though she had taken good care of herself. She still went to the gym two or three times a week and had a weekly full body massage which helped her manage the stresses of life.

"Are you working Debbie?" Janet asked.

"Yes, I am. I am manager of a hotel in town."

"Why does that not surprise me" said Janet, "You were born to that role, just thinking about all you did for me and the others in the other place."

"Yes, well they say to stick to what your good at. But nowadays I give the orders to my team. I worked in hospitality as soon as I got back home." Debbie explained. "What are you doing now?"

"Me, well I am working on a project with disadvantaged people. I give them a chance to work," said Janet.

"Now, here is somewhere calling the kettle black. You were always about giving people a voice as well as fighting for what you feel is right" Debbie said. The waiter came back with the wine they had ordered and poured a bit into a wineglass for Debbie to taste. She took a glug then nodded her approval. The waiter poured them both a glass full of the red liquid then withdrew. They picked up their glasses to toast each other then took a mouth full before launching back into chatter. It felt they had never been apart. About ten minutes later the waiter came with their food. It all looked beautifully prepared and on tasting both agreed the food was good. Janet remarked that it must be odd for Debbie to be on the receiving end of being served than her role at the hotel where she worked. Debbie said that she didn't do it enough and should try to get out and about more. She worked long shifts and then came home to her young family. There didn't seem to be much me time, she said.

Janet finished her food first and drained the wine from the glass. She picked up the bottle of red and poured them both a generous helping of the wine. When Debbie had finished eating, the waiter returned and removed the empty plates. Janet ordered another bottle of wine when they selected their desserts. The wine arrived with the high calorie servings of lemon meringue pie for Janet and profiteroles for Debbie. The desserts were delicious and the wine went down a dream. Janet remembered after her third glass full that she was meant to be driving home after this so ordered a coffee and a carafe of water in the hope she could dilute the wine. If need be, she thought, she could stay at the hotel if they had rooms and drive home tomorrow. Janet relayed this to Debbie and asked her if she could stay as well. Debbie said that she would just need to phone home to let them know and got out her phone to make the call. While she did that, Janet went up to the reception desk to see if she could book them in for that night. They had one twin left so Janet booked it then went back to the table where Debbie was finishing her call. They left the table and went into the lounge finding some nice big comfy chairs to sit and carry on their chat. Janet asked Debbie if she wanted another drink and suggested cocktails. Debbie was willing so Janet went to the bar to order them both a pina colada. The evening passed quickly, at some point through the haze of alcohol they made it to their hotel room and let themselves in. They both went to test the beds by throwing themselves on them then lay on their backs to look up at the ceiling.

"Do you remember when they had that wedding on Second Chance?" Janet reminisced.

"Yes, the day you did your back in" Debbie said.

"Yes, it was wasn't it. It was a long time ago, but I still think back to those days. I wonder if they have introduced another season, being spring all the time was nice in a way but got a bit boring" Janet said.

"Yes, it was, wasn't it. It's made me appreciate the seasons more, especially the winter."

'Do you ever think of where you would be if you hadn't have left Second Chance the way we did?" Janet asked.

"I guess I would still be managing the wing like I was before I was Graduated" Debbie replied.

"Don't you find it odd that the Resistance went to all that bother to expose the truth about Graduation and in the end it turned out to be so right. Maybe the Inner Circle knew what happens and didn't want people to leave so created this fear about it?" Janet mused.

Debbie was quiet for a moment then said, "They got it so wrong, didn't they. We did OK in the end."

"Yes, we did, didn't we," Janet said, then sat up and checked the time. "I had better let my lot know that I'm staying over; I won't be a sec." With that, she searched in her handbag for her mobile phone and realised that she had shut it down. She rebooted it, then found the number for Tim and pressed the dial. The number dialled came up with a busy noise, but on the third attempt, she got through to Tim. She started to explain things to Tim when he interrupted her.

"I've been trying to get in touch with you. Why did you have your phone off? Something has happened. Its Katie. She's in a bad way; they are not sure she is going to make it. There was an accident; she was driving. She's in the hospital. You really need to come." Tim said in a jumble.

"Hold on Tim, start again. Where is she, which hospital?"

"The Royal Infirmary," Tim replied.

"Janet you must go, let me call you a cab," said Debbie. Janet nodded at her giving her her consent.

"Tim, what happened? She was driving, you said?" Janet asked.

"Yes, she was hit by some bastard being chased by the police. The stolen car went straight into her. She is in a bad way." Tim explained.

"Your taxi will be here in ten minutes. We need to get down to reception," Debbie said. Janet nodded at her again and reached for her handbag and her shoes which she had kicked off.

"Are you at the hospital, Tim?" Janet asked him.

"Yes, I'm in the A and E. They won't let me see her while they are working on her."

"What do you mean working on her? Did she crash?" Janet asked, tripping over the words. It's amazing how undrunk you can feel in light of bad news. Janet was immediately fearful that they were trying to get her heart to start beating again. It really was bad. Janet and Debbie took the lift to reception to wait for the taxi. Janet had finished the call to Tim and stood with Debbie, fearful for the fate of her daughter. She was quiet but thankful for Debbie's company. She didn't need to say anything; Debbie knew what she was going through.

Just then they saw the taxi driving up outside so went out of the building to where it had pulled up. Debbie checked with the driver that they had the right taxi then climbed on board. The journey to the hospital seemed to take ages. Debbie sat next to Janet holding her hands in quiet support. Janet was fearful about saying anything, all that was going through her mind was that her daughter may be dead by the time they get there. The traffic was light that time of day which meant they got to the hospital nice and quickly. Once there, Janet paid the driver then they both got out of the taxi. It had stopped right near the A and E department so they had only a short distance to go.

Janet led the way in the building to the reception area where she asked where she might find Katie. The receptionist called for a member of staff to come out to see her which happened quickly. Janet knew instinctively that that was not a good omen. But Debbie and her followed the nurse into the critical care area. Janet saw Tim sitting in an area set aside for relatives. He looked ashen but seemed pleased to see Janet. Janet and Debbie went over to where he was sitting and Janet introduced Debbie to him.

"Is there any news, Tim?" Janet asked. He scratched his head held her gaze then looked away with what looked like tears in his eyes. "Are they still working on her?"

"Yes, it looked like she was responding, and then she went again. They need to get her stabilised to take her into surgery. She is just too ill at the moment." He explained. Janet touched his arm with her hand, and he responded by placing his hand on hers. Debbie offered to go and get them a drink which was well received, so she set off in search of coffee. While she was gone, a woman came out from one of the rooms and came over to where Janet and Tim sat.

She introduced herself as a doctor who was looking after Katie. She asked them to come with her into the relative's room. There were other people in the waiting area; clearly, what needed to be said had to be said in privacy. That was not good, thought Janet. Nevertheless, they followed the young woman into the room, who asked Janet how she was related to Katie. Janet told her she was her mother and then asked her how Katie was doing.

The doctor took a deep breath then launched into a monologue that went over Janets head. Or at least some of it stayed put. The bit where she told them that Katie was dead. Janet asked the doctor if she could see her daughter who said that they just needed to clear things up a bit in the room, she said she would come and get them when they were ready if they wanted to stay in the relatives room. Janet said that she would prefer to sit in the reception area where Debbie would know where they are. Tim agreed with that so they moved back to the area they sat in previously. Debbie was already there with a cardboard tray in her hands containing three cardboard cups of coffee. She looked at Janet and mouthed "has she gone."

"Yes said Janet, a bit louder than she intended. It was at that point, saying that one word when her loss hit her like a tonne of weight. She felt herself drop to the floor, Tim tried to catch her, but she fell too quickly. Once on the floor, she allowed help from Debbie and Tim to get up and sit in one of the chairs. She was ashen and shaking from the shock of the news about her lovely daughter. Debbie sat next to her and held one of her hands. She could feel the tremor coming from her body. After a short while, Debbie handed her a coffee which she drank in silence. Tim looked like he was going to burst into tears but got into practical mode and said he needed to phone his family and friends. He took out his phone and scrolled through the contacts list, selecting whom to ring first. Janet didn't want to hear him relaying the same message over and over again and asked Debbie if they could go outside together.

Debbie nodded yes then they walked arm in arm out of the building to the area the smokers go. It was times like these that Janet wished she was still a smoker as the ritual of smoking would be a good distraction. Janet gulped in the fresh air feeling somewhat liberated for some reason. She knew she had to go and say goodbye to Katie which would be hard, but she knew she would regret it if she didn't. After about five minutes the silence began to eat both of them, so Debbie decided to break it.

"Do they know what happened?" she asked. Janet took a moment to digest the words and then answered her quietly.

"No, just that she had ruptured a major blood vessel. They were resuscitating her, but the chances are that whatever they would have done it would be fruitless."

"Yes, your right. Do you want to see her in the state she's in?" asked Debbie.

"Yes, I must. No matter how bad she looks. She is my baby," replied Janet. With that and signalling the end of the conversation, Janet headed back to the reception area of the A and E to find Tim. Tim was holding his phone in his hand but had an odd look on his face.

"What is it, Tim? Are you OK?" Janet asked, putting her arm around his shoulders. Now it was her turn to nurture.

"She's gone. I didn't want to say the words. I couldn't tell them" Tim explained. Janet took the phone out of his hand and put it in her handbag. "We can call them together later, it's the middle of the night. Let's let them sleep." Just then one of the nurses came up to them asking if they wanted to see Katie. Janet and Tim got up to follow her while Debbie stayed in the reception area. Janet didn't know what to expect but seeing her looking like she was just asleep was not what she had prepared for. Somehow seeing all the blood and gore would have made it all real but the sanitised room gave the wrong message. Janet went over to where her daughter lay and picked up one of her dead hands. She still felt warm, again, she expected her to be cold. Katie never liked the cold; she would be happy hibernating during the winter months if given half a chance. Maybe she was just hibernating. Yes, that's it. They have made a mistake. Janet's head spun with all these thoughts, so she put her hand down by the side of her body and leant over her to give her a kiss on her forehead.

Tim was on the other side of the bed not too sure what he should be doing or saying. They kept their own council just looked over at each other now and then to see if they needed support. After five minutes, Tim stood up and kissed Katie on the cheek then let Janet know he was leaving. He needed to get in contact with loved ones and now felt like he could phone them. Janet sat with Katie a few more minutes before getting out her phone to use the camera to take one last picture of her baby. She took several shots from various angles, so she had choice to use as her screen saver. Janet then kissed Katie one last time then left the room to go to the reception area where Tim was on the phone to Katies sister Kim. Tim was clearly finding this hard, so Janet gestured for her to take over the conversation which he gladly did.

He thrust the phone into Janet's hand who calmly relayed what had happened to her youngest. Kim wanted to come and say goodbye to Katie. Janet was not sure how long it would be before they took Katie to the morgue. But assumed she could see her there. They usually had a room in the morgue for loved ones to go. Maybe if Kim can't get there on time, that was something she could do. Kim lived a fair distance away but was keen to drive to the hospital now. Janet could hear her bustling around she presumed, finding clothes to put on ready for the journey.

At least Kim hadn't cried, Janet was not sure how she would have coped with that. Kim was the main person they felt needed to know now, the rest, including her friends could wait until the morning. Katie had divorced her husband several years ago. They had one daughter who was old enough to stay at home alone. Katie was on her way home when the accident happened. Tim couldn't face ringing Stacy, his granddaughter, but she needed to know. Janet used her phone to ring her. She let it ring three times before it was finally answered by a sleepy sounding teenager. Janet had arranged for Kim to pick up Stacy if she wanted to see her mum which she did. Stacy sounded OK on the phone.

Maybe it would hit her later. While Janet was on the phone, Debbie went off to get more coffee. Janet sat down on the plastic chair wondering what to do now. Did they have to wait for a death certificate, how did it all work? Tim googled it but the sites he visited did not give the same information, so he was no better off. Janet approached one of the nurses who had been caring for Katie and asked her if they needed to stay. The nurse went to find a senior member of staff who explained what would be happening next. Katie would be moved to the morgue in the next half an hour and the doctor had filled in the death certificate which she handed to Tim. It was in a sealed envelope. Janet was ready to go home. She was feeling drained but before she could rest, she needed to go back to the hotel with Debbie to pick up their cars.

Tim said that he would drive them there so they could pick up the cars. Janet was half in the mind of staying put to wait until Katie had been moved but didn't want to see her body in the metal coffin wheeled by two porters. She was worried they wouldn't be gentle, that they may harm her or drop her. What if she was really just playing some joke with them and would sit up of her own accord and scare the living daylights out of them. Or maybe, just maybe, she was dead.

On arrival at the hotel, Janet and Debbie got out of Tim's car. Janet realised that this would be goodbye unless, of course, they planned to meet again. Janet hoped that they could, she knew this had not gone according to plan, but Debbie had been a good source of support. The girls hugged in the carpark, and Debbie asked Janet if she was OK.

"I will be fine; I have to be. I have a teenager to look after now," Janet replied. Tim stayed in the car, keeping a respectful distance between the friends. He didn't understand how they had got to know each other they were very different in age. He didn't pry; he had learnt over the years when to pry and when to stay quiet.

"Thank you for staying with me. I'm so sorry this had to happen," said Janet holding Debbie's hands.

"Please, you know you would have done the same for me. I know how kind you were on Second Chance." Debbie replied.

"We must meet up again. How about two years' time, same place, same time?" suggested Janet.

"Yes, that would be great. Now, are you safe to drive?" asked Debbie.

"Yes, I feel sober and calm. I will be fine; what about you?"

"Likewise," with that said, they hugged again then both turned around to go to their vehicles. Janet left with a heavy heart. She felt as if she had a tonne of tears to cry but would do her crying later. Stacy would need her now; she had no one. Janet strapped herself into the car and put on the radio. There was some sort of a chat programme on which she thought would be good company on the journey home. Tim had already set off, as had Debbie. Janet released the hand brake and pressed the accelerator, and the car moved smoothly towards the exit of the hotel car park. It felt like an age ago that she had driven here and met Debbie for the first time in forty years. Janet half listened to the radio and half listened to her own inner dialogue on the journey home. She didn't like the idea of Katie being on her own in the hospital. What if she got scared? She would need her mum then; what if she felt deserted by her parents? What if, what if, what if.

Chapter 22
Prologue

Two people waited for their delivery, knowing that three people were on their way. A third person came in and joined them a few minutes later. Each one of them held a clipboard and pen with a few sheets of paper attached to the board. They chatted a bit while they waited; it was always a worrying time, wondering what they would have to deal with. It was late at night, with only the night-time lights illuminating the room. The shadows were long and distorted the physiques of the three Fetchers. One of them checked his watch. It was going to be a long night with new arrivals to deal with. Just then, a woman entered the room,

"Are they here yet?" she said, looking around towards the door.

"Anytime now", said one of the men moving towards one of the chairs in the room. He sat down and then stretched out his arms in a stretch. The youngest of the men looked down at a sheet of paper and told the woman,

"One lady and two men this time." He said, shuffling from foot to foot.

"What do we know about them?" asked the female.

"Not a lot, one of them, the woman was involved in a car crash, and the men, well, one of them was shot, the other a suicide, hanging." He said, reading from his page. They were all prepared for the new people. Now they just needed the bodies. With that, the woman left the room, closing the door behind her. After ten minutes or so, the man who sat on the chair got up and looked at the time on the clock on the wall. The room was quite small, with no windows and just two doors. It had little in the way of furniture, just two uncomfortable chairs and a small table between them. The young man put his clipboard down on the table.

"I hate this bit. You never know what they will be like. I've been hit once or twice, you know. We don't get danger money, do we?"

"We don't get money full stop. We do this out of love," said the young woman. She moved over from where she was standing near the door to sit on the second chair sighing as she lowered her body.

"Where are they? I hope everything has gone OK on their end; we would be the last people to know if there was a problem," said the second man. The three of them kept on checking the two lights above the second door, which was opposite the entrance door. The lights were both red in colour, flickering gently now and then. The lights conveyed some kind of a message to them; each one of the three people kept glancing at the lights. They sat in silence for a moment or two,

"I could have had that cup of tea if I knew they were late," said the woman. She started to tap her index finger rhythmically on the table. She had a ring on her finger from her past life signalling that she was loved once upon a time. She could not not wear it; it was now so much part of her that without it she may as well be naked. She had blond hair tied up into a bun with little whiskers of hair hanging down doing its own thing. She was young, it was hard to determine her age but probably about thirty.

Around the same age as one of the men. He had short blond hair with a floppy fringe that he kept on flicking off his face. He had no jewellery on his body but did have a couple of discreet tattoos that he had done in a past life. The third man was much older than the others and had barely any hair though his baldness added to his good features. The three of them were dressed identically in light blue tunic and trousers with white clog shoes. Why they dress them in a light colour to do this job didn't make a lot of sense, but it gave the right image of them being carers.

"I'll give them five more minutes then I got to go. My bladder is calling me," said the bald man.

"Go now, in case it all kicks off," said the woman. The man stood up and headed for the door but before he could open the door to leave, the other man called him back.

"They are coming, the lights" he said. The three of them stopped to look at the lights above the door. One of the two lights had changed colour to green. A moment later the second red light turned green then they heard the noise of the door opening. It was a woosh door, one of those electric ones that opened quietly, barely audible they woosh open. When the door had fully opened, they walked over to it seeing what was in the space beyond. The bald man saw a gurney inside the space and pulled it through the door frame and into the room. On the gurney was a middle-aged man covered in a white sheet. He was not conscious and had been put in the recovery position.

The carer went to gurney and reached down to the mans head and checked for a pulse in the carotid artery. Satisfied he could feel a pulse, he moved the gurney to the end of the room creating space for the woman carer to bring out a second gurney baring a young man. Again a check was made for a pulse then the gurney was moved next to the middle aged man. The third gurney was pulled out and the check made. At that point the door with the lights above it closed and the lights turned back to red. The two male carers took the gurney with the female on it out through the entrance door and wheeled it to a room down at the other end of the corridor. The carer with the fringe stayed with the young woman while the other carer went back to the holding room. The two carers then wheeled the gurney with the young man to a separate room down the corridor then they did the same for the other man. The carers went to assist their patients and do the necessary checks. They would be unconscious for a good couple of hours so they would need to check vital signs until they finally wake.

The young man with the fringe looked in from the door frame to the young woman asleep. He thought she looked familiar but for the life of him could not recall from where or when. She looked so peaceful he thought. He withdrew and went to make himself a cup of tea. He fancied having a slice of cake with his tea so went in search of the cake tin. His comrades always seemed to get there before him leaving him with the ginger cake, the less glamorous of the cakes on offer. It's just as well he didn't mind; folk have fallen out over less than that. He went into the staff room and put down his clip board then went in search of the tin. Someone kept hiding it in one of the cupboards which he had sussed out a while ago. He had a look in the cupboard and moved a few items out of the way that were in front on the tin. He took the tin out then prised open the lid. To his delight there was ginger cake left but also a slice of carrot cake, one of his favourites. He found a clean plate then moved the slice of cake onto it then put the tin back where he had found it. The kettle had boiled at this point, so he went to it to pour the boiling water on to a tea bag. He found a clean teaspoon and mashed the bag until the tea was his preferred shade. Finally, he could enjoy the fruits of his labour, he sat down on the chair with the wonky leg and picked up the cake to sink his teeth into it. Boy, that tasted good, he thought then took a sip of his tea. He checked his watch to see how long he should leave it before checking up on the new woman. He was always nervous about this part; you never knew how they were going to behave. Once he had finished his break, he washed up then dried his hands on a rather grubby looking towel. His work colleagues always ribbed him about his need for cleanliness which he ignored in good grace. If he didn't wash up, it would remain unwashed and he, for one, wouldn't like to drink from someone's dirty mug. Still, he really didn't mind always doing the washing up for the others. He checked his watch again seeing that it was nearly time to go and see the new lady. He picked up the clipboard and went to the room she was sleeping in. He opened the door and peered in. It looked like she had stirred, she was lying in a different position. He went into the room to see if he could stir her without frightening her. He spoke her name a couple of times and she made a soft grunting sound like someone coming out of a deep sleep, which, to be fair, is what she was doing. He said her name again, but she stayed silent this time round. He noted her reaction on the paper on the clipboard then withdrew. He would leave it for another quarter of an hour before going in again. She should be properly awake soon if everything had gone to plan. This time in the staff room he picked up a magazine and flicked through the well-thumbed pages. The reading material was so out of date he thought but had a look at the horoscope to see if what it said for his month of birth had come true. Just then, Jon, one of his work colleagues came into the room and asked him if he had seen the wheelchair he needed for his male client. He responded with the negative then asked how he was doing. Jon said that he was happy with his progress and asked him about his new client.

"She is beginning to stir; I reckon if I give her another half hour, she will be awake. She has some serious injuries, but I am sure she will walk again" he said. Jon asked him if he would like a drink then put the kettle on. He said that he had just had a cup, so Jon just made one. Jon sat down at the table and picked up the magazine his colleague had just discarded.

"One day, they will get some decent reading material; this one has been here since early last year," Jon said. They sat in silence for a few minutes then Jon checked the time to see how much longer he could rest. His patient was quite new there and needed a lot of care. He felt that he could be left for short periods of time at this point in his recovery but wouldn't want to make it any longer. He finished his tea and then got up to leave.

"When are you next off?" Jon asked Mark.

"Not for a while. I am meant to be off the day after next, but with a new one to look after, that well might not happen, you know well what I mean," said Mark. Jon rinsed his mug under the hot tap, then said his goodbyes, and then headed off down the corridor. Mark stood up, picked up his clipboard, and then walked the short distance to the room where his charge lay. This time when he went in, he saw her sitting upright with an expression of fear on her face.

"Hello Katie, my name is Mark, I am here to help you" he kept on having to do double takes because she was so familiar. He couldn't work out where he had seen her before, he wondered if it was someone from his life on earth. Anyway, whatever, he had a job to do. He needed to break the bad news to her that she had died and that he was her Fetcher. He knew she had fractured her legs and back along with soft tissue damage. Mark hoped that the pain relief was doing its job because to clean and dress her wounds would have been very painful for her without it. He needed to find another Fetcher to give him a hand to reduce the fractures and get the bones in alignment. But for now, he had to help her to come to terms with her new reality.

"Katie, I know you are feeling really frightened, but no one is going to hurt you. I am here to help you recover from the car accident you had. You have come to Second Chance."

"Second Chance, I have heard of that from somewhere?" Katie said trying to think through her clogged brain where she had heard that. She rested back down on the gurney feeling exhausted. Katie felt herself drift back into sleep and tried to resist it. She sat back up and tried to move her legs over the side so she could stand up. She pulled off the sheet covering her body before she realised that she was nude underneath. She didn't care too much she just had to get away. She wanted to go home. Just then she looked down at her body and saw her legs. She yelled out in shock because her legs looked mangled. There was bone protruding out through the skin and it looked like her right ankle was nearly severed.

It hangs at an odd angle, but she was surprised not to see any blood. Horrified at the sight of her legs she pulled the sheet back over her hoping if she could not see it would not be real. All this time Mark watched her trying to suss out what she was thinking. He needed to give her a bit of space to start to come to terms of what was happening. She pulled the sheet up under her chin and looked over at Mark.

"What the fuck is going on."

"Katie, I know you are feeling scared, but please, there is nothing to worry about. You are safe here."

"Safe where? What on earth is Second Chance."

"It's a place where people who die too soon go to live out their lives," Mark said, a sentence he had said so so many times in the past. As if that helps someone in Katie's situation.

"I don't understand; why have I heard this before, somewhere." She tripped over her words, feeling suddenly very weary. She lay back down on the gurney and soon fell into a troubled sleep. Mark left her to rest and went to start doing some of the paperwork. He would check her every half an hour until she woke.

A couple of hours later, Mark went to see Katie, who was sitting up on the gurney. Mark went up to the gurney and asked her if she wanted a drink. She nodded yes to tea and yes to cake, so he took himself off to make up the order. She gulped back the tea, feeling very thirsty and ate the cake in big mouthfuls. She probably hadn't eaten for a while, Mark thought. It always took a while to get through the hospital system.

"Second Chance, I remember my mum used to tell me stories about a place called Second Chance when I was a little girl. Do you mean it is real?" she asked.

"Yes, it's real. Do you mind if I ask you who your mum is? Only you look familiar to me," Mark asked.

"My mum? Her name is Janet; why do you think you know her?" Katie said.

"Yes, I knew Janet. She never talked about having a daughter, though. I was her Fetcher. She caused quite a stir around here. Everyone knows her; I am so pleased she is OK." Said, Mark. He felt sure that she was going to do OK here; it would be so nice to have the daughter of such an inspirational woman here on Second Chance.

Katie said "So you are Mark, did you know you are behind the title of her book, yes, she always told me and my sister about you. She wrote a story about Second Chance, now I know it is real. She called her book 'The Fetcher'. Mark looked intently at Katie; he really was lost for words. He turned round making for the door saying, "I need to see to your legs, I won't be long". With that he approached the door which opened with a woosh.

THE END

Milton Keynes UK
Ingram Content Group UK Ltd.
UKHW051329200224
438172UK00012B/204